Martyn,

thank you for two successful years
of cooperation in a challenging and
learning environment. Perhaps you
will come back sometimes to Europe...

cheers

Friedrich

Skiing Europe

Gabriella Le Breton and Matt Barr

Ask ten people why they love skiing in Europe and you're likely to get ten different answers: the spectacular beauty of the mountains, the exhilaration of hurtling down the slopes, the food, the après-ski, the off-piste, the rustic mountain huts or simply being in picture-perfect Alpine villages surrounded by glistening snow.

It's the fact that skiing is much more than simply a sport that makes it so special. Yes, it's guaranteed to make your thighs feel like they've been in a vice (especially when a long day on the pistes is followed by a night of dancing on tables) but as you share the day's highlights with your mates over an après-ski beer or Glühwein, the aches are soon forgotten.

We believe that skiing should be as much about relaxing on a sun terrace admiring some of the planet's most spectacular scenery, taking long lunches in cosy mountain restaurants, whooping loudly as you bag fresh tracks on a powder day and singing your heart out to cheesy Euro-pop in a freezing outdoor bar before skiing (like a legend, of course) down to a little Alpine village for fondue, as it is about perfecting your skiing technique.

Recreational skiing has come a long way since its birth in the early 1900s. Arguably one of the most important aspects of this evolution is that it's no longer exclusive. Once regarded as the domain of the wealthy, skiing has become accessible to people of all budgets and all abilities. While novice skiers on a budget can find their skiing feet on the warm slopes of Andorra for a mere £300 per week, others will blow £10,000 on a week on a fully-catered chalet or on a private heli-skiing trip. Of the million-plus Britons who went skiing in the 2007/08 winter season, it's safe to say the majority found something in between.

So, given this abundance of choice, how do you decide which country, let alone which resort, to visit each season? As with all travel, research is key to making the right decision; about where to spend your time and money. There are several skiing guidebooks already in existence, but we were inspired to create a guide based entirely on our personal experiences of each resort that would provide useful and current information about both the destination's facilities and skiing.

We asked locals, friends, professional skiers, barmen, chalet staff, lift operators, tourists, children and journalists for their opinions and let their views temper and inform our own. We've tried to depict the resorts warts and all and address the needs of a wide variety of skiers.

Essentially, we've pooled several decades of skiing experience (and pleasure) and shared our very best secrets and top tips with you. We hope it will help you make some key decisions about where your future skiing adventures will take place.

Essentials

Andorra and Spain

Austria

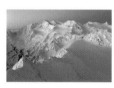

Bulgaria and Slovenia

France

Contents

Italy

Scandinavia

Switzerland

Contents

About the authors

Gabriella Le Breton was bitten by the ski bug the first time she stood on skis aged three in a tiny German village. Now 31, she might no longer don a yellow all-in-one ski suit but Gaby still gets totally over-excited by the sight of snow and battles to keep up with her big brother on the slopes. Growing up in Austria

and Switzerland meant that her love for snow developed into a full-blown ski obsession and, after graduating from Durham University, she travelled the world for three and a half years, spending two winter seasons in Aspen, Colorado. Settling down to a regular job in London proved virtually impossible for Gaby, who was forever dreaming of adventures in far-flung lands, so she took the plunge into the world of freelance travel writing - a move she's never regretted. In addition to doing her dream job of writing a ski guide, she contributes to a range of newspapers and magazines, including the *Sunday Telegraph* and *Metro*, writing about everything from luxury cruises in French Polynesia to exploring lesser-known countries in Western Africa.

Matt Barr has managed to spend most of his adult life visiting the mountains and managing to pass it off as work – not a bad effort for somebody brought up in the middle of Manchester. It didn't look likely on his first school ski trip to Zell am See aged 13, when he posted the worst time of the end-of-week race. Yet, bug duly caught, he spent the next few years ripping his trousers on the dendix of Rossendale dryslope before heading back out to the real mountains as soon as he could. He did his first winter season after finishing a degree in English Literature and went on to become Senior Editor of White Lines Magazine and co-founder of the ACM Writing Group (acmwriting.com) in 1999, giving him the freedom to explore the world. As a journalist Matt is happiest going off the beaten track, and his dispatches from some of the world's more unusual corners (recent trips have included Iran, Russia, Uzbekistan and Lebanon) makes him a favourite among the UK's more discerning national travel editors. In recent years he helmed Footprint's *Snowboarding The World* project and worked with Motorola on promoting their international snowboard team. As well as putting together *Skiing Europe*, he is currently contributing to a wide range of worldwide media titles, from *FHM* and *The Guardian* to *Transworld Snowboarding* and the *Daily Mail Ski and Snowboard Magazine.*

Acknowledgements

Thanks to the following people:

Andorra and Spain
Andrew at Millennium PR, Giles Birch for all help, TAG, Jaime Lahoz.

Austria
Eckard, Mary Stewart Miller, Lynsey Devon, Sam Baldwin, Nicholas Boekdrukker, Sophie Brendel, Edith Danzer, Kathrin Mitterer, Wilma Himmelfreundpointer, Ruth Hall, Christian Piccolruaz, Daniela Pfefferkorn, Joan Devey, Stefanie Falkner, Stefan Pühringer, Dominik Walser, Matthias Proneg, Max Salcher.

Bulgaria and Slovenia
Tina Kriznar, Zoe Anderson, James McPhail, SC Vogel, Balkan Holidays.

France
Gema Thompson, Susannah Osborne, Gemma Freeman, Maison de France, Erica Hutchins, Annie Martinez, Marie-Therese Smith, Richard Lett and the Altitude crew, Greg at Focus 52 for the outstanding pictures and help with various queries (check his site www.focus52.com), Eric Bergeri, Nico Guyet, Stephanie Briggs and all at Spring PR, Amelie and Alexis at Duodecim, Nik Hall, Zoom Agency, the guys at Meribel tourism, Yasmin Sethna, Jean-Louis Leger-Mattei, Héléna Hospital, Jeanne Mounaut, Melody Reynaud, Didier Grillet, François Badjilly, Philippe Amard.

Italy
Maria Grazia Matuella, Gabriella Talamini, Deborah Zani, Jolanda Senoner, Cath Argyle, Rob Smith, Deborah Zani, Helen Robinson, Susie Westwood and all at BGB, the amazing Trisha at Interski for all her help, James Crompton, Heidi Hauser, Nicole Dorigo.

Scandinavia
Linda Wassell, Susannah Osborne.

Switzerland
Guy Chanel, Richard Rigby, Heidi Reisz, Anne Pedersen, Martina Walsoe, Maria Ferretti, Eric Bélanger, Stefanie Tischhauser, Stephanie Bellwald, Aline Stämpfli, Rolf Bissig, Emilie Morard, Cornelia Lindner, Steve Scalzo, Sarah and Kevin, Eric Liechti, Sabine Willi and (last but not least) Sue Heady.

We'd also like to thank all our friends and colleagues in the ski industry for their help and endless enthusiasm about the book. Everyone says it, but it really wouldn't have happened without you guys: Lynsey Devon and Becky Horton at Inghams, Marion Telsnig at Crystal, Rob and Sue Freeman, Neil English, Brigit and Simon Booth, Kate Leah, Dan Egan, Dan Loutrel, Earl Knudsen, Christine Ottery, Rob Smith, Sam Haddad, Sam Baldwin, Jo Fernandez, Gemma Bowes, Tom Robbins, Roger Alton, Joe Mackie, Seb Ramsey, Toby Danos, Felix Milns, Pally Learmond, Pat Sharples, Dan Milner, James McPhail, Warren Smith, Melody Sky, Nick Southwell, Mark Junak, Hannah Engelkamp, Henry Druce, Cat Weakley, Nicolas Guyot, Eric Bergeri and Gema Thompson.

Matt and Gaby would also like to thank Ben, Chris and Ewan at ACM, and Alima, Dixy and Hugo Le Breton, and Duncan Bellamy for putting up with the endless deadline stresses and prolonged absences.

Final thanks to the unflappable team at Footprint, especially Alan 'safe hands' Murphy, Tim, Alice, Angus and Pat, and not forgetting Zoë, Catherine and Hannah.

Essentials

Planning a trip

Where?

"So, what's your favourite resort?" This has to be the question ski writers are asked most. What we've found is that we don't have one favourite resort – yes, we've got our personal top five but each has its own distinct appeal. There are places we go to ski and party hard with our mates, there are secluded little villages we go to with the family and romantic boltholes for special weekends.

There are thousands of ski resorts sprinkled all over Europe, from Andorra to Slovenia and we fully appreciate how daunting it is to pick and choose between them. We've therefore selected 114 key resorts that we're confident will appeal to a broad cross-section of skiers including beginners, families, intermediates and experts. We've tried to reflect the diversity of European skiing and highlighted the pros and cons of major international resorts like St Anton, Chamonix and Val d'Isère as well as smaller, lesser-known resorts such as Kühtai, Zinal and Geilo.

The length of each resort review is determined by a combination of factors: the size of the resort and scope of its ski area, the profile and reputation of the resort and our 'rating' of it.

Why?

Skiing has become a multi-million euro industry for most of the countries included in this guide. Each summer sees a whirlwind of activity, building new lifts, preparing new pistes and supporting local hotels, restaurants and transport services to entice more visitors the following winter.

While Fiat-founder Giovanni Agnelli pioneered Europe's first purpose-built ski resort in Sestriere, France caught on quickly and its colossal resorts such as Avoriaz and Les Arcs have led to the coining of the phrase 'factory skiing'. Although perfectly convenient and popular with families and committed piste-bashers, providing affordable on-slope accommodation and access to huge ski areas, these resorts do lack the 'Gemühtlichkeit' of more traditional resorts that is key to many visitors' enjoyment of the Alps.

There are few things more disappointing than arriving at a resort you're expecting to be cosy and family-friendly to find you're in teen-party central or to rock up with a bunch

of mixed-ability skiing mates in a town like La Grave that essentially caters exclusively for expert skiers. The intention of this guide is therefore to help you avoid these pitfalls as well as encourage you to explore new resorts and countries with informed, up-to-date recommendations to hand.

How?

A good guidebook performs two functions – reference and, more importantly in our case, comparison. The first provides you with the background and vital stats to establish whether a destination suits your needs and also provides recommendations and insider tips. Nobody likes to feel like a tourist but invariably you end up knowing the best shortcuts, pistes, restaurants and bars by the time you're due to leave. We've tried to save you that hassle so when you arrive in town you've already got some local knowledge up your sleeve.

A scale of comparison that all readers will find useful, despite their varied needs, is more difficult to accomplish. We've therefore devised a key for each resort that allows you to quickly see whether it's going to be the right one for you, while supporting the vital stats with a review of the resort and its skiing.

How to use the key

Deciding where to take your skiing holiday requires having an instant comparability chart at your fingertips, with all the possible factors and scenarios that are high, or low, on your list of priorities clearly marked. Under each resort heading is a quick reference key which lists all the most important statistics that you'll need to make the right choice. Note that for resorts which are part of larger ski areas, the figures in the categories below cover the entire ski area. See pages 28-29 for a full explanation of these areas.

Town altitude The height of the resort above sea level in metres.

Km to airport This is the nearest international gateway airport to the resort in kilometres.

Airport This is the nearest airport to the resort.

Highest lift Height in metres of the top of the highest lift. Note that hiking may be available above this limit. Highest peaks are not a great indication of a resort's skiable area.

Vertical drop Height in metres from the top of the highest lift to the bottom of the skiable area. Note that this number may be different than the highest lift minus the resort height if the skiable terrain extends below the resort, as is often the case in purpose-built resorts.

Km of pistes Distance of all the pistes added together in kilometres.

Nursery areas Number of areas set aside for absolute beginners.

Blue/red/black runs Number of runs - designated by the resort - as being beginner (blue), intermediate (red) or advanced (black) friendly runs.

Funicular/cable cars Number of funiculars (mountain trains) and cable cars (two cars on one wire) in resort.

Gondolas/chairs Number of gondolas (tens of enclosed 'pods' on one wire) and chairlifts (from one- to eight-person sit-down lifts) in resort.

Drags Number of draglifts (t-bars or any lift that requires you to stand and ride uphill) in resort.

Night skiing Yes or No indication to whether resort has floodlit skiing capabilities. Note some resorts are open every night, while others, such as La Clusaz, have only one monthly floodlit session.

Terrain parks Number of parks the resort maintains within its boundaries.

Glühwein factor ★☆☆ – Early nights all round (best for families or couple looking for quiet life); ★★☆ – Decent après and the odd club (best of both worlds); ★★★ – Prepare to stay up all night, ski all day and need a liver transplant by the end of it (best for night owls).

Ski in/ski out Accessibility on and off the slopes for the majority of accommodation in resort, using the following rating: ★☆☆ – Car or public transport almost certainly required; ★★☆ – Some walking to the lifts but no car or public transport required; ★★★ – Virtually fall out of bed onto the pistes.

Environmental rating Number rating using six criteria designed by climate change charity Respect the Mountain. The rating aims to flag up the resorts with the most environmentally friendly policies.

Where to stay

Deciding which resort you're going to visit is only the first step of planning a ski trip – now you've got to establish what kind of accommodation you should choose.

Your choice will be determined by budget, convenience, the size and needs of your group and personal preference. Virtually every resort in this guide offers a wide choice of hotels, B&Bs, chalets and apartments. The local Tourist Office is often an invaluable source of information – explain your budget and key requirements and staff will advise you of the best matches, check availability and offer combined accommodation and ski pass packages.

Broadly speaking, hotels (and their less expensive cousin the B&B) are ideal for couples and small families. They're convenient, plentiful and available to suit most budgets. As Daniela Pfefferkorn, owner of the Hospiz Alm hotel in St Christoph, says, "Staying in a hotel is convenient and luxurious for couples as well as families. Rooms are large and cleaned twice a day, you can get up whenever you want, as breakfast is served until noon, and the pistes start right in front of the hotel. A large part of the appeal is escaping the daily routine".

Apartments, on the other hand, are ideal for families and groups on a tighter budget. Lynsey Devon of Inghams finds they offer flexibility: "Apartments are ideal for families who want a bit of space and independence – the more relaxed it is in the place you call home for a week, the less stressful the holiday will be. You can eat what and when you like, dine out if you chose and the kids can play in a relatively large, self-contained area. Apartments are always better value than hotels of equivalent standard and more spacious, particularly in Austria and Switzerland."

Finally, there is the most luxurious option – the chalet. Chalet holidays come in such a wide variety of pricing options that they cater for virtually everyone from a small group of friends to extravagant corporate outings. The unique selling point here is providing a pampered bespoke experience. As Andrew Dunn, founder and MD of Scott Dunn puts it, "At Scott Dunn we pride ourselves on offering a luxury chalet experience with added extras such as car pick-ups to and from the slopes, spa pampering and indoor pools – personal touches that make a chalet ski holiday all the more enjoyable and relaxing".

So how do you decide? Fortunately, in addition to this book, numerous agents exist to help you negotiate your way through this maze of choice including tour operators, chalet providers and independent specialist ski companies.

All the major tour operators including Inghams, Crystal, Neilson, Mark Warner and Thomson have dedicated winter portfolios, offering a hassle-free and cheap ski holiday – neatly packaging up transport, accommodation, tuition and ski hire. Ideal for families, they're flexible too, enabling you to pick and choose which parts of the package you want. However, there can be a feeling of being herded from Southend-on-Sea to Southend-on-Snow, with many of the hotels dominated by English holidaymakers.

Companies like Powder Byrne and Scott Dunn offer packages to more upmarket hotels (the latter also has chalets in its portfolio) and also provide excellent childcare facilities. At the very top end of the market, VIP Chalets and Descent International provide deeply luxurious chalet holidays that come with those everyday necessities like a dedicated chauffeur, cook, nanny, sommelier, outdoor hot tub, sauna, entertainment system and Champagne on tap. Want a romantic lunch on the mountain on a hand-carved ice bench strewn with rose petals? Ask and you will receive.

Specialist ski agents such as Alpine Answers, Ski Solutions and Peak Retreats (France only) create bespoke packages for you to suit your needs and budget. They'll sort out flights, transfers, accommodation and equipment hire and ensure you get the best price for each element. There are companies that specialize in long weekends, trips for women travelling alone, gay and lesbian holidays, blind-date ski trips; you can even buy a bespoke ski season online, simply turning up with your kit and having your meals cooked for four months.

Best Luxury Breaks

Skiing has always offered those with the means limitless ways of disposing of their income. Although today it is possible to go skiing without having your bank manager's number on speed dial, for many the annual ski trip is a welcome excuse to splash out and let somebody else do the fetching and carrying for once. The ski industry has not been slow to take this idea and run with it, and it means that there are ever more elaborate and decadent options out there for skiers with a copy of Forbes on the coffee table and a particularly forgiving credit limit. Operators such as Crystal tip their hat to the trend with their 'Crystal Finest' range of chalet holidays (crystalfinest.co.uk), while in other areas companies such as Scott Dunn (scottdunn.com) and Descent International (descent.co.uk) are leading the way. Here we've picked our favourites (and yes, we have been lucky enough to stay in them). Just remember: if you need to ask the price, you probably can't afford it!

La Ferme de Moudon chalet, Les Gets
Sleeping 10 people, the 17th century Ferme du Moudon offers guests a sauna, massage room, a private chef to prepare all meals and a wine cellar, as well as a chaffeur on standby. **Contact**: descent.co.uk. **Price**: £32,000 (for the entire chalet).

Mont Cervin Palace Hotel, Zermatt
Mont Cervin has been the poshest hotel in Zermatt since 1851. A horsedrawn carriage will pick you up from the station, while many rooms have jacuzzis and open fireplaces. **Contact**: seilerhotels.ch. **Price**: £265 (CHF545) per night for a double room during high season.

Thurnhers Alpenhof hotel, Zürs
This family-run hotel publishes its own magazine and offers 15 rooms and 26 suites, a gourmet menu and a well-appointed wellness centre. **Contact**: thurnhers-alpenhof. at. **Price**: €1560-1620 per night (two-bedroom suite during peak February season).

The Eagle's Nest chalet, Val d'Isère
Sleeping 12, the Eagle's Nest chalet overlooks La Face piste, has an indoor pool in the basement and a beauty therapist on call. **Contact**: scottdunn.com. **Price**: £2245 per week per adult (guide price).

The Lodge, Verbier
Yes, this is Sir Richard Branson's own chalet. Sleeping nine, it has a 9-m pool, 'party room' with games consoles and plasma screen and even its own private ice rink. **Contact**: thelodge. virgin.com. **Price**: £43,500 for the entire chalet (winter 08-09).

Six of the best

Underground classics

❶ Grimentz, Switzerland
Outstanding intermediate terrain in a picture-perfect setting – Grimentz's low profile is something of a mystery.

❷ Alpe d'Huez, France
Forget the dashed-off-on-a-napkin village and concentrate on the glorious skiing for all levels.

❸ Andermatt, Switzerland
Muscular advanced skiing in an uncrowded setting. Advocates of Chamonix and St Anton take note.

❹ Montgenèvre, France
Inexpensive by French standards and linked to the Milky Way Ski area.

❺ The entire Monte Rosa range, Italy
Monte Rosa has about 180 km of pisted runs, world-famous off-piste skiing and several beautiful ski-in villages. So why is it so quiet?

❻ Champéry, Switzerland
Experience the Portes du Soleil by the backdoor in this charming village.

Mountain restaurants

❶ Hospiz Alm, St Christoph
The legendary Hospiz Alm is located directly on the pistes at the base of St Christoph. The wine cellar dates back to 1386.

❷ Jimmy's Hütte, Alta Badia
The sun terrace of Jimmy's Hütte looks straight out onto the spectacular Sella Massif and Jimmy himself will actively encourage you to try each of his different flavoured homemade grappas.

❸ La Bergerie Kanata, Les Deux Alpes
La Bergerie Kanata is an atmospheric spot on the quieter Pied Moutet side of Les Deux Alpes. Don't forget to visit the loo – they're the quirkiest mountain bathrooms we've ever seen.

❹ Chez Vrony, Zermatt
One of Zermatt's many culinary institutions, Chez Vrony in Findeln somehow manages to successfully mix traditional Swiss cuisine with Heston Blumenthal-type experimental flair.

❺ Nederhütte, Obergurgl
Neck glühwein, dance on the tables and then ski home woozily as the moon shines down. The Nederhütte is an Obergurgl institution.

❻ Alpenhaus, Ischgl
Membership of the VIP club in Ischgl gains you access to the VIP lounge in the Alpenhaus, which is as flash as it gets.

Bars

❶ Yucatan, Engelberg
Friendly, up-for-it bar with legendary happy hour offers.

❷ MBC, Chamonix
Unique Anglo-Canadian bar with live music and micro-brewed beers - heaven.

❸ Kandahar, St Anton
It stays open till 0600. Surely this is all you need to know?

❹ Scotland Yard, Mayrhofen
Mayrhofen's lovingly rendered British pub spoof serves up dodgy Guinness and wild parties.

❺ Rondpoint, Méribel
Was toffee vodka invented here? Either way, no trip to Méribel is complete without a session on the stuff at 'Ronnies'.

❻ Crap Bar, Laax
Handily situated just next to the gondola, the Crap Bar overflows during après sessions.

Must-do runs

❶ The Duty Free run, Ischgl
Ski down into Switzerland from Austria on this lengthy red.

❷ Vallons de Chancel, La Grave
One of La Grave's main descents, this is a tough, committing ski.

❸ Weissflühjoch to Klosters Dorf via Schifer, Davos-Klosters
Runs like this underline why these two resorts are combining into one new super-resort.

❹ La Sarenne, Alpe d'Huez
At 16 km, it is reputedly the longest piste in the Alps.

❺ Vallée Blanc, Chamonix
An obvious choice, but still one of the most spectacular routes in skiing.

❻ The Wall, Portes du Soleil
La Chavanette, to give it the correct name, is supposedly the most ferocious black in the Alps.

Six of the worst

Queues

❶ Val d'Isère, France
Val's brand name popularity means queues are inevitable – especially on the routes linking to Tignes. Don't get caught out!

❷ Chamonix in February
The French holidays, and lengthy bus and lift queues, make Chamonix a 'must avoid' resort in February.

❸ Valluga in St Anton on a powder day
It is on every serious skiers tick list, which means setting the alarm for 0500 on a powder day if you want to stand a chance.

❹ Mayrhofen, Austria
As well as making our scariest lifts list, the Penken is also a natural bottleneck, particularly at the end of the day.

❺ Bansko, Bulgaria
Although the infrastructure is on the up, queues for the gondola have been reported to snake down into town.

❻ Canazei, Italy
Another uploading bottleneck, get there early or expect huge queues.

Scariest lifts

❶ Penkenbahn, Mayrhofen
Only one pylon and a big kink in the middle; just don't look down!

❷ Aiguille du Midi, Chamonix
An awe-inspiring example of engineering ingenuity; just how did the French put this up back in the mid-20th century?

❸ Valluga II, St Anton
A guide is required before you're allowed on this lift. Serious stuff.

❹ Nashorn, Zermattt
As far as we're aware, the X7 drag on Klein Matterhorn is Europe's highest draglift, ascending from 3883 m to 3899 m. The ride itself isn't so scary, but the altitude is quite something – and it gets seriously cold!

❺ Falloria, Cortina
Built in 1939, they certainly don't make 'em like this any more. Thank God.

❻ Vanoise Express, France
It links Les Arcs and La Plagne and rises 380 m above the deck. Yikes.

Transfer times

❶ Madonna di Campiglio, Italy
At 127 km to the closest airport, you'll be itching for a Génépi by the time you get there.

❷ Zermatt, Switzerland
It is a surprising 244 km from Zermatt to Geneva. Get the train and enjoy the spectacular views.

❸ Livigno, Italy
Livigno is way out on a limb in its own enclosed valley 190 km away from Brescia.

❹ Baqueira-Beret, Spain
Fly to Toulouse, still a hefty 170 km away. Barcelona, another option, is 340 km!

❺ Arinsal, Andorra
A Pyrenean theme is developing – Arinsal to Toulouse is another hefty four-hour schlep.

❻ Espace Killy
170 km away from Geneva, but usually takes around four hours thanks to snarled up transfer day traffic on the roads through the Tarantaise.

For experts

❶ Chamonix, France
If only because there are so many decisions to make when it is good – which resort, which lift, which queue to avoid.

❷ Levi, Finland
It's a lovely place, but too flat for the real steep pitch lovers.

❸ Borovets, Bulgaria
The epitome of the 'pile 'em high, pack 'em in' beginner friendly resort.

❹ Vogel, Slovenia
Another resort suffering from a lack of pitch. Good job the incredible views compensate.

❺ Campitello, Italy
There is some good terrain, but it is a tiny area.

❻ Pas de la Casa, Andorra
If only because you're likely to have a hangover every morning.

What to take

Increasing numbers of skiers carry rucksacks on the slopes today, but what exactly have they got in there? While in many cases they're simply on-slope handbags filled with suncream, camera, sarnie and wallet, for some serious off-piste skiers the pack and its contents are quite literally lifesavers.

We've asked Klaus Kranebitter, an Austrian State-certified ski and mountain guide and Head of Guides at SAAC (Snow & Avalanche Awareness Camps) to give us a brief lowdown on avalanche safety and explain precisely what every skier who ventures off the beaten track should carry with them:

"A rucksack is an essential tool for any freerider – it's vital to carry all the safety gear listed below every time you go off-piste. The safety gear isn't just a list of equipment that will enable you to react in the case of an avalanche, it also includes sufficient kit to *prevent* an accident. A spare pair of gloves, goggles and a jacket – these can help prevent frostbite or loss of orientation on stormy days. The food and drink will help you to stay concentrated and hydrated.

The safety equipment used specifically in the case of avalanche accidents includes a beacon, used both to find a buried skier and be found yourself, and the shovel and probe, which enable you to locate precisely the buried skier and dig him out. To use the equipment efficiently and successfully, sign up for training initially, check your kit each time you go out and attend refresher avalanche awareness courses.

The safety gear list:
▶▶ Rucksack, minimum 20 litres volume
▶▶ Avalanche beacon
▶▶ Avalanche shovel and probe
▶▶ First-aid pack

▶▶ Mobile phone to call for help
▶▶ A map to tell rescue teams where you are
▶▶ Spare gloves, goggles and clothes
▶▶ Bivouac pack to keep injured people warm
▶▶ Thermos bottle for warm drinks, water and some granola bars

The best rucksack you can choose is an AAS (Avalanche Airbag System) pack. Should you be caught in an avalanche, you pull a cord, the pack inflates and you'll float on top of the snow. This invaluable pack will reduce your chances of getting buried to about 1%."

Avalanche awareness

As more skiers embrace the thrill of off-piste skiing, resorts are becoming increasingly aware of the need to inform visitors about avalanches: how they're created, how to avoid getting caught in one and how best to react should you become involved in an avalanche incident.

Subsequently, avalanche training courses and parks are becoming increasingly widespread throughout Europe and many resorts provide free seminars and avalanche transceiver training. For example, Les Deux Alpes runs the 'Free Respect' programme, which provides free evening seminars and daytime instruction about avalanche risk and even has a small exhibition and avalanche simulator at the base of the slopes.

A good way to get an introduction to avalanche awareness is to book a guide for a day of off-piste instruction – if you don't have your own safety gear, your guide will issue you with the kit and explain how to use it all. If that whets your appetite and you get the powder hunger, invest in the safety equipment that Klaus lists (see page 17), get acquainted with it in a transceiver training park and/or take an avalanche awareness course.

Davos in Switzerland was the site of the first **Avalanche Training Centre** (ATC), a snow park in which several active transmitters are buried at varying depths in order to enable skiers to practice tracking them down using their avalanche beacons

and probes in a safe environment. There are now several ATCs across the Alps in Switzerland (Leysin, Andermatt, Zinal, Zermatt and Mürren), Austria (the Arlberg) and France (Courchevel, Méribel and La Grave). Free tuition is offered at all the ATCs – check with the local Ski Patrol team to find out which days they'll be there.

Similar transceiver training parks exist in other resorts in France, where they're called ARVA parks (named after the leading French brand of transceiver). You'll find ARVA parks in Les Trois Vallées, La Plagne, Les Arcs, Val d'Isère, Serre Chevalier, Pelvoux and Tignes. Again, ask the local ski patrollers which days they offer free tuition. Skiers in Val d'Isère, Chamonix or Méribel should definitely drop by one of **Henry's Avalanche Talks** (henrysavalanchetalk.com) – regular, informal and very informative talks by avalanche expert Henry Schniewind for just €10.

In order to really understand why avalanches occur and learn to read the snowpack confidently, try an avalanche awareness course. We recommend that every serious freerider tries one of the excellent **Snow & Avalanche Awareness Camps** (SAAC; saac.at) courses. Held at various Austrian resorts, SAAC offer free two-day introduction courses, the SAAC Basic Camp, as well as more intensive three or five-day courses. Basic theory is covered but there's also plenty of off-piste guiding.

For the seriously dedicated, the **European Avalanche School** (EAS; euro-avalanche.com), the result of a partnership with the Canadian Avalanche Association and British Mountain Guides Association, runs a programme of in-depth, certified avalanche training courses for experienced off-piste skiers in Sweden, Finland, France and Scotland. The location of the courses varies but the main objectives are to give participants an in-depth knowledge of snow structure, the processes of change within it and, through on-slope experience, learn to read snowpack stability and become confident in ascertaining potential avalanche risk.

A history of modern skiing

1843: The first known civilian ski race takes place in Tromsø, Norway.

1864: St Moritz welcomes its first British winter tourists.

1868: Norwegian ski pioneer Sondre Norheim introduces the 'Telemark' ski, a short, curved, flexible wooden ski that enables easy turning in soft snow. He also develops a form of ski tuition based on the 'Christiania' or 'Stem Christi' turn.

1888: The Norwegian Fridtjof Nansen makes the first crossing of Greenland on skis. The report on his expedition, published in 1890 in both Norwegian and English, arouses great interest in skiing in Europe and the United States. Skiing becomes a regular news item and is soon adopted as a pastime and sport by wealthy Europeans.

1903: Sir Arnold Lunn organizes the first packaged ski holidays from England. He takes skiers to Adelboden, Switzerland.

1920: Johannes (Hannes) Schneider from Stuben near St Anton, Austria revolutionizes skiing by creating the 'Arlberg Technique' tuition system. Not only does he formalize the progression from snowplough to connected turns, he also dictates a set of ethical standards for the profession of ski instruction, truly establishing skiing as a popular recreational activity.

1931: Sir Arnold Lunn organises the first World Championships in Downhill and Slalom Racing at Mürren, Switzerland.

1928: The world's first solid aluminium skis are tested in France.

1932: Erna Low places an ad in the personal columns of the London Times: "Young Viennese graduate seeks other young people to join her Christmas skiing". It's the first step to building what will become Erna Low Consultants, the UK's largest self-drive tour operator to the French Alps in 2008.

1934: The first t-bar opens in Davos, Switzerland. Giovanni Agnelli builds Europe's first purpose-built ski resort: Sestriere, Italy.

1936: The world's first overhead chairlift opens at Sun Valley, Idaho .

1950: Warren Miller releases his first annual ski film *Deep and Light*.

1958: Joseph Martin launches the first ski pass in Les Deux Alpes.

1964: Lange launches the first all-plastic ski boots.

1968: Fibreglass skis supplant both wood and aluminium for use in most recreational skis and slalom racing skis.

1970s: The rise (and fall) of the mono-ski.

1973: Les Trois Vallées becomes the world's largest ski area connected by ski lifts and slopes with a single ski pass.

1980s: The birth of snowboarding.

1985: France bans heliskiing.

1993: The launch of 'parabolic' skis by Elan – shorter, fatter skis with deep sidecuts than enable better carving and turning capabilities. Traditional skiing technique changes dramatically as ski instructors are hauled back to school to learn 'modern skiing'.

2005: Italy decrees it's compulsory for all under-14s to wear ski helmets on the slopes.

Skiers' tales
Tignes spirit

Tignes today is a new town – one look at the concrete apartment blocks tells you that. Less well known is that its heritage goes back a long way – back to the Middle Ages, when the secluded village of Les Breniers (it translates literally as 'where the goats are reared') was renowned for its blue cheeses and lacework. By the early 1800s, Les Breniers existed in relative seclusion, faintly notorious for the produce the villagers exported to the rest of France via nearby Bourg St Maurice (the major town in the region – situated at the bottom of the valley from Tignes). But in the mid-20th century, two things had a dramatic effect on the hamlet. The first was in 1937, when the Iseran Pass connecting nearby Bourg St Maurice with Italy opened. Its immediate effect was to inflate the importance of Tignes' neighbour Val d'Isère. When the pass opened, Val had two hotels. By 1966, there were 62. To say it hasn't looked back is to flirt dangerously with understatement. Although at the time Tignes, a few kilometres off the beaten track, couldn't compete, the local die had been cast. Tourism would be the new lifeblood of the area.

The second event took place in the early fifties. Rumours of a dam had been doing the rounds in the Alps as far back as 1928, but the local communities had always vehemently – and often violently – opposed any construction work, often making raids on those undertaking evaluation work. But with so many of those against the project killed in the Second World War (it is estimated that three in four men of working age did not return to Tignes after the conflict), the French government moved in on Tignes and announced plans to build a dam across the Isère river at a natural rock bottleneck half a mile downstream from Les Breniers.

According to legend, only the local priest had any understanding of the consequences of building the dam, so with sly timing the authorities waited for him to pass away before announcing their plans. He died in 1952, and according to one source had only just been put in the ground when the first bulldozers moved in. Over the next five years, some 5000 workers lived, breathed and toiled on the ambitious dam project. Local factions, having regrouped after the losses in the war, put up a fight, disrupting the building and resisting the might of the project. But inevitably the 'Barrage de Tignes' went up, opening with the impressive boast that it would soon supply up to 10% of France's electricity needs with its hydroelectric generators.

But what about the ensuing local havoc caused by such a huge engineering project? Les Breniers was buried as the lake rose, never to be seen again. Though furious at this outcome, the locals did recognize the economic benefits. Workers had injected enough cash into the region over the previous five years to enable bars, restaurants and hotels to flourish. Almost by accident, the infrastructure had been laid for tourism to take hold. With a donation of cash from the government, they did a remarkably forward thinking thing: they built a ski lift. Tignes as we know it now was up and running.

Of course, it helped that next door in Val d'Isère they were one step ahead of the game. But while their growth was slow, steady and based on traditional housing, Tignes embraced (some people would say a little too eagerly) the modernist architecture movement prevalent at the time. The ensuing development gave birth to the modern towns of Les Boisses, Le Lac, Val Claret and Lavachet at the higher end, and the smaller, quainter town of Les Breviers underneath the dam at the bottom of the valley, where the bulk of the construction

workers lived. But if they got the style of building wrong, one thing is certain – the hills around the place couldn't have been better designed had Wren, Gaud' and Rennie Mackintosh all sat down and designed them specifically with snowboarding in mind. And when the bulging network of lifts from Tignes and Val d'Isère was finally combined to form the outstanding Espace Killy (named in honour of Jean Claude Killy, the region's 1968 Olympic downhill gold medallist), the previously ridiculous concept of this unassuming French hamlet idea being one of the world's finest winter sports destinations suddenly didn't seem so stupid. Killy's notoriety also brought untold publicity to the valley. What these new visitors discovered was an area boasting some of the best runs in the world and catering for every conceivable budget. From the 1970s onwards, Tignes and Val d'Isère attracted everyone from King Juan Carlos of Spain to the lowliest ski bum in his camper van. Tignes had made it.

These days Tignes is enjoying a brilliant rebirth. With a glacier guaranteeing snow, a longer season than most resorts can offer and a newer, more responsible approach to its architecture, Tignes is now considered one of the resorts of the millennium. And the best part about the whole story is that at its heart is the most delicious of ironies: the dam, the unwanted catalyst behind the changes wrought to the valley, has never actually been used to generate electricity.

The piste less skied

There are some truly legendary off-piste routes in Europe. When you stand at the top of any of the six routes below, you'll find yourself in a truly high-Alpine environment. And slightly terrified.

Before thinking about tackling any of these routes, book a certified mountain guide to lead the way and ensure you're fully equipped with avalanche safety equipment. Do not attempt them on your own.

Cheminées de Mascle, Alpe d'Huez

The two 'Mascle Chimneys' are clearly visible from the Marmottes 3 DMC cablecar and the sight of these steep, narrow gullies snaking down from the top of the Grandes Rousses deters all but the most determined skiers. The left chimney (on skiers left of the cablecar) is the steeper of the two with short sections of a 50° pitch. The couloirs are west-facing and need plenty of snow to make them skiable, so don't attempt them until spring.

Valluga north face, St Anton

There are three main routes off the north face of the Valluga into Zürs – our favourite incorporates the Valluga Bridge Couloir, where you make your way down roped steps to an old wooden bridge that spans the couloir. Clamber under the bridge and negotiate your way down the short, steep gully onto the west face of Valluga to be rewarded with the stupendous Paziel Tal powder bowl.

Pas de Chevre, Chamonix

Just one of so many epic off-piste routes in Chamonix, Pas de Chevre is reached from the top of Grands Montets and brings you out by the Montenvers train at the Mer de Glace. It offers spectacular views of the Drus and Aiguille Verte and good variation, leading you down wide open powder bowls and into tight couloirs before bringing you into the Vallée Blanche.

Pan de Rideau, La Grave

La Grave's Trifides t-bar accesses the four infamous Les Trifides couloirs as well as the challenging Pan de Rideau run. Just above the lift you'll find the Brèche de la Girosse (Girosse Gap), which leads to the aptly-named Glacier du Râteau ('se prendre un râteau' means to fall badly in French). Climb above the Gap and you emerge at the top of the northeast couloir and Pan de Rideau – seriously steep and exposed gullies which bring you down into Vallons.

La Table d'Orientation and Le Cairn, Val d'Isère

While the well-known La Banane in Bellevarde is easily accessible and long, with a vertical drop of nearly 900 m, a short hike from the beginning of the 1992 Olympic Downhill piste to La Table d'Orientation gives you a more varied and challenging run. A narrow couloir brings you onto the long Le Cairn run.

The back of Montfort, Verbier

Despite having destroyed a knee while skiing on the back of Verbier's spectacular Montfort, we still can't resist the tingle of anticipation that accompanies the noise of clipping into the rope at the bottom of the cablecar as we start to traverse into the main couloir. The descent is long, varied and offers outstanding views.

7443

DURING CHRIS DAVENPORT AND STIAN HAGEN'S ALPS PROJECT, THE TWO ACCOMPLISHED SKI MOUNTAINEERS SKIED 7,443 VERTICAL METERS ON FOUR OF EUROPE'S MOST ICONIC MOUNTAINS. 7,443 METERS OF STEEP, TECHNICAL, EXPOSED, HEART-IN-YOUR-THROAT SKIING. BUT THE PROJECT WASN'T JUST ABOUT QUENCHING THE TWO SKIER'S THIRST FOR ADRENALIN AND ADVENTURE. FOR CHRIS, IT WAS ALL ABOUT BRINGING THE SKIING POSSIBILITIES OF THESE PEAKS TO A BROADER AUDIENCE. FOR STIAN, WHO LIVES IN CHAMONIX, THE PROJECT REPRESENTED A RETURN TO HIS SKI MOUNTAINEERING ROOTS. TO FIND OUT MORE ABOUT THE ALPS PROJECT AND THE GEAR THAT MADE IT POSSIBLE, VISIT **HELLYHANSEN.COM**

H/H ®

STIAN HAGEN & CHRIS DAVENPORT. POINT LACHENAL, MONT BLANC MASSIVE.
PHOTO: CHRISTIAN PONDELLA.

HELLYHANSEN.COM

Ten cult powder days

Once you've experienced the exhilaration of slicing through deep, fluffy, virgin powder, with little pockets of snow bouncing up over your knees and into your face and nothing to be heard but the whooping of your fellow skiers, you will be officially hooked on skiing in powder. A fully-fledged powder hound, you'll find yourself going to increasing lengths to track down the magical white stuff; visiting resorts known for their off-piste, hiking further to reach untracked bowls, waking up at the crack of dawn on powder days ...
Here are some of the most satisfying powder runs:

❶ La Grave, France
Regarded by extreme skiers as one of the world's finest powder destinations. La Grave only has three chairlifts and two marked pistes, which pretty much says it all.

❷ St Anton, Austria
A perennial favourite for all European powder hounds. Stuben and Rendl are best for short, relatively quiet powder hits, while the Valluga is a must for any powder devotee.

❸ Verbier, Switzerland
A magnet for off-piste skiers, Verbier has a fantastic choice of long, varied and incredibly scenic powder routes. The only hard bit is deciding which one to do first.

❹ Lech and Zürs, Austria
Zürs is by no means 'simply' the end of the epic Valluga-Zürs freeriding route: both it and its neighbour Lech are mini powder wonderlands in their own right.

❺ Ischgl, Austria
Although well-known in Europe, Ischgl is seriously underrated as a powder destination in the UK. It's high, north-facing, has wide, steep powder bowls and gets tracked out much more slowly than most resorts on this list.

❻ Engelberg, Switzerland
Home to the famous 'Laub' run, a glacier and more off-piste than you can shake a ski pole at, it's no wonder that Engelberg is home to a host of extreme ski photographers and film makers.

❼ Alpe d'Huez, France
Probably a surprise entry for many readers but we love ADH for it's relatively quiet but extensive and seriously challenging freeriding terrain, particularly the runs down into Vaujaney.

❽ Andermatt, Switzerland
Small, mountain-lovers town with hardcore off-piste routes off Gemstock mountain and virtually deserted runs on Winterhorn.

❾ Chamonix, France
One of the world's finest and most challenging resorts. You have to wake up at the crack of dawn to beat the crowds but get fresh tracks on Grands Montets and you certainly won't be yawning.

❿ Val d'Isère, France
Couloirs, powder bowls, steeps, trees – Val really does have it all on a powder day.

Country price comparision

					@	
Andorra	€1	€3	€3	€1	€5	€1.50
Austria	€1.50	€3	€4	€1	€4	€2
Bulgaria	BGN1	BGN2	BGN2.50	BGN1	BGN2	BGN1.20
Finland	€2	€4	€5	€1.60	€5	€1.30
France	€2	€4.50	€5	€1	€4	€1.50
Italy	€1	€2.50	€2.50	€1	€3	€1.30
Norway	NOK22	NOK30	NOK50	NOK12	NOK10-15	NOK10.50
Slovenia	€1	€2	€1.50	€0.50	€1.50	€1.15
Spain	€1	€3	€3	€1	€5	€1.50
Sweden	SEK25	SEK30	SEK40	SEK13	SEK19	SEK12.22
Switzerland	CHF3.50	CHF6	CHF5	CHF2	CHF12	CHF2.50

Skiers' tales
Aosta Valley by Rob Smith

"The French Alps without the queues" is a description that springs to mind when skiing in the Aosta Valley. It's a well-known fact that Italy's Alpine neighbours – France, Switzerland and Austria – are home to some of the best skiing in the world, and therein lies the problem: it's a well-known fact! But nip through the Mont Blanc Tunnel into Italy's Aosta valley and you'll be surrounded by the same Alpine peaks (including the two highest – Mont Blanc and Mont Blanc de Courmayeur) while skiing wide open slopes with practically nobody around. Quite how this anomaly has come about is something of a mystery. Could it be a type of ski snobbery? A stigma attached to a bad safety record from the eighties? Or is it that Italy's military pilots have just a tad too much bravado? Whatever the reason, it means that those in the know can experience queue-free skiing with no fuss.

Geographically, the Alps separate Italy from continental Europe, with the Aosta Valley cutting deep into the heart of the range, right up to the base of the highest peak, the Mont Blanc massif. This has made the region incredibly important in the past, as historical trading routes used passes over the mountains surrounding the valley. These passes are now used by the ski resorts and make it possible to ski in three different countries.

The valley has five main ski regions all within a short drive of each other and they are all linked. It gives the skier many options, such as the ability to ski Courmayeur, La Thuile or Pila on the same pass. There's even a special Aosta Valley pass that grants you access to all the resorts, which is great if you've got a hire car and want to explore.

Another plus is that most of the resorts are family orientated, which is reflected in the skiing. The pistes are wide, safe and well groomed. Also, with new lifts going up and improvements to the infrastructure going on every year, queues are at a minimum and you'll be whisked to the top of the peaks in comfort and double-quick time. Apart from Aosta, the capital, which is the liveliest place in the valley, the towns have a quiet Alpine ambience.

Perhaps as a result of the valley's uniqueness, certain ski companies are now considered to be Aosta specialists. **Interski** (interski.co.uk) have been organizing trips to the region for years and have just started 'Interski Classics' that aim at the adult market. With so much experience they're acknowledged as the Aosta experts and are well worth checking out. But there are other specialists, such as **Ski2** (ski-2.com), who are able to add that personal touch to your trip. They're based in Champoluc where you can make use of the largest ski area in the valley, the Monte Rosa. They provide some fantastic packages for different budgets and personally vet every hotel on their books.

If this all sounds too good to be true, it's probably worth mentioning at this juncture the embarrassment of off-piste riches on offer in the region. There is truly too much to explore during the average week. At Courmayeur, where the Italian Alpine Guide Association was founded, you've got access to the daddy of all 'Alpine Hors Piste' runs – La Vallée Blanche. In the San Bernadino region, you'll find forests to ski through and an off-piste area patrolled by pisteurs in an effort to ensure skiers can get their powder technique down and ski in safety without paying for a guide. At the Monte Rosa area, there's the Col d'Olen and the surrounding territory that goes with it, making it something of an off-piste Mecca.

Italy is the cheapest country in the Alps to ski and one of the only places you can enjoy heli-skiing. If you haven't tried it, try it in the Aosta Valley. It won't crack your credit card, you've got incredible peaks, descents and glaciers to take on and the organizations that run the flights have years of experience. Head there now before the crowds descend.

Ski areas explained

Sometimes the ski industry is all about numbers – number of runs, kilometres of pistes, hourly lift capacity, number of beds. And although we know that such stark figures are rarely representative of the true worth of a ski area (La Grave, for example, with its one lift, is considered by the cognoscenti to be one of the world's best backcountry resorts), statistics can be especially persuasive when you're trying to narrow down your resort options. Especially when you're a lesser known resort trying to compete with Chamonix for terrain, say, or St Anton for nightlife.

Long established multi resort areas have long seen the value in flagging up this side of their operation. It is generally accepted that the French started it all when they linked the Trois Vallées (roughly Courchevel, Méribel and Val Thorens) and the Espace Killy (Tignes and Val d'Isère) areas. These were logical moves: large 'name' resorts in adjacent valleys were involved, and the result for skiers was more choice, better facilities and, ultimately, better value for money.

Obviously there were other, perhaps not unexpected by-products of this, and there's kudos in being the biggest. Soon other resorts cottoned on and local planners, tongues hanging out of the corners of their mouths and armed with setsquares, compasses and overactive imaginations, began to enthusiastically redraw resort boundaries in the manner of fevered First World War generals. The establishment of the Portes du Soleil (Avoriaz, Morzine, Châtel, Flaine, Le Crozet), Milky Way (various French and Italian resorts), Grand Massif (Flaine, Les Carroz, Samoens, Morillion and Sixt Fer a' Cheval) and Dolomiti Super Ski (almost every resort in the Dolomites) regions followed. Such is the popularity of this marketing approach that right now the ski industry is witnessing more tenuous amalgamations than the Monopolies Commission.

In recent years, Les Arcs and La Plagne have joined forces to become 'Paradiski', while Davos and Klosters are trying to pretend that they aren't two separate villages at all and are really one homogenous resort known as 'Davos-Klosters'. Then there are areas such as the Andorran Grandvalira and Vallnord 'resorts', or the Swiss Alpes Vaudoises area, who seem to be taking things to an even more tenuous extreme, with resorts only connectable by road included in increasingly imaginative super areas.

For the modern holidaying skier, faced with a bewildering number of options even in Europe, it is a good idea to be wise to this increasingly used ruse. Check the piste map before you go, and try to work out if you can actually ski as many different areas as promised, or whether a car or bus journey is essential. After all, sometimes biggest doesn't necessarily mean best. The resorts in this book which feature as part of larger ski areas are as follows:

Portes du Soleil Avoriaz, Châtel, Les Gets, Morzine, Champéry.

Paradiski Les Arcs, La Plagne, Bourg St Maurice and Champagny.

Trois Vallées Courchevel, La Tania, Méribel, Mottaret, St Martin de Belleville, Val Thorens.

Espace Killy Val d'Isère, Tignes.

Grand Domaine Valmorel.

Dolomiti superski Alta Badia, Campitello, Canazei, Cortina, Plan de Corones and Val Gardena.

Ski Welt Westendorf and Ellmau.

Espace San Bernardo La Thuile and La Rosière.

Monte Rosa Alagna, Champoluc and Gressoney.

Forêt Blanche Risoul and Vars

Grandvalira includes Grau Roig, Pas de la Casa and Soldeu-El Tarter, Canillo and Encamp.

Vallnord includes Arinsal, Pal, La Massana, Arcalis.

Opposite page: *Grand Domaine*, Valmorel.
Top: *Espace San Bernardo*, La Rosière.
Left: *Espace Killy*, Val d'Isère.
Right: *Espace Killy*, Val d'Isère.

Ski schools

Andorra & Spain
Baqueira-Beret
Baqueira British Ski School T+44 (0)1903-868249 (bbskischool.co.uk)

Austria
Zell am See
Skischule Zell am See T+43 (0)654-273207 (ski-zellamsee.at)

France
Alpe d'Huez
Ecole de Ski Internationale T +33 (0)476-804277 (ecoledeskiinternationale.com)
Avoriaz
Avoriaz Alpine Ski School T + 44 (0)1237-451099 (avoriazalpineskischool.com)
Chamonix
BASS Chamonix Ltd T+44 (0)845-4681003 (basschamonix.com)
Freedom 2 Ski T+33 (0)673-049412 (freedom2ski.com)
Courchevel
Around-Ski T+33 (0)616-567838 (around-ski.co.uk)
First Tracks Ski Coaching T+33 (0)479-079993 (first-tracks.fr)
Magic Snowsports Academy T+33 (0)479-081199 (magicfr.com)
New Generation Ski & Snowboard School T+ 33 (0)479-010318 (skinewgen.com)
Rtmsnowboarding T+33 (0)615-485904
SKI EXCEL T+33(0)7949 387699 (skiexcel.com)
Supreme Ski & Snowboard School T+33 (0)479-082787 (supremeski.com)
Flaine
Ski Ecole International T+33 (0)450-908441 (skiecoleflaine.com)
La Tania
First Tracks Ski Coaching T+33 (0)476-250422 (first-tracks.fr)
Les Arcs
Ecole de Ski Internationale Arc Aventures T+33 (0)479-076002 (arc-aventures.com)
Les Deux Alpes
Bliss Snow School T+33 (0)476-795676 (blisssnowschool.fr)
Easiski T+ 33 (0)476-795884 (easiski.com)

Les Gets
British Alpine Ski & Snowboard School T+44 (0)1485-572596 (britishskischool.com)
Méribel
First Tracks Ski Coaching T+33 (0)476-250422 (first-tracks.fr)
Parallel Lines T+44 (0)1702-589580 (parallel-lines.com)
Rtmsnowboarding T+33 (0)615-485904 (rtmsnowboarding.com)
Ste Foy
Progression Ski and Snowboard School T+44 (0)208-1233001 (progressionski.com)
Serre Chevalier
EurekaSKI T+33 (0)492-245647 (eurekaski.com)
Snow Connections T+33 (0)492-462832 (snow-connections.com)

Tignes
Alliance Snowboarding T+33 (0)677-577860
(alliancesnowboarding.com)
Alpine Logic T+44 (0)1248-671058
(ski-instruction-tignes.co.uk)
ESF Tignes Le Lac T+33 (0)479-063028 (esf-tignes.com)
Progression Ski and Snowboard School
T+44(0)208-1233001 (progressionski.com)
Ultimate Snowsports T+44 (0)7772690746
(ultimatesnowsports.com)
Val d'Isère
British American Ski School T+33 (0) 671-758225
(valdisereskischool.com)
Martin Mckay Skiing T+44(0)7710 237 094
Progression Ski and Snowboard School
T+44 (0)208-1233001 (progressionski.com)
the development centre T+33 (0)615-553156 (tdcski.com)
Val Thorens
Prosneige T+33 (0)479-010700 (prosneige.fr/en)

Alta Badia
Ski and Snowboard School Dolomites
T+39 (0)4710-844018 (skidolomites.it)
Cervinia
Scuola di Sci del Cervino T+39 (0)166-948744
(scuolacervino.com)
Cortina
Cristallo Cortina Ski School T+39 (0)436-879483
(scicristallocortina.com)
Livigno
Ski & Snowboard School Galli Fedele T+ 39 (0)342-970300
(scuolascilivigno.net)
Sauze d'Oulx
Scuola Sci Sauze Sportinia T+39 (0)122-850218
(scuolascisportinia.com)
Sestriere
Scuola Nazionale Sci Sestriere T+39 (0)122-77060
(scuolascisestriere.com)

Switzerland
Davos
Schweizer Schneesportschule Davos T+41 (0)814-162454
(ssd.ch)
Saas Fee
Eskimos Sports GMBH T+41 (0)279-574904 (eskimos.ch)
St Moritz
Ski Cool St Moritz (BASS) T+41 (0)793-645292
Verbier
Adrenaline International Ski School T+41 (0)277-717459
(adrenaline-verbier.ch)
Skier's Toolbox T+41 (0)796-519286 (skierstoolbox.com)
Villars
Ecole Suisse de Ski T+41 (0)244-952210 (ess-villars.ch)
Villars Ski School LLC T+41 (0)244-954545
Zermatt
Summit Ski & Snowboard School T+41 (0)279-670001
(summitskischool.com)

Essentials Ski schools

Andorra and Spain

Andorra & Spain rating

Value for money
★★★★★

Nightlife
★★★★☆

Off-piste
★★★☆☆

Family
★★★★☆

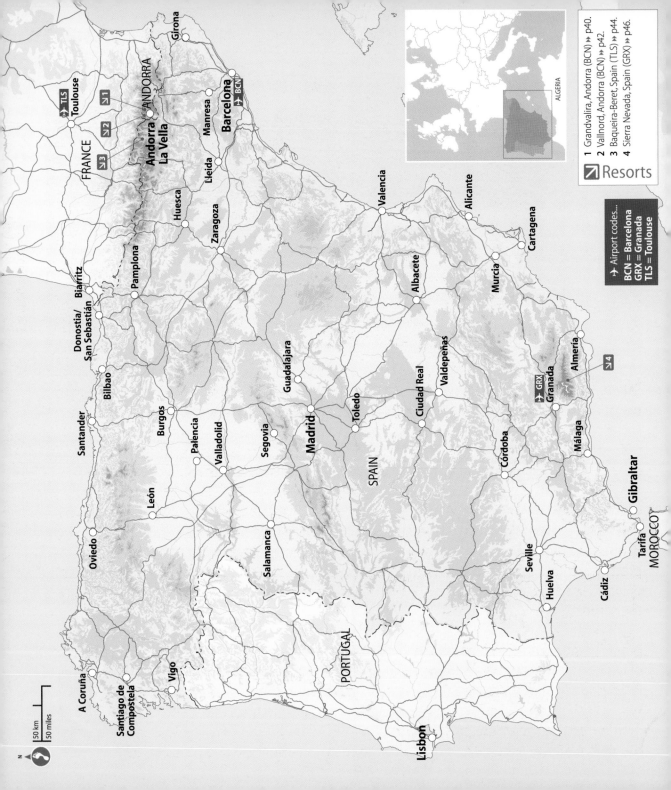

1 Grandvalira, Andorra (BCN) ➤ p40.
2 Vallnord, Andorra (BCN) ➤ p42.
3 Baqueira-Beret, Spain (TLS) ➤ p44.
4 Sierra Nevada, Spain (GRX) ➤ p46.

➤ Resorts

✈ Airport codes...

BCN = Barcelona
GRX = Granada
TLS = Toulouse

FRANCE

Toulouse
✈ TLS
➚ 1
➚ 2
➚ 3

ANDORRA
Andorra La Vella

Girona

Barcelona
✈ BCN

Manresa
Lleida
Huesca
Zaragoza
Pamplona
Biarritz
Donostia/
San Sebastián
Bilbao
Santander

Valencia
Alicante
Cartagena
Murcia
Albacete
Valdepeñas
Ciudad Real
Guadalajara
Toledo
Madrid
Segovia
Valladolid
Palencia
Burgos
León

SPAIN

Almería
✈ GRX
Granada
➚ 4
Málaga
Córdoba
Seville
Huelva
Cádiz
Tarifa
Gibraltar
MOROCCO

ALGERIA

Oviedo
A Coruña
Santiago de Compostela
Vigo
Salamanca

PORTUGAL

Lisbon

50 km
50 miles

N

Skiing in Spain? The uninitiated might baulk at the prospect, but there is some serious fun to be found in this neglected (at least for winter holidays) corner of Europe. True, the Spanish resorts of the Pyrenees are generally less celebrated than those of their distinctly more snowy-sounding neighbour Andorra. But they share many similarities, starting with their position on the flanks of that particular mountain range, which is actually older than the Alps – fact fans – and, if possible, more rugged in appearance. Both are blessed with plenty of snow and lots of sunshine, and have local cultures that thrive in their own Petri dish-like environments, far from the mainstream. As part of the Iberian peninsula, resorts such as Baqueira-Beret in Spain and Soldeu in Andorra are subject to the same climate and, thus, pretty much the same conditions. Truly, these are ski areas separated only by the constructs of language and custom. In terms of their natural position and geography, they are basically the same place.

And then there is Sierra Nevada, Europe's most southerly winter sports outpost, sitting proud in the south of Spain and overlooking the Mediterranean. Just the cultural uniqueness of a trip here is enough to warrant inclusion in the guide. Sure, going skiing or snowboarding in Spain in sight of Africa might sound daring or even slightly risky, when you're all but guaranteed snow and crazy nightlife in the familiar surroundings of somewhere like Méribel or St Anton. But weren't winter sports meant to be daring? And what could be more daring than travelling outside your comfort zone to see what else the world has to offer?

Skiing Andorra and Spain

Spain and Andorra might share the same environment, but they are very different places and the development of their skiing industries has unfolded along sharply contrasting lines. Andorra has long been known as king of the budget package holiday, especially among skiers attracted by its cheapness and suitability for beginners – a kind of proto-Bulgaria, if you like. As a result, Andorra's profile has benefited greatly from this popularity, and the resorts themselves have responded by investing heavily in their infrastructures and marketing – as seen by the establishment of the Grandvalira and Vallnord areas. Spain, in contrast, rarely troubles the mainstream skier. Think Spain and understandably the immediate connotations are of beaches and partying rather than mountains and powder. Nevertheless, it is home to a

fantastic local skiing and snowboarding scene, and in Baqueria-Beret the Spanish have a resort unique among its European peers.

The other hugely appealing aspect of any ski trip to Spain is the chance to combine it with a city break or a surf trip. The surf breaks of the Basque country are among the best in Europe, and this bounty is all confined to a relatively small area. With some flexibility and a hire car, those 'ski in the morning, beach in the afternoon' clichés can become a reality here.

Above all, Iberian snow offers a different take on an old theme. As Thomaz Garcia, editor of the Spanish *Snow Planet* magazine says, "...while the more celebrated Alps might be described as quaint, Pyrenean mountain culture is definitely rougher round the edges. Ancient villages,

whose inhabitants haven't changed their lifestyle in centuries, dot the mountainside." Away from the Alpine heartland, with its predominantly Franco-German culture, there's a freshness about a trip to Spain and Andorra that causes you to re-evaluate the old associations you might lazily have begun to foster. Tapas after skiing instead of *tartiflette* or fondue? Such a simple difference changes the context entirely. Consider the amazing riding as well, and you've got quite a trip.

Conditions

The Pyrenean resorts are subject to weather systems coming in from the sea. This humidity can bring huge amounts of snow in a short period of time – but it also means the resulting cover can melt quickly, and the area is characterized by a melting cycle far more rapid than that which takes place in the Alps. The moral is to make sure you're up early on a powder day to take quick advantage of it. Sierra Nevada is even more of a paradox, managing to combine limitless sunshine (it's often touted as Europe's 'sunniest' resort) with a long-lasting base, much of which is thanks to the resort's height and slick snowmaking system. Unsurprisingly, the spring conditions here are pretty amazing. And look out for the snow taking on a reddish tint – the result of sand blowing over from the Sahara and staining the snow. You don't get that in Val d'Isère

When To Go

Thanks to an obvious difference in latitude, Andorra and Spain are subject to slightly warmer temperatures than the other main European ski centres, even if the resorts tend to have similar opening times (Sierra Nevada, for example, stays open until the end of April). As with the other European countries, January and February are the best months to go for guaranteed snow and low temperatures, but early March is probably the best time to go if you're planning a city break as well. By this time of the year, the temperature is pleasantly rising in the cities and along the coast, while there is still plenty of snow in the mountains.

Off-Piste Policy

Perhaps the main thing to say is that heli-boarding and snowmobiling are legal here, unlike in France. Immediately, this opens up plenty of options for those prepared to pay the money to experience real Pyrenean backcountry conditions. That said, private sled rentals and private heli ops are the norm, so speak to some locals to find out more.

In resort, everything is on limits to inquisitive riders, although it goes without saying that the same dangers are very prevalent and you should make sure you're fully kitted out with full avalanche equipment. Resort boundaries are well defined,

PROS

Friendly locals, great nightlife.

As you'd expect, it's generally sunnier here than in the rest of the mainland, so pack some mirrored lenses.

By mixing in a city break, make the trip more unusual.

The food! It's one of the main reasons for making the trip.

Cheaper than the rest.

CONS

Check the snow before you go. Late season in particular is a bit of a lottery.

Freestylers should choose their spot carefully. Good parks do exist, but they are by no means widespread.

Some antiquated lift systems, although this part of the world is catching up quickly.

but there is plenty of scope for exploration, particularly in Baqueira-Beret and Andorra's Vallnord.

Secret Spots

Andorra and particularly Spain's slightly isolated position in the alpine world means that the resorts don't have as huge an influx of foreign skiers as the French and Austrian resorts do. As such, the atmosphere here is one of inquisitive friendliness rather than the hostility that can arise in France when it comes to the testy subject of local powder rights.

Andorra & Spain Skiing Andorra and Spain

Essentials

Getting there

One of the best parts about doing a trip to Spain or Andorra is the opportunity it affords to spend some time in one of the great Spanish cities. For Spain and Andorra, the handiest point of entry is Barcelona. Carriers to Barcelona include **easyJet** (easyJet.com), **Swiss Air** (swiss.com), **KLM** (klm.com), **Air France** (airfrance.com), **Lufthansa** (lufthansa.com), **Iberia** (Iberia.com) and **British Airways** (ba.com). Another option is to fly into Bilbao and spend some time in San Sebastián before heading into the mountains. Airlines flying into Bilbao include **easyJet**, **British Airways**, **Alitalia** (alitalia.com), **Air France** and **Lufthansa**. Other airport options include Biarritz (**easyJet**, **Air France**, **BMI.com**, **BA** and **Lufthansa**) and Toulouse (**BA**, **KLM**, **Air France**, **Alitalia**).

Red Tape

Spain is a fully paid-up EU member, so member nationals only need a valid passport to travel to and from the country. Other foreign nationals can stay for 90 days on a valid passport. A few exceptions require a visa – check spain.info for more information. Note that all flight entries now require strict submissions of extra information on top of your booking. Your airline should let you know of the increased security measures, and should include an additional form for you to fill in on the booking. Andorra is not a member of the EU, but in most cases a valid passport is enough to gain entry.

Getting Around

Although there are public transport facilities (see below) driving is probably the easiest way of making this trip. The Spanish and Andorrans drive on the right, and a full driving licence (photo type or International Driving Permit) is required plus liability insurance – you need a 'green card' certificate to prove this. You also need to carry two warning triangles by law and it's worth noting that there is a new law in effect that requires all drivers to have a reflective vest in their cars, which should be donned every time one leaves the car while on a highway. Fines for not having one are steep, so all rental companies now provide one. In Spain, roads are generally good. New and improved road links are opening regularly, and the motorway network is expanding rapidly right across the country. Make sure your papers are in order, because unless your Spanish is top notch you're going to have a hard time understanding what is going on should you be pulled over.

Car Hire Most major hire car companies (easycar.com, hertz.com, avis.com) have offices in airports and cities. Usual age restrictions apply.

Public Transport Public transport is possible – to get to Andorra, try novatel@andorrabybus.com, who run bus services from Barcelona and Toulouse. Eurolines also run services from Barcelona airport to Andorra (info@autocars-nadal.ad). Once in Andorra La Vella, buses run across the principality – check the andorra.ad/ang/transports/index site for more on each of these options. In Spain, the rail network is worth a look, although they are likely to charge for ski carriage. **RENFE** (renfe.es) is useful for major routes. Try euskotren.es for options from the Basque country.

Opening Hours and Traditions

Everything glides to a halt at lunchtime in Spain, which typically lasts for a few hours from 1400 till 1700. Shops tend to close around 2000, and are open from Monday to Saturday. Larger supermarkets have longer opening hours. Andorran shops follow similar opening hours.

Eating

Eating in Spain is a huge social occasion, and one of the main draws for any rider thinking of making the trip. Tapas (*pintxos* in

Fact File

Currency Euro €

Time Zone GMT +1

Country Code +34 (Spain) +376 (Andorra)

Emergency Numbers

Ambulance T112 (Spain), T118 (Andorra)

Police T092 (Spain), T110 (Andorra)

Fire T112 (Spain), T118 (Andorra)

Euskadi) culture rules across Spain, and it's a cheap, social way of taking care of the après-ski munchies and the evening meal. The bustling tapas bars fill up with families and locals in the early evening, and it's a great experience to get stuck in with a glass of *vino tinto* and a plate full of *pintxos*. Dishes range from *tortilla* (a potato and egg omelette) to more local delicacies of which seafood is a primary ingredient. Grab a plate from the barman, load it up and either make a note of how many you've taken or ask him to tot it up for you.

In the Pyrenees, the local cuisine is an even more mouth-watering prospect, and in the Val d'Aran in particular it is almost impossible to get a bad meal. A good rule of thumb when it comes to choosing a restaurant is that if there are locals present, dive in. Be warned though – locals here share the worldwide Latin habit of dining late, with most restaurants only get going at around 2200.

Breakfast can be a bit of a disappointment, thanks to the puzzling Iberian predilection for liberally dousing their pastries in sugar and cloyingly sweet chocolate. In Andorra, it's pretty much the same story, although in the larger resort areas the British angle is well taken care of with fry-ups, roast dinners and other UK mainstays available in the ex-pat bars – although that would be to miss the point somewhat. If you're serious about food, check out Iberia.

Language

Spanish is the main language in Spain, while in Andorra Catalan is the main language, although most Andorrans speak Spanish as well. In Andorra, English is relatively well understood, but in Spain it is not widely spoken, so make an effort to learn some key phrases. In the Basque area of the Northern Pyrenees (known as Euskadi), Euskara is also spoken or written down as well as Spanish. It's worth noting that Catalonia is a largely autonomous part of the country, proud of their language and culture and not that happy to be lumped in with the rest of Spain.

Crime and Safety

Crime is not a massive problem although when it comes to Spain there are a few precautions worth taking. Among the European nations, Spain has suffered from a higher than average level of terrorist activity, although that is on a downward slope following a change of government. In popular Spanish cities such as Barcelona and San Sebastián, tourists are targeted by street criminals fairly regularly. In both Spanish and Andorran resorts, board or ski theft from outside restaurants or apartment balconies is on the increase, so keep an eye on your set-up or use a lock if you're super paranoid. In Spain, report anything lost or stolen to the Policia Nacional, who handle urban crimes. The Guardia Civil handle roads,

Top Tips

1 **Dive** into the tapas culture, and don't be afraid to eat somewhere new every night. It's cheap and a great way of getting into the rhythm of the place.
2 **Visit** Caldea in Andorra on a down day. It is one of the best spa complexes in Europe.
3 **Take** advantage of Andorra's lax duty-free regulations.
4 **Make** sure you spend a night either side of your skiing time in either Barcelona or San Sebastián.
5 **Speak** to the locals. They're incredibly friendly, and surprisingly helpful when it comes to pointing out favourite eating or skiing spots.

borders and law and order away from towns, while the Policia Local/Municipal also deal with some criminal investigations. In Euskadi, nationalistic sentiments are still very prevalent so be sensitive to this situation when interacting with locals. Drunkenly singing 'Y Viva Espana' in the street is unlikely to go down well. This also applies to the Catalonians, who are equally anti-Spanish and also hate being lumped in with the Castilians.

Health

Spain is governed by European health standards, so EU residents should carry a European Health Insurance Card (EHIC), which replaces the old E1-11 form. In Spanish resorts or towns, try to find an on-call pharmacy, which will be open round the clock. Health insurance is highly recommended for any trip as an additional safety net. Andorra is not an EU member so the EHIC is not valid for health cover while in the country. Health insurance is pretty much obligatory if you're going to make the trip.

↘1 Grandvalira, Andorra

Town altitude	n/a	Km of pistes	193 km	Funicular/cable	
Km to airport	200 km	Nursery areas	5	cars	0/1
Airport	Barcelona	Blues	38	Gondolas/chairs	3/30
Highest lift	2640 m	Reds	32	Drags	32
Vertical drop	930 m	Blacks	22	Night skiing	yes

Terrain parks	3
Glühwein factor	★★★
Ski in/ski out	★★★
Environmental rating	★★★★☆☆

PROS

- ✔ Fantastic for rowdy groups and those wanting a classic ski-and-booze holiday.
- ✔ Cheap.
- ✔ Great lifts, and surprisingly good skiing.

CONS

- ✖ Can suffer from bad snow due to latitude and altitude.
- ✖ Young, rowdy crowds in Pas de la Casa.
- ✖ Long transfer.

A supergroup of resorts – Grau Roig, Pas de la Casa and Soldeu-El Tarter and Canillo and Encamp – form the 'Grandvalira' area.

Unlike Andorra's other super-ski-area, Vallnord, the Grandvalira lift system is actually geographically connected. That said, it is hardly what one would call a natural ski area, being stretched rather thinly along a 15-km valley that bends from Encamp eastwards to the French border. In reality there are two ski areas: the peaks above Soldeu and El Tarter (which Canillo and Encamp access by way of a cable car and a smaller ski hill); and further to the east – and connected via the Llac del Cubil – the higher peaks belonging to Grau Riog and Pas de la Casa. The Porte des Neiges area was added in 2008 by extending the Pas de la Casa terrain over the French border by way of a six-seater chairlift. Grandvalira plans to build more lifts in this area over the coming seasons, adding another 60 km of pistes onto its – already impressive – 193 km of skiable runs. Given that a reported €112 million has been spent upgrading the lift system and creating the Grandvalira brand, expect speedy chairs, state-of-the-art gondolas and some impressive cable cars.

Beginners Andorra's fame as a perfect place to learn is well-grounded. There are plenty of wide, open (and often empty) pistes, especially above El Tarter, Canillo and Encamp.

Intermediate Confident skiers have some fantastic challenges on the slopes above Soldeu, and there's always the tempting geographical test of lapping from El Tarter to the edge of the Porte des Neiges and back.

Expert The treeless slopes of Pas and Grau Roig are perhaps best for good skiers, although the entire Grandvalira is packed with secret stashes and steeper pistes.

Powder Grau Riog has always been the area's best bet for powder snow. But the new Porte des Neiges could open up new possibilities in the coming years.

Trees Soldeu and El Tarter have the best tree-skiing.

Book a guide There are some brilliant peaks to hike above Soldeu-El Tarter. The peak of the Tosa del Espiolets has some great chutes to ski, taking you down to the funpark at El Tarter – a run that encompasses every conceivable type of skiing.

Tuition The **Soldeu Ski School** (T+376 890591) is widely recognized as being one of the best English-speaking schools in the world.

Kids The **Soldeu Ski School** takes kids from as young as three years old.

Bad light The Soldeu-El Tarter area is best for trees. If the bad light keeps you off the hill, head for Andorra la Vella for its shopping and a dip in the Caldea spa or, if you're still in need of excitement, try the **Grandvalira Circuit** (T+376 801074), a winter rally course.

Not to miss The new Porte des Neiges area. It's growing every year so ski it while it's still unique.

Remember to avoid Heading higher than the trees at Grau Roig or Pas de la Casa if there's cloud cover. You won't see a thing.

Pitstop and sunbathe The **XiriPizza** restaurant on the La Solana pistes of Soldeu is the perfect place to stop for a few rays, a cocktail and some pizza-style tapas.

Best mountain restaurant **Refugi Llac de Pessons** (T+376 759015), a mountain restaurant at the top of Grau Riog, has perhaps the best views in Grandvalira.

Practicalities

Pas (as most call it) is widely hailed as an ugly collection of modern buildings built primarily for those looking to pop over the border and indulge in some duty-free shopping. It is also the undisputed party capital of Andorra, catering for the younger crowd who want to hit the bars as hard as they hit the slopes. If you're looking for a picturesque town with plenty of activity at night then Soldeu is the place to head. Its neighbour El Tarter is a slightly quieter, more family-friendly version, but with good links to Soldeu.

Sleeping Four-star Hotel Himàlaia (T+376 878515) is right in the middle of Soldeu town, has easy access to the slopes and used to be the place to stay in town, but many are hailing the new five-star SportHotel Hermitage, reflecting the recent investment in the area. Young groups will love Pas de la Casa. For a cheap self-catering apartment, try Grifo Vacances (T+376 855250). Hotel Magic Canillo offers rooms and apartments in a renovated building in Canillo, while Apartments Austria and Hotel Piolets are great examples of traditional Andorran buildings given a modern brush up. All can be booked through T+376 801064, grandvalira.com.

Eating Pas de la Casa is full of bar/restaurants that do après-ski and evening meals then morph into nightclubs. KSB and El Tupi are perhaps the most popular. In Soldeu, a quick snack can be had from the Fun Food or Espress'Oh chain. The Borda del Rector (T+376 852606), just outside Soldeu on the way to El Tarter, is one of the best restaurants in the area, well known for its traditional Catalan cuisine.

Au pair/crèche There are crèches in Pas de la Casa (T+376 871920) and Grau Roig (T+376 872920), while the Mickey Snow Club has crèches in Soldeu (T+376 890591), Canillo (T+376 890691) and El Tarter (T+376 890641).

Best après-ski In Pas, Milwaukee, the Underground and Mulligans are but three of the best après-ski spots. In Soldeu, the entire main street bristles as the lifts close.

Bars and clubs In Pas, the KSB bar, Pas 83 and the Havana are worth a visit if you're under 30. Soldeu has a wider age range including the Roc Bar, Avalanche Bar, Pussycat's, Ice Berg and the ever-popular Fat Albert's.

Shopping Andorra la Vella is half an hour down the road from Canillo, where you'll find boutiques, electrical shops and – because it's right on the French border – plenty of cigarette and booze shops offering bulk discounts.

Hire shop/rental Esqui Calbo (T+376 870500) is based in the cable-car station at Soldeu, while the functionally named Rental Ski (T+376 755850) is in Pas de la Casa.

Health and wellbeing The spa/swimming pool complex Caldea (caldea.com) is an absolute must if you're in Andorra – it's well worth the drive down to Andorra la Vella. Otherwise, head for Hotel Piolets Park (T+376 871787) or the Sport Wellness Centre Spa (T+376 870500; sportwellness.ad).

Down days with kids There's only one place to go – Caldea (caldea.com).

Internet Most bars in Pas and Soldeu are Wi-Fi enabled.

Transfer options Andorra suffers from a lack of easy transfers. Most people arrive as part of a package-holiday deal, with coach transfer included. If you're making your own arrangements, the only real options are to fly to Toulouse (180 km away) or Barcelona (200 km) and grab a coach or hire a car. Barcelona is generally the preferred option with better budget airline links, more frequent transfers and a faster road into Andorra.

You can also ski here ... Pas de la Casa, Grau Riog, Canillo, Soldeu-El Tarter, Encamp, the Porte des Neiges.

If you like this ... try Vallnord ▶▶ p42.

Andorra & Spain Grandvalira, Andorra

OPENING TIMES
End Nov to early May: 0830-1600

RESORT PRICES
Week pass: €196
Day pass: €41

DIRECTORY
Website: grandvalira.com
Tourist office: T+376 801074
Medical centre: T+376 971010
Pisteurs: T112
Taxi: T+376 863000

↘2 Vallnord, Andorra

Town altitude	1550 m	Km of pistes	63 km	Funicular/cable	
Km to airport	205 km	Nursery areas	4	cars	0/1
Airport	Barcelona	Blues	19	Gondolas/chairs	2/12
Highest lift	2560 m	Reds	18	Drags	10
Vertical drop	1010 m	Blacks	5	Night skiing	yes

Terrain parks	2
Glühwein factor	★☆☆
Ski in/ski out	★★★
Environmental rating	★★★★☆☆

PROS

- ✔ Cheap skiing and cheaper duty free.
- ✔ Great for beginners and intermediates.
- ✔ Really good fun.

CONS

- ✖ The best and worst of Brit culture.
- ✖ Flat spots on the mountain mean plenty of poleing around.

⊙ OPENING TIMES
End Nov to early May: 0830-1600

⊛ RESORT PRICES
Week pass: €150
Day pass: €34.50

⊙ DIRECTORY
Website: vallnord.com
Tourist office: T+376 737000
Medical centre: At Arinsal main gondola station
Pisteurs and snowphone: T+376 864389
Taxi: T+376 863000

Arinsal and Pal have joined forces with valley town La Massana, and nearby resort of Arcalís, to form the 'Vallnord' area.

This is where things get a little complicated. In practical terms, Vallnord can be divided into two ski areas. Arinsal and Pal are separate villages that share a linked, fully skiable area. Arcalís is connected to this main area in name only: if you're staying in Arinsal and plan to ski at Arcalís, you'll need to take a bus journey of around 40 minutes. For good skiers (or adventurous intermediates), Arcalís is unquestionably worth visiting, as it has Andorra's best steep and off-piste skiing. The Arinsal-Pal area – like most of Andorra – is primarily known for its great cruisey slopes, lined with trees and offering those getting into the sport a relatively cheap introductory holiday. Powder skiers are probably best looking elsewhere, although

if the snow falls it's as good here as anywhere in the world. Because of Arinsal-Pal's southern latitude, combined with its open, mostly south-facing slopes, fresh snow turns to fun, slushy snow quite quickly. Arcalís is generally north-facing so holds its powder longer.

Beginners Arinsal offers great skiing for those just coming into the sport, with an almost equal amount of blue and red runs. The Prat de la Coma is the place to start, and those feeling up to it can have a crack at the La Solana run, 6.5 km of gentle, tree-lined descent back to town.

Intermediate Since the gondola opened in 2000, the best place for intermediates has been the area above Pal. It's filled with switchback cat-tracks through the forest, and the views back to the Arinsal area are fantastic. If you're feeling like a challenge, head to Arcalís and ski some beautiful and usually quieter runs.

Expert There are only two black runs in the Arinsal-Pal area – La Devesa (claiming the title of 'steepest run in Andorra') and La Comellada, which is often pegged out

as a slalom course. Otherwise, Arcalís is the place to go with bumps and more challenging terrain in spades. Those wishing to hit the funpark or the halfpipe should head to the link lift between Arinsal and Pal.

Powder You'd be foolish to book a holiday to Andorra expecting powder, but should it snow while you are there, then Arcalís is the undisputed best area in the country, featuring steep chutes, fantastic tree runs and some good, open bowls.

Trees In good snow conditions it is possible to ski between Arinsal and Pal, but it is best to get a guide. The whole area is untouched tree-skiing at its best.

Book a guide For the route between Arinsal and Pal, guides can be booked through the tourist office.

Tuition The **Arinsal Ski School** (T+376 737008) is the best in the region, with plenty of English-speaking instructors.

Kids Arinsal's **Snowpark Ski Kindergarten** (T+376 737014) takes kids from four years upwards.

Bad light Much of the ski area is below the treeline, so if it's snowing or there's a

⊛ LOCALS DO

- ✔ Head to Arcalís if it has been snowing – the powder stays good for longer.
- ✔ Make the most of the Club Vallnord card.
- ✔ Take advantage of the flyer offers.

⊗ LOCALS DON'T

- ✖ Head too high if it's windy.
- ✖ Spend much time in the rowdy après-ski. It can be a bit Brit-centric.

white-out there should still be plenty of visibility. If it's a no-go on the mountain, head for the Caldea spa in Andorra la Vella.

Not to miss Getting a Club Vallnord card (bookable online at vallnord. com), which gives a 5-50% discount on everything from restaurants and shops to lift tickets.

Remember to avoid Thinking that the whole Vallnord area is linked. Stay in Arinsal if you don't want to be sitting on a bus for much of your holiday.

Relive a famous moment Ski the track used for the Mountain Bike World Cup downhill events.

Pitstop and sunbathe Stop by the main bar area in Arinsal where you'll find **El Cau**, **Quo Vadis** and **The Derby**, all of which have sun terraces.

Best mountain restaurant Again, ski down to Arinsal base for your pick of the best mountain food stops.

Practicalities

Of the four towns Arinsal is perhaps the only one that fits the accepted term of what a ski resort should be. It is still popular with Brits, Scandinavians and those looking for a good deal or an introduction to skiing, and although many of the buildings are now on an architectural par with Verbier and Méribel, there is still an undeniable Brits-abroad feel to the place.

Sleeping The resort's best hotel is probably Arinsal's four-star **Princesa Parc** (T+376 736400; hotelprincesaparc. com), offering easy access to the slopes as well as in-house bars, cafés and clubs. Others choices in Arinsal include the cheap and cheerful **Hostal Poblado** (T+376 835112; hotpoblado.com) and the slightly more upmarket **Verdú** (T+376 737140; hotelhusaxaletverdu. com), while most people coming to the resort would opt for self-catering at somewhere like the **Besolí** (T+376 836336; hotelhusaxaletbesoli.com).

Eating Arinsal is full of touts vying for your custom and handing out flyers for restaurants offering everything from Tex-Mex, Thai and Chinese to traditional British fry-ups. For those wanting an authentic Andorran meal, **The Restaurant 360** is the place to head. Otherwise, **Cisco's** (Tex-Mex), **El Moli** (Italian), **Surf** (steak), or the **Palarine**, (British-owned Chinese cuisine) should replace some lost energy. For something

a little different, **Rocky's** is a Moroccan/Catalan restaurant on the mountain slopes that operates a free minibus service for groups, while for genuine haute cuisine, **El Rusc** (T+376 838200), in La Massana, is the place to head.

Au pair/crèche The Arinsal Ski School (T+376 737008) operates a crèche for under-fours and has a kindergarten open to older kids.

Best après-ski Again, Arinsal is full of touts handing out flyers for drinks promotions. The **Quo Vadis**, **Off Piste** and **El Cau** are generally the most competitive places to head to at the bottom of the mountain. **Cisco's** has a Mexican 'Cave' and serves free nachos to après-skiers. **El Derby** is an Irish bar in town, while **El Moli** has cocktails. The **Bull Bar** is always popular.

Bars and clubs Bogart's in the Princesa Parc is the upmarket nightclub, while the **Surf** regularly imports famous Ibizan and British DJs.

Shopping If you're self-catering, Arinsal has two supermarkets. For anything else, including the fabled tax-free electric goods, tobacco and alcohol, head to the capital, Andorra la Vella, 30 minutes away.

Hire shop/rental Esports Pic Negre (T+376 737720), **Loaded** (T+376 837717), and the inappropriately named **Esports St Moritz** (T+376 737878) are Arinsal's ski-hire shops.

Health and wellbeing The Princesa Parc has a great spa and massage area, but for real indulgence it's worth making the journey to the **Caldea** (caldea.com) in downtown Andorra la Vella.

Down days with kids The Caldea (as above) is a fantastic water-park excursion. Otherwise, there's a great sports centre in Ordino, and if you have transport, the ice-rink in Canillo (around 25 km down the valley) is worth a visit. Kids will also love the **Snowmobile Tours** (T+376 324010) around the Grau Roig valley. They have mini-skidoos for the nippers.

Internet Wi-Fi in virtually all bars in town.

Transfer options Andorra suffers from a lack of easy transfers. Most people arrive as part of a package-holiday deal, with coach transfer included. If you're making your own arrangements, the only real options are to fly to Toulouse (180 km away) or Barcelona (200 km) and grab a coach or hire a car. Barcelona is generally the preferred option with better budget airline links, more frequent transfers and a faster road into Andorra.

You can also ski here ... Arcalís, Pal.

If you like this ... try Grandvalira ▶▶ *p40*, Baqueira-Beret ▶▶ *p44*.

↘3 Baqueira-Beret, Spain

Town altitude 1500 m	Km of pistes 104 km	Funicular/cable cars 0/0	Terrain parks 1
Km to airport 160 km	Nursery areas 3	Gondolas/chairs 1/20	Glühwein factor ★★☆
Airport Toulouse	Blues 37	Drags 5	Ski in/ski out ☆☆☆
Highest lift 2510 m	Reds 25	Night skiing no	Environmental rating n/a
Vertical drop 1100 m	Blacks 6		

PROS

- ⊘ Gorgeous valley.
- ⊘ Good for all levels.
- ⊘ Fantastic food.

CONS

- ⊗ Short season, and unreliable snow.
- ⊗ A car is pretty much essential to get the best of it.

Spain's best resort combines versatile intermediate skiing with a fantastic, homely welcome.

Baqueira-Beret basks in its reputation as the best resort in Spain. Although it has suffered from a couple of lean years snow-wise, it often enjoys unique conditions thanks to an Atlantic-facing aspect that seems to create a snow/sun cycle when conditions are good. Terrain-wise, it is also surprisingly large and challenging. The resort can be divided into three main areas: Baqueira, Beret and Bonaguia, which is the backside of the mountain. Baqueira is the 'main' mountain, while Beret's slopes are more mellow.

Beginners There are easy green beginner areas at the base of Baqueira and over in Beret. The area in Baqueira is particularly well thought out. Later in the week, there is much to enjoy by lapping the Argulls chair on the way to Bonaguia (make sure you take the blue run down!) and the runs in Beret. There is a cheaper pass for beginners.

Intermediate Intermediates will have great fun in Baqueira. The Mirador lift is the obvious place to start. Almost all of the routes down from this lift are a great way to stretch your legs.

Expert You'll find the steepest terrain underneath the Manaud chair; there are two blacks here that link up with the Argulls side. If there is snow and you want to try some easy powder turns, take the Teso dera Mina chair, head back along the ridge, then drop back down onto the Argulls piste. On the front face, there are some options on skier's right of the main Mirador chair but these are only for extremely confident skiers.

Powder If it is really good, go heli-skiing! Baqueira is one of the cheapest spots to try this fantastic experience (T+34 629-278968).

Moguls Head for the Manaud chair – this is usually where you'll find the best bumps.

Tuition We like **Era Escòla** (eraescola. com) but there are many options, including **Free Mountain**, **Ski Techno** and **Ski Class**.

Kids Baqueira British Ski School (bbskischool.co.uk) offer private lessons for under-fives as well as group lessons for those a little older.

Bad light Lack of tree cover means that, when it's cloudy, it's probably time to check into the spa...

© LOCALS DO

✓ Eat tapas at après-ski.

✓ Stay down in the valley.

⊗ LOCALS DON'T

⊗ Take the Bonaguia pass if driving from Barcelona – they head for the Vielha tunnel instead.

⊗ Dilly-dally if the snow is good. The sun can blast it within hours.

Not to miss ... or head down the valley and check out some of the beautiful hamlets and villages.

Remember to avoid Getting stuck in Baqueira if you've parked the car in Beret. Or vice-versa.

Relive a famous moment As noted, BB is suddenly the resort of choice for Spanish celebs. King Juan Carlos apparently has a chalet in town, so it has the royal seal of approval.

Best mountain restaurant Restaurante 1800 at the base of the Pla de Baqueira serves a good mix of local and international snacks.

Practicalities ⊟/♨⊟

Baqueira-Beret, in the heart of the Pyrenees, is one of Europe's best-kept secrets, where the night-time pursuits are of a classier bent, the tapas is cheap and plentiful and there is a huge, oversized Pacha nightclub should you feel the need to enjoy a sizeable night out.

Sleeping Baqueira sits at the head of the beautiful Val d'Aran, giving you a choice of places to stay – in the resort itself or a little farther down the valley. Just up the hill from town, **La Pleta** (T+34 973-645550; lapleta.com) is the resort's most exclusive hotel and spa operation. Mid-priced **Tuc Blanc** (hoteltucblanc.com) is a cheerful hotel next to the lifts and is usually packed. For cheaper Val d'Aran options, **Hotel Lacreu** (T+34 973-644222) in Salardú is homely with great service. For enquiries about renting apartments, phone the dedicated line T+34 973-639027.

Eating The food in the valley is one of the main attractions and Baqueira Beret is dotted with great tapas bars. El Sol (T+34 973-644297) in Salardú is a little gem, while **La Pleta** has two fantastic restaurants with **Del Gel al Foc** serving Catalan and fusion dishes. In town, the **Escornacrabes Diner and Bar** (T+34 973-644088) is a great place for families to take kids, serving burgers, milkshakes and other diner fodder. Locals also rate **La Borda Lobato** and **Ticolet** (ticolet.com) in town as great restaurants.

Au pair/crèche There is a children's snow park at the **Borda Lobato** (parquesinfantilesbaqueira.es) for kids aged 3 months to 2½ years.

Bars and clubs Pacha dominates the nightlife but doesn't get going until late. There are plenty of tiny local tapas bars at the base near the **Tuc Blanc** complex.

Shopping Beso and Multipropiedad provide in-resort basics, but everything is cheaper in Vielha, 13 km down the valley.

Hire shop/rental Tanau Sports (htanau.es) has a branch in the resort and is a local Val d'Aran specialist.

Health and wellbeing The Occitania Spa at La Pleta (lapleta.com) is the best place for a pampering.

Down days with kids Take them down to Vielha, which is a busy town with sightseeing, walks, a leisure centre and other attractions. It's also usually a bit warmer down there.

Internet Most hotels have Wi-Fi and the odd terminal. In town, the **Tuc Blanc** is convenient and next to the lifts.

Transfer options Taxi Val d'Aran (taxivalledearan.com) organize transfers from Toulouse and Barcelona.

You can also ski here ... No local partners.

If you like this ... try Sauze d'Oulx ▶▶ p240, Hemsedal ▶▶ p256.

© OPENING TIMES

29 Nov to 5 Apr: 0845-1645

⑤ RESORT PRICES

Week pass: €215

Day pass: €42

Season pass: €875

① DIRECTORY

Website: baqueira.es

Tourist office: T+34 973-639010

Medical centre: T+34 973-645107

Pisteurs: T+34 973-639025

Taxi: T+34 617-401445

⬊4 Sierra Nevada, Spain

Town altitude	2100 m	Km of pistes	87 km	Funicular/cable	
Km to airport	45 km	Nursery areas	2	cars	0/0
Airport	Granada	Blues	5	Gondolas/chairs	2/16
Highest lift	3300 m	Reds	36	Drags/conveyors	2/4
Vertical drop	1200 m	Blacks	5	Night skiing	yes

Terrain parks	1
Glühwein factor	★★☆
Ski in/ski out	★☆☆
Environmental rating	★☆☆☆☆

PROS

- ✓ Long season and pristine runs.
- ✓ Good for all levels.
- ✓ Best suntan ever!

CONS

- ✗ Prone to high winds and lift closure.
- ✗ Very busy getting to the slopes on the gondolas during high season.
- ✗ Car ideally required to get the best of it.

Guaranteed snow, nightlife and long sunny days create a perfect family package.

Sierra Nevada has the geographical benefits of being one of Europe's highest resorts. While it is also Europe's sunniest resort, the altitude and Mediterranean humidity create a greater guarantee of snowfall than many of its lower-altitude counterparts. When the snow doesn't fall as expected, the advanced snowmaking installation is activated; it has proved its worth on more than a few occasions. The skiing is spread over three main areas: Borreguiles (including Veleta, Rio and Parador); Laguna de las Yeguas; and Lomar de Dilar. While Lomar de Dilar and Laguna are areas in their own right, Borreguiles forms the central hub of the resort.

Beginners Borreguiles opens out to wide gentle nursery and green slopes, making a perfect environment for initiation and lower intermediates. If the winds get up and the gondolas are unable to function, a small area is prepared in the Lomar de Dilar area accessed by a lower chair from the village.

Intermediate Sierra Nevada is the perfect resort for intermediates, with long rolling blue and red pistes everywhere. The Lomar de Dilar area gets you away from most of the crowds at busy times to enjoy some fantastic blue-run cruising.

Expert When the snow is plentiful, Sierra Nevada is simply a playground with easily accessible off-piste terrain and long descents. The Laguna de las Yeguas offers some testing cornices and ridges while the Barranco de San Juan attempts to lure you down past the point of no return. The Ascensor is accessed via a narrow tongue of snow between crags to reveal a fantastic steep open descent, but beware – people will be watching you from the gondola!

Powder If it's good, you can go anywhere (within reason) and at the minimum of risk.

Moguls The short but steep black, Visera, is the place to go.

Tuition The **British Ski Center** (britishskicenter.co.uk) is the resort's only ski school to guarantee quality English-speaking tuition for all ages and levels.

Bad light Being above the treeline makes the resort susceptible to rapid changes in weather conditions.

Not to miss Exploring the Genil river valley via the Carretera del Duque from El Dornajo to Güejar Sierra, Granada city and the Alhambra Palace.

Remember to avoid Weekends! They get busy.

Relive a famous moment Ex-President Clinton swore he witnessed the best sunset from the lookout at San Nicolas church in Granada's Albaicin district.

Best mountain restaurant The **Nevasur** is away from the crowds with a great sunbathing and people-watching terrace.

☺ LOCALS DO

- ✓ Eat tapas at après-ski.
- ✓ Stay down in the valley.

☺ LOCALS DON'T

- ✗ Arrive late in resort during high season and weekends.
- ✗ Dilly-dally if the snow is good. The sun can blast it within hours.

Practicalities

The Sierra Nevada ski village has developed significantly over recent years but still suffers from a complete lack of profile in much of Europe. This is hardly surprising; for most, the idea that you can ski almost on the southern shores of the Mediterranean with views out to the Rif Mountains in Morocco sounds a little far fetched. But with one of the longest ski seasons in Europe it is not uncommon to be skiing from the end of November to the beginning of May.

Sleeping The ski village lies at the base of the pistes so it's not hard getting to the lifts from most of the accommodation. The hotels **Meliá Sierra Nevada** (T+34 958-481204; solmelia. com) and **Meliá Sol y Nieve** (T+34 958-480300; solmelia.com) provide modern, cosmopolitan accommodation and a range of facilities including kids' club, swimming pool and the **YHI Spa** complex. The **Kenia Nevada** (T+34 958-480911; kenianevada.com) and **Vincci Rumaykiyya** (vinccisierranevada. com) hotels conform to the more rustic image associated with many Alpine and Pyrenean resorts. Self-catering skiers looking for the pure convenience of being right down in the centre of things will do well to consider the **Alfa Apartments** (sierranevada.co.uk).

Eating The majority of cafés and restaurants offer a good standard of tapas, rations and everyday dishes suitable for all the family. Particular favourites are **La Visera** (T+34 958-480595), **Vertical** and **Tia Maria** (T+34 958-340432). For something more traditional, the **Ruta del Veleta** (T+34 958-486134; rutadelveleta.com) and **La Cariguela** are top-class restaurants offering select cuisine and quality service in comfortable environments. For meat lovers, go to **Bar Mazon** for the optimum steak freshly grilled in their open fireplace.

Au pair/crèche The crèche below the entrance to the Al-Andalus gondola caters for kids aged six months to three years. On piste, the **Snow Garden** offers a great base in Borreguiles with a large, open segregated area containing four belt lifts for three- to seven-year-olds.

Bars and clubs Most nightlife does not really get going until beyond midnight so be prepared to get into 'siesta' mode to keep up! What does hit hard after lift closure is the tapas scene in the **Mont Blanc** gallery where for every drink you buy, there is a free tapa. The **Crescendo** has ample outdoor terraces to lap up the sun, while inside is a cosy environment of split-level lounge areas and open fireplace (perfect for enjoying your hot wine and Lumumba). Live musicians occasionally play here to jazz up the après-ski ambience.

Shopping The main supermarkets are located in the lower squares. **Las Gondolas** is particularly popular for its bakery products, log cabin bar and terrace. There are plenty of clothing stores and souvenir shops to keep most shoppers happy.

Hire shop/rental We recommend **Intersport Rio Sport** (intersport.es) who offer quality English-speaking assistance with well-maintained equipment that is renewed on a two-year cycle.

Health and wellbeing The new YHI spa at the Meliá Sol y Nieve offers all the relaxation therapies you could need with a full range of pools, jacuzzis and massages.

Down days with kids With Granada just 30 minutes' drive away, you'll find ample opportunities to keep everyone occupied. A visit to the coast is 45 minutes' drive further on.

Internet Many hotels have Wi-Fi while the cybercafé beside the **Hotel Ziyab** opens from mid-afternoon until late.

Transfer options With Granada airport just 45 minutes away, taxis are the usual means of getting to and from the airport. The local bus company **Autobuses Bonal** (T+34 958-465022) runs to a limited timetable with just three daily services (four at weekends).

You can also ski here ... No local partners.

If you like this ... try Vars ▶▶ *p196*, Plan de Corones ▶▶ *p239*.

If you like this ... try Vars ▶▶ *p196*, Plan de Corones ▶▶ *p239*.

⊚ OPENING TIMES

Late Nov to late Apr: 0900-1645

⊙ RESORT PRICES

Week pass: €196.50-256

Day pass: €32.50-40

Season pass: €1000 (family discount available)

⊙ DIRECTORY

Website: sierranevada.co.uk

Tourist office: T+34 958-249100

Medical centre: T+34 958-249138

Pisteurs: T+34 958-100749

Taxi: T+34 608-058709

Andorra & Spain Sierra Nevada, Spain

Austria

Austria rating
Value for money
★★★★★
Nightlife
★★★★☆
Off-piste
★★★★★
Family
★★★★☆

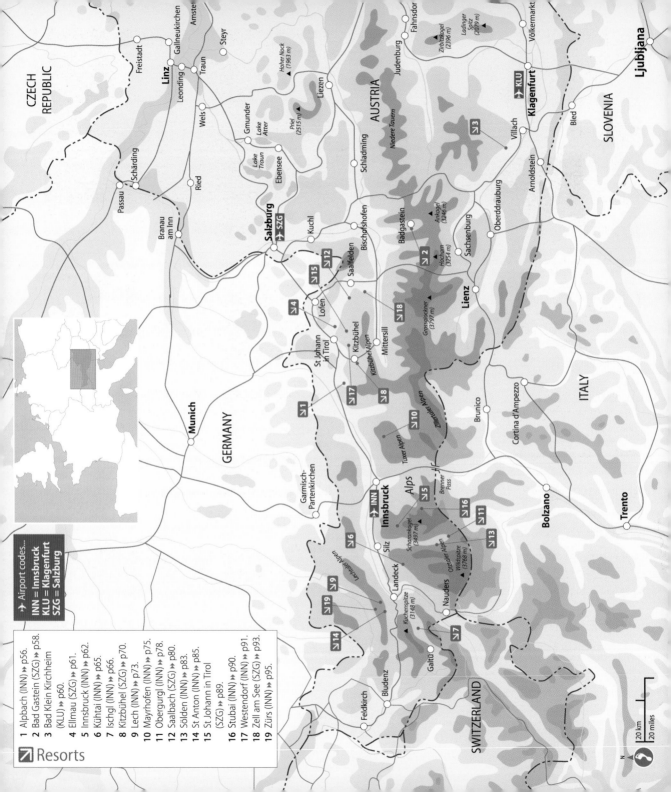

CZECH REPUBLIC

AUSTRIA

SLOVENIA

Ljubljana

Linz

Freistadt
Gallneukirchen
Amste
Steyr
Traun
Leonding

Fahnsdorf
▲ Lodinger Spitz (2079 m)
▲ Zirbitzkogel (2396 m)
Völkermarkt
✈ KLU
Klagenfurt
Bled

Passau
Schärding
Branau am Inn
Ried
Wels
Gmunden
Ebensee
Lake Atter
Lake Traun
▲ Priel (2515 m)
Liezen
Judenburg
Niedere Tauern
▲ Hoher Nock (1963 m)
Schladming
Villach
Arnoldstein

Salzburg ✈ SZG
Kuchl
Bischofshofen
Saalfelden
↗ 12
↗ 15
↗ 4
Lofen
Badgastein
▲ Ankogel (3246 m)
↗ 2
Hochnar (3254 m)
Sachsenburg
Oberddrauburg
Lienz
↗ 3

GERMANY

Munich

Garmisch-Partenkirchen

St Johann in Tirol
Kitzbühel
Kitzbühel Alpen
Mittersill
↗ 18
▲ Grossglockner (3797 m)
↗ 17
↗ 8
↗ 1
Tuxer Alpen
↗ 10
Zillertaler Alpen
Brunico

✈ INN
Innsbruck
Alps
↗ 5
Brenner Pass
↗ 16
↗ 11
↗ 13
Cortina d'Ampezzo
ITALY

Silz
↗ 6
Lechtaler Alpen
▲ Schrankogel (3497 m)
Ötztaler Alpen
▲ Wildspitze (3768 m)
Landeck
↗ 6
↗ 19
↗ 14
Nauders
↗ 7
▲ Kühtai (3148 m)
▲ Rüthenspitze (3148 m)
Bolzano
Trento

Feldkirch
Bludenz
Galtür
SWITZERLAND

Airport codes...
✈ INN = Innsbruck
KLU = Klagenfurt
SZG = Salzburg

1 Alpbach (INN) » p56.	
2 Bad Gastein (SZG) » p58.	
3 Bad Klein Kircheim (KLU) » p60.	
4 Ellmau (SZG) » p61.	
5 Innsbruck (INN) » p62.	
6 Kühtai (INN) » p65.	
7 Ischgl (INN) » p66.	
8 Kitzbühel (SZG) » p70.	
9 Lech (INN) » p73.	
10 Mayrhofen (INN) » p75.	
11 Obergurgl (INN) » p78.	
12 Saalbach (SZG) » p80.	
13 Sölden (INN) » p83.	
14 St Anton (INN) » p85.	
15 St Johann in Tirol (SZG) » p89.	
16 Stubai (INN) » p90.	
17 Westendorf (INN) » p91.	
18 Zell am See (SZG) » p93.	
19 Zürs (INN) » p95.	

↗ **Resorts**

20 km
20 miles

N

Austria is justly regarded as one of the world's finest winter sports destinations. It's the birthplace of the Arlberg skiing technique and countless international skiing superstars, the villages are heartbreakingly perfect, it has attractive wooded slopes as well as stark glaciers and its legendary après-ski is as cheesy – and as fun – as it gets.

Add to this the fact that locals are genuinely friendly (and invariably Lederhosen-clad), accommodation is comfortable and scrupulously clean whether in hotels or family-run B&Bs, food is tasty (assuming you like cheese and eat meat) and affordable and you'll understand why several of our favourite resorts are found here.

We're not saying that Austria's ski scene is perfect, if you love freeriding but want chocolate-box pretty surroundings and loud, unpretentious après-ski it might just be your spiritual ski home.

Skiing Austria

Austria, and the Arlberg in particular, prides itself on being the 'cradle of skiing' thanks to Hannes Schneider, who was born in the small town of Stuben and founded the Arlberg Ski School in 1921, which revolutionised downhill skiing techniques. Since then, Austria has spawned a host of skiing superstars who have consistently dominated the international ski scene and the ski industry now accounts for up to a quarter of the economy in regions such as the Tyrol.

Austria attracts a fairly eclectic clientele. For many visitors, its appeal lies in reviving the rosy-cheeked charm of skiing in the 1950s – gliding down empty tree-lined slopes into small villages with onion-domed churches to sip glühwein in front of a roaring open fire. For others, it's the glamour of resorts like Kitzbühel and Lech or the wellness scene of spa towns like Bad Gastein. For a significant few it's simply the lure of vast quantities of beer and Jägermeister and table-top dancing in ski boots while still others come in search of the renowned off-piste terrain of resorts like St Anton and Mayrhofen. Can one small country cater for all these diverse tastes? We think it can, and does.

Conditions

Austria's weather systems come in from all angles. Generally speaking, weather from the north, and especially from the northwest, brings cold and snowy conditions. Weather from the east can bring snow, while anything straight from the south can bring snow as well. This unique set-up basically means there's always snow to be found.

When To Go

Austria has classic Alpine weather. Early snowfalls are common (November/December 2007 was a fantastic time to be in the Austrian Alps) but it would be foolish to book a trip for the end of November and expect there to be snow. Most resorts gear up to a full opening the week before Christmas although Ischgl usually opens at the end of November. The other exceptions are the glaciers – Kitzsteinhorn and Hintertux

PROS	CONS
A great choice of party central resorts (St Anton, Ischgl, Mayrhofen), quiet, picture-perfect family resorts (Zürs, Alpbach) and even a city-based resort (Innsbruck).	Famously difficult to get hold of good vegetarian food that's not cheese.
Cheap by European standards.	Mountain access is normally via cable car from town, often resulting in big down and upload queues.
Has four of Europe's best spots for glacier skiing – Hintertux, Kitzsteinhorn, Sölden and Stubai.	Resorts are, generally speaking, lower and smaller than their French and Swiss equivalents.
The spiritual home of après-ski – think table-top dancing in ski boots, loud singing, umbrella bars, igloo bars. And very large beers.	Several key resorts are made up of small villages and mountains connected by time-consuming bus journeys.
Faultlessly clean, welcoming and comfortable accommodation.	

remain open all year apart from a few weeks in June while Sölden's glaciers and the Stubaital open in October and stay open through May. The best weather is traditionally through early February until the end of March, although clearly this is subject to fluctuation.

Off-Piste Policy

Austria has a very relaxed attitude to off-piste riding. However, follow the resort rules and read the warnings closely. Austria has a high fatality record for avalanches.

With a fierce local scene, secret powder stashes are jealously guarded and some of the more organised local skiers even insist on having filming rights to their local out-of-bounds areas. However, few Austrians are ever that aggressive, and any situations can be usually be diffused with some respectful discussion. The Zillertal Valley is particularly well-known and guarded, but even here the locals are open to outsiders (though they're unlikely to guide you around). That said, Austria's mountains have been the source of backcountry books for decades now, and a library of secret spots awaits any skier intrepid enough to delve into the local book market.

Essentials

Getting There

Austria's resorts are best served by either Salzburg's W.A. Mozart International Airport (salzburg-airport.com) or Innsbruck Airport (flughafen-innsbruck.at) in the heart of the mountains. Carriers to Salzburg include **Aer Lingus** (aerlingus.com), **Austrian Airlines** (austrian.com), **BMI Baby** (bmibaby.com), **British Airways** (ba.com), **Fly Be** (Flybe.com), **KLM** (klm.com), **Lufthansa** (lufthansa.com), **Monarch** (flymonarch.com), **Ryanair** (ryanair.com, **Thomson** (thomsonfly.com) and **Sky Europe** (skyeurope.com); while Innsbruck has **Austrian Airlines** (austrian.com), **British Airways** (ba.com), **Sky Europe** (skyeurope.com) and **Welcome Air** (welcomeair.com). Visitors to the Alps also often arrive via Germany's Munich International (munich-airport.de/EN), which has a multitude of international carriers and the smaller **Klagenfurt** (klagenfurt-airport.at).

Austria's train network (raileurope.com) is excellently maintained, while bus services throughout Europe to Austria can be booked through Eurolines (eurolines.com). Austria's road system is also very good with high-speed links to Switzerland, Germany, Italy and Slovenia. A *vignette*, or road tax sticker, must be bought if you intend to use Austria's motorway network.

Red Tape

Austria has been a member of the EU since 1995. Member states require no visas but foreign nationals from the rest of the world need to apply for permission to enter.

Getting Around

Driving is standard European (right-hand side). A valid driving licence from your home country is fine. Generally speaking, people drive with care and consideration and tend to obey all signs. Be aware that the high speeds you may have enjoyed in Germany can't be applied once the border is crossed, and traffic offences are enforced with immediate fines.

Mountain Passes If you're planning on taking a mountain pass between resorts, check whether it's open before you travel and if you're relying on sat nav, be sure to check whether the route it selects involves a pass.

Car Hire Most major hire car companies (easycar.com, hertz.com, avis.com etc.) have offices in airports and cities. Usual age restrictions apply.

Public Transport Austria's superb public transport network has been designed from the ground upwards, and is based on the idea that intercity transport is by train, with connections by local bus companies at major stations to complete the local network. There are several discount schemes in operation on the trains, including the VorteilsCard (for around €20), which gives under 26s a discount of 45% for every journey. Most resorts have train links to their nearest major airport. The ÖBB website is a fantastic resource when planning trips by public transport (oebb.at).

Opening Hours and Traditions

Shops are generally open from 0900 until noon, before reopening again from 1400 until 1900. For cheap supplies (often with an attached café), the supermarket chain M-Preis is unbeatable.

Eating

Like France, Austria is full of restaurants covering a narrow area of the culinary spectrum. Happily, they do it well, and traditional Austrian cuisine is the stuff of banqueting legend. Roasted pigs, chicken parts, breaded hams and potatoes abound, and of course there are more schnitzels, strudels and sausage dishes than any sane person could attempt on a week's holiday. Deserts are not for the faint-hearted or weight-conscious either – there's Austria's famous Kaiserschmarren desert (shredded pancake stuffed with raisins and served with fruit compote), rich Sachertorte and apple strudel drowning in whipped cream.

For the modern traveller however, this culinary cul-de-sac can pose a problem. While traditional dishes – possibly served by buxom wenches in *dirndls* – are undeniably part of Austria's charm, such a conservative approach to the joys of worldwide cuisine is also limiting. For those with special dietary needs it might be enough to put you off going at all. As one recent commentator noted, "In Austria, even the vegetarians eat meat."

That aside, a huge part of Austria's appeal for the mainstream eater is its forthright approach to grub. Mountain restaurants are usually filled to bursting point at lunch times, serving stodge

---

Fact file

Currency Euro €

Time Zone GMT +1

Country Code +43. (Phone calls from the UK to Austria can be made at local rate by calling T0845 2442442 first, followed by the local number.)

Emergency Numbers

Ambulance T144
Police T133
Fire T122
Mountain Rescue T140
General Emergency (multi language) T112

stalwarts such as burger and chips, pizzas and spag bol. Austria has realised that holidaymakers just need some cheap energy during the day to keep going. For many skiers, this truism makes a refreshing change, and means that it's often cheaper to eat on the mountain than go out for an evening meal.

Top tips

1 **Take** cash. Credit card machines and ATMs do exist, but many villages are still very much a cash society.
2 **Get** up early for breakfast – many B&Bs stop serving by 0930.
3 **Hit** the slopes early too – Austrian powder hounds don't seem to sleep.
4 **Nearly** 80% of the country is Roman Catholic, so stock up on Saturdays as there's no Sunday shopping.
5 **Obey** road signs, speed limits, parking signs and no entry signs as the traffic cops are some of the most efficient in the world.

Green Travel Tip

To avoid air travel, take the Eurostar from London to Brussels, where you can pick up the excellent (and we think underrated) Bergland Express (berglandexpress.com). This is an overnight service that runs from Brussels directly to various resorts in the Austrian Tyrol including Innsbruck, Kitzbühel, St Johann in Tirol and Zell am See.

There are of course, exceptions to this generalisation. St Anton, Kitzbühel and Ischgl have several world class restaurants both on and off the mountain, as well as upmarket après ski joints and trendy cafés. And Austrian supermarkets – M-Preis in particular – are well-stocked with fodder for health food fanatics and specialist foods for those with dietary requirements. However, for the moment, it would be safe to say that while a cultural revolution is well underway on the slopes, Austria's kitchens still lack variation and non-meat and/ or dairy eaters will seriously struggle.

Language

The official language is German, although Austrians speak a version with several everyday words changed. English is widely spoken, especially in the resorts.

Crime and Safety

Crime is generally at levels lower than in European cities. Skis and belongings can be left on balconies and outside restaurants, but thefts do occur, especially in the bigger, thriving resorts. Despite issuing on the spot fines (for traffic or street offences), which must be paid immediately, the Austrian police are generally fair. Motorway drivers should be aware that a *vignette*, or road tax sticker, is essential, as it's difficult to drive too far without meeting random checkpoints.

Health

As part of the EU, Austria is governed by European health standards. Health insurance is recommended and EU citizens should carry a European Health Insurance Card (EHIC).

Austria Essentials

↘1 Alpbach

Town altitude	1000 m	Km of pistes	52 km	Funicular/cable cars	0/0
Km to airport	60 km	Nursery areas	2	Gondolas/chairs	3/5
Airport	Innsbruck	Blues	3	Drags	13
Highest lift	2030 m	Reds	10	Night skiing	yes
Vertical drop	1030 m	Blacks	3		

Terrain parks	no
Glühwein factor	★☆☆
Ski in/ski out	★☆☆
Environmental rating	☆☆☆☆☆

PROS

✔ Chocolate-box beautiful village.

✔ Excellent for families and skiers who want to relax as well as ski.

✔ Surprisingly lively nightlife.

CONS

✖ Shuttle bus required to reach the slopes from the heart of the village.

✖ Limited ski terrain (unless you travel to other resorts in Kitzbüheler Alpen).

'Austria's prettiest village' – friendly, safe and atmospheric.

Austria Alpbach

The nursery slope above the village church is the only slope in Alpbach that's not a (free) five-minute bus ride away on the Wiedersberger Horn. At 52 km, the main area isn't big but slopes are well maintained and combine open snowfields with tree-lined runs. The small area of Reith is part of the Alpbach ski area and shouldn't be neglected – particularly on busy or bad light days.

Beginners Novices thrive on the sunny nursery slopes above the church. Once you've gained confidence, there are a couple of blues on Wiedersberger Horn but it can be a big jump to the reds for tentative beginners.

Intermediate There are great runs for intermediates in Alpbach like the long red 8 down from Gmahkopf. However, the amount of terrain is limited and

confident intermediates should tackle the expert terrain below or explore the Kitzbüheler Alpen area for more reds.

Expert Locals argue that, although small, Alpbach boasts great skiing for experts. This is partly because much of the off-piste remains untouched but also because there are some 1000-m vertical descents. The most challenging runs are route 1 to the Achenwirt mid-station, after which you can cut through the trees to the base station and route 5 to InnerAlpbach.

Powder Take a guide on a powder day to make the most of the virtually deserted backcountry. A popular route is Kohlgrube, down the back of the mountain. Intermediates will enjoy their first taste of powder on the wide red 9 on Wiedersberger Horn or on Reith if it's dumping.

Moguls Route 5 to InnerAlpbach is popular with mogul-seekers.

Tuition There are three schools, all of which have English-speaking instructors and keep classes small.

Kids Alpbach is very popular with families – most hotels cater well for kids, all three ski schools offer ski kindergartens and there's plenty of easy terrain for them.

Bad light Stick to the tried and tested rule: stay low.

☺ LOCALS DO

✔ Ski at Reith on weekends to escape the 'crowds'.

✔ Chill out with mates at The Halle in Böglerhof.

☹ LOCALS DON'T

✖ Hold back on karaoke nights at the Waschkuchl.

✖ Get lost sledging back to town after dinner at Gasthof Rossmoss.

Not to miss Tucking into fresh, locally caught trout at **Gasthof Jakober**.

Relive a famous moment Alpbach is known as 'The Village of Thinkers', having hosted the annual European Forum since 1945.

Best mountain restaurant The **Berggasthaus Hornboden** restaurant does good food although a burger at the **Almhof** will set you up for the afternoon. The best views are from **Wiedersberghorn Hütte**.

Practicalities

If Hollywood ever needs a picture-perfect Alpine village, Alpbach should be first to audition. Stuffed with beautiful chalets and with a church at its heart, the resort offers a good range of accommodation and off-piste entertainment.

Sleeping Families love the cosy Böglerhof (T+43 (0)5336-52270; boeglerhof.at) for its proximity to the nursery slopes. **Hotel Post** (T+43 (0)5336-5203; hotel-post.cc) is another firm favourite. Mrs Moser runs **Pension Edelweiss** (T+43 (0)5336-5268; tiscover. at/edelweiss.alpbach) – a comfy B&B by the nursery slopes. Book self-catering accommodation like **Haus Schönblick** through the tourist office (alpbachtal.at).

Eating **Gasthof Post** does Tyrolean and international favourites served with local wines while **Messner's** does great pizza. **Am Eck** and **Gasthof Jakober** are popular with locals. For something special, take a horse-drawn sleigh to **Gasthof Rossmoss** or **Bischoferalm** and sledge back to town.

Au pair/crèche Juppi's Kids Club offers full-day care for children (2-12 years) and evening babysitting. Register in advance with the tourist information centre in Reith (T+43 (0)5337-62674).

Bars and clubs For a small village, there's a surprisingly lively après scene. Popular spots include **The Halle** in the Böglerhof and the **Jakober**. Later on, **Post Alm** and the tiny **Waschkuchl** (next to the Jakober kick off). Thursday karaoke at the Waschkuchl is legendary.

Hire shop/rental Alpbachtal Ski & Sportshop is next to the gondola, **Iggy's** is by the church, while **Sport Hannes & Norbert** in Reith provides free ski and boot storage.

Health and wellbeing The Indoor Adventure Pool **Erlebnisbad** in the village has a sauna and steam room. The spas at **Böglerhof** and **Alphof** are open to non-residents (only €3 to access the Alphof spa).

Down days with kids Sledging is really popular, with plenty of well-maintained tracks (rent from Iggy's).

OPENING TIMES

End Nov to mid-Apr: 0830-1600

RESORT PRICES

Week pass: €147.50
Day pass: €31
Season pass: €285

DIRECTORY

Website: alpbach.at
Tourist office: T+43 (0)5336-200941
Medical centre: T+43 (0)5336-20044
Pisteurs T+43 (0)5336-523325
Taxi: T+43 (0)5336-5616

The Indoor Adventure Pool provides plenty of entertainment.

Transfer options Fly to Innsbruck and take a train to Brixlegg (oebb.at) where you can take a bus to Alpbach or book a private transfer (a-t-s.net).

You can also ski here ... Extend your pass to include the Kitzbüheler Alpen area.

If you like this ... try Westendorf ▶▶ p91, Ste Foy ▶▶ p178, Saas Fee ▶▶ p301.

↘2 Bad Gastein

Town altitude 1002 m	Km of pistes 201 km	Funicular/cable cars 1/1	Terrain parks 1
Km to airport 95 km	Nursery areas 2	Gondolas/	Glühwein
Airport Salzburg	Blues 16	chairs 10/17	factor ★☆☆
Highest lift 2686 m	Reds 40	Drags 15	Ski in/ski out ★☆☆
Vertical drop 1443 m	Blacks 6	Night skiing yes	Environmental rating ★★★☆☆☆

PROS

- ✔ Uncrowded slopes.
- ✔ Plenty of terrain for intermediates.
- ✔ Excellent for non-skiers and families.

CONS

- ✖ Limited skiing for beginners and experts.
- ✖ Negotiating the steep streets of Bad Gastein in ski boots is terrifying.
- ✖ Atmosphere of a spa town rather than a ski town.

Attractive town with decent skiing, but better thermal spas.

Each of the four Gastein villages accesses its own ski area, providing lots of terrain, most of which is best suited for intermediates. Reliable ski buses link the resorts. Bad Gastein and Bad Hofgastein access the largest linked area – Schlossalm/ Stubnerkogel. Dorfgastein is linked to Grossarl and has the most varied terrain, modern lifts and good mountain restaurants. Sportgastein is the highest and most exposed hill while Graukogel is steepest with plenty of trees – both are self-contained.

Beginners Angertal is the best place for beginners. Generally speaking, however, nursery slopes are dispersed and blues are either too flat or too steep.

Intermediate We particularly like Dorfgastein with its tree-lined runs and connection with Grossarl. Schlossalm/ Stubnerkogel offers lots of varied runs and the brilliant 8 km-long H1 Hohe Scharte piste. Confident intermediates should progress to Graukogel.

Expert Limited black runs and accessible off-piste. Graukogel is steepest, there are long reds on Schlossalm/Stubnerkogel, while Sportgastein has some challenging blacks.

Powder Get fresh tracks on Sportgastein on a clear day before shredding the trees on Graukogel.

Moguls Sportgastein and the black B20 down to Angertal.

Tuition There's one school in Bad Gastein, two in Dorfgastein and two in Bad Hofgastein. **Schneesport Schule** operates in both Bad Gastein and Dorfgastein.

Kids Schneesport Schule ski kindergarten (from four years). There's a dedicated Children's Ski Area at the base station of the Dorfgastein lift, good nursery slopes at Angertal and the **FunCentre** on Stubnerkogel. In Dorfgastein, children from three staying in a Pongi hotel can join the **Pongi Children's Club**.

Bad light Head for Graukogel or indulge yourself at the spas.

Not to miss Admiring Bad Gastein's famous waterfall from the bridge in the centre of town.

Remember to avoid Drinking too many *flugels* in the **Silver Bullet**.

Relive a famous moment Bathe in history – former devotees of Bad Gastein's springs include Empress Sissi, Bismarck, Franz Schubert and Thomas Mann.

Best mountain restaurant Treat yourself to gourmet food on the slopes at the **Angertal 1180**. Stubnerkogel's **Gipfel** restaurant has superb views while the **Bellevue Alm** does excellent Austrian specialities.

Practicalities ☐ ☐ ☐

Visitors first came to Gastein in Roman times to take the curative spring waters. Today, skiing still plays second fiddle to the wellness industry – the steep streets of Bad Gastein, distance between chairlifts and the centre and time-consuming bus journeys between slopes being less than ideal for skiers. However, with glamorous boutiques and more spas than you can shake a towel at, non-skiers will love it.

Sleeping Four villages make up the resort, each with its own distinctive feel. Bad Gastein is the largest, Bad Hofgastein is stuffed with modern facilities, Dorfgastein is sleepy and rural and Sportgastein the most spartan. Most accommodation is in hotels. Arcotel-Elizabethpark (T+43 (0) 6434-2551; arcotel.at) in Bad Gastein is modern, central and has a wellness centre, while **Pension Kurhaus Orania** (T+43 (0) 6434-2224; gastein.com) is comfortable and good value. Bad Hofgastein's 5-star **Park Hotel** (T+43 (0) 6432-6356; grandparkhotel.at) is located on the piste.

Eating Try the cosy, traditional **Hofkeller** and **Jägerhäus**, historic **Lutter & Wegner** and trendy restaurant and wine bar **Prälatur**. Dorfgastein's **Römerhof** is good for gourmets.

Au pair/Crèche The tourist office has a list of babysitters.

Bars and clubs For glitzy après head for the **Casino**, which keeps going until late. **Silver Bullet** (with live band and DJ), **Hagblöms** and **Gatz** nightclub attract a younger, lively crowd. For more relaxed drinks try **Joe's Bar** or **Prälatur**.

Shopping Zentrale for essentials and a smattering of high-end boutiques.

Hire shop/rental TOP-RENT **Schober** has outlets and storage at the Stubnerkogel and Sportgastein base stations. **Intersport Fleiss** has three outlets in Bad Hofgastein and one in Bad Gastein.

Health and wellbeing Highlights include **Felsentherme** in Bad Gastein, **Alpen Therme Gastein** in Bad Hofgastein and the **Healing Gallery** in Sportgastein (a naturally heated underground chamber reached by a 2-km train journey into the mountain).

Down days with kids Ice-skating in Bad Gastein and Bad Hofgastein, the **FunCentre** at Stubnerkogel and evening tobogganing at Bad Hofgastein (**Aeroplan**) or Dorfgastein (**Fulseck**).

Internet At most hotels and there are machines at the **Stubnerkogel FunCentre**.

Transfer options Fly to Salzburg and take a shuttle bus (salzburg-airport.com) or train (oebb.at).

You can also ski here ... Bad Hofgastein, Dorfgastein and Sportgastein. Bad Gastein is also part of the Ski Amadé area – Austria's largest ski area with 860 km of pistes and 270 lifts.

If you like this ... try Kitzbühel ▶▶ *p70*, St Moritz ▶▶ *p304*.

⊙ OPENING TIMES
End Nov to early May: 0800-1700

⑤ RESORT PRICES
Week pass: €182

Day pass: €38

Season pass: €400

❶ DIRECTORY
Website: skigastein.com

Tourist office: T+43 (0) 6432-3393 560

Medical centre: T+43 (0) 6432-141

Pisteurs: T+43 (0) 6432-645550

Taxi: T+43 (0) 6434-6633

↘3 Bad Klein Kircheim

Town altitude 1100 m	Funicular/cable cars 0/0
Km to airport 50 km	Gondolas/chairs 4/6
Airport Klagenfurt	Drags 16
Highest lift 2055 m	Night skiing no
Vertical drop 955 m	Terrain parks 0
Km of pistes 103 km	Nursery areas 2
Nursery areas 2	Glühwein factor ★☆☆
Blues 3	Ski in/ski out ★☆☆
Reds 26	Environmental
Blacks 6	rating ★☆☆☆☆

Good for intermediate skiers after a comfortable ski and spa break.

Austria Bad Klein Kircheim

BKK oozes civilized, luxurious comfort. The old spa town spreads along a narrow valley in southern Austria and is littered with hotels, restaurants and spas. Downhill ski legend Franz Klammer was born nearby and still plays an active role in the resort. Like the town, Bad Klein Kircheim's (BKK) slopes are civilized – beautifully manicured, wide, mostly tree-lined cruisers. Three quarters of the runs are red, with little challenging terrain, making it ideal for intermediates.

Beginners BKK and St Oswald have their own nursery slopes. However, being north-facing BKK gets cold. Find your ski legs on St Oswald and build up to the long blue run from Nockalm.

Intermediate Perfect technique and build up stamina on the longer runs (the K70 from Kaiserburg is a must), practise cutting through the trees and build up to the steeper blacks.

Expert Pretty limited once you've covered the World Cup runs. Book a

Practicalities 🛏️🍴🚌

Sleeping Luxury seekers can choose from over 30 four- and five-star hotels. There are plenty of cheaper options (and family discounts) – visit badkleinkirchheim.at for the full selection.

Eating Gourmet favourites include **Thermenhotel Ronacher** and Hotel Pulverer's **Loy Stub'n**. Gasthof Alt Kirchheim, **Gasthof Hinteregger** and St Oswald's **Berghof** do hearty local food. Piste-side, feast in the **Maibrunhütte** and enjoy the views at **Kaiserburg**.

Bars and clubs BKK après is, generally speaking, civilized and concentrated in hotel bars. Regular haunts include **Almstube**, **Viktoria Pub**, **Club MC 99** and the **Take Five Dancing Club**.

Hire shop/rental Plenty of (upmarket) rental shops including the large **Intersport Gruber**.

Transfer options Fly to Klagenfurt or Salzburg and take a shared transfer (kaernten-transfer.at) from €20 one-way or train (oebb.at) to Villach and bus.

You can also ski here ... St Oswald.

If you like this ... try Bad Gastein ▶▶ p58, Kitzbühel ▶▶ p70.

guide to explore off-piste on Falkert and off St Oswald.

Tuition Three ski schools in BKK and one in St Oswald.

Bad light There are plenty of trees but why not check out the designer shops and soak in the fantastic **Römerbad** pool.

Not to miss Meeting Franz Klammer at his Skibar on Strohsack.

Remember to avoid Skiing without a piste map – visitors can find the on-piste signage confusing.

⊙ OPENING TIMES
Early Dec to early Apr: 0900-1600

Ⓢ RESORT PRICES
Week pass: €179
Day pass: €37
Season pass: €330

ⓘ DIRECTORY
Website: badkleinkirchheim.at
Tourist office: T+43 (0)4240-8212
Medical centre: T+43 (0)4240-4105
Pisteurs: T+43 (0)4240-8282
Taxi: T+43 (0)4240-227

↘4 Ellmau

Town altitude	820 m	Funicular/cable cars	1/0
Km to airport	80 km	Gondolas/chairs	11/37
Airport	Salzburg	Drags	32
Highest lift	1220 m	Night skiing	no
Vertical drop	1020 m	Terrain parks	1
Km of pistes	250	Glühwein	
Nursery areas	yes	factor	★☆☆
Blues	26	Ski in/ski out	★★☆
Reds	43	Environmental	
Blacks	11	rating	★☆☆☆☆

Traditional ski village ideal for families and beginners looking to cruise the SkiWelt area.

Ellmau is a picturesque resort with sweeping views of the Wilder Kaiser mountains and the SkiWelt area – Austria's largest linked ski area – at the back of the village. The SkiWelt area is paradise for beginners and intermediates with all but eight of the trails rated easy or moderate: that's 227 km of gentle, tree-lined cruisers. New lifts make travel across the mountain quick, easy and comfortable.

Beginners There's a nursery slope in the village centre complete with magic carpet lift and miles of easy runs from the Astberg chair near Going and the Hartkaiser above Ellmau.

Intermediate Take the funicular up the Hartkaiser Mountain for a great choice of terrain and enjoy plenty of open cruising. The plateau at the top of Astberg offers snow-sure, easy slopes.

Expert Expert terrain is fairly limited but the steeps off Hohe Salve summit and the moguls between Brandstadl and Neualm will keep you entertained.

Tuition Of three ski schools in the village, **Top Skischule** (T+43 (0)5358-3700; skischule-ellmau.at) comes highly recommended, particularly for children.

Practicalities 🛏🚻🚌

Ellmau caters for a sedate family-orientated audience, so those looking for nightlife should head to the neighbouring resorts Söll and Kitzbühel.

Sleeping The expensive option is upmarket **Hotel der Bär** (T+43 (0)5358-2395; hotelbaer.com). Mid-range hotels include **Hotel Hochfilzer** (T+43 (0)5358-2501), bang in the centre of town, who also run two cheaper properties opposite. Budget options include **Pension Claudia** and **Haus Garden** – stay here, use the Hochfilzer facilties!

Eating The **Ellmauer Alm** does traditional on the piste, while **Gasthof Lobewein** offers the same in the centre of town.

Bars and clubs The **Cafe Pub Memory** for après, **Pub 66** and **Ötzi** for karaoke evenings. Thursdays at **Stangl-Leit'n** are lively.

Hire shop/rental **Sport 2000 Fuchs** is the largest shop in town.

Transfer options Trains run from Innsbruck and Salzburg to Wörgl, St Johann in Tirol or Kufstein where you can pick up a bus to Ellmau (T+43 (0)5334-051717; oebb.at).

You can also ski here ... SkiWelt: Westendorf, Going, Itter, Scheffau, Hopfgarten and Brixen im Thale.

◉ OPENING TIMES
End Dec to end Mar: 0830-1630

⑤ RESORT PRICES
Week pass: €193
Day pass: €35.50
Season pass: €469

ⓘ DIRECTORY
Website: ellmau.at
Tourist office: T+43 (0)5358-505410
Medical centre: T+43 (0)5358-2738
Pisteurs: T+43 (0)5358-225155

Austria Ellmau

↘5 Innsbruck

Town altitude	575 m	Km of pistes	282 km	Funicular/cable		Terrain parks 6
Km to airport	4 km	Nursery areas	3	cars 2/3		Glühwein factor ★★☆
Airport Innsbruck		Blues	28	Gondolas/chairs	9/26	Ski in/ski out ★★☆
Highest lift	3150 m	Reds	44	Drags	39	Environmental
Vertical drop	1400 m	Blacks	11	Night skiing	yes	rating n/a

PROS

- ✅ You can be skiing within an hour of landing at Innsbruck airport.
- ✅ There's a wide range of mountains to ski on and towns to stay in, each with its own atmosphere.
- ✅ Innsbruck offers all the facilities of a major city and doesn't charge ski-resort prices.

CONS

- ❌ Innsbruck itself lacks typical skiing ambience.
- ❌ If you make Innsbruck your base, you'll need to travel at least 30 minutes to the various ski areas (apart from Nordpark).

Cosmopolitan skiing at its best with an international airport on its doorstep.

With up to 11 mountains to ski on with one pass, you have to plan your days carefully to get the most out of your visit to Innsbruck. If you're based in the city, be prepared to spend some time in the (free) ski buses reaching the various resorts – you'll be rewarded with fantastically varied skiing.

Beginners Kühtai, Mutters, Rangger Köpfel and Schlick 2000 offer gentle, quiet slopes ideal for anyone learning to ski.

Intermediate Axamer Lizum is a high-altitude ski station with acres of high-speed cruising runs as well as good off-piste and tree-skiing opportunities. Glungezer is quieter with long red slopes, including the longest piste in the Tirol (15 km). Nordpark will challenge you with its steeper top sections and dense trees lower down.

Expert Although small, Nordpark has some excellent, challenging terrain, with steep chutes cutting down to the Seegrube base from the top of Hafelekar. There's good freeriding on Axamer Lizum and some tough ski routes on the Stubai glacier.

Powder If it dumps on a weekday, hit Nordpark early for steep and deep powder runs. On weekends, freeriding off the Götzner Grube and Pleisen chairs on Axamer is quieter than Nordpark, or try the virtually untouched powder bowls in Kühtai.

Trees There are great tree runs on the lower sections of Nordpark and Axamer Lizum.

Book a guide Probably not worth taking a guide to the Olympia SkiWorld resorts (they're too small) but definitely worth it when you ski on St Anton and/or Kitzbühel.

Ski school Virtually each resort has its own ski school, so you can chose the one most convenient for you. The **Innsbruck Ski School** (skischool-innsbruck.com) offers instruction for all ages and levels on all the mountains in the Olympia SkiWorld area.

Kids Mutters and Kühtai are fantastic for children, with gentle slopes and excellent ski kindergartens. There's a very popular **Micky Mouse Ski Club** on the Stubai glacier.

Bad light Buy a 24-hour Innsbruck City Pass for unlimited public transport use and entry to the city's best museums and galleries.

Not to miss Nordpark's Friday 'Ride & Dine' evenings; eat in the mountain restaurant way above the twinkling lights of Innsbruck (T+43 (0)512-303065).

Remember to avoid Nordpark on a weekend powder day – way too crowded.

Relive a famous moment Franz Klammer won Olympic gold in the 1976 Winter Olympics in spectacular style on Patscherkofel.

Pitstop and sunbathe Admire Innsbruck from **Leingartner's Restaurant** on Nordpark, enjoy excellent apple strudel at **Jagdschloss** in Kühtai, chill out at **Swing In** snow bar at the base of Mutters and enjoy the views at **Panorama Restaurant Kreuzjoch** on Schlick 2000.

Best mountain restaurant **Kühtaier Dorfstadl** does good food, **Hoadl Haus** on Axamer is lively, **Rosskogel Hütte** and **Tufenalm** on Rangger Köpfel and Glungezer respectively are both good.

Practicalities

Innsbruck is a beautiful, historical yet lively city in the heart of the Tyrolean Alps. It's certainly the only one we've ever been to where you stroll past world-class galleries, museums and restaurants in your ski boots on the way to the ski lift. Innsbruck is ideal for skiers who like to benefit from the attractions of a modern European city when they're not on the hill and makes a great base from which to explore the nine resorts in the Olympia SkiWorld Innsbruck ski area, which range from Nordpark (10 minutes from the centre of town on a new funicular) to the Stubai glacier (one hour away by ski bus).

Sleeping The tourist office offers a range of excellent packages that combine accommodation with a ski pass for the best value – visit Innsbruck.info. Most major hotel chains are represented here but some more atmospheric favourites include the small and ancient **Gasthof-Hotel Weisses Rössl** (T+43 (0)512-583057; roessl.at) and the welcoming **Gasthof Innsbrücke** (T+43 (0)512-281934; gasthofinnbruecke.at). The **Grand Hotel** (T+43 (0)512-5931; grandhoteleuropa.at), the city's only five-star hotel, is large, plush and central. The traditional exterior and public areas of the **Schwarzer Adler** (T+43 (0)512-587109; deradler.com) are cosy and comfortable while the bedrooms are modern with vast bathrooms.

Eating Being a city, there's a vast choice of eateries. **Magic Pizza** on Herzagfriedrich Strasse in the Old Town does affordable Italian, the **Stiftskeller** offers traditional Austrian food and **Kenzi** is an excellent Korean and Japanese restaurant. Watch your dinner being prepared at the modern open kitchen of **Thai Li Ba**. Chef Alfred Miller has created a gourmet temple with

the **Schöneck** restaurant, named the city's best restaurant by the *Gault Millau* guide. For seriously delicious Austrian food, dine at the **Schwarzer Adler**.

Au pair/crèche Various childcare services are available in each resort. Contact the tourist office for information specific to your location.

Best après-ski Each resort in the Olympia SkiWorld has its own après scene (see separate reviews for Kühtai and Neustift in Stubai). Innsbruck doesn't have a huge après atmosphere during the week, with evening entertainment starting later.

Bars and clubs Again, each resort has its own scene. In Innsbruck, **Jimmy's Bar** and the **Couch Club** offer chilled out drinks while later partying goes on at **Bacchos** and the **Casino**.

Hire shop/rental The funky **Die Boerse** (dieboerse.at) in Innsbruck has modern kit. You'll find various rental shops in each of the other resorts.

Lift tickets Buy ski passes at the tourist office in Innsbruck (thus avoiding the queues at the base of the funicular) and at all the lifts in the Olympia SkiWorld.

Health and wellbeing The **Alpine Wellfit Eagles Hotel** (T+43 (0)512-377481) is just 5 km out of town in nearby Igls and offers a wide choice of spa facilities.

Down days with kids Innsbruck is the place to be with restless children. A 24-hour Innsbruck City Family Pass gives you unlimited public transport use and entry to the city's best attractions including the world-famous **Swarowski Crystal World**.

Internet Free internet at the tourist office and a **Telecome** office with internet at the

main Post Office opposite the train station. Various internet cafés in Innsbruck.

Transfer options It couldn't be easier – fly to Innsbruck Kranebitten airport (just 4 km from the centre of Innsbruck) and grab a cab or bus to your hotel (ski-innsbruck.at).

You can also ski here ... Olympia SkiWorld Innsbruck incorporates Axamer Lizum, Glungezzer, Kühtai, Mutters, Nordpark, Patscherkofel, Rangger Köpfel, Schlick 2000 and the Stubai glacier. Furthermore, if you buy a Super Ski Pass you can ski for one day in both St Anton and Kitzbühel.

If you like this ... try Serre Chevalier ▶▶ *p180*.

⊙ OPENING TIMES

Early Oct to early May: 0900-1630

⑤ RESORT PRICES

Week pass: €170

Day pass: €36

Season pass: €450

① DIRECTORY

Website: innsbruck.info

Tourist office: T+43 (0)512-59850

Medical centre: T144

Ski passes: T+43 (0)512-562000

Taxi: T+43 (0)512-5311

↘6 Kühtai

Town altitude	2020 m	Funicular/cable cars	0/0
Km to airport	35 km	Gondolas/chairs	0/4
Airport	Innsbruck	Drags	7
Highest lift	2820 m	Night skiing	yes
Vertical drop	800 m	Terrain parks	1
Km of pistes	37 km	Glühwein	
Nursery areas	3	factor	★☆☆
Blues	4	Ski in/ski out	★★★
Reds	10	Environmental	
Blacks	5	rating	★★★★★★

Austria's highest Alpine village and one of its prettiest: perfect for families and beginners.

OPENING TIMES

Early Dec to mid-Apr: 0900-1600

RESORT PRICES

Week pass: €148

Day pass: €28.50

Season pass: €345

DIRECTORY

Website: schneegarantie.at

Tourist office: T+43 (0)5239-5222

Medical centre: T+43 (0)5239-5219

Pisteurs: T+43 (0)5239-21616

Lift information: T+43 (0)5239-5284

Practicalities

Kühtai is a pint-sized winter wonderland 45 minutes' drive from Innsbruck. This makes the city accessible but not ideal for 'popping out' for nightlife, something Kühtai lacks. However, for most visitors the peace is what they're here for.

Sleeping The Count of Stolberg-Stolberg has welcomed guests to his family's hunting lodge, **Jagdschloss Kühtai** (T+43 (0)5239-5201; jagdschloss.at), for over 50 years. The all-inclusive **Moritz Hotel** (T+43 (0)5239-5400; hotelmoritz.com) is child heaven.

Eating Most guests are here on half- or full-board, so dining is generally in hotels. Notable are the **Mooshaus** and **Elisabeth**. **Pizzeria Rustica** does decent Italian.

Bars and clubs Nightlife isn't a priority here but fun can definitely be had at **Yeti Bar**, **Kühtaier Dorfstadl** and **Yellow Umbrella**.

Hire shop/rental There are three well-equipped shops in the centre of town.

Transfer options Free (slow) post buses from Innsbruck (timetables at schneegarantie.at). Taxis cost approximately €60 each way (innsbruck-airport.com). Some hotels offer a shuttle service.

You can also ski here ... Axamer Lizum, Norpdpark-Seegrube, Schlick 2000, Mutters, Patscherkofel, Glungezer and the Stubai glacier.

If you like this ... try Arosa ▶▶ *p276*, Saas Fee ▶▶ *p301*.

Austria Kühtai

Yes it's small but Kühtai has 1600 beds and a lift capacity of 1600 people per hour – so queues are rare. The Kaiserbahn chair, scheduled to open in 2008/09, will take skiers to the top of Schwarzmoos, opening up more terrain for advanced skiers.

Beginners An idyllic place to learn – it's picturesque and quiet, with three nursery areas and wide, well-maintained pistes with plenty of snow.

Intermediate The majority of runs on the mountain are red, making this a good place to perfect your technique.

Expert Kühtai makes an entertaining day trip for expert skiers based in Innsbruck. The blacks round the Gaiskogel and Wiesberg T-bars are fun and the off-piste is barely touched.

Tuition There are three ski schools – **1st Ski School** has a popular Kids Club.

Bad light Given the altitude, there are no trees, so explore Innsbruck.

Not to miss The views from the **Zum Kaiser Maximillian** mountain restaurant.

Remember to avoid Being shown up by kids half your age in the K-Park.

↘7 Ischgl

Town altitude 1377 m	Km of pistes 205 km	Funicular/cable cars 1/2	Glühwein factor ★★★
Km to airport 62 km	Nursery areas 1	Gondolas/chairs 3/23	Ski in/ski out ★★☆
Airport Innsbruck	Blues 14	Drags 12	Environmental
Highest lift 2872 m	Reds 41	Night skiing yes	rating ★★★★★★
Vertical drop 1472 m	Blacks 8	Terrain parks 1	

PROS

- ✔ Relatively undiscovered outside Austria.
- ✔ Legendary nightlife.
- ✔ Significant investment in modern lifts and excellent piste-grooming make for a slick hill with minimal queues.

CONS

- ✘ Expensive.
- ✘ The runs into town are steep and crowded.
- ✘ Limited trees for bad visibility days.

Rated by Europeans as Austria's best resort after St Anton – yet overlooked by Brits.

Like its better-known big brother, St Anton, Ischgl is more suited to intermediate and advanced skiers than beginners. The resort is high – all the runs except those into the resort are above 2000 m – and most are north-facing, meaning the snow quality is typically excellent. The Silvretta Arena ski area is Austria's largest continuous ski area – there are long cruisers, steep blacks and plenty of excellent freeriding terrain, which is skied out considerably less quickly than that of St Anton. The resort also boasts one of the best terrain parks in the Alps, the snowARTpark.

Beginners Ischgl's nursery slopes are located on the mountain, which means good snow but also crowded slopes overrun by faster skiers. And at the end

of the day, you have to negotiate the rather treacherous piste down to the village or queue to download.

Intermediate Confident intermediates will thrive in Ischgl. There are loads of long cruisers (slopes are generally quieter on Alp Trida), more challenging pistes round Vesil from the top of Palinkopf and plenty of short, accessible off-piste hits. The long Duty Free run into Switzerland won't disappoint with gentle slopes and stunning views.

Expert Expert skiers will find more challenges off-piste than on, although the blacks off Höllenspitz and Greitspitz are entertaining. Freeriding terrain is accessible and relatively untouched, with even the marked ski routes getting relatively little traffic.

Powder Get an early start and you'll be rewarded with fresh tracks for several hours. Some favourite routes are off the Gampen chair into Vesil; dropping into the Höllenklar valley from the Höllenspitz chair or by cutting across into it from Greitspitz; and the number 9 ski route under Videf Joch.

Trees Limited, with just a few decent runs under the Bodenalp lift.

Book a guide Drop off the back of Palinkopf down into the Fimbatal, an area that will be opened up when the planned Piz Val Gronda lift opens. A classic route involves a short hike from the Visnitzbahn chair before a long descent to Kappl, bringing you out by the valley road opposite the village.

Ski school Schneesport Akademie is Ischgl's only ski school. Lessons start late (1030) up on Idalp – make sure to request an English-speaking instructor when you book lessons. They also offer off-piste guiding.

Kids Children under eight ski free in Ischgl and, if two kids and one parent buy a pass, the rest of the brood go free. The **Schneesport Akademie**

☺ LOCALS DO

⊘ Make the first lift while visitors are nursing their hangovers.

⊘ Avoid the crowds on the home run by staying on the mountain until 1700 or leaving early to bag a spot at Niki's or Trofana Alm.

⊘ Ski on the Samnaun slopes when the resort is busy.

☹ LOCALS DON'T

⊗ Stock up on duty-free at (inflated) prices in Samnaun.

⊗ Hold back in Trofana Arena – dance like your life depends on it!

⊗ Spread the word about Ischgl too loudly.

offers ski kindergarten for children from three to five years.

Bad light Given the lack of trees, release your inner child in the Adventure Pool in the **Silvretta Centre**. Then get some fresh air hurtling down one of Europe's longest tobogganing runs – it's 7 km long and drops 950 vertical metres (open Mondays and Thursdays, 0700-2030, T+43 (0)5444-606).

Not to miss Skiing over to Switzerland for lunch at **Haus Chronik**.

Remember to avoid Being on Idalp when the ski schools meet at 1030 and trying to take the Silveretta or Fimba lifts down at 1530.

Relive a famous moment Sting, Tina Turner, Lionel Ritchie and Elton John have all opened Ischgl's winter season.

Pitstop and sunbathe **Alp Bella** on Alp Trida has a large sun terrace with sweeping views. Escape the crowds at the tiny **Bodenalpe** restaurant and treat yourself to real Swiss hot chocolate at the **Schmuggler Alm** in Samnaun.

Best mountain restaurant **Paznauer Thaya** does authentic local food in cosy surroundings while the new **Pardorama** is modern with good food and fast service. Feeling flash? Join the Mountain VIP club – membership gets you access to the VIP lounge and restaurant in the **Alpenhaus**, priority queuing at Silvretta, parking and more (silvretta.at/mvc).

Practicalities

Ischgl is a compact, traditional farming village dating back to the 10th century. It's largely pedestrianized, with a walkway cut through part of the mountain to facilitate access to lifts and bars, and successfully combines the old-fashioned luxury of resorts like Kitzbühel and St Moritz with the modern party scene of St Anton (with a touch of Moscow).

Sleeping There are 72 four-star hotels in Ischgl in addition to numerous B&Bs and apartments. Favourites include **Hotel Madlein** (T+43 (0)5444-5226; madlein.com) for its über-trendy, slick looks and gorgeous spa; **Hotel Solaria** (T+43 (0)5444-5205) for its friendly, unpretentious feel; the large and central **Hotel Post** (T+43 (0)5444-5232; post-ischgl.at); and small, welcoming and affordable **Hotel Neder** (T+43 (0)5444-5390; neder.at). The **Trofana Royal** (T+43 (0)5444-600; trofana.at) is Ischgl's five-star hotel and one of the finest in Austria. It's suitably plush, takes pride of place in the centre of town and has a legendary nightclub

Eating Hotel Madlein offers modern cuisine and the best salad buffet we've ever seen. The family-run **Jägerhof** and **Trofana Alm** do traditional local dishes in cosy settings while **Salz und Pfeffer**, **Allegra** and the **Steakhouse** (Hotel Grillalm) all provide value for money.

Michelin-starred chef Martin Sieberer oversees the **Paznauer Stube** at the **Trofana**. For those who can afford it, it's worth it!

Au pair/crèche SkiSchule Ischgl (T+43 (0)5444-5257) has a kindergarten at the base of Silvretta open from 1000-1600. **Mrs Lenz** offers evening babysitting (T+43 (0)5444-50073).

Best après-ski Ischgl's nightlife is as legendary as its skiing, if not more so. Après kicks off at **Niki's Stadl** by the Pardatschgrat chair, the **Trofana Alm** and **Romantik Hütte** at the bottom of the toboggan run and at the **Elisabeth Hotel's Eisbar**. The **Kühstahl** opposite the Silvretta lift often warms up a little later and keeps going till 0300.

Bars and clubs Kühstahl, as above, offers loud Austrian après action. Head for **Guxa** and **Fire & Ice** for cocktails or the **Golden Eagle Pub** if you're craving English beer. Finally, a night in Ischgl isn't complete without a boogie in the Moscow-style **Trofana Arena** nightclub and/or **Pacha** in Hotel Madlein.

Shopping Ischgl is shopping heaven if you have a penchant for diamonds, fur and designers. You can even indulge in tax-free shopping when you ski over to the Swiss border, although the savings are questionable.

Hire shop/rental Chose a shop with storage facilities at the lifts to avoid lugging your kit around. We recommend **Intersport Mathoy**, which has a shop opposite the Post Hotel and at the base of Pardatschgrat. **Silvretta Sports** has shops at the base of Silvretta and on Idalp and free storage facilities.

Lift tickets Buy at the lift stations in the afternoon to avoid the morning queues.

Health and wellbeing The majority of hotels in Ischgl have a sauna and steam room. **Hotel Madlein** has a designer spa, outdoor sauna and hot tub while the luxurious **Trofana Spa** is one of Austria's largest.

Down days with kids The Silvretta Sports Centre has lots of facilities. Alternatively, take a horse-drawn sleigh to nearby Mathon to visit the animals at **Niki's Ranch** (T+43 (0)5099-0100).

Internet There's an internet café at the Silvretta Centre with seven machines and Wi-Fi. Many of the hotels also have Wi-Fi.

Transfer options Fly to Innsbruck and take a taxi the whole way (taxi-ischgl.at) or train to Landeck followed by bus (oebb.at) or taxi.

You can also ski here … Samnaun, Galtür, Kappl and See.

If you like this … try St Anton ▶▶ *p85*, Chamonix ▶▶ *p126*, Verbier ▶▶ *p308*, Zermatt ▶▶ *p316*.

Austria Ischgl

◉ OPENING TIMES

End Nov to early May: 0830-1600

⑤ RESORT PRICES

Week pass: €219.50

Day pass: €41.50

Season pass: €597

① DIRECTORY

Website: ischgl.com

Tourist office: T+43 (0)5099-0100

Medical centre: T+43 (0)5444-5243

Pisteurs: T+43 (0)5446-5266

Taxi: T+43 (0)5444-5999

↘8 Kitzbühel

Town altitude	761 m	Km of pistes	168 km	Funicular/cable	
Km to airport	80 km	Nursery areas	3	cars	0/1
Airport	Salzburg	Blues	21	Gondolas/chairs	8/28
Highest lift	2004 m	Reds	26	Drags	15
Vertical drop	1600 m	Blacks	13	Night skiing	yes

Terrain parks	1
Glühwein factor	★★☆
Ski in/ski out	★☆☆
Environmental rating	★★★★★★

PROS

- ✔ Probably the ultimate 'traditional Austrian' resort.
- ✔ The well laid out mountain area caters for most abilities.
- ✔ Most visitors are here for the non-skiing attractions, leaving the off-piste unexplored.

CONS

- ✘ The low altitude of the slopes can leave slopes bare.
- ✘ The excessive, showy wealth of many visitors will turn some people off.
- ✘ Relatively limited challenging skiing for experts.

A beautiful town with diverse terrain, spread over several mountains that sadly suffer from low altitude.

Mention Kitzbühel – think **Hahnenkamm**. But Kitzbühel is not a one-slope wonder – it boasts diverse terrain on several mountains, including a freeriding hill and snowboarding/beginners hill, and access to the vast Wilder Kaiser Brixental SkiWelt area. To help visitors get to grips with the area, there are six clearly marked routes for skiers of all abilities. They've (finally) recognized the need to modernize the lift system, resulting in a currently eclectic mix of slick new lifts and antiquated chairs. However, Kitzbühel can't change its major disadvantage – its desperately low altitude.

Beginners Start at Jochberg, where the nursery slopes are at the base of the mountain. Then move on to Kitzbüheler Horn for quiet, gentle slopes to build technique and confidence.

Intermediate Your dream terrain, with long blues, reds of varying levels, wooded slopes, accessible powder fields and breathtaking scenery. Build up to the Ski Safari or Master Tour, enjoy the blues down into Kirchberg from Ehrenbachhöhe and spend at least a day on Kitzbüheler Horn.

Expert The seriously challenging Hahnenkamm and Jufen Steilhang (literally steep slope) simply have to be skied. Other Pengelstein favourites include the long ski route 34 down to Jochberg and ski route/red 32a to the Pengelstein II chair. Pass Thurn is generally quieter, with steep runs under the Trattenbach and Zweitausender chairs.

Powder If you anticipate a dump, book a guide for Bichlalm. Otherwise, get to Resterhöhe early for the best snow and try the ski routes 33 and 34 off Steinbergkogel. Kitzbüheler Horn offers accessible hits for powder virgins and experts, particularly under the Raintal chair.

Moguls It seems that the more fur on show in a resort, the more moguls there'll be on the hill, so there's no shortage of bumps here. Try the blacks and ski route off Steinbergkogel, black 55 by the Hochsaukaser chair and black 63 on Bärenbadkogel.

Trees The (only) benefit of Kitzbühel's low altitude is the number of trees on each mountain. Experts will enjoy cutting through the trees around the black 56 down to Aschau, the off-piste route from the Gauxjoch hut down into Alte Wacht and Bichlalm.

Book a guide Alpin Experts (T+43 (0)5356-177) offer guided trips on Bichlalm, a small mountain by the Kitzbüheler Horn that's used exclusively for freeriding and ski touring and currently serviced by snowcat (plans are afoot to install a lift).

Ski school Rote Teufel and element3 (which offers ski hire, tuition and guiding and is pitched at a younger, more adventurous audience) are based in Kitzbühel, with further schools in the other Kitzbüheler Alpen villages.

Kids Best off on Jochberg and Kitzbüheler Horn. **element3** runs special courses for teens aged 15 and above, teaching jumps and tricks as well as basic technique.

Bad light Stick to the trees mentioned above or indulge your inner waterbaby at the **Aquarena**.

Not to miss Book dinner at the **Bichlalm** mountain hut (T664-139 7982) and ski down in the moonlight.

Remember to avoid Beginners should steer clear of the legendary Streif run, which quickly gets icy and bumpy.

Relive a famous moment Visit the grave of mountaineer Peter Aufschnaiter in Kitzbühel's churchyard. His life was featured in the film *Seven Years in Tibet*.

Pitstop and sunbathe The **Gipfelhütte** on the sunny Kitzbüheler Horn has exceptional views and **Sonnbühel** above Hahnenkamm has a lively atmosphere.

Best mountain restaurant The **Bärenbadalm** on Jochberg cleverly combines modern facilities with traditional decoration. The local family who runs it also raises Angus cows, meaning the steaks are delicious. **Bruggeralm** by the Talsen chair is cosy with excellent food.

Practicalities

The medieval town of Kitzbühel (Kitz to locals) is the definitive Austrian ski resort, featuring an all-time great ski race (the Hahnenkamm in January), buzzing nightlife and locals straight from the set of National Lampoon's European Vacation. The resort incorporates five satellite villages, which appeal to families and anyone after less expensive accommodation.

Sleeping Find affordable accommodation with **Inghams, Crystal** and the tourist office. Our favourites include **Hotel Edelweiss** (T+43 (0)5356-75252; tiscover.at/edelweiss.kitzbuehel), which is quiet and near the Hahnenkamm lift; family-

OPENING TIMES

Early Dec to late Apr: 0830-1600

RESORT PRICES

Week pass: €196
Day pass: €41
Season pass: €525

DIRECTORY

Website: kitzbuehel.com

Tourist office: T+43 (0)5356-777

Medical centre: T+43 (0)5456-63009

Pisteurs: T+43 (0)5356-62265

Taxi: T+43 (0)5356-66222

---

friendly **Gasthof Eggerwirt** (T+43 (0)5356-62455; eggerwirt-kitzbuehel. at); **Villa Mellon** (T+43 (0)5356-66821; villa-mellon.at), a secluded and charming B&B; and the traditional **Hotel Zur Tenne** (T+43 (0)5356-64444; hotezurtenne.com). The five-star **Weisses Rößl** (T+43 (0)5356-71900; roesslkitz.at) is a Kitz institution that oozes luxury from every brick. Also excellent is the **Schwarzer Adler** (T+43 (0)5356-6911; adlerkitz.at).

Eating **Barrique** does authentic pizza and pasta, **Bergsinn** offers light bites in a trendy setting, **Landhäusl** is traditional and affordable. For something special, the **Lobster Dock** does seafood and **Zur Tenne** is consistently excellent. There are two Michelin-starred chefs in Kitzbühel – Thomas Dreher at **Tennerhof** and Stefan Hofer at the **Schwarzer Adler** – and one in Aurach, Andreas Wahrstätter at **Gigglingstube**. Dress up, tuck in.

Au pair/crèche A list of babysitters is held at the tourist office. **Reith Ski School** runs the Bobo Bambini Club kindergarten by the nursery slopes (from two years).

Best après-ski Kitzbühel is more about cocktails and clubbing than oompah-style après – unless it's World Cup weekend, when the partying doesn't stop – with **Streifalm** and **Chizzo's** your only options. Nearby Kirchberg offers more in this department, with **London Pub** and **Eis Bar** both very lively.

Bars and clubs Locals start with pre-dinner cocktails at the trendy **Café Bergsinn** or **Jimmy's**, moving on to **Fünferl** after dinner and finishing the night in **Club Take Five**. If you're more into beers than bellinis, try **The Londoner** pub or **Stamperl** before boogieing in **Highways**.

Shopping Retail therapy heaven, if you're loaded. There's also a good selection of food shops, from supermarkets to delicatessens.

Hire shop/rental Intersport Kitzsport has six branches in the resort, including the vast flagship store at the base of Hahnenkamm.

Lift tickets Check kitzbuehel.com before you book for seasonal packages combining ski pass and accommodation. Otherwise, buy at all lift base stations.

Health and wellbeing The **Aquarena** in the centre of town has pools, saunas and steam rooms – get 50% off with your ski pass (two days or more). For luxurious pampering, visit **Weisses Rößl's** two-storey spa and **Schwarzer Adler's** rooftop pool.

Down days with kids The **Aquarena** is always popular, as is feeding and petting the animals at Aurach's **Wildpark** (wildpark-tirol.at).

Internet There's wireless at the trendy **Bergsinn Bar** and machines and Wi-Fi at **Kitz Video Internet Café** on Schlossergasse.

Transfer options Kitzbühel Alpen Shuttle transfers from Salzburg airport to your hotel cost the same as the bus – book up to 24 hours in advance (T+43 (0)5356-66222; kitzalps.com/shuttle).

You can also ski here ... Reith, Aurach, Kirchberg, Pass Thurn, Mittersill/Oberpinzgau. The Kitzbüheler Alpen Ski Pass gives access to Kitzbühel, Alpbach, Brixen im Thale, Wildschönau and St Johann (704 km of pistes).

If you like this ... try Cortina ▶▶ *p222*, Davos ▶▶ *p280*, Klosters ▶▶ *p294*, St Moritz ▶▶ *p304*, Zermatt ▶▶ *p316*.

↘9 Lech

Town altitude 1450 m	Km of pistes 276 km	Funicular/cable	Terrain parks 4
Km to airport 120 km	Nursery areas 2	cars 0/6	Glühwein factor ★☆☆
Airport Innsbruck	Blues 37	Gondolas/chairs 4/38	Ski in/ski out ★★☆
Highest lift 2450 m	Reds 36	Drags 36	Environmental
Vertical drop 1000 m	Blacks 6	Night skiing no	rating ★★★★☆

PROS

- ✅ Wonderfully atmospheric village with predominantly ski in/ski out accommodation.
- ✅ Lots of beginners and intermediate terrain.
- ✅ Easy access to off-piste terrain as well as St Anton.
- ✅ Modern, comfortable ski lifts.

CONS

- ❌ Expensive.
- ❌ Hotels and ski instructors are booked up months in advance.

Chocolate-box perfect luxury Alpine village, Lech is one of the world's finest resorts.

Lech is the Bentley of the ski resort world, offering unrivalled comfort, speed if you want it and beautiful curves from every angle. It's also quiet, thanks to parking restrictions and a rigidly enforced ceiling on ticket sales. It benefits from access to the neighbouring resorts of Zürs and St Anton. Surprisingly, it also boasts one of Europe's best funparks.

Beginners Start at the nursery slopes by the Flühen T-bar, graduate to the blues off the Schlegelkopf chair and build up to the descent from the summit of Kriegerhorn in Oberlech.

Intermediate Whizz round the White Ring circuit, cruise the long red from Madlochjoch to Zug, find your powder feet under the Hassensprung chair and spend a day in St Anton.

Expert The marked ski routes off Stubenbach are a delight in powder, developing into moguls by the end of the day. There's acres more unmarked

Austria Lech

freeriding – take a guide to tackle the terrain under Rüfikopf, in Paziel Tal and the Warth-Schröcken ski area as well as St Anton.

Powder Lech regulars drink Champagne and ski in champagne powder. Take a guide to explore the areas above as well as Zürs, Stuben and St Anton.

Moguls Marked ski routes 40, 41 and 44.

Tuition The **Alpin Centre** (T+43 (0)5583-39880) is excellent for skiers looking for off-piste thrills. Instructors at the **Lech Ski School** (T+43 (0)5583-2355) are often booked for the entire season by regular visitors.

Kids **Miniclub Lech** takes children from three years and the **Oberlech Ski School** from 3½ years.

Bad light Skiing in the trees is forbidden for environmental reasons. Check out the entertainment in St Anton.

Not to miss A glass of the **Tannbergerhof**'s legendary glühwein.

Remember to avoid Buying a pair of handmade Strolz ski boots on impulse, unless you're a millionaire.

Relive a famous moment *Bridget Jones – The Edge of Reason's* skiing scenes were filmed in town, with Gasthof Post and the Schlegelkopf chair featuring heavily.

Best mountain restaurant Disappointingly limited, with the pick of the bunch in Oberlech's hotels – **Goldener Berg** and **Bergkristall**.

Practicalities

On a snowy night, it's hard to imagine Lech has changed in the past 700 years. Old chalets that now house luxurious hotels and restaurants are set on either side of a river that meanders through the town centre, past an onion-domed church. Lech regulars tend to be rich, famous and/ or royal and, perhaps because they're so 'common', the resort remains refreshingly unpretentious. Oberlech is a tiny cluster of hotels above Lech accessible only by skis or cablecar (which runs until 0100).

Sleeping Lech and Zürs are the most exclusive resorts in Austria with 6 five-star and 49 four-star hotels between them. The five-star **Gasthof Post** (T+43 (0)5583-22060; postlech. com) is everything a small, luxury Alpine hotel should be. The traditional four-star **Hotel Tannbergerhof** (T+43 (0)5583-2202; tannbergerhof.com) is central and welcoming; **Hotel Kristiania** (T+43 (0)5583-25610; kristiania.at) is faultless. In Oberlech, **Goldener Berg** (T+43 (0)5583-22050; goldenerberg. at) offers unforgettable views, food and spa facilities.

Eating Lech has more award-winning restaurants than any village in Austria, most of them in hotels. These include **Gasthof Post**, **Tannbergerhof**, **Hotel Arlberg** and **Goldener Berg**. Favourite restaurants are **Hüs Nr. 8**, **Rudi's Stamperl** and – sniggering aside – **Fux**.

Au pair/crèche Kinderland Oberlech (T+43 (0)5583-2007) cares for children aged 2½ upwards.

Bars and clubs Champagne flows from 1600 in Oberlech at **Hotel Montana** and **Goldener Berg** before action moves down to Lech's **Tannbergerhof** and **Pfefferkörndl's**. Both of these spots keep going until late, as do the **Fux** jazz café and **Archiv Bar**. Disco queens head for **Hotel Kröne's Side Step** disco and the **Arlberg's Scotch Club**.

Shopping Relatively limited and expensive. Shops in St Anton are better.

Hire shop/rental **Strolz** is to ski shops what Hamley's is to toy shops – enjoy.

Health and wellbeing The concept of 'welltain' ('wellbeing in the mountains') originated in Lech (welltain.at/lech-zuers). Hotel spas are virtually standard.

Down days with kids There's an ice rink at **Hotel Monzabon** and a 1200-m toboggan run from Oberlech.

Internet Available at most hotels. **Café Fritz's** coffee shop has machines.

Transfer options Fly to Innsbruck and take a train to Langen am Arlberg (oebb. at). Travel the last 17 km by bus or book a taxi (taxi-lech.at).

You can also ski here … St Anton, St Christoph, Zürs, Stuben, Pettneu and Klösterle.

If you like this … try Méribel ▶▶ *p166*, Klosters ▶▶ *p294*, Zermatt ▶▶ *p316*.

⊘ OPENING TIMES

Early Dec to early May: 0830-1630

Ⓢ RESORT PRICES (Arlberg ski pass)

Week pass: €199

Day pass: €41.50

Season pass: €665

ⓘ DIRECTORY

Website: lech-zuers.at

Tourist office: T+43 (0)5583-2245

Medical centre: T+43 (0)5583-2032

Pisteurs: T+43 (0)5446-2565

Taxi: T+43 (0)5583-2501

↘10 Mayrhofen

Town altitude 630 m	Km of pistes 157 km	Funicular/cable	Terrain parks 2
Km to airport 75 km	Nursery areas 3	cars 0/8	Glühwein factor ★★★
Airport Innsbruck	Blues 20	Gondolas/chairs 8/17	Ski in/ski out ☆☆☆
Highest lift 3286 m	Reds 27	Drags 27	Environmental
Vertical drop 2656 m	Blacks 5	Night skiing yes	rating ★★★★★★

PROS

- ✅ If you're young and looking to party, Mayrhofen is the place for you.
- ✅ Accommodation and dining is affordable and good quality.
- ✅ Off-piste terrain is excellent and barely touched.

CONS

- ❌ Huge amounts of drunken après-ski action.
- ❌ Queues to buy lift tickets, queues to get onto the lifts and queues to download at the end of the day.
- ❌ Although the Ziller pass gives access to a lot of terrain, you do have to travel to reach it.

Atmospheric town with boisterous nightlife and great terrain – shame about the queues ...

Mayrhofen sits between two mountains: the small Ahorn and Penken. Ahorn has snow-sure nursery runs at the top and one long red top-to-bottom run while Penken has a bit of everything. To reach the Penken slopes you have to take the gondola from one end of town (think queues) or bus it to the gondolas at Hippach and Finkenburg (think more queues). With the exception of two ski routes to Hippach and Finkenburg, the only way to get off the mountain is by gondola (think queues at 1500). You've been warned. Advanced skiers should invest in a Zillertal SuperSki Pass to access some 500 km more terrain.

Beginners The clearly marked 'Penken Tour' follows blue runs and appeals to families and tentative beginners. If you're feeling adventurous, explore Ahorn's blues before taking the 5.5-km valley run home.

Intermediate The 'Gaining Elevation Tour' will appeal to intermediates after glory. Burn down the reds and blacks on Ahorn and Penken and the lift ticket cashiers will calculate the altitude difference you've covered (approx 13,000 m), give you a certificate and post your name on the Mayrhofen website.

Expert At first glance, there don't seem to be many expert skiers here – that's because they're dropping off the back of the Tux150 lift or in Zell am Ziller and Kaltenbach. Here you'll find quieter lift queues and challenging steep terrain.

Powder The Tux150 gives access to great runs down the Penken face, particularly under the lift. In good snow, the Ski Route from Rastkogel to Eggalm is great.

Moguls Pick of the bunch are the lines underneath the Schafskopf, Knorren and Nordhang chairs.

Trees Slightly limited with some good runs from Knorren down to the Penkenbahn and round Zell am Ziller.

Book a guide There's a lot of excellent freeriding to be had in and around Mayrhofen. Locals won't share their secrets, so it's worth booking an experienced local guide. Try **Schischule Mayrhofen Total** (T+43 (0)5285-63939).

Ski school The **Roten Profis** ski school is closest to the Penkenbahn and does ski hire. **SMT** is very child-friendly, with weekly races and prize-giving.

Kids **Roten Profis** looks after children from three months while **Mayrhofen Total** accepts children from two years.

Bad light Battle through the fog looking for trees or join the kids in the **Erlebnisbad** – we know what we'd rather do.

Not to miss Even if you don't ski down the 'Harikari' run (Austria's fabled steepest piste), take a look at it – if only to admire the winch-operated piste-grooming machines.

Remember to avoid The lift queues on Penken to get back into Mayrhofen at the

end of the day. Leave the mountain before 1500 and chill out on Ahorn instead.

Relive a famous moment Rent your skis from the Uli Speiss shop – perhaps his World Downhill Champion skills will rub off on you ...

Pitstop and sunbathe Ahorn's **White Lounge** igloo bar (ironically billed as 'this season's hottest venue') is open from 1000 and 1630 (and on Tuesday evenings). Expect deck chairs and lounge music set amongst sculpted igloos.

Best mountain restaurant On Ahorn, **Josef's Biohütte** serves organic food while the **Schneekarhütte** is known for fresh seafood (and high prices). On Penken, **Schiestl's Sunnalm** is popular, as is **Grillholfalm** by the terrain park, which does great (and cheap) pizza and pasta.

⚫ LOCALS DO

✔ Plan their days to avoid the queues – take the 0800 bus to avoid crowds at Hintertux.

✔ Go further afield to Zell am Ziller and Kaltenbach to escape the crowds and bag the best powder.

✔ Enjoy quiet après-ski beers at the Gasthof Brücke away from all the tourists.

⚫ LOCALS DON'T

✖ Join the tourists downing Jägermeister in the après-ski bars but save their ski legs for early starts.

✖ Go to Hintertux when it's cold and windy.

Practicalities

Mayrhofen is a pretty town in the Ziller valley that's been popular with Brits since the 1970s for its lively atmosphere and large amount of terrain, including the Hintertux glacier. Today, it's part of the Zillertal 3000 ski area, opening up 620 km of pistes and making it the biggest resort in the valley. Thanks partly to 'Snowbombing' every April – a week-long party-cum-ski holiday with live music – Mayrhofen attracts a young, boisterous crowd.

Sleeping Hotel-Gasthof Perauer (T+43 (0)5285-62566; perauer.at) is close to the lifts, has great spa facilities and a suite costs only €10 more than a standard double. Families love the **Alpenhotel Kramerwirt** (T+43 (0) 5285-6700; kramerwirt.at). Be at the heart of the après action at **Gasthof Brücke** (T+43 (0)5285-62232; gasthof-bruecke.com). The über-trendy **White Lounge** (white-lounge.at), 2000 m up the Ahorn mountain, opened 10 'igloo suites' in 2008. Guests travel up by cable car, are welcomed with Champagne, served dinner in the dining igloo and left to snuggle up in double sleeping bags.

Eating For local food, head for the **Bruggerstube** or **Café Tirol**. **Manni's** does good pizza while **Ciao** is also good for Italian food and does takeaway. **Mo's Esscafe & Music Room** does steaks

and burgers accompanied by live music while the trendy **Coup Kitchen** delivers tasty basics. The dining igloo in the **White Lounge** serves up excellent food in an unforgettable setting while the **Grillküchl** in town is less exotic but also intimate.

Au pair/crèche The public kindergarten and crèche **Wuppy's Kinderland** (T+43 (0)5285- 63612) takes kids from three months to seven years.

Best après-ski Head for **The Ice Bar** and **Nikki's Schirmbar** – Ice Bar claims to serve more Grolsch than any bar in Europe. **Happy End**, owned by skiing legend Uli Spiess, is also popular.

Bars and clubs **Scotland Yard** is an institution – après-ski here is large, loud and late. **Mo's Esscafe & Music Room** also fills up before the partying masses head for the **Schlusselalm** disco at the Brücke Hotel, **Arena** at the Strass Hotel or the **Speakeasy**.

Shopping Mayrhofen offers eclectic retail therapy, selling everything from crampons to Swarovski crystal-studded toasters. The best supermarket is **M-Preis** next to Kaltenbach.

Hire shop/rental Uli Speiss has quite a monopoly on ski rental shops, with outlets in town and at the Penken and Ahorn lifts.

Lift tickets Buy tickets at all lift stations – do so the afternoon before to avoid the morning queues.

Health and wellbeing The Strass Hotel has a large wellness area with a pool, saunas and beauty treatments. The **Solarice Wellness Centre & Spa** does excellent massages.

Down days with kids The Erlebnisbad (Adventure Pool) has water slides and a

spa. The Sennerei Zillertal dairy on the outskirts of town makes a fun day out.

Internet Tirol has three computers (try some of the cakes while you're surfing), **Videothèque** has computers and games, and most hotels offer Wi-Fi (for a fee).

Transfer options Trains run from Innsbruck, Salzburg and Munich to Mayrhofen (T+43 (0)5285-62362; zillertalbahn.at). Each airport website also has details of coach and rail transfers (munich-airport.de, innsbruck-airport.com and salzburg-airport.com).

You can also ski here ... Eggalm, Rastkogel, Penken and Hintertux. A Zillertal 3000 pass includes Mayrhofen, Hippach, Finkenberg, Vorderlanersbach and Lanersbach.

If you like this ... Try Sölden ▶▶ *p83*, St Anton ▶▶ *p85*, Chamonix ▶▶ *p126*.

Austria Mayrhofen

☺ OPENING TIMES

Dec to early Apr: 0900-1600

⑤ RESORT PRICES

Week pass: €176 for 6 days or €197 for 7 days

Day pass: €36

Season pass: €413/€506

ⓘ DIRECTORY

Website: mayrhofen.at

Tourist office: T+43 (0)5285-67600

Medical centre: T+43 (0)5285-62550

Pisteurs: T+43 (0)5285-62277

Taxi: T+43 (0)5285-62260

↘11 Obergurgl

Town altitude	1930 m	Km of pistes	110 km	Funicular/cable	
Km to airport	100 km	Nursery areas	3	cars	0/0
Airport	Innsbruck	Blues	9	Gondolas/chairs	7/8
Highest lift	3082 m	Reds	15	Drags	8
Vertical drop	1152 m	Blacks	5	Night skiing	no

Terrain parks	0
Glühwein factor	★★☆
Ski in/ski out	★☆☆
Environmental rating	★★★★☆

PROS

- ✔ Traditional Austrian village.
- ✔ Large, fun mountain.

CONS

- ✘ Might be too staid for some.
- ✘ Altitude means bad weather can be common.

A lovely old-fashioned Austrian resort that has kept pace with modern ski tourism.

Oberburgl is a great mountain and one that definitely appeals to a certain type of skier. Not for nothing are most visitors you speak to repeat visitors on their second, third or fourth trip. They're attracted to the place for a couple of reasons, first of which is the quality of the snow. Obergurgl is so high when compared to other Alpine resorts that the snow always seems to be of a high

standard. True, the weather can come in as a result, but that's a fair pay-off. The other good news about Obergurgl is the new lift investment, which has really helped to solve some queuing issues.

Beginners First timers should head to the Mahdstuhlift beginner area. Those with some confidence will find a lot to like here, as the resort is very well planned, especially with the new Hohe Mut Bahn gondola, which is probably where you should start. Once confidence levels are on the rise, take the Roßkarbahn chair and explore the many blues. There is a long, winding blue to get you home.

Intermediate You'll probably start on the Roßkarbahn lift and spend time getting used to the many fun, swooping pistes on offer. Over to the skier's left, if conditions are good, head to the top of the Hohe Mut Bahn and tackle some of the reds. Later in the week, head over to neighbouring Hoch Gurgl.

Expert There is a surprising amount of solid terrain here, and strong skiers will enjoy exploring their way around. The majority of the steeper blacks are in Hoch Gurgl, but it is easy to find open powder stashes and some long, challenging descents.

Powder Obergurgl's height gives it an edge: with many lifts topping out at well over 2500 m, there is usually a lot of powder to be had. The higher sections of

✔ LOCALS DO

- ✔ Afford visitors an old-fashioned welcome.
- ✔ Ski the entire area.
- ✔ Live in busier Sölden and ski Obergurgl.

✘ LOCALS DON'T

- ✘ Snowboard in any great numbers.
- ✘ Mind showing visitors the best runs.

Hohe Mut Bahn are worth investigating initially, but to really make the most of it hire one of the excellent local guides for half a day.

Moguls Traditionally the best places to test your knee ligaments are the Top-Wurmkogl II, under the Top Mountain Star in Hoch Gurgl, and the piste at the top of Hohe Mut in Obergurgl.

Tuition Obergurgl has an excellent ski school (skischule-obergurgl.com), with good English-speaking instructors.

Kids The **Obergurgl Ski School** caters for children aged four and up, with lessons usually including a supervised lunch. **Bobo's Kinderclub** also looks after the little ones.

Bad light Great tree riding is another string to Obergurgl's bow, with the trees under the **Steinmannbahn** in Obergurgl and down to the **Hochgurglbahn** very stimulating.

Not to miss It has to be a session in the Nederhutte. The place is quite literally the talk of the town.

Remember to avoid The upper slopes in bad light. It is very easy to get yourself lost.

Relive a famous moment Auguste Piccard, the first man to fly a balloon into the stratosphere, ended his historic flight on a nearby glacier.

Best mountain restaurant Without question, it is the **Top Mountain Star** in Hoch Gurgl. At 3082 m the views are spectacular, and the hot chocolate isn't bad either.

Practicalities

If nearby Sölden sounds too much like hard work, Obergurgl might be the answer. While it might not share the profile of its near neighbour or other Austrian behemoths such as St Anton, it is the type of timeless resort that inspires a fierce loyalty. Its altitude makes it very snow-sure, and a day spent gliding through the lower trees is a little like going back in time, thanks to a dearth of snowboarders and a social scene centred around the après sessions at the semi-legendary Nederhütte.

Sleeping The four-star **Edelweiss and Gurgl** (edelweiss-gurgl.com) is one of those family-run places the Austrians do so well, with great food and attentive staff. **Hotel Alpenland** (hotelalpenland. at) also adheres to this homely, high-service approach. **Hotel Josl** (josl.at), meanwhile, is flying the flag for the boutique hotel craze.

Eating **Hotel Jenewein** (hotel-jenewein.com) serves up snacks next to the new gondola, while other more substantial options include the elaborate à la carte at the **Wiesental** (hotelwiesental.com) and the restaurant at the **Josl**, which the locals seem to rate.

Bars and clubs The fame of the Nederhutte has spread far and wide and is a must-do. In town, the **Josl Keller** gets busy at happy hour, as does the Edelweiss Bar.

Hire shop/rental Plenty of options, but **Ski Set** has a large presence in the resort and a dedicated website at obergurgl.skiset.com.

Health and wellbeing This being a relatively upmarket Austrian resort, there are many wellness options to keep you

occupied. The **Josl** is very proud of the **Sky Sphere** area, while the **Edelweiss and Gurgl** also has an enormous facility, with hay baths, solariums, saunas and outdoor pools.

Down days with kids Still plenty to do, including horse riding, indoor golf and, our favourite, curling on the outdoor rink. Just remember to wrap them up warm.

Internet Most hotels have internet access, the **Edelweiss and Gurgl** being a typical example with its couple of terminals and wireless access in the bar.

Transfer options The best way of arranging a transfer is through the online **Otzal Shuttle** (obergurgl.com), which usually costs around €40 per person.

You can also ski here ... Obergurgl is linked to Hoch Gurgl and your pass enables you to ski the entire area.

OPENING TIMES
Mid-Nov to mid-Apr: 0830-1630

RESORT PRICES
Week pass: €235.50
Day pass: €42.50

DIRECTORY
Website: obergurgl.com
Tourist office: T+43 (0)57200-100
Medical centre: T+43 (0)5256-6423
Pisteurs: T+43 (0)5256-6260
Taxi: T+43(0)5256-6540

Austria Obergurgl

↘12 Saalbach

Town altitude	1003 m	Km of pistes	200 km	Funicular/cable cars	0/15
Km to airport	100 km	Nursery areas	3	Gondolas/chairs	15/16
Airport	Salzburg	Blues	34	Drags	24
Highest lift	2020 m	Reds	28	Night skiing	yes
Vertical drop	1070 m	Blacks	6		

Terrain parks	3
Glühwein factor	★★★
Ski in/ski out	★★★
Environmental rating	★★★★★

PROS

- ✓ Excellent resort for intermediate skiers and families.
- ✓ Lively and family-friendly après-ski scene.
- ✓ A large ski area with modern lifts which is easy to navigate.

CONS

- ✗ Regular influx of businessmen visiting from nearby cities has pushed prices up in bars and discos.
- ✗ Fairly limited off-piste skiing.
- ✗ Snow on south-facing slopes can suffer from sun and low altitude.

A large, easily navigable ski area – great for intermediates – and lively après-ski.

Austria Saalbach

The mountains surrounding Saalbach were created for skiing. Divided on either side of the Saalbach valley to give both north- and south-facing slopes, there are gentle blues, reds of varying difficulty, steep blacks, open powder bowls and wooded glades. Add to this an outstanding lift system, excellent mountain restaurants and breathtaking scenery and it's clear why visitors keep coming back.

Beginners Nearby Hinterglemm has the best nursery slopes – they're self-contained and snow-secure. Buy block tickets (up to 10 rides) to save money on a full lift ticket. Build up to the long, gentle blues from Bernkogel and Kohlmaiskopf but beware of the blue Schattberg-Vorderglemm run, which gets busy and icy at peak times.

Intermediate Confident intermediates can (just) complete a circuit of the SkiCircus in one day – completed clockwise or anti-clockwise (better for following the sun), it's easy to pull out at any stage by dropping into the valley and grabbing a ski bus home. However, don't neglect the terrain under Reiterkogel, off Seekar or towards Leogang. Consider building up to the circuit by familiarizing yourself with the terrain first rather than regarding it as an orientation exercise.

Expert Freeriding enthusiasts might be disappointed, but experts looking for mileage will love Saalbach. Challenging black pistes include the Nordabfahrt on Schattberg Ost and Zwölferkogel, while the off-piste ski routes by Hintermaisalm (Schattberg West), Walleggalm (Spieleckkogel) and into Leogang will test most experts.

Powder In addition to the itineraries above, traverse right from the Hochalm chair to access a powder bowl; pick your lines in the steeper Seekar bowl; and traverse along the ridge on Schattberg Ost to access light trees before joining the Jausnerabfart to Vorderglemm.

Moguls The Zwölferkogel-Nordabfahrt down to Hinterglemm, black 7a under Schattberg Sprinter and red Kollingalm run off Hochalm.

Trees The most challenging trees are on Schattberg West, Schattberg Ost and Zwölferkogel. The mountains on the south side of the valley offer easier, gladed skiing.

Book a guide Sepp Mitterer, local ski and mountain guide, guides off-piste tours (T+43 (0)664-2420236).

☺ LOCALS DO

- ✓ Burn down the World Cup run from Zwölferkogel chair.
- ✓ Toboggan back from dinner at the Spielberghaus and Pfefferalm mountain huts.
- ✓ Sing cheesy songs at the top of their lungs at Bauer's Schi Alm.

☹ LOCALS DON'T

- ✗ Forget to validate their parking tickets before 1600 to get free parking.
- ✗ Drink copious quantities of Jägermeister and wear the orange hats to prove it.
- ✗ Do their food shopping between 1600 and 1700 when the shops are rammed.

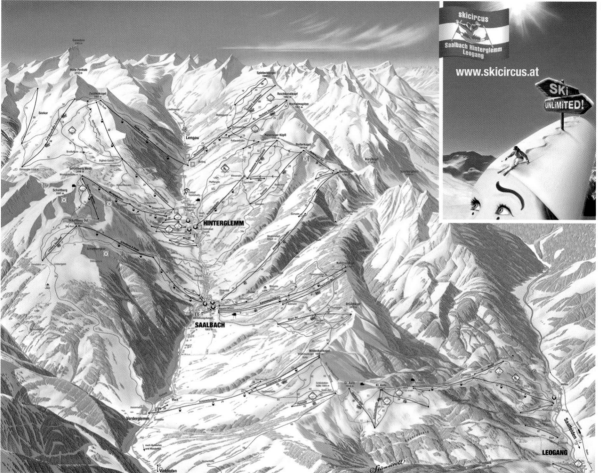

Ski school Ten ski schools is arguably excessive. Saalbach's **Hinterholzer** classes start at 0930 to avoid the 1000 rush while Hinterglemm's **Thomas Wolf & Bartl Gensbichler** is good for children.

Kids Children are highly rated citizens here, particularly in Hinterglemm and Leogang. Kids under six ski free, there are good offers at peak periods (visit skicircus.at) and ski schools offer ski kindergarten from three years, as do some of the hotels.

Bad light Most of the terrain is below tree level but why not go tobogganing

to a mountain hut for lunch or visit nearby Zell am See.

Not to miss The breathtaking views from the top of Spieleckkogel and Zwölferkogel on a clear day.

Remember to avoid The queues for the Spieleck and Hochalm chairs between 1000 and 1100.

Relive a famous moment Follow in the ski steps of World Championship skiers as you burn down the 1991 Downhill World Championship course under the Zwölferkogel chair.

Pitstop and sunbathe The **Pfefferalm** is 280 years old, has no electricity, a sun terrace you'll never want to leave and food matched only by the views.

Best mountain restaurant Mountain restaurants are excellent and numerous (44 in total). Our pick of the bunch are the **Xandlstadl** at the bottom of Westgipfelbahn; **Alte Schmeide** above Leogang; and the **Rosswaldhütte** by the Hochalm chair.

Practicalities

The villages of Saalbach, Hinterglemm and Leogang make up this popular resort near Salzburg. Saalbach is the largest, with a rocking nightlife, Hinterglemm (2 km from Saalbach) is slightly quieter with more self-catering accommodation, while Leogang is furthest away and popular with young families. Fortunately, a slick lift system joins all three and shuttle buses enable non-skiing transport between them.

Sleeping Saalbach: **Hotel Kendler** (T+43 (0)6541-6225; kendler.at), at the base of the Bernkogel chair, has excellent children's facilities and a spa. **Alpenhotel** (T+43 (0)6541-6666; alpenhotel.at) has everything from a spa to disco and several restaurants. **Haus Schnargel** (T+43 (0)6541-62840; haus-schnargl.at) is a comfortable, central B&B.

Hinterglemm: **Hotel Egger** (T+43 (0)6541-63220; hotel-egger.at) is perfect for families, with five swimming pools and direct access to ski school. Wolf Hotels runs the four-star wellness **Hotel Haus Wolf** (T+43 (0)6541-7408; wolf-hotels.at) in Hinterglemm and opens the resort's only five-star hotel, the **Alpine Palace**, in 2008.

Eating With nearly 70 restaurants, visitors are spoiled for choice. Saalbach: **Peter's Restaurant** is great for carnivores and the pizzeria in **Hotel Haider** is good value. Hinterglemm: the Goaßstall at the base of Reiterkogel (a rustic, goat-themed restaurant famous for its 'Hot Goat' dish – actually steak), **Heurigenstube** and **Knappenhof** for traditional Austrian dishes. **Restaurant Kendler** in Saalbach has fresh seafood and international cuisine. For an atmospheric evening, you can't beat a meal at the mountain huts **Spielberghaus** (T+43 (0)6541-7253)

or **Hinterhagalm** (T+43 (0)6541-7212), accessed by toboggan or snowcat. Reservations essential at peak times.

Au pair/crèche Many hotels (particularly in Hinterglemm) offer day care. Contact Mrs Annaliese Kröll for private babysitting (T+43 (0)6541-7183).

Best après-ski Après kicks off early, with the mountain restaurants and schirmbars (umbrella bars) full of cheery skiers by 1500. The **Hinterhagalm hut's** '5 pm tea bar' warms people up for the ski down to **Bauer's Schi Alm** – consistently voted Austria's best après-ski bar, Bauer's is made up of several well-staffed schirmbars, a 'sausage heaven bar', playground and hearty singing. More gentle après takes place at the **Saalbacher Hof** (until Castello's opens in the cellar).

Bars and clubs Saalbach: **Zum Turm**, within staggering distance from Bauer's, **Pub Stamperl** by the Shattenberg Express and **Kuhstall** in the Hotel Arena. Move on to **King's**, **Arena** and **Crazy Bear** later for dancing. Hinterglemm: start at **Goaßstall** and **Hexenhäusl** before moving to **Glemmerkeller**, **Road King** and **Tanzhimmel**. There's a night bus between the two villages until late on week nights and 0230 on Saturdays.

Hire shop/rental Intersport Bauer is in the centre of town on four floors with huge rental choice, friendly staff and a café. There's a depot service at the Intersport by the Kohlmais chair.

Lift tickets Available at all base stations. Avoid queues and buy passes from **Intersport Bauer** and **Sportalm Scharnagl**.

Health and wellbeing The public swimming pool in Hinterglemm has a sauna. **Vital Tempel** by the Bergkogel lift offers beauty treatments and massage (T+43 (0)6541-62250).

Down days with kids Free guided walks start from the tourist offices in Saalbach and Hinterglemm at 1000 on Tuesdays and Thursdays respectively.

Internet There are machines in **Intersport Bauer** and the Zwölferkogel and Schattberg Express base stations. The internet cafés **Hexenhäusl** and **The Tunnel** have Wi-Fi.

Transfer options Fly to Salzburg and take a shuttle bus that runs to Saalbach four times a day (three on Sundays). A return costs €65 (salzburg-airport.com) or €70 with the five-times-daily resort shuttle (holiday-shuttle.at).

You can also ski here ... Saalbach, Hinterglemm and Leogang.

If you like this ... try Ischgl ▶▶ *p66*, Mayrhofen ▶▶ *p75*.

⊙ OPENING TIMES
Early Dec to mid-Apr: 0830-1630

⑤ RESORT PRICES
Week pass: €186

Day pass: €38.50

Season pass: €465

⑥ DIRECTORY
Website: saalbach.com

Tourist office: T+43 (0)6541-6900

Medical centre: T+43 (0)6541-6287

Pisteurs: T+43 (0)6541-6670

Taxi: T+43 (0)6541-6261

↘13 Sölden

Town altitude	1377 m	Km of pistes	150 km	Funicular/cable	
Km to airport	80 km	Nursery areas	2	cars	0/2
Airport	Innsbruck	Blues	51 km	Gondolas/chairs	5/19
Highest lift	3250 m	Reds	62 km	Drags	8
Vertical drop	1680 m	Blacks	27 km	Night skiing	yes

Terrain parks	1
Glühwein factor	★★★
Ski in/ski out	★★☆
Environmental rating	★★★★★★

PROS

- ✅ Two high-altitude glaciers and good snowmaking facilities ensure consistent conditions throughout the season.
- ✅ Vibrant party atmosphere: ski hard, party hard.

CONS

- ❌ If you don't want party central, you don't want Sölden.
- ❌ Beginners slopes can get crowded.

> *"Think Big, Think Sölden" – a slogan equally applicable to the skiing terrain and the party scene.*

☺ LOCALS DO

- ✅ Wrap up warm when skiing on the glacier – it gets seriously cold!
- ✅ Head for the glaciers when it gets busy on Giggijoch and Gaislachkogl.
- ✅ Enjoy cocktails at Candela's before the dancing kicks off.

☹ LOCALS DON'T

- ❌ Get caught in the queue to download from Giggijoch – ski down from Rotkogljoch to Gaislachkogl and grab a bus.
- ❌ Ski off-piste on the glacier unless they know what they're doing.

With two glaciers (Rettenbach and Tiefenbach) and two mountains (Gaislachkogl and Giggijoch), Sölden provides varied terrain for all skiing levels and is virtually guaranteed snow. It can take 45 minutes to reach Tiefenbach from Giggijoch but the views are breathtaking and the lifts comfortable.

Beginners Ski schools meet on Giggijoch, where there are lots of gentle blues, but escape the crowds and head for the wide open blues on the Tiefenbach glacier, taking in the awe-inspiring views.

Intermediate The entire ski area is great for intermediates, so explore it by following the Big 3 Rallye – a tour that takes in Sölden's three peaks over 3000 m, covering 50 km and 10,000 m in altitude. Try the 15-km descent from Schwarze Schneide to Gaislachkogl (a vertical descent of 1370 m).

Expert Do the Big 3 Rallye, explore the steep blacks off Hainbachjoch and Schwarzogl, play in the excellent BASE Winter Park and the runs under the 3SB Wasserkar lift and Tiefenbachkogl gondola.

Powder Visitors to Sölden attach more importance to first beers than first tracks, so get an early start and reap the

Austria Sölden

rewards. However, skiing off-piste on glaciers is dangerous so book a guide to learn the terrain.

Moguls Black 14 down from Hainbachjoch and red 11 off the Gampe chair.

Tuition All four ski schools are based in Giggijoch and keep class sizes below 10.

Kids The Giggijoch kindergarten takes children from three years.

Bad light Glaciers aren't great on bad-visibility days, so visit the **Aquadome** in Längenfeld – there's a pool, thermal baths, saunas and herb chambers.

Not to miss The views from the (kind of scary) glass viewing platform at the top of Tiefenbachkogl (3309 m).

Remember to avoid Falling into the river after too many après-ski beers – it does happen.

Relive a famous moment Sölden's self-professed claim to fame is its après-ski, so steel yourself and head for the bars!

Best mountain restaurant The **Schwarzkogel** restaurant is modern and popular with colossal windows. **Gampe Thaya**, accessible from red 11, is rustic and serves local food.

Austria Sölden

Practicalities

This pint-sized town packs the punch of a shot of Jägermeister. It's essentially a mile of (busy) road flanked by buzzing bars, clubs and restaurants that attracts a young and lively crowd. Sölden is bisected by a river, with the main strip under the mountain and quieter hotels and guesthouses on the other side. Further removed from the fray is Hochsölden – a sprinkling of ski in/ski out hotels on the mountain.

Sleeping Virtually every building in town offers some sort of accommodation, with affordable B&Bs in demand from younger visitors. **Haus Ulrich** (T+43 (0)5254-22030; hausulrich.at), on the quiet side of the river, is kept scrupulously clean by Annie Lackner. **Hotel Liebe Sonne** (T+43 (0)5254-22030; liebesonne. at) is at the heart of the action, while **Rosengarten** (T+43 (0)5254-2674; hotelrosengarten.at) is popular with families.

Eating Otzi Wein & Dine in Hotel Berglan has excellent food and wine, **S'Pfandl** does good Austrian food while **Pizzeria Gusto** is busy till late.

Bars and clubs Après action starts early at **Phillip** and **Grüner's Almstube** at the top of Innerwald or **Cuckoo Bar** and **Liebe Sonne's Schirm Bar** at the bottom of Giggijoch. **Nanu** and **Candela's** are good for early cocktails while **Fire & Ice** and **Partyhaus** rock on until late.

Hire shop/rental Sport 4 You (T+43 (0)5254-30610) will pick you up, fit you for kit and return you to your hotel.

Health and wellbeing The Freizeit **Arena** has public pools and saunas.

OPENING TIMES

Early Dec to late Apr/early May: 0830-1600

RESORT PRICES

Week pass: €205.50

Day pass: €41.50

Season pass: €501

DIRECTORY

Website: soelden.com

Tourist office: T+43 (0)57200-200

Medical centre: T+43 (0)5254-2040

Pisteurs: T+43 (0)57200-203

Taxi: T+43 (0)5254-3232

The five-star **Central Spa Hotel** (T+43 (0)5254-22600; central-soelden.at) offers more exclusive facilities.

Down days with kids Entertain children at the Freizeit Arena or **Aquadome** in nearby Längenfeld (aquadome.at).

Internet There's wireless in **Freizeit Café** and several machines in the apparently nameless café next to **Hotel Hubertus**.

Transfer options Trains run frequently from Innsbruck to Otztal (oebb.at), where you take a bus (40 minutes) or taxi (25 minutes). Alternatively, take a direct airport shuttle (airport-transfer.com).

You can also ski here ... The Five Tirol Glaciers (Stubai, Kaunertal, Pitztal and Hintertux).

If you like this ... try Mayrhofen ▶▶ *p75*, Zell am See ▶▶ *p93*, Les Deux Alpes ▶▶ *p156*.

↘14 St Anton

Town altitude	1304 m	Km of pistes	276 km	Funicular/cable		Terrain parks	4
Km to airport	100 km	Nursery areas	2	cars	0/6	Glühwein factor	★★★
Airport	Innsbruck	Blues	37	Gondolas/chairs	4/38	Ski in/ski out	★★☆
Highest lift	2450 m	Reds	36	Drags	36	Environmental	
Vertical drop	1350 m	Blacks	6	Night skiing	No	rating	★★★★☆☆

PROS

- ✅ Arguably some of the world's most exciting and challenging terrain, most of which is easily accessible.
- ✅ Excellent après-ski and a friendly, lively atmosphere in the car-free town.

CONS

- ❌ Powder dogs are out in force, so terrain gets tracked out within hours of a dump.
- ❌ No matter how well you ski, you'll always feel inadequate.
- ❌ Not the resort of choice for beginners.
- ❌ The slopes do get busy and queues (particularly for the Zammermoos chair) can be lengthy.

Makes dreams of epic freeriding and extreme après action come true.

St Anton fully deserves its cult status. Located in Austria's Arlberg region and considered to be one of Europe's best, it boasts guaranteed snow, limitless freeriding (nearly 5500 ha of off-piste), dramatic Alpine terrain and efficient lift systems. A mountain guide is essential to your enjoyment of the resort, which means it can be expensive – but worth every penny, particularly if you're lucky with the weather.

Beginners Arguably not the best spot for novices. The gentlest nursery slopes are at Nasserein and above the restaurant at Gampen but you'll have to progress quickly to feel comfortable on the busy Kapall and Galzig blues. Consider sticking to Lech and Zürs.

Intermediate St Anton is great for intermediates hungry to improve, with few better ways to get miles under your ski belt than skiing down from the peaks of Valluga, Kappal, Madloch-Joch and Zuger Hochlicht during a week. Build up your legs skiing from Valluga to town without stopping; practise carving in relative peace on the 17 to Rauz or 11 to Arlenmähder and at speed on the Kapall World Cup piste; get acquainted with powder on the Albonagrat; conquer the relatively quiet blacks on Pettneu; and make Rendl your friend.

Expert The ultimate aim of any expert skier coming to St Anton is to ski the north face of the Valluga. Accessed by a tiny lift from the top of the Valluga 1 gondola (when accompanied by a qualified guide), the initial descent is seriously steep before opening out into open powder fields to Zürs. Other must-dos are: the 34 from Kapall to Mattun; the 3 under Galzig cable car; and S3 and S13 on the Albonagrat. Don't neglect Rendl, particularly good for bad-light days.

😊 LOCALS DO

✔ Take off-piste seriously and equip themselves accordingly.

✔ Head for Lech when St Anton is tracked out.

✔ Enjoy the relatively quiet slopes on Rendl and Stuben.

✔ Queue for the Valluga cable car on a powder day – it's worth the wait.

😟 LOCALS DON'T

✖ Drive into town – parking is limited.

✖ Go to the free Ski Show on Thursday evenings with demos by the ski schools – but visitors should.

✖ Pay €2 for the ski 'cloakroom' at the Krazy Kangaruh – but do split their skis (and remember where they left them).

Powder Essentially, the entire mountain area is skied on powder days – quickly. Our favourite powder runs include: all the variations on the north-facing Albonagrat (snow magnet) but particularly the Maroikopf-Langen route; dropping off Rendl into Hinteres Rendl or cutting through the Malfon valley from Rendl to Pettneu; itinerary 18 down to Alpe Rauz under the Valgefahr chair; and tackling the less-skied west face of Valluga. For shorter hits, stick under the Zammermoos, Mattun and Valfagehr lifts.

Moguls Most runs get bumped out quickly. Long mogul runs include ski routes 16 and 33 down Mattun and 15 down Schindler Kar.

Trees Head for the legendary (and surprisingly quiet) tree runs through Langen forest accessed by the Albonagrat lift by Stuben or stick on Rendl.

Book a guide If you want to experience the real St Anton, book a guide. We recommend British-run guiding company **Piste to Powder** (T664-174 6282; pistetopowder.com). Guides have excellent local knowledge and can sniff out fresh powder several days after a dump.

Ski school Long before St Anton gained cult status with partying freeriders, skiing grandaddy Hannes Schneider revolutionized skiing when he opened the **Arlberg Ski School** here in 1921. Today it has some 300 instructors and also owns the smaller **St Anton Ski School**. Both schools offer excellent tuition for beginners to off-piste guiding.

Kids Skischool Arlberg has **Kinderwelt** centres at St Anton, Nasserein and St Christoph. They offer child care (from 2½ years) and ski kindergarten for over threes. The Snowman Ticket enables children born in 2000 and after to get an Arlberg season pass for €10.

Bad light Visit the Skiing Museum, chill out in the **ARLBERG-well.com** leisure centre or simply abandon yourself to the lure of the bars.

Not to miss Skiing down Valluga to Zürs (weather permitting) and celebrating at the end of the day in the Krazy Kangaruh.

Remember to avoid Breaking every bone in your body skiing down from the Mooserwirt in the dark.

Relive a famous moment *Die Weisse Rausch* (The White Thrill), one of the first ski films ever made, was filmed in St Anton in 1931. Today, the Weisse Rausch lives on in the form of a chaotic 9-km free-for-all race from Valluga down to the valley every April.

Pitstop and sunbathe Sample some of the **Hospiz Alm**'s renowned wines in St Christoph or bag a deckchair at **Taps** (above the KK). The **Ice Bar** at **Rendl Beach** is legendary.

Best mountain restaurant The **Verwallstube** at the top of Galzig does (pricey) posh nosh on a sunny terrace; the hundred-year-old **Ulmerhütte** just off the top of the Arlenmähder lift does Tyrolean food; while the restaurant at the top of **Valluga** has awesome views. Further afield, ski down to Stuben for excellent food on the large sun terrace of the **Hotel Arlberg Sport Café** or cosy up in Hannes Schneider's birthplace – **Café Restaurant Dorfstuba** (closed on Wednesdays).

Austria St Anton

Practicalities 🛏️⚡🚌

The pretty town of St Anton positively hums with a palpable energy. This energy is generated by the sheer enthusiasm of the people who make the pilgrimage to what's become a Mecca for off-piste skiing, equalled only by its party scene. Pilgrims include seasonaires, Scandinavians and Brits staying for weeks and powder hounds who drop everything to come out when conditions are good.

Sleeping The resort of St Anton incorporates St Christoph, Stuben, Lech and Zürs, Nasserein, St Jakob, Pettneu, Oberdorf and Klösterle – that's a lot of accommodation. Lech and Zürs are covered separately in this book so here's a breakdown of the rest. St Anton: best for access to lifts and bars are **Aparthotel Anton** (T+43 (0)5446-2408; hotelanton. com), **Haus Erwin Falch** (tiscover.com/hotel-garni-falch) and **The Old House** chalet (theoldhouse.at). The five-star **St Antoner Hof** (T+43 (0)5446-2910; st.antonerhof.at) does old-fashioned luxury in the centre of town. Nasserein: good for beginners and families is **Nassreinerhof** (T+43 (0)5446-3366). Stuben: direct access to awesome Albona ski area, **Kohler Haus** chalet (arlberg-stuben.at/kohlerhaus). St Jakob, Pettneu, Oberdorf and Klösterle: distant but cheap, **Pension Sonnenblick** in St Jakob (T+43 (0)5446-2445). The five-star **Arlberg-Hospiz** in St Christoph has various restaurants, a wine cellar dating back to 1386, a spa and a children's nursery.

Eating Funky Chicken, Pizza Pomodoro and **Maximillian's** in the pedestrianized area of town offer good value food with a lively atmosphere. **Underground on the Piste** does great seafood while **Kandahar** does Thai food in a buddah-bar style setting. The oak-panelled rooms of the **Ski Museum** make an unlikely but delightful location for fine dining. Alternatively, indulge in a six-course dinner in **Hospiz Alm's** historical Ski Club Stube, which has one of the world's largest Bordeaux wine collections.

Au pair/crèche The tourist office can arrange babysitter services (T+43 (0)5446-2269).

Best après-ski The **Krazy Kangaruh** and the **Mooserwirt** are international après-ski phenomena – Mooserwirt sells 5000 litres of beer each day. **Underground on the Piste** is a cosy, candlelit antidote to its noisy neighbours, tucked away on the skiers' right after Moosewirt and before Galzig. Drinking at the **Anton Café** by Galzig will decrease your chances of glühwein-induced ski injuries.

Bars and clubs Following a brief 'disco nap' lull, action kicks off at **Scotty's**, **Pub 37**, **Bobo's** and **Funky Chicken** before moving to **Piccadilly** and the **Postkeller**. The über-cool **Kandahar** comes alive later – and keeps going until 0600.

Shopping Locals love kit – there are several shops selling expensive mountain equipment. There are two (busy) supermarkets in town but M-Preis, about 1.5 km down-valley, is better.

Hire shop/rental Local Reinhard Alber runs **Alber Sport** in the centre of town, which stocks high-quality equipment and offers a depot service at Galzig and Nasserein.

Lift tickets Buy tickets at all the main lift stations – Galzig stays open until 1900. Buy tickets for the next day from 1400.

Health and wellbeing The ARLBERG-well.com leisure centre has a large pool, saunas, massage, gym etc.

Down days with kids Drop by the leisure centre, take a guided walk, go sledging and visit the Skiing Museum in the beautiful old Arlberg Kandahar House by the Galzig gondola.

Internet Mail Box on the main street has Wi-Fi, cable and machines to use and there are machines at **Surfer's Paradise** snowboard shop and **Sportshop Kirschbaum**. There are public Wi-Fi hot spots at the Zielstadion, Valugasaal, Seminarraum Patterioll and Arlbergsaal.

Transfer options Innsbruck, Vienna and Zürich have direct train connections while Friedrichshafen and München are within transfer reach. **Arlberg Express** (arlbergexpress.com), **Loacker Tours** (airportbus.at) and **Four Seasons Travel** (airport-transfer.com) run transfers from Zürich, Friedrichshafen and München respectively. Visit seat61.com for trains from Vienna.

You can also ski here ... The Arlberg ski pass gives you access to St Anton, St Christoph, Lech, Zürs, Stuben, Pettneu and Klösterle.

If you like this ... try Ischgl ▶▶ *p68*, Chamonix ▶▶ *p126*, Verbier ▶▶ *p308*.

⊙ OPENING TIMES

Early Dec to early May: 0830-1630

Ⓢ RESORT PRICES (Arlberg ski pass)

Week pass: €199

Day pass: €41.50

Season pass: €665

ⓘ DIRECTORY

Website: stantonamarlberg.com

Tourist office: T+43 (0)5446-22690

Medical centre: T+43 (0)5446-6580

Pisteurs: T+43 (0)5446-2565

Tyrolean Avalanche Warning Service: T+43 (0)512-1588

Taxi: T+43 (0)5446-2315

⬂ 15 St Johann in Tirol

Town altitude 670 m	Funicular/cable
Km to airport 65 km	cars 0/0
Airport Salzburg	Gondolas/chairs 3/4
Highest lift 1700 m	Drags 10
Vertical drop 1010 m	Night skiing no
Km of pistes 60 km	Terrain parks 1
Nursery areas 3	Glühwein
Blues 16	factor ★★☆
Reds 12	Ski in/ski out ★☆☆
Blacks 1	Environmental
	rating ★★★★★

Small, family-friendly resort with more mountain restaurants than black runs.

St Johann's slopes, on the back of the Kitzbüheler Horn, are north-facing and generally snow-sure. Terrain is best suited for beginners and intermediates. A four-day pass or more gives access to the Schneewinkel area (55 lifts, 170 km of pistes).

Beginners Several nursery slopes and five free beginners' lifts. Build confidence on the quiet Baumoos blues before

◉ OPENING TIMES

Early Dec to end Mar: 0830-1630

Ⓢ RESORT PRICES

Week pass: €173

Day pass: €34

Season pass: €375

◔ DIRECTORY

Website: ferienregion.at

Tourist office: T+43 (0)5352-633350

Medical centre: T+43 (0)664-473 9207

Pisteurs: T+43 (0)5352-62293

Taxi: T+43 (0)664-342 7768

heading up to the Harschbichl mid-station.

Intermediate The whole mountain is yours. Eichenhof is quieter for warm-ups. Explore the Schneewinkel area and Kitzbühel.

Expert Very limited, despite some off-piste opportunities.

Tuition Schischule St Johann is established, with Bobo's ski kindergarten. The smaller **Wilder Kaiser** school promises smaller classes.

Bad light Virtually all the mountain is in trees. Alternatively, visit Kitzbühel or soak in the **Freizeitzentrum**.

Not to miss Trying to dine in all 14 mountain restaurants – they're all excellent.

Remember to avoid Queues for the Harschbichl gondola by taking the Bauernpenzing gondola from Oberndorf instead.

Practicalities

🛏 🍴 🚌

This old Tyrolean town has a pedestrianized centre, where comfortable hotels are housed in frescoed buildings. Locals are welcoming and the resort is popular with families and visitors keen to relax as much as ski. Kitzbühel is just 10 minutes away.

Sleeping First, choose whether to stay in town (atmospheric) or by the lifts (10 minutes' walk away). Second, check with the tourist office for offers. Town: **Hotel Post** (T+43 (0)5352-62230; hotel-post.tv) and **Hotel Gruber** (T+43 (0)5352-61461; hotelgruber.at). Slopes: **Hotel zur Schönen Aussicht** (T+43 (0)5352-62270; schoene-aussicht.com).

Eating **Edelweiss** for traditional Austrian, **La Rustica** and **Villa Masianco** for Italian, **Ambiente** in Hotel Bruckenwirt for special. **Gasthof Hochfeld** on the mountain is good for lunch and open in the evening.

Bars and clubs **Café Rainer** and **Bunny's Pub** for après. **Max Pub** followed by **Crowded House** for youngsters, **Chez Paul** and **Scala** for older visitors.

Hire shop/rental Schischule St Johann also does ski hire.

Transfer options **Kitzbühel Alpen Shuttle** transfers from Salzburg airport to your hotel – book in advance (T+43 (0)5356-66222; kitzalps.com/shuttle).

You can also ski here ... Oberndorf, Kirchdorf and Erpfendorf. Also Schneewinkel and the Kitzbüheler Alpen Ski area.

If you like this ... try Alpbach ▶▶ *p56*, Westendorf ▶▶ *p91*.

↘16 Stubai

Town altitude 1000 m	Funicular/cable
Km to airport 30 km	cars 0/0
Airport Innsbruck	Gondolas/chairs 5/7
Highest lift 3150 m	Drags 8
Vertical drop 1400 m	Night skiing no
Km of pistes 110 km	Terrain parks 1
Nursery areas 2	Glühwein
Blues 12	factor ★☆☆
Reds 8	Ski in/ski out ☆☆☆
Blacks 2	Environmental
	rating ★★★★★★

Ideal for families and spring skiing.

⊙ OPENING TIMES

Early Oct to early May: 0830-1630

Ⓢ RESORT PRICES

Week pass: €169 (€187 for Stubai Super Ski Pass)

Day pass: €36

Season pass: €450

ⓘ DIRECTORY

Website: stubai.at

Tourist office: T+43 (0)501-8810

Medical centre: T+43 (0)5226-2737

Pisteurs: T+43 (0)5226-8151

Taxi: T+43 (0)5226-2877

Practicalities

Sleeping In Neustift, SPA-Hotel Jagdhof (T+43 (0)5226-2666; hotel-jagdhof.at) is Stubai's five-star property. The **Stubaier Hof** (T+43 (0)5226 2450; stubaierhof.at) has large rooms and generous meals. Book self-catering apartments through the tourist office (stubai.at).

Eating In Neustift, **Grillstube** does good steaks, **Bellafonte's** pizzas are popular and **Hotel Jagdhof** is excellent. **Gasthof Grobenhof** in Fulpmes is Stubai's answer to gourmet.

Bars and clubs **Eissee Snow Bar** on the glacier is best for early après-ski, followed by **Aumi's Pub, Rossini** and **Dorf Pub** in Neustift.

Hire shop/rental There are three Intersport shops and a vast ski depot on the glacier, making the 'commute' to the hill painless.

Transfer options Fly to Innsbruck and take a taxi (airport-transfer.com), bus (stubai.at) or hotel transfer.

You can also ski here ... A Stubai Super SkiPass gives access to Schlick 2000, Serles Cableways and Elfer Cableways.

If you like this ... try Hochsölden (Austria), Alta Badia ▶▶ *p208*.

The 40 km-long Stubai valley is dotted with villages leading up to the Stubai glacier. Neustift is the largest with the liveliest nightlife (this is relative – it's still quiet). While Neustift does have a small ski area for novices, skiing happens largely on the Stubai glacier, 20 minutes' drive away. While the bus service is efficient, families might find a car more convenient, enabling exploration of Schlick 2000, Serles and Elfer.

Beginners Idyllic spot to learn with gentle, open slopes.

Intermediate Enjoy the long, open groomers, perfect your carving on the giant slalom race course and learn some tricks in the fun park.

Expert Limited black runs and unguided off-piste on the glacier isn't advised. However, there are challenging marked ski routes. Book a guide to explore properly (T+43 (0)5225-63490).

Kids Stubai is ideal for children. Under-10s ski free and the Mickey Mouse Club (the first in Europe) offers full-day childcare from three years (skiclub-mickymaus.com).

Tuition The Neustift-Stubai Glacier School has offices in the five key Stubai villages.

Not to miss A pitstop at the **Jochdohle**, Austria's highest mountain restaurant at 3150 m.

↘17 Westendorf

Town altitude	800 m	Km of pistes	250 km	Funicular/cable		Terrain parks	1
Km to airport	80 km	Nursery areas	yes	cars	1/0	Glühwein factor	★★☆
Airport	Innsbruck	Blues	26	Gondolas/chairs	11/37	Ski in/ski out	★★☆
Highest lift	1900 m	Reds	43	Drags	32	Environmental	
Vertical drop	800 m	Blacks	11	Night skiing	yes	rating	★☆☆☆☆

PROS

- ✔ Small, cosy town feel and great family resort.
- ✔ Relatively quiet on the pistes, which is good for beginners and intermediates looking for some high-speed cruising.

CONS

- ✘ Although the SkiWelt area is huge, Westendorf itself is small and advanced skiers will get bored quickly.
- ✘ Après-ski is fun but ends early – party-goers are better off at larger resorts in the SkiWelt area.

Picturesque, family-friendly resort with massive SkiWelt area on its doorstep.

Terrain at Westendorf is immaculately groomed and over two-thirds is covered by snow cannons. The runs are ideal for beginners, intermediates and families. There's limited action for advanced skiers who would do well to use **Westendorf** as an atmospheric and affordable base from which to explore the SkiWelt (9 resorts, 90 lifts and 250 km of pistes). That said, you do need to take a bus to the Kitzbühel/Pass Thurn ski area.

Beginners Stay in Westendorf for a couple of days to find your feet on the long blues off the Alpenrosenbahn before exploring SkiWelt.

Intermediate Once you've mastered the reds around Fleiding, which offer great variety in terms of pitch and terrain, choose a 'SkiWelt Route' – clearly marked tours of the SkiWelt area. The Salven and Westendorf routes follow blue and red runs, with stunning views.

Expert Advanced skiers will exhaust Westendorf quickly so grab a ski bus to Brixen im Thale to tackle the steep runs off Hohe Salve or the Brixen SkiWelt route through the trees between Choralpe and the Kandleralmlift.

Powder Westendorf can be great on a powder day as most skiers stick to pistes – first tracks galore!

Moguls Under the Alpenrosen gondola from the middle station down to town.

😊 LOCALS DO

- ✔ Whoop it up at the large annual events held in the town – the Hahnekamm Warm Up and 'Jump and Freeze'.
- ✔ Ski from Choraple down to Ziepl – if they know the area well.
- ✔ Go après tobogganing with their children.

😞 LOCALS DON'T

- ✘ Sleep in on a powder day.
- ✘ Queue to take the Alpenrosen gondola down to town – the blue run is great for cruising at the end of the day.

Tuition **Top Schischule** in the centre of town offers private lessons and fun activities for children.

Kids Westendorf is family heaven – children under seven ski free and there are plenty of family deals. Visit skiwelt.at for information.

Bad light There are tree runs on both sides of the Gampenkogel lift and under Laubkogel, but why not indulge yourself at Kitzbühel's **Aquarena**.

Not to miss Hanging out with the world's best skiers during the Hahnenkamm Warm-Up (January).

Remember to avoid Rush hour on the lifts at 1000.

Relive a famous moment The 'famous' Austrian singer Hansi Hinterseer films his music videos in Westendorf.

Best mountain restaurant The **Alpenrosenhutte** is popular with locals and **Jausenstation Fleidingalm** is great for Austrian atmosphere and food.

Practicalities 🍴🎿🚌

⊘ OPENING TIMES

Early Dec to late Apr: 0900-1600

⊘ RESORT PRICES

Week pass: €173
Day pass: €35.50
Season pass: €469

ⓘ DIRECTORY

Website: kitzbuehel-alpen.com
Tourist office: T+43 (0)5334-6230
Medical centre: T+43 (0)5334-6390
Pisteurs: T+43 (0)5334-2000 or T140
Taxi: T+43 (0)5334-30044

Health and wellbeing Hotel Scheermer, Hotel Glockenstuhl and Hotel Jackobwirt have spa facilities. For more serious attention, visit the Therapiezentrum Westendorf.

Down days with kids Weekly family torchlight walks on Mondays and farm walks on Thursdays –book up until the night before at the tourist information office.

Internet The tourist office, Dieters Sport Shop and in larger hotels.

Transfer options Trains run from Innsbruck and Salzburg to Wörgl, where you change for Westendorf (T+43 (0)5334-051717; oebb.at).

You can also ski here ... The entire SkiWelt area, which includes Ellmau, Going, Itter, Scheffau, Hopfgarten and Brixen im Thale. A new gondola is due to open in December 2008 linking SkiWelt with Kitzbühel, making it one of the world's three largest interconnected ski areas.

If you like this ... try Alpbach ▶▶*p56*, Obergurgl ▶▶*p78*.

Westendorf is a picture-perfect little Austrian ski village. It attracts families more than party-goers thanks to its gentle nursery slopes and diminutive size. Bars and discos are quiet during the week but twice a year the town is transformed as thousands of people descend upon it for the legendary Hahnenkamm Warm-Up Week and 'Jump and Freeze' night (which involves people skiing into a pool of freezing water wearing fancy dress).

Sleeping The friendly Hotel Bichlingerhof (T+43 (0)5334-6326), just off the main street, has large rooms and good food. Vital Land Hotel Scheermer (T+43 (0)5334-6268) is the smartest address in town, while self-catering options can be found at skiwelt.at.

Eating The bar and restaurant FeinSinn (T+43 (0)5334-30111) on the main street does fantastic steaks, La Vita is great for Italian, while Bruchstall (T+43 (0)5334-30422) on the piste does traditional Alpine après-ski and early supper.

Au pair/crèche Kindergruppe Simba (T+43 (0)5334-20603) cares for non-skiing children from 18 months.

Bars and clubs Westendorf is largely a family resort but there's still après action at Gerry's Inn and Moskitobar. Wunderbar is the best disco.

Shopping Billa and Spar in the centre of town but head down-valley for larger shops.

Hire shop/rental Staff at Dieter's Sport Shop by the ice rink are knowledgeable and throw free glühwein parties on Mondays (1600-1800).

↘18 Zell am See

Town altitude 757 m	Km of pistes 136 km	Funicular/cable	Terrain parks 3
Km to airport 80 km	Nursery areas 1	cars 0/5	Glühwein factor ★★★
Airport Salzburg	Blues 20	Gondolas/chairs 6/17	Ski in/ski out ★☆☆
Highest lift 3029 m	Reds 22	Drags 13	Environmental
Vertical drop 1243 m	Blacks 13	Night skiing yes	rating ★★★★★★

PROS

- ✓ A wonderful family resort.
- ✓ A year-round destination with established town and extensive facilities – good for non-skiers.
- ✓ Lively nightlife enjoyed by young and old.

CONS

- ✗ Limited terrain for expert skiers.
- ✗ While it's fantastic for early and late season skiing, you have to share the Kitzsteinhorn glacier with crowds from Salzburg and Kitzbühel.

Beautiful lakeside resort that combines family facilities with lively nightlife.

With skiing split over three mountains, there's plenty of intermediate-friendly terrain. Schmittenhöhe is accessed directly from Zell. Kaprun, with Maiskogel and the Kitzsteinhorn glacier, is a short ski bus-ride away.

Beginners Maiskogel and the lower blues on Schmittenhöhe are uncrowded. The slopes on Kitzsteinhorn's glacial plateau are gentle and give you the thrill and beauty of altitude skiing but they can get busy.

Intermediate Long blues on Schmittenhöhe by the three-stage Areit gondola, more challenging reds off Sonnkogel and essentially the whole of Kitzsteinhorn. Confident intermediates will discover black pistes are more dark red than black.

Expert Advanced skiing is limited, with a handful of (easy) blacks and marked ski routes. The terrain parks are good for freestylers.

Powder Hit the marked ski routes on Kitzsteinhorn early –our favourite is the Magnetköpfel under the Gipfelbahn. Book a guide to drop off the back of Kitzsteinhorn into the Niedernsill valley.

Moguls Under the Osthanglift on Schmittenhöhe and the black 5 runs on Kitzsteinhorn.

Tuition There are 12 ski and snowboard schools and guides in Zell am See and Kaprun. **Sport-Alpin Zell am See** has experienced, English-speaking instructors. **Outdoor Adventures** in Zell is small, aimed at young, adventurous types and promises small groups.

Kids Children under 12 ski free – one of the best deals we've found in Europe. **Schmidolin's 'Kinderland'** is at the Hahnkopflift and there's a winter playground at the Sonnkogel-Pfiff.

Bad light Stick to Schmittenhöhe, where there are plenty of trees. Alternatively explore town, stroll round the lake, skate across it or go snow-kiting on it.

Not to miss The spectacular views of Hohe Tauern National Park and Grossglockner from the top of Kitzsteinhorn.

Austria Zell am See

☺ LOCALS DO

✓ Ski in the morning and windsurf on lake Zell in the afternoon in spring.

✓ Have a favourite beer at the Bierstadl (there are over 30 brews).

✓ Master the art of snow-kiting on the lake, at speeds up to 75 kph!

☹ LOCALS DON'T

✗ Encourage tourists to ride off-piste on the glacier.

✗ Forget to bring their swimmers if they fancy hot-tubbing at Panorama-Pfiff.

Remember to avoid The queues for the Schittental cable car by taking a ski bus to the Schüttdorf gondola.

Relive a famous moment Aged Brit rockers Smokie (greatest hit, *Living next door to Alice*) headlined Zell's annual Snow, Sun & Party week in 2008 – a precedent has been set.

Best mountain restaurant At **Panorama-Pfiff** on Schmittenhöhe, there's an outdoor hot tub for guests (towels provided) – the food's good too. The atmospheric **Jaga Alm** does local specialities and **Breiteckalm** is excellent. On Kitzsteinhorn, the **Gletschermühle** has it all – good food, stunning views and deckchairs.

  # Practicalities

Zell am See is a pretty town on the shores of a lake surrounded by towering mountains. Its pedestrianized centre dates back to the 13th century and positively buzzes in the evenings. Zell is popular in summer and winter, meaning the tourist infrastructure is excellent. It is so family-friendly that it has won various awards, while the lively nightlife appeals to 20-somethings.

Sleeping Inghams offers several properties including the five-star **Salzburgerhof** and historic **Grand Hotel**. We love the central **Hotel Lebzelter** (T+43 (0)6542-7760; hotel-lebzelter.at) and ski in/ski out **Hotel Alpin** (T+43 (0)6542-769; alpinhotel.at). The tourist office offers great inclusive packages.

Eating Schloss Prielau (T+43 (0)6542-729110) above the lake has a Michelin-starred restaurant. In town, **Bar Einkehr** is chic, **Kupferkessl** does colossal steaks, **Steinerwirt** does traditional Austrian food and Villa Crazy Daisy's **Crazy Restaurant** is unforgettable.

Au pair/crèche Joys (T+43 (0)664-3325665) kindergarten caters for one-year-olds and up. **Babyboom** (T+43 (0)664-376 2553) offers babysitting.

Bars and clubs Après starts on Schmittenhöhe at **Schnapps Hans Eisbar** and Berghotel's **Jaga Alm**. Continue at **Hotel Alpin's** umbrella bar, **Bar Einkehr** and Hotel Lebzelter's **Sportstüberl**. Youngsters party hard at **Diele's**, **Crazy Daisy** and **Flannigan's** before dancing at **Viva** and **Baum Bar Reiteralm**, on the outskirts of town. More mature revellers frequent **Greens XL**, **Insider** and **Einkehr**.

Hire shop/rental Intersport has various outlets in Zell and Kaprun, with a large shop and depot at the base of cityXpress.

Health and wellbeing The spa at **Salzburgerhof** is sensational. The **Freizeitzentrum** has pools, saunas and steam grottos.

Down days with kids Choices are endless: ice-skating on the lake, swimming at the **Freizeitzentrum**, caving, horse riding.

Internet Computers and Wi-Fi at **Estl's Café** on the main street.

Transfer options Fly to Salzburg and take a bus or train to Zell (oebb. at). Alternatively, book the Vorderegger express bus (vorderegger.at) or a shuttle (holiday-airportshuttle.at).

You can also ski here ... Kitzsteinhorn glacier.

If you like this ... try Sölden ▶▶ *p83*, Les Deux Alpes ▶▶ *p156*.

⊙ OPENING TIMES

End Nov to end Apr: 0830-1630

⑤ RESORT PRICES

Week pass: €192

Day pass: €40

Season pass: €480

① DIRECTORY

Website: zellamsee-kaprun.com

Tourist office: T+43 (0)6542-770

Medical centre: T+43 (0)6542-56766

Pisteurs: T+43 (0)6542-73694/6547-8621

Taxi: T+43 (0)664-33 44 888

↘ 19 Zürs

Town altitude	1716 m	Funicular/cable	
Km to airport	110 km	cars	0/6
Airport	Innsbruck	Gondolas/chairs	4/38
Highest lift	2450 m	Drags	36
Vertical drop	750 m	Night skiing	no
Km of pistes	276 km	Terrain parks	4
Nursery areas	2	Glühwein	
Blues	37	factor	★★☆
Reds	36	Ski in/ski out	★★☆
Blacks	6	Environmental	
		rating	★★★★☆

Exclusive yet unpretentious and great off-piste.

Zürs is essentially a cluster of luxury hotels conveniently located on the slopes. On-piste terrain here is easier than in St Anton with its long, gentle cruisers making it ideal for intermediates and families. The popular 22-km White Ring circuit takes you round Zürs, Oberlech and Lech covering 5500 m of altitude. However, Zürs' best-kept secret is its champagne powder and awesome freeriding.

Beginners Start on the village nursery slopes before heading for the blues higher up or to the sunny meadows of Oberlech.

Intermediate Confident intermediates will quickly exhaust Zürs' blues and reds. However, the White Ring circuit opens up plenty of terrain and a day trip to St Anton is a must.

Expert The off-piste in Zürs is fantastic thanks to consistently excellent snow, lots of space and few freeriders. Book a guide to take you off Trittkopf into Paziel-Tal or Stuben, across Monzabon into Lech, down the Gamsroute and Erzburg routes. Possibilties are endless.

Tuition The **Zürs Ski School** has nearly 300 instructors, reflecting the fact that some 80% of visitors take private tuition. Instructors are predominantly Arlberg locals and speak English. Book off-piste guiding with the school or with the **Alpin Centre** in Lech (T+43 (0)5583-39880).

Bad light Skiing in the trees is forbidden, for environmental reasons, and is closely monitored. Explore Lech and St Anton instead.

Not to miss A champagne powder day in Zürs.

Remember to avoid Not booking an instructor in advance in peak season.

◉ OPENING TIMES

Early Dec to early May: 0830-1630

⑤ RESORT PRICES (Arlberg ski pass)

Week pass: €199
Day pass: €41.50
Season pass: €665

ⓘ DIRECTORY

Website: lech-zuers.at
Tourist office: T+43 (0)5583-2245
Medical centre: T+43 (0)5583-4242
Pisteurs: T+43 (0)5446-2565
Taxi: T+43 (0)5583-2442

Austria Zürs

Practicalities 🛏🍴🚌

Sleeping The five-star **Hotel Zürserhof** comes complete with spa and rental shop; the four-star **Hotel Edelweiss** (T+43 (0)5583-2662; edelweiss.net) is welcoming; foodies should stay at **Albona Nova** (T+43 (0)5583 2341; albonanova.at). **Haus Küng** (T+43 (0)5583 2556; hauskueng.at) is a delightful, family-run guesthouse.

Eating Gourmets are spoiled for choice. Top venues include **Hotel Albona Nova, Chesa** (Hotel Edelweiss) and **Hirlanda**. **Flexenhäusle** does excellent fondue.

Bars and clubs Party and people-watch at the **Kaminstübel, Mathies-Stüble** and **Vernissage**. Champagne flows at **Zürserl** disco until late. Explore Lech too – the James night bus costs €4 and runs until 0400.

Kids Little Zürs (T+43 (0)5583-224 5252) looks after children from three years. Contact the tourist office for babysitters.

Hire shop/rental There are five rental outlets – chose the closest to your hotel.

Transfer options Fly to Innsbruck and take a train to Langen am Arlberg (oebb.at). Travel the last 17 km by bus or book a taxi (taxi-zuers.com).

You can also ski here ... The Arlberg ski pass gives you access to St Anton, St Christoph, Lech, Stuben, Pettneu and Klösterle.

If you like this ... try Lech ▶▶ *p73*, Westendorf ▶▶ *p91*, Ste Foy ▶▶ *p178*.

Bulgaria and Slovenia

**Bulgaria and
Slovenia**
Value for money
★★★★☆
Nightlife
★★★☆☆
Off-piste
★★★☆☆
Family
★★★☆☆

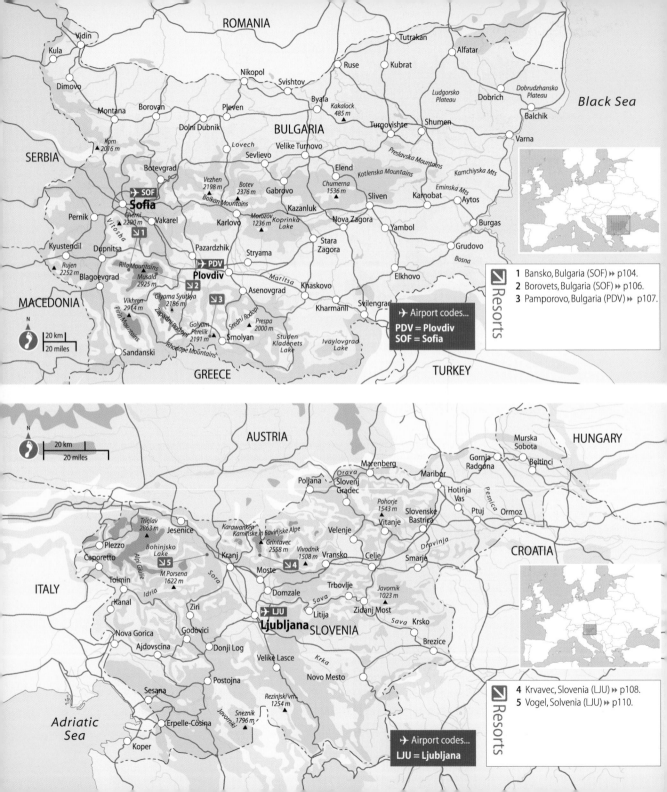

Map 1 (Bulgaria)

ROMANIA

Vidin
Kula
Dimovo
Montana
Borovan
Nikopol
Svishtov
Byala
Tutrakan
Alfatar
Ruse
Kubrat
Ludgorsko
Plateau
Dobrich
Dobrudzhansko
Plateau
Black Sea
Balchik
Varna

Pleven
Dolni Dubnik
BULGARIA
Kakalock
485 m
Turgovishte
Shumen
Preslavska Mountains
Kamchiyska Mts
Eminska Mts

SERBIA
Kom
2016 m
Botevgrad
Lovech
Sevlievo
Velike Turnovo
Elend
Kotlenska Mountains
Vezhen
2198 m
Botev
2376 m
Chumerna
1536 m
Gabrovo
Sliven
Kamobat
Aytos

SOF
Sofia
Cherni
2290 m
Vakarel
Balkan Mountains
Kazanluk
Morozov
1236 m
Koprinka
Lake
Nova Zagora
Stara
Zagora
Yambol
Burgas

Pernik
Vitosha
↘1
Karlovo

Kyustendil
Dupnitsa
Rila Mountains
PDV
Plovdiv
↘2
Pazardzhik
Stryama
Elkhovo
Bosna
Grudovo

Rujen
2252 m
Blagoevgrad
Musala
2925 m
Maritsa
Khaskovo

MACEDONIA
Vikhren
2914 m
Glyama Syutkya
2186 m
↘3
Asenovgrad
Kharmanli
Svilengrad

Zapadni Rodopi
Sredni Rodopi
Golyam-
Perelik
2191 m
Smolyan
Prespa
2000 m
Studen
Kladenets
Lake
Ivaylovgrad
Lake
TURKEY

N
20 km
20 miles
Rhodope Mountains
Sandanski
GREECE

Resorts (Bulgaria)

1 Bansko, Bulgaria (SOF) ▸ p104.
2 Borovets, Bulgaria (SOF) ▸ p106.
3 Pamporovo, Bulgaria (PDV) ▸ p107.

✈ Airport codes...
PDV = Plovdiv
SOF = Sofia

Map 2 (Slovenia)

N
20 km
20 miles
AUSTRIA
HUNGARY

Marenberg
Gornja
Radgona
Murska
Sobota
Beltinci

Poljana
Drava
Slovenj
Gradec
Maribor
Hotinja
Vas
Ptuj
Pesnica
Ormoz

Triglav
2863 m
Jesenice
Karawanken
Kamniške in Savinjske Alpe
Pohorje
1543 m
Vitanje
Slovenske
Bastrica

Plezzo
Bohinjsko
Lake
Grintavec
2558 m
Velenje
Dravinja
CROATIA

Caporetto
↘5
M Porsena
1622 m
Kranj
Vivodnik
1508 m
Vransko
Celje
Smarjé

Tolmin
Alpi Giulie
Idrio
Sora
Moste
↘4
Trbovlje
Javornik
1023 m

Kanal
Ziri
Domzale
Sava
Zidanj Most
Krsko

ITALY
Nova Gorica
Godovici
LJU
Ljubljana
Litija
Sava
SLOVENIA
Brezice

Ajdovscina
Donji Log
Krka
Novo Mesto

Sesana
Velike Lasce
Postojna

Erpelle-Cosina
Javornik
Rezinjski vrh
1254 m
Sneznik
1796 m

*Adriatic
Sea*
Koper

Resorts (Slovenia)

4 Krvavec, Slovenia (LJU) ▸ p108.
5 Vogel, Solvenia (LJU) ▸ p110.

✈ Airport codes...
LJU = Ljubljana

Bulgaria, located in the Europe's far east, has a solid share of the British ski market. The country, which is still scraping off the rust from the Iron Curtain, offers good intermediate skiing at its premier resorts of Borovets, Pamporovo and rising star Bansko.

The big draw of Bulgaria is definitely the price, and is the main reason for its inclusion in this guide. The country boasts the cheapest package deals in Europe and as a result attracts an increasingly large number of UK skiers each year who would ordinarily be priced out by the usual Alpine big hitters. However, this does have downsides, and those looking for an unspoiled après ski experience should definitely look elsewhere. Skiing in Bulgaria is undeniably cheap and cheerful but if you're in the market for a bargain, it is hard to beat.

Slovenia is the most western nation of the Balkans, both geographical and economically, and many Slovenians don't actually consider themselves to be part of the Balkans. The county is about 40% mountainous and skiing is a national sport which Slovenians claim was invented there (Scandinavians might well disagree!). Fathers of skiing or not – Slovenians are snow babies, picking up the sport at an early age, meaning there is a thriving ski scene in the country, reflected by their prowess in international ski racing competitions. Slovenians are a very friendly and polite people, most of whom seem to speak excellent English, so getting around is a smooth operation, and the country is known for its deep natural beauty and traditional ski resorts.

Skiing Bulgaria and Slovenia

The ski resorts of the Balkans have a similar, though slightly shorter season than the Alps, and slightly lower altitudes, yet they still offer good intermediate skiing at great prices. Neither country can boast the massive interlinked ski zones further west, but bigger doesn't always mean better, and even advanced skiers should be able to keep themselves entertained if they head off piste or, in the case of Slovenia, visit a few different resorts.

Slovenia's resorts aren't huge; but the country does offer about 20 small to medium sized ski areas, the highest of which is Kanin – perched on the border with Italy at around 2300m. With plenty of powder and parks, the larger resorts will keep intermediate skiers content for a couple of days, and the country's small size makes it ideal for a road trip.

The clientele that Slovenia and Bulgaria attract is very different. Slovenia is known as a fairly gentle, family friendly country, with a strong traditional feel, and it doesn't feature heavily in the major tour operators brochures, instead attracting a more niche clientele. Bulgaria on the other hand has much more

of a production line feel to it and is popular with binge drinking Brits who are there for the extensive après ski drinking opportunities as much as the powder.

The beauty of skiing the Balkans can be found in their low prices, attractive landscape (Slovenia's spiky Julian Alps especially) and a culture that is different enough from usual Western resort experiences to make things interesting for seasoned ski travellers. These two countries which lie at opposite ends of the Balkan region also showcase the diversity of Eastern Europe, with distinctly different languages, people and food, that offer distinctly different ski holidays; Bulgaria most definitely fits the cheap and cheerful tag, whereas Slovenia's ski resorts have more in common with an Austria of days gone by, than any of the former Eastern Bloc.

Conditions

Slovenia's Julian Alps are kept well fed with snow though most resorts in the country are relatively low, so they have slightly shorter seasons. Kanin, is the only resort in the country to offer slopes over 2000m high, and as such, has a longer

season, lasting until May. Bulgaria also boasts a good length season, with Bansko opening lifts from mid December to mid May.

When To Go

Both Bulgaria and Slovenia have slightly shorter seasons than in the high Alps – but generally a trip between Early Jan and late March would be a safe bet for snow. Neither country has any glacial resorts, so summer skiing is out, though the snow can hang around until summer in the highest parts of the mountains, and offer backcountry spring skiing for the more adventurous.

The slightly lower altitudes of Bulgarian and Slovenian resorts may become a worry in this age of global warming, though for now, greater investment in snow making systems is helping to ensure that seasons are still a respectable length.

PROS

Bulgaria is probably the cheapest ski trip in Europe with great bargain basement package deals on offer.

Bulgaria is a party capital so ideal for younger skiers after a good après booze up.

Slovenia is one of the most beautiful countries in Europe, if not the world, and offers a traditional ski experience, untainted by Brit influence or overdevelopment.

Slovenia offers Western standard accommodation and service at Eastern prices.

The Balkans offer a ski trip that is a little off the beaten track and more of a cultural adventure than traditional favourites.

CONS

Bulgaria is very Brit heavy, and traditional Bulgarian culture is being eroded to make way for an Anglo invasion.

Bulgaria's eastern location means it takes a little longer to get there.

The words "good" and "service" are rarely used together in descriptions of Bulgarian restaurants and hotels.

Slovenia's resorts are small compared to many French, Swiss and Austrian areas, with nothing in the way of large interlinked areas.

Both countries are a little lacking in challenging terrain, so aren't ideal for advanced skiers looking to be tested – though off piste this can still be found.

Essentials

Getting there

Getting to Eastern Europe is as easy as getting to France these days. You can fly to Slovenia's capital, Ljubljana (lju-airport. si), from Manchester, Birmingham and London Stansted. Check out their national carrier **Adria Air** (adria-airways.com) or **easyJet** (easyJet.com) for flights. It's also worth looking at Slovenia's neighbours for feasible travel options – Klagenfurt (klagenfurt-airport.at) and Graz (flughafen-graz.at) in Austria are close to the Slovenian boarder, as is Trieste in Italy (aeroporto. fvg.it) and Zagreb (zagreb-airport.hr) and Pula (airport-pula.hr) in Croatia. **easyJet** and **BA** fly to Bulgaria's capital Sofia (easyJet. com, BA.com) which is just over an hours drive from Borovets. To find and compare all European flights, check out Skyscanner. net – a very useful flight search engine.

Driving in Slovenia is very chilled, with little traffic on the road compared to the UK. A *vignette* (road tax sticker) has just been introduced to replace the toll roads on the motorway network – make sure you've got one or face a fine. Bulgarian drivers are nuts and the roads aren't well maintained, so it's only for the brave.

Red Tape

Both Slovenia and Bulgaria are members of the EU, so EU passport holders don't need a visa. Foreign nationals from the rest of the world need to apply for permission to enter.

Getting Around

Driving in both Bulgaria and Slovenia is standard European (right-hand side). A valid driving licence from your home country is necessary. The local drivers in this part of the world aren't the greatest and seem to have little consideration for oncoming traffic, so be particularly cautious when driving round blind bends, as it's quite common to meet careless over takers on the wrong side of the road.

Mountain Passes If you're are driving to resorts, double check your route to ensures it's open before you travel; some of the higher mountains passes will close in heavy snow, meaning journey times can be longer in winter.

Car Hire Most major hire car companies (europcar.si, easycar.com, hertz.com, avis.com etc.) have offices in airports and cities. Usual age restrictions apply.

Public Transport Bulgaria's public bus system is antiquated, though private buses (the biggest company being Etap-Grup – EtapGroup.com) cover many major routes and offer more comfortable transport and are cheap. Almost all timetables are written in Cyrillic so brush up on your Bulgarian before taking the bus. The Bulgarian rail network (bdz.bg) is quite extensive, but the rolling stock is aging and quite slow meaning private buses are often the preferred choice for those travelling between cities.

Public transport in Slovenia is of a high standard and your journey is likely to run smoothly and offer a very scenic experience. The train network (slo-zeleznice.si) is inexpensive, clean and reliable; ideal for travelling between cities or even to neighbouring countries. Slovenia's bus system (ap-ljubljana. si) is a little more far reaching than the rail network, though getting to rural areas can still be difficult with an infrequent service; always check timetables first.

Opening Hours and Traditions

The Slovenian supermarket chain TUS has infiltrated almost every town in the country and is open from 0800 to 1900 on weekdays, and 0800 till 1300 on Saturdays. Most shops are closed on Sundays and public holidays except for some pharmacies and some tourist attractions. Banks and Post Offices are open from 0830 to 1230 and again from 1400 till 1700 Monday to Friday, and 0830 till 1130am on Saturdays. All banks are closed on Sundays and public holidays. Bulgarian supermarket and grocery stores have similar opening hours – Monday to Sat – 0900 till 1800, and they are closed Saturday afternoons. Banks are open 0900-1600 but are closed on weekends.

Eating

The Balkan countries aren't renowned for their culinary excellence – but that doesn't mean you can't eat well. Slovenia's cuisine is heavily influenced by its neighbours Italy, Austria and Hungary, so expect to find plenty of pizza (which are huge!), Wiener Schnitzel and Goulash at mountain restaurants. Wash them down with one of Slovenia's excellent lagers – Lasko Zlatarog and Union are favourites and Slovenian

Fact File

Currency BGN (Bulgaria) Euro € (Slovenia)

Time Zone GMT+2 (Bulgaria) GMT +1 (Slovenia)

Country Code +359 (Bulgaria) +386 (Slovenia)

Emergency Numbers
General emergency T112
Ambulance T150 (Bulgaria)
Police T124 (Bulgaria)

Top Tips

1 **Impress** your mates by learning the Cyrillic alphabet – which will allow you to read Bulgarian words
2 **Being** a small compact country, a ski road trip is an ideal way of exploring Slovenia's ski resorts.
3 **Don't** come to Bulgaria if you don't want to party – ski punters here enjoy a rowdy time.
4 **While** in Slovenia, try and visit Lake Bled or Bohinj, which are enchantingly beautiful spots
5 **Check** you restaurant bills and change, as it's not unheard of for the locals to take advantage of tourists.

Going green
Take the train from London to Slovenia for a relaxed journey that allows you to enjoy the scenery that you miss from the air. It takes about 18 hours – nice if you have time.

wine is also of a high calibre. Salads are also fairly common so veggies should find plenty to eat. 10% is not expected but it's polite to round up the bill in way of a tip.

Bulgaria has a similar variety of good, wholesome inexpensive fodder served in generously sized portions which hit the spot after a day on the slopes. Spit-roasted pig is a favourite in resorts such as Borovets and Brit-friendly food like steak and chips is everywhere. To drink in a bit of Bulgarian culture, try some of their beers; *Astika*, *Zagorka* and *Kamenitza* are all tasty crisp brews and are cheaper than the foreign lagers on sale. At local supermarket, a bottle of Bulgarian brewed beer will cost around just 30p. Bulgarian wine is also well worth a try and make sure you try the *Rakiya* – Bulgarian brandy made of grapes or plums which is traditionally drunk as an aperitif. Bulgarians have a habit of reminding you how poor their country is and those working in the service industry will expect a sizeable tip (at least 10%) from western visitors

In both countries, you will have no problem finding western junk food such as kebabs, hot dogs and chips, and Slovenians are keen on horse, which can often be found in burger form. Some of Bulgaria's larger resorts also have international restaurants such as Chinese, Indian and Mexican.

Language
Bulgarians speak Bulgarian, which is written in the Cyrillic alphabet, making things trickier for those not familiar with it. But as you might expect, most Bulgarians in the tourist industry speak English. Slovenia's official language is Slovene (also called Slovenian), though English is widely spoken in most tourist areas.

Crime and Safety
Bulgarians often grumble about the *Mutri* – (the Bulgarian Mafia) and their corrupt officials, but this is something unlikely to affect the average tourist. That said, don't be too alarmed to see 'No Handguns' signs at the entrance to some nightclubs! You're most likely to have a run in with the Police if you are driving in a foreign car – so be careful and be prepared to part with a few small "fines" (read: bribes) if you want to avoid lengthy delays.

Slovenia is much more developed than many imagine, and has a very low crime rate. You'd be very unfortunate to come across any problems here.

Health
As part of the EU, both Slovenia and Bulgaria are governed by European health standards. Health insurance is recommended and EU citizens should carry a European Health Insurance Card (EHIC). Slovenian facilities rival those of any in the west, while medical services within Bulgarian ski resorts are of a high standard. As long as you're insured, you should have no worries about winding up in hospital here.

↘1 Bansko, Bulgaria

Town altitude	990 m	Km of pistes	70	Funicular/cable cars	0/0
Km to airport	150 km	Nursery areas	1	Gondolas/chairs	1/7
Airport	Sofia	Blues	5	Drags	6
Highest lift	2600 m	Reds	8	Night skiing	no
Vertical drop	1610 m	Blacks	1		

Terrain parks	0	
Glühwein factor	★★★	
Ski in/ski out	★★☆	
Environmental rating	☆☆☆☆☆	

PROS

- ✓ Cheap. And then some.
- ✓ Good size hill.
- ✓ Bulgarian culture is hanging on in there.

CONS

- ✗ Little England expatriate influence strong.
- ✗ Varying standards of accommodation.
- ✗ Some accommodation a long way from the base station.

Bulgaria's flagship resort combines an exciting town with surprisingly good infrastructure.

Of all the fast-rising Bulgarian resorts, Bansko seems to be the most promising. The mountain is easily the most versatile in the country, and the town itself hasn't fully succumbed to the temptation to turn itself into Magaluf or Benidorm-on-snow as sister Bulgarian Borovets and Pamporovo have. Whether things stay like this is open to question but for now it is unquestionably the best ski destination in the country. Lifts here are quick, modern and well situated. Confident intermediates in particular will find much to enjoy.

Beginners Complete beginners should book a lesson, but those with a modicum of confidence can start with the runs on the skier's right side of the resort. Here you'll find wide-open blues accessed by quick chairs. The run down is fun, if flat at points.

Intermediate Head to the summit and the entire resort opens out for you. There are long routes down to the right-hand side, and some interesting trees to explore on the left.

Expert Bansko's size means there is still plenty to occupy experts, although you'll probably find yourself gravitating towards the Shiligarnik side and taking the right-hand chair, which leads to most of the steeper runs. And try the run from the summit all the way down to the base on the way home – fun, varied terrain and thigh-burningly long.

Powder There are plenty of fun, obvious tree runs to explore if the snow is good, although to find the best stashes you'll need to book a guide.

Moguls Bankso is on the whole extremely well groomed, although some moguls can develop on the steeper pitches towards the summit.

Practicalities 🛏️🍴🚌

Sleeping There are plenty of accommodation options. **Hotel Pirin** (T+359 7443 8051) is a large, friendly and clean four star with great service and a pool. Closer to the main lift is the new five-star **Kempinski Hotel Grand** (kempinski-bansko.com), with a great spa and plenty of dining options. **Balkan Holidays** (balkanholidays.co.uk) offer a wide range of well-appointed self-catering apartments such as the **Mountain Paradise Apartments**.

Eating As with all Bulgarian resorts, fry-ups, roast dinners and other British comfort food seems to be everywhere. But it is possible to try some authentic local cuisine. **Mehana Bansko** (T+359 7443 4231) is popular, while **Bakanova Mehana**, in the main square, is good for pizzas. Locals also seem to rate the curries at the British-run **Hotel Avalon** (avalonhotel-bulgaria.com).

Au pair/crèche The Blues Kangaroo crèche (T+359 8865 88515) is a popular spot to leave the little ones.

Bars and clubs Hangovers are basically issued with your lift pass in Bansko. Check in for après-ski at the **Happy End** bar, next to the gondola, before heading into town to check out one of the many other options: **Buddah Bar**, **Lion's Pub**, **Amnesia** and the **No Name**.

Shopping Bansko is a large town with plenty of shopping facilities and the prices are ridiculously cheap. You'll be able to find anything you want here, and the prices make self-catering a particularly appealing prospect.

Hire shop/rental Again, numerous options but **Bansko Ski School** (banskoskischool.info) are as good as any.

Health and wellbeing Bansko's recent exploding popularity means there is now an embarrassing number of pampering options – we like **Bansko Spa** (banskospa.com) and the on-site facilities at the **Kempinski Hotel Grand** (kempinski-bansko.com).

Down days with kids Given the size of the place, there are plenty of options, but great day-trip options include a visit to **Rila Monastery** or the **Dancing Bears Park** at Belitsa, 33 km away, where captive bears are rehabilitated.

Internet Almost every hotel seems to have Wi-Fi, but assuming yours doesn't, head to **Plan B Internet Cafè** at 79 Stefan Karadja Street.

Transfer options Buses run from either Sofia or Plovdiv airports. Try bulgariaski.com or sofiaairporttaxis.co.uk.

You can also ski here ... No local partners.

If you like this ... try Megève ▶▶ p164.

⏰ OPENING TIMES
Early Dec to early Apr: 0830-1600

💲 RESORT PRICES
Week pass: BGN280
Day pass: BGN50
Season pass: BGN1340

ℹ️ DIRECTORY
Website: banskoski.com
Tourist office: T+359 7443 8048
Medical centre: T+359 7443 8388
Pisteurs: T+359 7443 8911
Taxi: banskoservices.moonfruit.com

Bulgaria & Slovenia Bansko, Bulgaria

Tuition Bansko Ski School (banskoskischool.info) are one of the best, so you can sort your lessons and kit at the same time. Ask them for advanced guiding options as well.

Kids Kids are well looked after, with kids aged four to seven looked after at an on-site nursery next to the top of the gondola. See banskoski.com for full details.

Bad light Bansko still works well in bad light as most of the runs are in the treeline and there are some easy-to-find gullies below the Banderiza piste.

Not to miss Cheap hot dogs and a beer for lunch at one of the on-hill tents after a long morning spent swooping down the many wide pistes.

Remember to avoid The home run if you're tired after a day learning the ropes. It is deceptively long and flat, meaning you need to maintain your speed.

Relive a famous moment The FIS Europa Cup was held on the Banderiza piste in 2008 – see if you can match their skills!

Best mountain restaurant The restaurant at the foot of Todorka, in the Shiligarnika area, is a popular spot for coffee and sunbathing.

↘2 Borovets, Bulgaria

Town altitude	1300 m	Km of pistes	58 km	Funicular/cable cars	0/0
Km to airport	72 km	Nursery areas	3	Gondolas/chairs	1/3
Airport	Sofia	Blues	5	Drags	8
Highest lift	2560 m	Reds	11	Night skiing	yes
Vertical drop	1260 m	Blacks	5		

Terrain parks	0
Glühwein factor	★★★
Ski in/ski out	★★☆
Environmental rating	★★☆☆☆

The oldest and biggest ski resort in Bulgaria, playing host to skiers who come for low prices and lively nightlife.

Borovets is probably one of the cheapest ski trips in Europe. At just one hour's drive from the capital, Sofia, it's also the most popular resort in the country, which means crowded slopes at the weekend. Borovets has three separate zones which aren't yet fully linked: Borovets Central, Yastrebetz and Markudjik. Built on the slopes of Mount Musala, the highest point accessible by lift is a respectable 2540 m. The orange gondola takes around 25 minutes to deliver skiers to the top, with the option of getting out at mid-station.

Beginners At the bottom of the Borovets area the vast majority of runs are wide, open and gentle. Watch out for the drag lifts though; many start with quite a jolt which can deposit beginners on their bums, so hang on tight.

Intermediate The Yastrebetz area offers some good, long cruising runs, from the top of the gondola all the way down to the bottom.

Expert This is not the ideal place to come if you're looking to be challenged as most of the slopes are gentle with little in the way of steep or testing terrain, but experts can amuse themselves for a while up at the Markudjik portion of the mountain where you can ride off-piste after a heavy snowfall.

Tuition The **Borovets Ski School** has more than 200 ski instructors, fluent in many different languages, and many are former professional skiers.

Bad light Stick to the lower half of the mountain in Yastrebetz or Borovets Central, where you'll find better contrast in amongst the pine trees.

Not to miss Eating a spit-roasted pig on a bar terrace while the gypsy horse and carts trot past in town.

Remember to avoid The lower half of the Suhar run is a beginners' bottleneck.

Practicalities

🛏 🍴 🚌

Sleeping Most people come to Borovets on a package tour; operators use the large hotel complexes such as the **Samokov** (samokov.com, T+359 (0)7-503 2306) and **Hotel Rila**, which is at the foot of the slopes (rila@borovets-bg). The **Alpine Hotel** also offers eight attractive pine chalets (alpin-hotel.bg).

Eating For traditional Bulgarian food try the **Green King** or **Bar Deva**; for steak visit **Katy's**, and for a decent full English breakfast, head to **Chilli Peppers** or **Marmacitas**.

Bars and clubs Chilli Peppers is popular, with welcoming staff, live music, prizes, Brit-friendly fodder and DJs.

Hire shop/rental The Rila has an extensive ski-rental depot, and there are also skis and boards available behind the gondola base station.

Transfer options Private transfers start at around BGN80 per vehicle; try motoroads.com or transportia.bg.

You can also ski here ... Malyovitsa (23 km), Vitosha (44 km).

If you like this ... try Pas de la Casa (Andorra), Livigno ▶▶ *p232*.

⊙ **OPENING TIMES**
Dec to early Apr: 0900-1630

$ **RESORT PRICES**
Week pass: BGN299
Day pass: BGN44

ⓘ **DIRECTORY**
Website: borovets-bg.com
Tourist office: T+ 359 (0)2-835 219
Medical centre: T+359 (0)8-762 7479
Pisteurs: T+359 (0)7-128 2450
Taxi: gogotaxis.com

↘3 Pamporovo, Bulgaria

Town altitude	Vertical	Blacks 1	Terrain parks 0
1650 m	drop 1926m/276m	Funicular/cable	Glühwein
Km to airport	Km of pistes 17.5	cars 0/0	factor ★★★
83 km	Nursery areas 1	Gondolas/chairs 0/5	Ski in/ski out ☆☆☆
Airport Plovdiv	Blues 3	Drags 13	Environmental
Highest lift 1971 m	Reds 4	Night skiing no	rating ★☆☆☆☆

Beginners and intermediates looking for a cheap, cheerful trip with plenty of nightlife will find lots to keep them occupied.

Although they might claim otherwise, Pamporovo is essentially a very mellow ski hill. Gradients are generally gentle and the place supposedly gets 270 sunny days a year. Which means that it is hardly going to be blasted with snow, but is perfect beginner/intermediate territory. The resort is basically on Snejanka peak – look for the TV tower, which is the summit.

Beginners As a cheap, non-intimidating introduction to skiing, Pamporovo is perfect.

Intermediate Once you've graduated from the drag-accessed nursery slopes, the whole hill is your playground. There are only eight runs in Pamporovo and most of them are mellow reds. Work up to 'The Wall' by week's end.

Expert Pamporovo isn't really for expert skiers or those with a yen for powder. The only serious pitch is short and mogul-filled, meaning you'll be hitting the bars by Wednesday. There is a GS run, but again not really enough to occupy a week.

Tuition There is a well-equipped ski school in town – book through bulgariaski.com.

Bad light Most of Pamporovo's slopes are in the trees, so you should be able to get around in all but the thickest of pea-soupers.

Not to miss A night in the **White Hart** – preferably on the last evening of the trip. Hangovers guaranteed.

Remember to avoid If you're an expert skier.

Practicalities

Pamporovo is based around a central complex of hotels, bars and restaurants along one strip. Other hotels dot the local area, although access to the slopes is usually by shuttle bus wherever you stay.

Sleeping Balkan Holidays (balkanholidays.co.uk) seem to be the major English-speaking package holiday operators in town and place tourists in complexes such as **Grand Hotel Murgavets** (murgavets-bg.com), **Hotel Pamporovo** (victoria-group.net) and **Aparthotel & Spa Royal Lodge** (hotelroyallodge.com).

Eating The British influence is writ large in Pamporovo, with pubs such as the **White Hart** packed to the rafters and serving endless full English breakfasts and other pub grub. Locals like **Chevermeto** (chevermeto-bg.com) for local cuisine.

Bars and clubs The **White Hart** and **Daks** get rowdy and offer liver-scaring drink promotions.

Hire shop/rental Hire shops are available at the base of the lifts, or there are a raft of options on line from bulgariaski.com, Bulgaria-hotels.com and others.

Transfer options If you book a package, your operator will have this sorted. If not, try motoroads.com for deals from Plovdiv airport

You can also ski here ... No local partners.

If you like this ... try Vogel ▶▶ *p110*, Åre ▶▶ *p260*.

◉ **OPENING TIMES**
Dec to early Apr: 0830-1630

Ⓢ **RESORT PRICES**
Week pass: BGN276
Day pass: BGN45

ⓘ **DIRECTORY**
Website: pamporovo.net
Tourist office: T+359 (0)9 302 1236
Taxi: gogotaxis.com

Bulgaria & Slovenia Pamporovo, Bulgaria

↘4 Krvavec, Slovenia

Town altitude	Vertical drop 1971 m	Blacks 5	Terrain parks 1
1450 m	Km of pistes 26	Funicular/cable cars 0/1	Glühwein factor ★☆☆
Km to airport 25 km	Nursery areas 1	Gondolas/chairs 0/7	Ski in/ski out ★☆☆
Airport Ljubljana	Blues 5	Drags 3	Environmental
Highest lift 1971 m	Reds 12	Night skiing no	rating ★★☆☆☆

PROS

- ✔ Spectacular view.
- ✔ Quiet midweek slopes.
- ✔ Good value.

CONS

- ✖ Not for experts.
- ✖ Infrastructure quite basic compared to other resorts.

Slovenia's steepest and, thanks to its proximity to the capital, most versatile resort.

Krvavec is a quiet resort with a local feel. Queues are due to the limited number of lifts rather than the number of people. The locals watch the weather avidly and sprint up the mountain when it's clear so it can get busy quickly if conditions are good.

Beginners Complete beginners will enjoy the nursery area with its moving carpets and drag lifts. There are limited blue runs: stay between Dom na Krvavcu, Krisna Planina and Krzisce for a couple of decent blues to keep you occupied.

Intermediate Go to Zvoh, the highest point in the resort at 1971 m, and take either a steep red or try a black off-piste down. This will provide the longest run possible.

Expert Like many of its Balkan cousins, Krvavec suffers from a lack of pitch and the shortness of the runs on offer. That said, it is steeper than most and has a couple of blacks at the top. Most advanced skiers should only really consider it for a weekend.

Powder Pistes 14 and 20 are always left unstamped, but this isn't really the place to come to satisfy a powder fix.

Moguls No specific areas set aside, but 14 and 20 rut up well enough.

Tuition With beginners such an important part of the market, tuition is

☺ LOCALS DO

- ✔ Drive to the resort to avoid the inevitable cable car queues.
- ✔ Wait for favourable weather.
- ✔ Welcome visitors – this is a very friendly resort.

☹ LOCALS DON'T

- ✖ Mind the loud music emanating from most bars.
- ✖ Pass up the opportunity of a midday snifter.
- ✖ Ski much in the week.

strong here. Book through **Smucisce Krvavec** (krvavec@solasmucanja.com).

Kids Kids will find the 80-m 'Wonder Carpet' useful, and there's a dedicated ski play area as well.

Bad light Although the slopes are lined with trees, you'll need to stay low during bad-light spells – that or head into the city.

Not to miss A drink in the igloo village.

Remember to avoid The lunchtime rush at the restaurants – they get busy and play thumping Euro house music.

Relive a famous moment Krvavec a contestant for the 'resort closest to major airport' award, although they don't really seem to have cottoned on to the marketing potential of this claim.

Best mountain restaurant Plansarija Vizencar on the other side of the mountain offers good traditional food from local produce.

Practicalities

Krvavec's trump card is its proximity to Ljubljana. Some authorities think the 15-minute journey time to the airport makes it the closest ski area in the world to a capital city airport. As with most Slovenian resorts, there isn't a great deal up at the hill, so staying in the capital and commuting each day is the best way of making the most of your trip.

Sleeping In resort, **Pension Tiha Dolina** (T+386 (0)4-201 2801) is clean, simple and straightforward. For the more adventurous, the **Igloo Village** (info@koren-sports.si) is an experience. **Apartment Paula** is brand new and has modern facilities and friendly staff (apartmaji-paula.si). In Ljubljana, **Hostel Celica** (souhostel.com) – a former prison converted into an achingly trendy hotel – is worth a look. It is close to the bus station, the departure point for shuttle buses to Krvavec, as is **City Hotel** (cityhotel.si).

Eating Krvavec dining tends to err towards the 'authentic', and the food served in the local pensions and hotels tends to be wholesome stuff. **Hotel Zlatorog** (T+386 (0)4-572 3381) is probably the pick of the bunch, serving great local produce in its restaurant. In Ljubljana, Italian and fusion cuisine abound, as does great local offerings. Check ljubljana.si for a comprehensive list.

Au pair/crèche Sky School Krvavec (T+386 (0)4-271 1803) is great, and there is also a children's playground for three- to six-year-olds every day between 1100 and 1300.

Bars and clubs For more serious clubs and bars you need to visit Ljubljana. The scene in Krvavec is limited but it is getting better. Head to **Brunarica**

Soncek, (affectionately known as 'The Beach') or the **Igloo Village**, which is lively.

Hire shop/rental Ski servis Strel Krvavec (T+386 (0)4-271 1808) is reliable, friendly and affordable, and the people seem to care.

Health and wellbeing The Atlantis resort (atlantis-vodnomesto.si) in Ljubljana is a water park with wellness facilities including thermal pools and saunas.

Down days with the kids Other than the obvious Ljubljana option, you could go south to the Karst region, a UNESCO World Heritage site with striking caves to explore.

Transfer options There are special ski buses from Ljubljana to Krvavec – get the timetable from ap-ljubljana.si/shop and buy the ticket on the bus. If you buy a combined bus and ski ticket you can get a 10% discount.

You can also ski here ... Stari Vrh, near Ljubljana. Offers night skiing.

If you like this ... try Pila ▶▶ *p238*, Lillehammer ▶▶ *p258*.

⊙ OPENING TIMES

End Nov to early May Mon-Fri 0700-1700; Sat/Sun 0800-1800

⊖ RESORT PRICES

Week pass: €113

Day pass: €24

Season pass: €380

⊙ DIRECTORY

Website: rtc-krvavec.si

Medical centre: T+386 (0)4-271 1805

Pisteurs: T+386 (0)1-541 5800

Taxi: T+386 (0)1-541 5800

Bulgaria & Slovenia Krvavec, Slovenia

↘5 Vogel, Slovenia

Town altitude **569 m**	Km of pistes	Funicular/cable	Glühwein factor
Km to airport **60 km**	**18 km**	cars **0/1**	★☆☆
Airport **Ljubljana**	Nursery areas **1**	Gondolas/chairs **0/3**	Ski in/ski out
Highest lift **1800 m**	Blues **7**	Drags **4**	★☆☆
Vertical drop	Reds **5**	Night skiing **no**	Environmental
1231 m	Blacks **0**	Terrain parks **1**	rating **n/a**

PROS

✔ Romantic, beautiful and peaceful.
✔ Those views.

CONS

✖ Prone to bad visibility.
✖ Limited skiing.

With incredible views, it's one of the most picturesque skiing locations in Europe.

Vogel is a pretty mountain range with lots of meandering slopes and opportunities to stop off and admire Lake Bohinj below. Its beauty makes it a popular destination but even when the weather is fine and the entire surrounding population have made the trip up the mountain, it feels a million miles away from a big commercial French ski resort. The lack of infrastructure can be frustrating but is also its charm.

Beginners Only 4 km of trails but enough spectacular views to keep you occupied. Head to Orlave Glave,

Practicalities

Vogel is located high above the beautiful Bohinj Lake and is part of the stunning Triglav National Park. Bohinj itself is a scattering of small hamlets with hotels and houses dispersed along the water's densely wooded southern shores. The area is an oasis of calm and tranquility with the clear lake and clean air giving it a unique sense of undiscovered beauty. If you are happy to put serious skiing to one side and explore the stunning scenery, this is the place to come.

Sleeping Hotel Bohinj (alpinum.net), a 10-minute drive from the cable car in Ribcev Laz, is a clean, well-presented hotel let down by a distinctly average restaurant in the basement. Up the mountain there are a few residential options including the grand looking **Ski Hotel Vogel** (skihotelvogel.com).

Eating Center Pizzeria (T+386 (0)4-572 3170) next to Hotel Bohinj serves decent pizza, as does **Zoisor grad** (T+386 (0)4-574 7590) in nearby Bohinjska Bistrica as well as hearty traditional Slovenian dishes and a good selection of regional wine. Up the mountain you'll find more pizza options and some pretty rustic eating haunts. **Orlove glav** is ideally situated for lunch stopovers.

Au pair/crèche Vogel's kindergarten programme runs daily between 1000 and 1400.

Bars and clubs Try **Vodni Park** (T+386 (0)4-577 0210): an aqua park with a nightclub open till 0400! Party animals won't find much to satisfy them in Vogel. When the lift stops, so does the action.

Hire shop/rental Ski servis Finzgar (ru-fi.si/) is the best option.

Health and wellbeing Breathing the air here makes you feel healthy. For specifics, **Hotel Golf** (T+386 (0)4-579 1702) in nearby Bled has high-end swimming pools and good beauty facilities.

Down days with kids Vodni Park is the obvious option. Nearby Bled is another lakeside town. It is busier and more commercial with lots of places to eat, drink and hang out.

Transfer options You can get to Vogel by bus (ap-ljubljana.si/) but its worth hiring a car – Slovenia's primary asset is it's outstanding natural beauty and you will want to stop to take in the views more frequently than in most ski countries.

You can also ski here ... Kanin, the only Slovenian ski resort with altitudes over 2000 m.

If you like this ... try Valmorel ▶▶ *p192*, Hemsedal ▶▶ *p256*.

◉ OPENING TIMES

Dec to early Apr: 0900-1600

⑤ RESORT PRICES

Week pass: €139

Day pass: €26

ⓘ DIRECTORY

Website: vogel.si

Tourist office: T+386 04-574 6010

Taxi info: intersiti.net/en/index.php

a cluster of blues in the centre of the resort, or Brunarica Zadnji, a leisurely 2-km trail through the great scenery.

Intermediate Notable spots include the Zagarjev Graben run through the trees or Sija Zadinji Vogel, which is the highest and steepest slope in Vogel. Intermediates will be right at home in Vogel.

Expert If the conditions are right, there are some decent off-piste opportunities. But within the main resort runs, there is nothing that will really challenge an advanced skier.

Powder Booking a guide is the best way to uncover any secret powder stashes. Try **Servis Finzgar** (T+386 (0)4-572 1722).

Moguls Nothing specific worth making the trip for, although there are the usual end-of-day bumps to play on.

Tuition As well as **Servis Fingzar**, try **Alpine Sport Ski School** (alpinsport@ siol-net) or **Ski & Fun Ski School** (T+386 (0)1-280 8080).

Kids **Servis Finzgar** organize lessons for kids. Book through servis.finzgar@ru-fi.si.

Bad light Clouds rather ruin the point of visiting pulchritudinous Vogel. Take the day off and spend the day exploring the nearby lake towns. Or take a day trip to Ljubljana.

Not to miss Get an Aquapass! It entitles you to skiing at Vogel, nearby Kobla and admittance to the Aquapark at Bohinjska Bistrica. More information at vogel.si/.

Remember to avoid If you are an expert skier – it might get tedious after a day or two.

Relive a famous moment Apparently, Vogel's alumni include Agatha Christie, who was taken with the incredible vistas.

Best mountain restaurant **Cottage Merjasec** (T+386 04-567 8790) takes care of decent on-hill lunches. Sit back and enjoy the views.

Bulgaria & Slovenia Vogel, Slovenia

France

France
Value for money
★★★☆☆
Nightlife
★★★☆☆
Off-piste
★★★★★
Family
★★★★☆

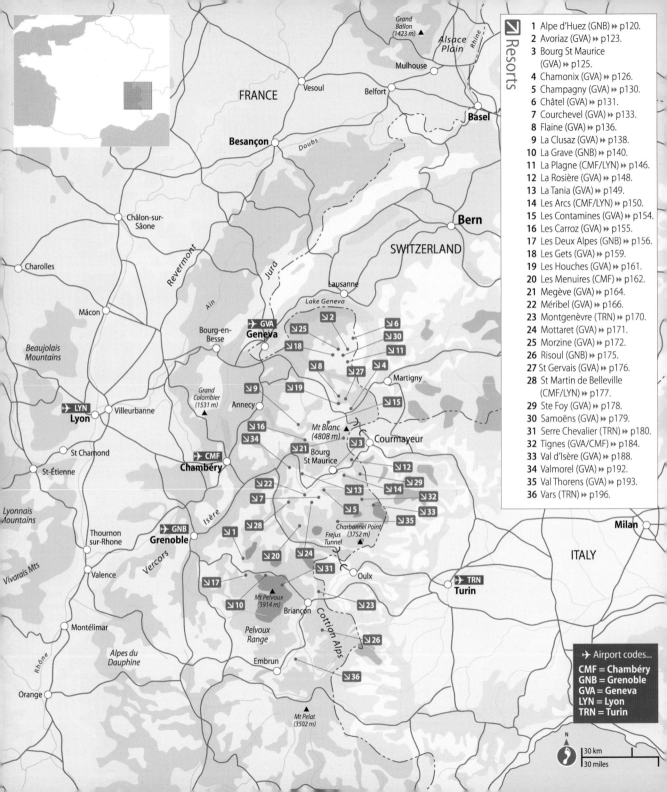

✈ Airport codes...
CMF = Chambéry
GNB = Grenoble
GVA = Geneva
LYN = Lyon
TRN = Turin

France attracts winter sports enthusiasts from all over the world. Many a bearded backcountry American has been heard to drawl with gushing pride, "I skied Chaaaam," while on the other side of Mont Blanc the boutiques and bling of Courchevel have Russian millionaires arriving by the (private) helicopter load.

But between the extremes are the reasons that *we* love France – the vast, well-linked areas of Espace Killy, Portes du Soleil, Trois Vallées and Paradiski, with their endless miles of groomed pistes; the relaxed attitude to exploring the snow off-piste; the choice of two mountain ranges; the mulled wine at lunch time; the fresh baguettes and the cheese.

Being France, there are the obvious crimes against architecture – Les Arcs, Les Menuires, Avoriaz and central La Plagne, to name a few – but it's not hard to find a more traditional French ambience in villages like Ste Foy, St Martin de Belleville and Châtel where the way of life has barely changed for 50 years.

Yes, it is true that some of the lift systems are in desperate need of updating but it has been noted that skiers don't like waiting in queues and there is evidence of heavy investment. If you like clocking up the mileage and loud après-ski then France is for you. And if you want freeriding and a laid-back attitude, France is for you, too.

Skiing France

France is hugely popular as a ski destination. With over 8000 km of pistes and hundreds of resorts, France claims to have the largest number of skiable slopes in the world: during the 2007/2008 winter season French ski lifts carried 499 million passengers.

British skiers have a fondness for France and French ski resorts, where one in three of us take our ski break. There are considered to be three generations of French ski resorts – traditional, state-built and purpose-built – all of which have a different appeal. This gives rise to an assorted ski crowd, peppered with über-rich Russians and seasoned with budget-conscious families.

Following the rapid expansion of the French ski industry in the 1960s and 1970s, bed-heavy resorts were developed to meet the demand for places to stay in the snow; any British skier to France will have surely stayed in a cabin-like apartment in Les Arcs or Tignes. But alongside the ungainly resorts you can still find hidden gems where the snow stays untracked for days and you rarely have to queue for a lift. For this reason, we still believe that France has something for everyone.

"France's position as the number one destination for British skiers looks unassailable, their high altitude resorts have guaranteed snow even during the occasional poor season. The French resorts have also invested heavily their lift systems over recent years with fast quad chairlifts and gondolas replacing the unpopular Poma draglifts. Accommodation has improved too, and although the shoe-box apartments still exist, there are now more options available. If you are worried about your carbon footprint, France is also the best option with the snow train running direct from London to Bourg St Maurice." *Graham Bell, Ski Sunday Presenter*.

Conditions

France's Alpine weather can be hugely changeable, as can the snowfall. Bluebird days can be followed by white-outs and seasons vary enormously. Occasional very high winds from the west, such as the Foehn, bring sand from north Africa, turning the snow yellow. The winter seasons of the Alps and Pyrenees are shorter than other mountain ranges but the variety of terrain and open access goes some way to make up for this.

When To Go

Some French resorts open at the end of November (Val d'Isère) but most open during December and you are unlikely to get perfect conditions before Christmas. Early January is considered low season and you are likely to get a cheap deal at this time of year – it can also be a time of huge dumps of snow accompanied, sadly, by low cloud and flat light. French school holidays and English half-term means that February should be avoided if possible. By March the days are lighter, brighter and high snow falls are common. Take to the terraces in April but have your skis to hand – you can be tanning one minute and knee-deep in powder the next.

Off-Piste Policy

One of the beauties of France is that there is a very relaxed attitude to going into the backcountry. With this, however, comes a huge risk. Winter sports enthusiasts travelling to France are warned by the Foreign and Commonwealth Office that there is "an acute danger of avalanches in the French Alpine" regions. There have been many avoidable deaths in the last few years. If you intend to ski off-piste you need to buy a Carte Neige when you buy your lift pass. This specific additional insurance will ensure that you are taken off the mountain without having to pay for the helicopter ride.

Secret Spots

Due to the number of visitors to France powder stashes are guarded and considered the private property of the people in the know – which is usually the locals and a handful of blessed seasonaires. However, the terrain is so vast that on a powder day there are freshies to be had in every resort. Powder does get tracked out very quickly – it's a numbers game – so you need to be on the first lift to get your share. The sheer volume of skiers in bigger resorts has started a trend among some for visiting smaller, lesser-known resorts and edge-resorts (those on the outskirts of larger ski stations) such as Vallandry, Villaroger and La Tania. Here you can sometimes spend hours in the trees or in powder with very few neighbours for company. **Piste Hors** (pistehors.com) is a backcountry website with useful information about off-piste routes and safety.

PROS

A huge choice of resorts with something for everyone - families, beginners and experts.

Four huge interlinked ski areas.

Four grades of piste with very easy runs for real beginners.

Generally good food and wine at affordable prices.

Alpine centres with a long history of winter sports and mountaineering.

CONS

Small cramped self-catering accommodation.

Expensive when compared to other European counties (and with the dollar still relatively weak, the USA).

Some lift systems are antiquated and lift queues can be enormous during February and early March.

Many on-mountain restaurants are of a poor standard.

France Skiing France

Essentials

Getting there

Most skiers enter France through Switzerland's Geneva International Airport (gva.ch) or Lyon Saint Exupéry (lyonairport.com), both of which require a two- to three-hour transfer to the Alpine resorts. Skiers visiting the Pyrenees enter via Toulouse (toulouse.aeroport.fr) or Spain's Barcelona (barcelona-airport.com). Carriers to Geneva include **Aer Lingus** (aerlingus.com), **BMI Baby** (bmibaby.com), **British Airways** (ba.com), **easyJet** (easyjet.com), **Fly Be** (Flybe.com), **KLM** (klm.com), **Jet 2** (jet2.com), **Lufthansa** (lufthansa.com), **SWISS** (swiss.com) and **Thomson** (thomsonfly.com); while Lyon has Aer Lingus, BMI Baby, British Airways, Easyjet and KLM. If you are traveling independently, coach transfers from Geneva and Lyon can be arranged through **Altibus** (altibus.com).

Driving to the Alps is a rite of passage for many skiers and the motorway network is excellent. Make sure you have cash or cards at the ready to pay tolls and get in the correct land when approaching the payage.

Red Tape

France was a founder member of the EU. Member states require no visas but foreign nationals from the rest of the world need to apply for permission to enter.

Getting Around

You should take particular care when driving in France as driving regulations and customs are different from those in the UK. Roads in France, particularly motorways, are of an excellent standard but speed limits are higher than in the UK and the accident rate is higher. Driving is standard European (right-hand side). A valid driving licence from your home country is fine.

Fact File

Currency Euro €

Time Zone GMT +1

Country Code +33

Emergency Numbers

Ambulance T15

Police T17

Fire T18

Mountain rescue (only available in some areas) T15 or T112

General emergency T112

Mountain Passes Check the route before you travel, especially if you're planning on taking a mountain pass between resorts. Many are closed over the winter.

Car Hire Most major hire car companies (easycar.com, hertz.com, avis.com etc.) have offices in airports and cities. Usual age restrictions apply. Note that if you fly in to Geneva and hire a car, you may need some Swiss Francs for parking.

Public Transport SNCF is the national railway of France. UK residents can make online bookings for train tickets to and within France. This includes travel on Eurostar, TGV high-speed trains and other local train services (autotrains).

Opening Hours and Traditions

Shops are generally open 0800-1200, before reopening again from 1400 until 1700 although most shops in the Alps stay open until 1900. Stock up in big towns at the larger supermarkets (Super U/ Carrefour); Alpine supermarkets, such as Sherpa, are expensive but stock all the essentials.

Eating

Say France, think bread, cheese and wine in any order, at any time of the day. Part of France's great appeal is its superior culinary tradition. Start the day with a buttery, just-baked, pain au chocolate or croissant, wash it down with un grand café and you are set up for a day on the slopes.

Michelin-starred restaurants can be found in Chamonix, Megève, and Saint Martin de Belleville and many make visiting these establishments a feature of their ski holiday. If your budget doesn't stretch to this, there are plenty of pizza/steak/fondue-style gaffs in most resorts. However, these can be pricey and don't always offer the best grub. Do as the locals do and you are more likely to get authentic rustic alpine food.

Lunch on the mountain can be a disappointing affair with the many self-service (referred to as 'self') restaurants serving expensive, bland, greasy food (€13 for a plate of chips anyone?). The French make their own, and come midday baguette and fromage picnics are enjoyed all over the slopes. If you are on a budget there are usually panini-serving snack bars to be found at the base of the lifts.

Language

The official language is French, although the accent varies hugely across the country. English is widely spoken, especially in the resorts.

Top Tips

1 **Take** cash. Credit card machines and ATMs exist in most villages and resorts but they do tend to run out of money.
2 **Eat** lunch early and enjoy empty slopes for two hours – French skiers still like to take long lunches.
3 **Avoid** the bigger resorts during the French school holidays (early February to mid-March).
4 **Only** go off-piste if you have the correct equipment (transceiver, shovel, probe) and you know how to use it. The laissez-faire attitude to backcountry skiing is liberating but potentially life-threatening.
5 **If** you go early season book a higher resort like Val Thorens – otherwise you could be skiing on grass.

Going green
Overland travel to the Alps is easy. From December to April **Eurostar** offers the brilliant (if pricey) train service from London St Pancras to the Alps calling at Moûtiers, Aime La Plagne and Bourg St Maurice. Prices start from £99. The legendary **Snow Train** (raileurope.co.uk), complete with disco carriage, leaves St Pancras and calls at Ebbsfleet (Kent), Chambéry, Albertville, Moûtiers, Aime la Plagne, Landry and Bourg St Maurice.

Crime and Safety
The crime level is generally low but it is not advisable to leave skis unlocked on balconies and outside restaurants – new season, sought-after skis are at most risk of walking. The biggest threat is car crime and there have been cases of tourist cars being targeted for valuables. Report any incidences of theft to the local police (Police Nationale).

Health
As part of the EU, France is governed by European health standards. Medical insurance is recommended and EU citizens should carry a European Health Insurance Card (EHIC). The EHIC is not a substitute for medical and travel insurance but entitles you to emergency medical treatment on the same terms as French nationals. Note that in the case of accident in a ski resort visitors to the départements of Savoie and Haute-Savoie may be transferred to Switzerland for hospital treatment.

↘1 Alpe d'Huez

Town altitude	1860 m	Km of pistes	249 km	Funicular/cable		Terrain parks	2
Km to airport	110 km	Nursery areas	2	cars	0/6	Glühwein factor	★★☆
Airport	Grenoble	Blues	32	Gondolas/chairs	10/25	Ski in/ski out	★★☆
Highest lift	3330 m	Reds	36	Drags	40	Environmental	
Vertical drop	2230 m	Blacks	17	Night skiing	yes	rating	★★☆☆☆

PROS

- ✔ Lots of sunny, high-altitude skiing to suit all levels.
- ✔ Extensive choice of accommodation – apartments, chalets, hotels and B&Bs.
- ✔ Ski pass gives loads of extra perks.
- ✔ Great for families and has lively nightlife.

CONS

- ✘ Too much sunshine on south-facing slopes leads to icy mornings and slushy afternoons later in the season.
- ✘ Very few trees for bad light days.
- ✘ Pyramid layout of the town means long walks back home at night.

A vast, sunny ski area suitable for all levels in a spectacular setting – shame about the village.

Located in the Grandes Rousses massif, Alpe d'Huez (ADH) has long been popular with the French for its breathtaking scenery, alleged 360 days of sunshine per year and huge ski terrain.

ADH boasts just 50 km fewer pistes than Val d'Isère and Tignes combined, the longest piste in the Alps (the 16 km-long Sarenne), excellent off-piste, one of Europe's largest nursery areas, modern lifts and good mountain restaurants. Unfortunately, the largely south-facing slopes often suffer from excessive sun, particularly in late season, and can get very crowded.

Beginners Gentle lower slopes make for a large network of green runs accessed by chairlifts rather than drags. Buy a dedicated beginner's lift pass, which accesses 11 lifts at a lower cost.

Intermediate Confident intermediates will find plenty here – practise carving on Auris and the long Fare slope down to Vaujany, find your powder feet on the Dôme des Petites Rousses and build up stamina for the iconic Sarenne and Champagne (2230-m vertical descent) runs. Less confident intermediates beware: some reds would be classified black in other resorts – approach Villard-Reculas and Signal with caution.

Expert ADH has plenty of black slopes and excellent freeriding. Warm up along the edges of Sarenne and on Dôme des Petites Rousses before tackling the classic routes below. These are best done with a guide and some require transport back to the resort. Extreme skiers will thrive on the Cheminées de Mascle, l'Impossible and Col de l'Herpie couloirs.

Powder Get an early start and, if you're an experienced off-piste skier, hit the classic Grandes Rousses routes. For more accessible hits, keep to the north-facing runs above Vaujany.

Moguls Love moguls? The precariously steep Tunnel run down the front of Pic Blanc will cure you.

Trees Given the altitude, trees are limited. You'll find some around Montfrais, down to Auris from Signal and down to Huez in early season.

Book a guide A guide will show you the classic Grande Rousses routes such as Pic Bayle, Grand Sablat and Le Glacier des Quirlies as well as the Combe du Loup by Sarenne. Hike 20 minutes from the cable car up La Pyramide to be rewarded with a 2000-m vertical

descent to Vaujany down either P10 or the Couloir de Fare. Check with the **Bureau des Guides** for information (guidesalpedhuez.com).

Ski school The **ESF** is the largest (350 instructors) but classes also tend to be large. The **British Masterclass** school guarantees small classes taught in English.

Kids Children under five ski free. Both the ESF and ESI run ski kindergartens in the resort – **La Garderie des Neiges** (from four years) and **Le Baby Club** (from 2½ to 3½ years) respectively.

Bad light Head for Serre Chevalier – one day's skiing is included in the Visalp ski pass.

Not to miss Skiing down Sarenne by the light of the full moon after a

gourmet meal on the glacier (T+33 (0)476-803473).

Remember to avoid The bus journey to Les Deux Alpes by taking a 10-minute helicopter ride from the Altiport directly onto the slopes – at €62 return it's worth it for the views!

Relive a famous moment Jean Pomagalski invented the drag lift at ADH in 1936 and went on to found the Poma lift company. His son now lives and skis in ADH.

Pitstop and sunbathe Soak up the views at **Le Signal** and enjoy the spectacular surroundings at the **Perce-Neige** on the way down to Oz.

Best mountain restaurant Chalet du Lac Besson, on the edge of a frozen lake and only accessible on foot or skis, and

the **Forêt de Maronne** hotel (Chatelard) both offer excellent food in secluded locations. **Auberge de l'Alpette** does tasty basics at good prices. **La Combe Haut** makes a great break after cruising the Sarenne – reservations essential (T+33 (0)476-806138).

😊 LOCALS DO

✅ Start early on Saturdays, taking advantage of change-over day and beating the weekend crowds.

✅ Save time by downloading on Vaujany-Villette to take the big gondola up to l'Alpette.

✅ Call the Grandes Rousses gondola the DMC.

😊 LOCALS DON'T

❌ Tire of the beauty of their surroundings.

❌ Miss the last cable car to Alpe d'Huez from Vaujany – it's an expensive cab ride home.

❌ Share the recipe for their home-made Génépi.

Practicalities

Unfortunately, the purpose-built town sprawls across four separate quarters, meaning accommodation and restaurants are far apart. The Altiport complex, where most chalets are, is particularly far away from the centre. However, you can stay in the more rustic villages of Vaujany and Huez, which are linked to ADH by chairlift.

Sleeping The large three-star Le Pic Blanc (T+33 (0)476-114242; hmc-hotels.com) at the base of Les Bergers has spacious rooms, a pool and spa. Three-star **Hotel Christina** (T+33 (0)476-803332; lechristina-alpedhuez. com), near the bars, is more traditional. Chalets in the Altiport are all ski in/ski out – try **Chalet Louisa** (skiworld.ltd.uk), complete with hot tub and sauna. **Ski Peak** (skipeak.com) offers excellent accommodation in Vaujany. **The Hotel Royal Ours Blanc** (T+33 (0)476-803550; hotel-royal-ours-blanc-alpe-huez.federal-hotel.com) and **Au Chamois d'Or** (T+33 (0)476-803132; chamoisdor-alpedhuez. com) are the resort's two four-star properties.

Eating There are some 60 restaurants in town but make sure you book during peak times. Favourites include **Au Dahu Grillé** (try Rodolphe's homemade Génépi), **Pizzeria La Roy Ladre** and **Génépi**. Younger crowds enjoy the laid-back atmosphere in **Les Caves de l'Alpe** and **Lily Muldoon's**. **Au P'tit Creux** and **Au Chamois d'Or** offer excellent food in atmospheric surroundings.

Au pair/crèche **Les Intrepides** (T+33 (0)476-112161) cares for children from six months to three years and **Les Crapouilloux** (T+33 (0)476-113923) from 2½ years.

Best après-ski **The Underground** is the spot for Austrian-style après until late, while **Melting Pot** does quieter drinks on the sun terrace.

Bars and clubs ADH has a lively nightlife, with 43 bars and clubs. **Le Sporting** on Avenue des Jeux appeals to an older audience (incorporating a bar, restaurant and disco), as do **Lilly Muldoon's** and **Les Caves de l'Alpe** in the old town. Youngsters go for **O'Sharkey's Bar**, **Underground**, **Crowded House**, **Zoo** and **Igloo** disco.

Hire shop/rental The Les Bergers commercial centre has loads of shops – **Cyril's Sport** is best for hi-tech kit. If you're based in the Cognet quarter, try **Sarenne Sport** or **Loup Sport**.

Lift tickets Buy tickets at lift stations or the tourist information office. A six-day pass gives free access to the Sports Centre on Avenue des Jeux, complete with swimming pools, climbing wall, tennis, indoor golf etc.

Health and wellbeing Use the Sports Centre or luxuriate in the **Au Chamois d'Or** spa.

Down days with kids Children love the Sports Centre and 'In Vertigo' in particular – an aerial adventure park without ropes but with a large safety net underneath.

Internet The **Agua Café** and **Mère Michel Café** offer customers free Wi-Fi. There are machines at the tourist office.

Transfer options Fly to Grenoble and take a shuttle directly to the resort (bensbus.co.uk). Alternatively, transfer to Grenoble coach station by bus and from there by coach (voyages-monnet.com).

You can also ski here ... Vaujany, Auris-en-Oisans, Oz-en-Oisans and Villard-Reculas as well as Les Deux Alpes, Serre Chevalier, Briançon, Puy Saint Vincent and the Milky Way.

If you like this ... try Avoriaz ▶▶ *p123*, Serre Chevalier ▶▶ *p180*, Tignes ▶▶ *p184*.

OPENING TIMES

Early Dec to late Apr: 0900-1645

RESORT PRICES

Week pass: €198.50

Day pass: €38.20

Season pass: €700

DIRECTORY

Website: alpedhuez.com

Tourist office: T+33 (0)476-114444

Medical Centre: T+33 (0)476-806432

Pisteurs: T+33 (0)476-803738

Taxi: T+33 (0)476-803838

↘2 Avoriaz

Town altitude	1800 m	Km of pistes	650 km	Funicular/cable cars	0/4	Terrain parks	9
Km to airport	90 km	Nursery areas	5			
Airport	Geneva	Blues	112			

Town altitude 1800 m   Km of pistes 650 km   Funicular/cable cars 0/4   Terrain parks 9
Km to airport 90 km   Nursery areas 5   Gondolas/chairs 9/80   Glühwein factor ★★☆
Airport Geneva   Blues 112   Drags 102   Ski in/ski out ★★★
Highest lift 2280 km   Reds 104   Night skiing yes   Environmental rating ★★☆☆☆
Vertical drop 1180 m   Blacks 28

PROS

- ✔ There's a great selection of funparks and man-made runs from beginner to expert.
- ✔ Ski straight from your doorstep.
- ✔ Snow until late in the season.

CONS

- ✖ Can get busy during the holiday periods.
- ✖ Can be a drag getting bags from the car park to the apartments.
- ✖ Crazy architecture people either love or hate.

Affordable ski in/ski out resort at the heart of the Portes du Soleil, a contestant for the 'world's biggest linked lift system'.

The Portes du Soleil covers an enormous area in the corners of both France and Switzerland. Avoriaz is perhaps the jewel in the crown of the area, being both staggering in its concept and – given the right light – beautiful to behold. Certainly, those skiing back to town as the sun sets over distant peaks will get a view that few other resorts can boast.

Beginners Open your front door and ski towards the eight-man Tour chair that goes back up through town. From there, head down the Proclou run until

you hit the area known as Super-Morzine (it is above the Super-Morzine gondola), perhaps the best beginner area in France. Ride around the whole area and back to Avoriaz and you've done a decent lap covering gentle terrain that includes skiing through a tunnel.

Intermediate From Avoriaz head to the top of the Chavanette where you'll encounter 'The Wall', a ludicrously steep mogul run. Don't worry – you can take the chair down. At the bottom keep heading for Crosets; when you get there find the funpark. You don't have to take on the jumps just yet, but definitely try out the fantastic gulley run. A return lap

Expert A near-complete lap of the PDS is within the realms of possibility if you start early enough and have a group consisting of good skiers. First head to Switzerland via the Chavanette (if you're feeling strong, ski down 'The Wall'), then lap all the resorts – Les Crosets, Champéry, Val d'Illez and Morgins. Return via Champoussin to the Montriand valley, then head through Morzine to Les Gets. If you do it this way round, getting stuck isn't a problem. The Prodains cable car runs from Morzine to Avoriaz until late at night, so even if you don't complete the lap you'll be able to make it home.

Powder If there is powder, the piste from Avoriaz to Les Prodains offers some incredible cat tracks to jump from or shadow on the way down. Otherwise, the area above the Avoriaz park has plenty of moonscape possibilities.

Moguls Bump skiers will find 'The Wall' absolutely heavenly.

Tuition As with all French resorts, the **ESF** (Ecole du Ski Francaise), (T+33 (0)450-740565) is the biggest, while the **Avoriaz Alpine Ski School** (T+33 (0)450-383491) is the town's best English-speaking school.

Kids Le Village des Enfants (T+33 (0)450-740446) will look after the kids for around €40 per day.

France Avoriaz

☺ LOCALS DO

- ☺ Get the Prodains cable car down to Morzine for a good knees-up.
- ☺ Head to the Crosets park for some man-made fun.
- ☺ Know that some of the best terrain can be found at the lower spots – the Mossettes chair in particular.

☹ LOCALS DON'T

- ☹ Walk uphill too much. Most buildings have public-access elevators and top-floor bridges to higher ground. Use the free lifts to get around.
- ☹ Head into Switzerland after 1500 and risk getting stuck.
- ☹ Ski down 'The Wall'. Unless they're showing off.

Bad light The Prodains home run down to Morzine offers the best trees nearby. Otherwise, the bottom three-quarters of the Montriand valley has a great coverage.

Not to miss The Montriand valley is often overlooked, which is a shame as it's probably the most picturesque part of the PDS.

Remember to avoid Getting stuck in Switzerland after 1630. Always make sure you've got enough time to get home as the taxi can cost upwards of €150.

Relive a famous moment Luc Besson started his film career by entering – and winning – the Avoriaz Film Festival in 1983, later going on to make *The Big Blue* (see Tignes RAFM) and *The Fifth Element* with Bruce Willis, Gary Oldman and Milla Jovovich.

Pitstop and sunbathe Try the ever-popular **Changabang** for a coffee and brownie.

 # Practicalities

Avoriaz is famous for its bizarre architecture and town planning, first proposed by French Olympian Juan Vuarnet in the 1970s. Perched high above Morzine and built to blend in with the surrounding cliffs, most buildings are futuristic in concept, have odd, eclectic shapes and are crammed with apartments that wouldn't look out of place on *The Jetsons*. Avoriaz is home to an annual 'Futuristic' film festival and yet – in contrast – the town is car free, meaning horse-drawn sledges whizz everyone around. It can be reached by either road or cable car from Morzine, and everywhere has incredible access to the slopes.

Sleeping Self-catering is king, with **Maeva** (maeva.com) being the largest apartment agency in town. It regularly has deals as low as €20 per person per night. **Club Med** (clubmed.com) has catered accommodation for around €40 per night, while **Les Dromonts** (T+33 (0)450-740811) has perhaps the best views in town for €140 per night.

Eating La Falaise (T+33 (0)450-741048) is perhaps the only pizza restaurant in the world next to a 300-m cliff, hence its name. For a less edgy meal, a fondue or traditional Savoyard meal in **La Reserve** (T+33 (0)450-74-02-01) would suit.

Au pair/crèche Village des Enfants d'Annie Famose (T+33 (0)450-740446),

Garderie Les Petits Loups (T+33 (0)450-740038) and **ESF Avoriaz** (T+33 (0)450-740565) all take care of the young ones on the slopes, while the cutely named **Jack Frosts** (jackfrosts.net; T+44 (0)1579-384993) does apartment/hotel visits.

Bars and clubs Shooters, Le Tavaillon and **Pub Le Choucas** are all worth a punt. For big nights out, get the Prodain lift down to Morzine town.

Shopping There is a supermarket island, between two pistes, in the middle of town but it's very overpriced. Morzine offers better competition but an out-of-town shop is very difficult from Avoriaz. In short, bring as many supplies as you can muster.

Hire shop/rental Oxygene Ski (T+33 (0)450-742246) and **Ski Sport Rene Collet** (T+33 (0)450-74 14 65) will look after you.

Health and wellbeing If the **Espace Thalgo Centre du Bien-être** (T+33 (0)450-740811) doesn't live up to its name in Avoriaz, there's always the **Galarie du Baraty** (T+33 (0)450-791068) in Morzine for spa, massage and sauna.

Down days with kids Get everyone shouting "Mush!" behind a team of huskies with a sledge day at the **Cheins de Traineau** (T+33 (0)450-731517).

Internet Surprisingly for such a futuristic place it lacks a true internet café, but the tourist office and the bowling alley have machines (€2 for 10 minutes). If you really need to get on line, there's Wi-Fi at the bakery **Manie Brioche**.

Transfer options From Geneva airport, bus transfers (T+33 (0)450-384208) take around an hour. Or for the flash, **Mont Blanc Helicopters** make the same trip in 10 minutes (T+33 (0)450-927821) for around €1000 per person.

You can also ski here ... The Portes du Soleil lift pass covers Morzine, Les Gets, Châtel, Les Crosets and Abondance, to name a few.

If you like this ... try Les Menuires ▶▶*p162*, Val Thorens ▶▶*p193*.

OPENING TIMES
End of Nov to end of Apr: 0830-1700

RESORT PRICES
Week pass: €189
Day pass: €39
Season pass: €724

DIRECTORY
Website: avoriaz.com
Tourist office: T+33 (0)450-740211
Medical Centre: T+33 (0)450-740542
Pisteurs: T+33 (0)450-741113
Taxi: Avoriaz is car-free
Local radio: Radio Morzine 97.9 FM

↘3 Bourg St Maurice

Town altitude 800 m	Funicular/cable
Km to airport 145 km	cars 1/1
Airport Geneva	Gondolas/chairs 3/31
Highest lift 3200 m	Drags 18
Vertical drop 2400 m	Night skiing yes
Km of pistes 425 km	Terrain parks 0
Nursery areas 5	Glühwein factor ★☆☆
Blues 43	Ski in/ski out ☆☆☆
Reds 43	Environmental
Blacks 26	rating ★☆☆☆☆

The main Tarantaise valley town, with fantastic access to Ste Foy, La Rosière, the Espace Killy and the Paradiski area.

Practicalities

As a valley town, Bourg's primary selling points are its access to Les Arcs via the funicular railway and Eurostar links to Paris and the UK. It is also cheaper to stay down here than up in one of the resorts. Roving skiers could hire a car and spend the week exploring the entire valley for a week or fortnight with a difference.

Sleeping The homely three-star **Hotel Autantic** (autantic.fr), two-star **Le Relais de la Vanoise** (relaisdelavanoise.info) and **Hostellerie du Petit Saint Bernard** (hostelleriedupetitsaintbernard.com) are all great options. For a cheaper option, try the extremely friendly **Chill Chalet** (chillchalet.com).

Eating Visit nearby La Pre for classic Savoyarde fare at **La Ferme** (la.ferme.free.fr). In Bourg, **Le Refuge** and **La Savoyarde** are popular.

Au pair/crèche Lucy Ward (snowlittle@fisheye.f9.co.uk) runs a stable of English-speaking babysitters.

Bars and clubs **Central Bar** is popular, as is **Cafè Flore** and **Bazoom Bar** opposite the station. Bourg isn't known for its incredible nightlife though.

Shopping As a large town, Bourg is a cheap option compared to the neighbouring resorts. Try the enormous **Super U** just before the Les Arcs turning for most supplies. If you can't bear to eat locally, **The Trading Post** (tradingpost.fr) seems to do a thriving trade.

Hire shop/rental The ever-reliable **Interski** (intersport-bourg.com) should take care of things. Experts might also want to check out **Zag Skis** (zagskis.com), a brand based in Bourg.

Health and wellbeing L'Oree des Cimes (cgh-residences.com) in nearby Piesey Vallandry has a luxurious spa and health club.

Down days with kids Bourg is better than most, its valley location meaning that it is easy to escape to larger towns such as Annecy (roughly 90 minutes away). In town, a skatepark, long walks, outdoor pools and climbing walls offer diversions.

Internet McDonald's has wireless access, as does **Super U** and **Bazoom**.

Transfer options The train is undoubtedly the best way of reaching Bourg (eurostar.com). For transfers try altibus.com.

You can also ski here ... Les Arcs, Paradiski, Espace Killy.

If you like this ... try Méribel ▶▶ *p166*, Serre Chevalier ▶▶ *p180*, Livigno ▶▶ *p232*.

▶▶ *p166*, ▶▶ *p180*, ▶▶ *p232*.

France Bourg St Maurice

⊚ OPENING TIMES

Dec to early Apr: 0900-1700

Ⓢ RESORT PRICES

Week pass: €216

Day pass: €47

Season pass: €935

ⓘ DIRECTORY

Website: lesarcs.com

Tourist office: T+33 (0)479-071257

Medical Centre: T+33 (0)479-070988

Pisteurs: T+33 (0)479-078566

Taxi: T+33 (0)686-242383

↘4 Chamonix

Town altitude	1035 m	Km of pistes	155 km	Funicular/cable cars	2/7
Km to airport	88 km	Nursery areas	4	Gondolas/chairs	5/20
Airport	Geneva	Blues	36	Drags	18
Highest lift	3842 m	Reds	31	Night skiing	yes
Vertical drop	2807 m	Blacks	14		

Terrain parks	2
Glühwein factor	★★★
Ski in/ski out	☆☆☆
Environmental rating	★★★★☆

PROS

- ⊘ Some of the world's steepest, most challenging and most scenic skiing.
- ⊘ Accommodation to suit all budgets.
- ⊘ Rocking nightlife.
- ⊘ Easy to reach from Geneva.

CONS

- ⊗ Skiing is spread across five separate mountains – prepare to commute.
- ⊗ Not ideal for beginners or intermediates.
- ⊗ The mountain gets tracked out quicker than you can say 'powder'.
- ⊗ You have to pay for the second stage of the Grands Montets cable car.

With epic off-piste, awe-inspiring scenery and a brilliant party scene it's arguably the best (expert) ski resort.

Skiers come to Chamonix for extreme off-piste, massive vertical descents and breathtaking high-alpine scenery, not for on-piste cruising or gourmet lunches. Other than getting tracked-out quickly, the main complaint about Chamonix is the fragmentation of its ski areas. There are five: Le Brévent and La Flégè (linked by lift), Grands Montets, L'Aiguille du Midi (ungroomed terrain only) and Le Tour. The solution: accept

Chamonix is the most scenic resort in the world. Every year when I ski this amazing resort I'm reminded how insignificant and small humans are compared to the size and scope of nature. Skiing the Vallée Blanche is an experience of a lifetime, it never gets old and leaves me with a proper perspective on my life

Dan Egan, US Extreme Skiing Pioneer
(skiclinics.com)

it, embrace the variety, plan your days carefully, and consider hiring a car. Les Houches, 6 km down the valley from Chamonix, is included in the Mont Blanc Unlimited pass but not Chamonix Le Pass.

Beginners Although there are nursery slopes, Cham isn't ideal for learners. Le Tour is the best area, with several blues accessed easily by the Vallorcine chair. Buy day passes for the nursery slopes.

Intermediate Tentative intermediates find Chamonix difficult to love as terrain is so dispersed. Le Tour is your best mountain, with wide, open pistes, a mellower gradient and the dreamy 8-km blue T19, which leads into trees down

☺ LOCALS DO

- ⊘ Pick up the weekly *Le Petit Canard* for the latest news and hottest après-ski (lepetitcanardchx. com).
- ⊘ Wear serious 'kit' – we're talking crampons, ice picks, harnesses ...
- ⊘ Wake up ludicrously early on powder days.

☹ LOCALS DON'T

- ⊗ Ski badly.
- ⊗ Eat in mountain restaurants but stick a sarnie in their rucksacks.

to Vallorcine. Confident intermediates will enjoy sunny Flégère, with easily accessible off-piste and challenging runs from the top of the L'Index chair. The Vallée Blanche is a Chamonix highlight: 22 km of (guided) off-piste down the stunning Mer de Glace glacier.

Expert Grands Montets above Argentiè re has long, steep itineraries (link the Point de Vue and Pylones itineraries with the Pierreà Ric red for a 2035-m vertical descent) and accessible off-piste above the Lognan cable car. Brévent/Flèg re have spectacular views, are often sunnier than other mountains and the black B1 from Brévent is one of the steepest in the valley. The north-facing T18 itinerary on Le Tour is (relatively) quiet after a storm.

Powder Powder is what Cham's all about although sadly its cult status means you need night-vision goggles to get fresh tracks. Observe three rules and, in the right conditions, you'll enjoy some of the world's finest skiing: start very, very early, carry appropriate avalanche gear and don't freeride on the glaciers without a guide. Blossoming powder hounds should head for Flégère and Les Houches. Expert skiers should try some iconic Grands Montets routes: Italian Bowl from la Herse; Combe de la Pendant and Canadian Bowl from Bochard; the Pas de Chevre couloirs into Vallée Blanche; and Grand Mur, reached from the Point de Vue run. Try less-travelled routes on the Vallée Blanche such as the Vraie Vallée, Envers du Plan or

Col du Plan. Another favourite is Le Tour's Possettes Couloir into Vallorcine.

Moguls Grands Montets isn't pisted, so terrain gets bumped out quickly after a storm. Pylones and Les Coqs are particularly challenging.

Trees On Grands Montets, the aptly named Dream Forest is between the Retour Pendant and Plan Roujon chairlifts. Domaine de la Balme off the back of Le Tour above Vallorcine is less steep and Les Houches has excellent tree-skiing.

Book a guide There are numerous guiding companies but our recommendations are: Denis at

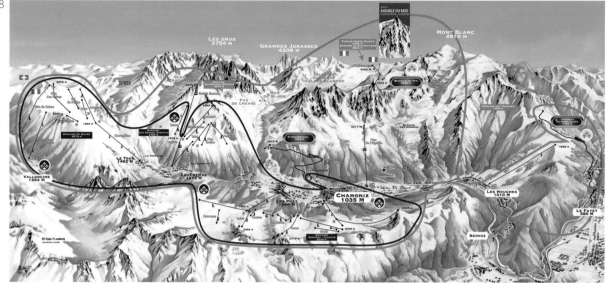

Chamonix Mountain Guide
(chamonixmountainguide.com),
Evolution2 (evolution2-chamonix.com),
Ski Sensations (ski-sensations.com) and
Mountain Guide Adventure (mountain-guide-adventure.com). In addition to
routes named above, try day-long tours
off Flégère and L'Aiguille du Midi.

Ski school We like **Evolution2** and
Ski Sensations as above.

Kids Evolution2 runs **Panda Club**
(T+33 (0)450-540888) for kids from three.

Bad light Stick to the trees above.
Alternatively, go **Winter Paint Balling**
(paintballcham.com).

Not to miss The unbeatable views from
the top of the Aiguille du Midi on
a blue-sky day.

Remember to avoid Tackling the
Vallée Blanche without a guide (and
disappearing into a crevasse).

Relive a famous moment The **Boss
des Bosses** ('bosses' are moguls in
French) takes place on Grands Montets
every March. Watch seasonaires from
various European resorts do battle
on the bumps and copy their moves
(carefully) on Les Coqs the next day.

Pitstop and sunbathe Brévent and
Flégère are sunniest, so head for La
Chavanne or **Panoramic** or soak up the
views from a rock at the top of the L'Index
or Cornu chairs. **Chalet de Charamillon** on
Le Tour has deckchairs and great views.

Best mountain restaurant Not
Chamonix's strong point although La
Crèmerie du Glacier (T+33
(0)450-540752) and **Chalet-Refuge de
Lognan** (T+33 (0)688-560354) on Grands
Montets are excellent (hence booking is
essential). **La Bergerie de Planpraz** on
Brévent is good. **Les Vieilles Luges**, **La
Tanière** and **Le Cha** in Les Houches are
worth a visit.

☉ OPENING TIMES

Early Dec to early May: 0800-1700
(peak); 0830-1630 (off-peak)

⑤ RESORT PRICES

Week pass: €185/225 (Chamonix Le
Pass/Mont Blanc Unlimited)

Day pass: €37

Season pass: €650/1045

① DIRECTORY

Website: chamonix.com

Tourist office: T+33 (0)450-530024

Medical Centre: T+33 (0)450-530326

Pisteurs: T+33 (0)450-5322275

Taxi: T+33 (0)607-263662

Practicalities

Chamonix is a large yet attractive town incorporating several satellite villages along a 12-km-long glacial valley. It has a long mountaineering history thanks to its location at the base of Mont Blanc and its bars buzz with happy, modern-day mountain-lovers from 1600 onwards. Yes, there's a Chanel shop but don't expect glamour – locals and regular visitors wear climbing harnesses and carry ABS rucksacks, and there's accommodation and dining to suit all budgets.

Sleeping Party-lovers should stay in Chamonix, committed skiers in Argentière, intermediates in Le Tour and families in Les Houches. Budget options include **Gite Vagabond** (T+33 (0)450-531543; gitevagabond.com) and **Hotel Le Dahu** (T+33 (0)450-540155) in Argentière. More expensive are **Hotel Gustavia** (T+33 (0)450-530031; hotel-gustavia.com), home to Chambre Neuf bar but quiet at night; **Le Prieuré** (T+33 (0)450-532072; bestmontblanc.com), which has shuttle buses to the lifts; and **Hotel La Vallée Blanche** (T+33 (0)450-530450; vallee-blanche.com), on the river, which serves vast breakfasts. **Le Hameau Albert 1er** (T+33 (0)450-530509; hameaualbert.fr) comprises hotel accommodation, a chalet and super-chic farmhouse in addition to two award-winning restaurants and a spa. **Clubhouse** (T+33 (0)450-909656; clubhouse.fr) is a boutique hotel and slick members' bar from the creators of Milk & Honey in London and New York.

Eating Mojo's sandwiches and **Beluga**'s cobs are legendary (slap a Beluga sticker on your skis for instant 'local' kudos). For more substantial meals, **Munchies** does Asian food, **MicroBrewery Chamonix (MBC)** does

excellent burgers, **Le Caveau** is an ancient cattle cellar accessed by a tiny door on Rue du Dr Paccard and **Casa Valeria** does great pizzas. **The Jekyll** is a gastro-pub while **Maison Carrier** (Albert 1er), **Le Chaudron**, **La Bergerie** and **Le National** are good for local specialities. Albert 1er's Michelin-starred restaurant deserves its two stars, chef Mickey at **Le Bistro** creates imaginative dishes, while **Le Panier des Quatre Saisons** might look unremarkable but serves remarkably good local food.

Au pair/crèche Maison des Jeunes et de la Culture (T+33 (0)450-531224) cares for 3 to 12 year-olds and **Baby-Cham** (T+33 (0)614-555287; baby-cham.com) offers babysitting.

Best après-ski Après-ski is well deserved in Chamonix and locals party as hard as they ski. **MBC**, **Chambre Neuf**, **Elevation**, **Jekyll** and **La Terrasse** rate among our favourite bars in the ski world.

Bars and clubs **Le Derapage**, tucked away in the centre of town, warms up after 2000. **Bar'd Up** attracts raucous crowds at Happy Hour. **No Escape** and **The Clubhouse** (members only) are trendy new bars, while **Le Lapin Agile** is an unpretentious wine bar. Also good are **Monkey Bar** in Chamonix Sud and **The Office** in Argentière. **Le Choucas** nightclub is expensive and has a miniscule dance space but is open late, while **The Garage** is old-school cheese, with a hint of sauciness.

Shopping A good combination of sports shops (**Sport Extreme** is a ski supermarket, selling cheap, own-brand kit), boutiques and supermarkets.

Hire shop/rental Snell Sports has a vast selection of kit and does custom boot fittings. For serious foot attention,

try **Footworks** in Chamonix Sud. **Sanglard**, next to the Argentière cable car, picks you up from your hotel, sorts out your equipment and delivers you back for free.

Lift tickets Book online before the season starts for reduced prices (compagniedumontblanc.fr). There's a bewildering array of passes, offering access to different parts of the Mont Blanc ski area – research before you buy.

Health and wellbeing There are physios galore in Cham – try **Angie Wardle** (T+33 (0)619-576000). The **Richard Bozon Sport Centre** has pools while **Granges d'en Haut** (grangesdenhaut.com) in Les Houches has a new spa.

Down days with kids Visit the **Alpine Museum**, go swimming in the **Richard Bozon Sport Centre** or take the Montenvers train to Mer de Glace for an ice-tunnel tour.

Internet Mojo's has several terminals. There's Wi-Fi at **Monkey**, **Le Lapin Agile** and **Grand Central Coffee**.

Transfer options Companies chamexpress.com and alpybus.com do shared transfers from Geneva for around €20 (single), while private transfers cost up to €200 (a.t.s.net). Public buses cost about €50 return (sat-montblanc.com).

You can also ski here ... A Mont Blanc Unlimited ski pass gives you access to L'Aiguille du Midi, Brévent/Flégère, Le Tour, Grands Montets, Les Houches, Courmayeur, La Funivia and the Montenvers train and Tramway du Mont Blanc.

If you like this ... try St Anton ▶▶ *p85*, Verbier ▶▶ *p308*, Zermatt ▶▶ *p316*.

France Chamonix

↘5 Champagny

Town altitude	Km of pistes 425 km	Funicular/cable	Terrain parks 2
1250-1450 m	Nursery areas 12	cars 1/3	Glühwein factor ★☆☆
Km to airport 140 km	Blues 129	Gondolas/chairs 13/66	Ski in/ski out ★☆☆
Airport Geneva	Reds 66	Drags 54	Environmental
Highest lift 3250 m	Blacks 35	Night skiing yes	rating ★★★★☆
Vertical drop 2050 m			

One of the few attractive villages in the Grande Plagne ski area, good for families and intermediates wanting to dip their toes into Paradiski.

Champagny-en-Vanoise is an old farming village tucked away in woods on the south-facing slopes of the Grande Plagne ski area. Champagny le Haut is a smattering of chalets in the spectacular Vanoise National Park above Champagny.

A high-speed cable car takes skiers up to Rocher de Mio in about 20 minutes, making access to Paradiski relatively painless.

Beginners Get a Champagny/ Montchavin ski pass and stick to the gentle blues above the resorts. You'll have to download initially as the only in-resort runs are red.

Intermediate Champagny is ideal for you: the two long reds into town are a joy, you can find your powder and tree-skiing feet in relative peace, and you can access the rest of Paradiski.

Expert The main advantage of staying in Champagny for you is the proximity of the Bellecôte Glacier – book a guide for the descent from the glacier to Champagny-le-Haut along the Cul du Nant.

Tuition ESF is based in town and runs the **Piou Piou** children's ski club.

Bad light Stick to the lower slopes.

Not to miss Visiting Champagny's beautiful 16th-century Baroque Church of St Sigismond.

Remember to avoid Not bringing an extra layer for skiing on the glacier.

Practicalities

Sleeping Hotel l'Ancolie (T+33 (0)479-550500) and **Les Glières** (T+33 (0)479-550552) are Champagny's two hotels. There are also the four-star **Les Chalets du Bouquetin** (T+33 (0)479-550113; bouquetin.com).

Eating Don Camillo does pizza, **La Poya** serves local food, while **Alpenrose** and **Chalets du Bouquetin** are more upmarket.

Bars and clubs Refuge du Bois (Champagny le Haut) for après-ski and **Don Camillo**, **Le Barillon** and **Le Barà Vin** for later. **Le Galaxy** is the village disco.

Kids Les Cabris (T+33 (0)479-550640) cares for two- to six-year-olds, with the option of including half a day's tuition with ESF.

Transfer options Fly to Geneva or Chambery and take an altibus.com bus. Alternatively, take the Eurostar (eurostar.com) to Moutiers followed by an Altibus.

You can also ski here ... Paradiski.

If you like this ... try St Johann in Tirol ▶▶ *p89*, Les Gets ▶▶ *p159*.

⊚ OPENING TIMES

Mid-Dec to late April: 0830-1700

⊚ RESORT PRICES

Week pass: €197.50

Day pass: €47

Season pass: €935

ⓘ DIRECTORY

Website: champagny.com

Tourist office: T+33 (0)479-550655

Medical Centre: T+33 (0)479-041799

Pisteurs: T+33 (0)479-097979

Taxi: T+33 (0)479-550528

⬊6 Châtel

Town altitude 1100 m	Km of pistes 650 km	Funicular/cable cars 0/4	Terrain parks 9
Km to airport 65 km	Nursery areas 2	Gondolas/chairs 9/80	Glühwein factor ★★☆
Airport Geneva	Blue 112	Drags 102	Ski in/ski out ★★☆
Highest lift 2466 m	Red 104	Night skiing yes	Environmental
Vertical drop 1366 m	Black 28		rating ★☆☆☆☆

PROS

✔ Fewer English-speaking visitors means fewer English-speaking shopkeepers, which will give you a great opportunity to practise your schoolboy/girl French!

✔ Good variety of terrain.

CONS

✘ The lower altitudes mean that sometimes you may have to go elsewhere for deeper snow.

✘ Taxis can be hard to find after a night out.

Peaceful, friendly and authentically French, with easy access to some great skiing.

Châtel is part of Les Portes du Soleil, the world's biggest linked winter playground, which joins eight resorts in France and four in Switzerland by chairlift and bus.

Beginners The main area, **Super Châtel**, is located above the village and home to the beginners' slopes. Take the TK Super Châtel, then the TK Châtel-Neuf, to find wide open, easy trails such as Bellevue and Le Lac. The green runs are generally close together and easy to find which takes the stress out of learning.

Intermediate Châtel is perfect for people who can ski well enough to brave a blue, like the challenge of trees, and enjoy going nice and fast. Don't miss Les Combes, where you can get some serious downhill speed, and La Perdrix Blanche, a big open bowl with widely spaced trees and little powder pockets.

Expert More advanced skiers in Châtel should head for Linga, with its steeper north-facing slopes and access to Avoriaz. Les Renards is a long black run,

with some narrow chutes and smaller cliffs to drop off. There is a nice little Snowpark too if you're up for it.

Powder There are some fantastic off-piste runs - from steep, narrow couloirs to extensive hidden powder

fields. Many of the areas are accessible from the lifts and with a small amount of hiking it is possible to discover some real gems. You can usually find some good powder under the Morclan chair, even after all the rest of the mountain has been tracked out.

Moguls Some of the steeper runs in Le Linga will get moguls, but are usually avoidable if you don't like them.

Tuition There are five ski schools in Châtel, offering everything from SnowPark lessons to tele-marking, in groups or privately. The biggest of these, **ESF** (Ecole du Ski Français, T+33 (0)450-732264), has branches throughout the Alps.

France Châtel

Kids Under fives ski free. Instructors will meet the kids at the ESF ski school at the top of Super Châtel and take them to the kiddies area where they can practise skiing and using the magic carpet ski lift.

Bad light Stick to the lower level trees in poor visibility. La Balette can be fun if you're at Linga.

Not to miss Après at the bars on top of the Super Châtel telecabin. Sit in the sun (or inside around the fire) and enjoy a hard-earned drink.

Remember to avoid Wearing shoes/boots that aren't non-slip when you're out walking around. Hard-packed snow turned to ice can easily lead to slippery embarrassment.

Relive a famous moment Head over to Avoriaz where Enrique Iglesias and Anna Kournikova were seen skiing last winter.

Practicalities

The holiday town of Châtel is tucked away in the Portes du Soleil, and though very popular with the French, does not get as many foreign visitors as some of its neighbours. This does have the advantage of lending it a very traditional rustic charm.

Sleeping There are good value self-catering apartments, or catered chalets like **Les Erines** right in the centre of the village. If you prefer hotels try **Fleur du Neige** (T+33 (0)450-732010), from €69-105 with sauna and hot tub to relax your tired muscles. As its name suggests, the three-star **Panoramic** hotel (T+33 (0)450-732215), from €58 per person per night, has spectacular views up Super-Châtel valley.

Eating **Chez Francis** does great pizza, **Le Grizzli** is good for grills and *tartiflette*, **La Table d'Antoine** is the place if you've got a date to impress. **Domain Chaux des Rosèes** does delicious crêpes on the pistes.

Au pair/crèche The **Mouflets** crèche costs €6 per hour plus meals, bookings essential. Alternatively contact the tourist office for local au pair phone numbers.

Bars and clubs Kick off après at **èvalanche**, move on to the **Le R'bat Bar**

for some live music to take you to dinner. **Le Break** next, then dance until first lifts at **The Discoteque** at the base of Super Châtel.

Shopping Every Wednesday morning, Châtel's farmers and craftspeople come into town to sell their wares at the local market.

Hire shop/rental SkiLinga rents some quality gear at fairly reasonable prices.

Health and wellbeing It's a 25-minute drive to Thonon and Evian, with health retreats and spas frequented by Europe's rich and famous. Take a dip in the natural thermal public baths, or be pampered in one of the town's many health clubs.

Down days with the kids Visit a traditional village farm or take a guided tour of Châtel with the miniature sightseeing train. There's a free sledging area located at Pré-la-Joux, with two sledging runs: one for two- to six-year-olds and the other for children aged six and over.

Internet The majority of the big hotels have internet access for about €9 per hour.

Transfer options Fly into Geneva and from around €22 per person you can hire a driver to pick you up and deliver you to your chalet door. Coaches are cheaper and do go from the airport to Châtel but may take three times as long to get you there.

You can also ski here ... Châtel is linked by chairlift to Avoriaz, Torgon and Morgins.

If you like this ... try Morzine ▶▶ *p172* and Avoriaz ▶▶ *p123*.

OPENING TIMES
20 Dec to 3 Apr: 0900-1700

RESORT PRICES
Week pass: €172
Day pass: €31.50
Season pass: €432

DIRECTORY
Website: chatel.com
Tourist office: T+33 (0)450-732244
Medical Centre: T+33 (0)450-733201
Pisteurs: T+33 (0)450-733424
Taxi: T+33 (0)450-733283

France Châtel

⬊7 Courchevel

Town altitude	Vertical drop 1055 m	Blues 41		Night skiing yes	
1350 m, 1550 m,	Km of pistes	Reds 40		Terrain parks 4	
1650 m and 1850 m	157 km (part of the	Blacks 12		Glühwein factor ★★☆	
Km to airport 149 km	600 km within the	Funicular/cable cars 1/0		Ski in/ski out ★☆☆	
Airport Geneva	Trois Vallées)	Gondolas/chairs 10/20		Environmental	
Highest lift 3230 m	Nursery areas 5	Drags 28		rating ★★★☆☆	

PROS

- ✅ Courchevel caters for all types of snow seekers so if skiing is not your thing, you'll always find something else to do.
- ✅ If you like your holiday to have a touch of luxury, you'll be spoilt rotten.
- ✅ As part of the Trois Vallées, it's difficult to get bored of the varied terrain.

CONS

- ❌ Easy access from neighbouring resorts leads to the best fresh snow being ransacked quickly.
- ❌ The cost – unless you're Roman Abramovich (who tried to buy the entire village of 1850 in 2003) you'll struggle to be able to afford to do everything you'd like.

Cornerstone of the Trois Vallées, the largest ski area in the world, Courchevel has a huge range of activities, nightlife and accommodation.

Courchevel attracts some of the wealthiest people from all over the world including plenty of nouveau-riche Russians.

They really look after their terrain and have attempted to cater for everyone with fun areas for kids, a supervised snow park and even an avalanche camp. Start with the Saulire, which will ferry you to the highest point possible at 2738 m from where you can take some of the long reds and blacks back down to Courchevel or over the hill to Méribel.

Beginners The nicest blues and greens are those that connect 1850 to 1650 and 1550. The pistes are wide and really well groomed so you can practise without the pressure of the busier slopes on Creux Noirs.

Intermediate Across the Trois Vallées, there are a tremendous number of excellent blue and red runs which you'll struggle to complete in a week. If it's long steady runs you're after, try the Chanrossa chair that will take you down through the stop zone or venture to Val Thorens or Méribel where you can take advantage of the stunning views from a different angle.

Expert There are a few tough runs that will take you down to Le Praz, or use your Trois Vallées pass and wander over to Les Menuires where the Col de la Chambre mixes long, steep runs with some that are slightly easier.

Powder Check out some of the off-piste around the Suisse chairlift and the Vizelle gondola. Just be prepared that powder-lovers from across the Trois Vallées might have the same idea ...

Moguls There's not a huge amount of bumpy terrain as the pistes are so well groomed. Try the Combe Saulire or Combe Pylônes from the Saulire Gondola.

Trees For some great tree-skiing, try the runs out of 1850 towards 1300 or La Tania.

Book a guide Hiring a guide will allow you to take advantage of local knowledge to find the best snow to suit you and your ability across all of the Trois Vallées so it's good value even for just a day. You can find **Courchevel Guides** (T+33 (0)479-010366) in Le Forum.

Ski school That's right – you've guessed it, **ESF** (T+33 (0)479-082107) is the main provider of ski tuition in Courchevel. **Supreme Ski** (T+33 (0)479-082787) guarantee English-speaking and BASI-trained instructors but you'll pay a bit more for them.

Kids Courchevel takes childcare very seriously and it's one of the only resorts in the world to have Magnestik safety packs. These keep the kids wriggle-free by using magnets inside the lifts and in their jackets. On the mountain there are dedicated 'zen zones' where parents can join their kids to learn how to stop properly.

Bad light Head to 1650 which is billed as "Courchevel for sun lovers". It's also at a lower altitude so the light's not so flat.

Not to miss Thinking "It doesn't look that bad" goes out of the window when you check out the ski jumps, Tremplins Olympiques, in 1300 – they're enormous.

Remember to avoid Overspending! This is one very expensive resort, especially for mountain eating.

Relive a famous moment The village of La Tania, also known as 1400, hosted the competitors for the 1992 Winter Olympics in Albertville. It's definitely worth a look before heading to Le Praz where the Olympic ski jump was held.

Pitstop and sunbathe Enjoy the sunshine and a beer in 1650 in **Le Bel Air** (T+33 (0)479-080093). The food is traditional and they do some great Savoyarde dishes.

Best mountain restaurant Ski down to the bottom of the Jardin chairlift and have lunch with the ski instructors at **Hôtel Les Grandes Alpes** (T+33 (0)479-000000). The prices are very reasonable and the quality of food is excellent. (Try the dessert buffet or, if you're brave, have a shot of Génépi.)

🙂 LOCALS DO

✅ Save their celebrations for huge family affairs in the nicest restaurants – you're advised to book.

✅ Get up early to bag the best powder.

🙁 LOCALS DON'T

❌ Head out much across the other resorts – the amount of terrain seems to be enough in Courchevel.

❌ Spend much time on the mountain – most tend to be working.

Practicalities

Based over four levels – Courchevel 1350 (aka La Praz), 1550, 1650 and 1850, named after their altitudes – the atmosphere varies greatly from village to village, with a different, younger clientele being drawn to the area in recent years. Regardless of where they are staying, everyone converges on the huge terrain of the Trois Vallées ski area to take advantage of long runs and short lift queues, all groomed to immaculate status. In short, it's a French classic.

Sleeping 1850 offers ultimate luxury with hotels such as **Le Kilimandjaro** (T+33 (0)479-014646) and **Le Saint Roch** (T+33 (0)479-082482) among the 12 four-star luxe hotels. Family-friendly hotels dominate 1650 and three-star **Les Portetta** (T+33 (0)479-009292) provide entertainment and accommodation for children. Hotels such as **Les Airelles** (T+33 (0)479-003838) and **Byblos des Neiges** (T+33 (0)479-009800) are price on application. Rooms at **Le Saint Joseph** (T+33 (0)479-081616) are finished with antiques, priceless paintings and enormous four-poster beds starting at €680 a night.

Eating The range of restaurants is enormous, from Japanese at **Le Ten Kai** (T+33 (0)479-411804) to roast game at **Le Bal** (T+33 (0)479-081383). For a cheaper night out, head to 1550 where

pizzas at **La Cortona** are great value. **Le Chabichou** (T+33 (0)479-080055) is owned by Michel Rochedy, who also runs the hotel's two-star Michelin restaurant from his kitchen. A *produit-régionale* menu sources the very best of local ingredients for €90 a head.

Au pair/crèche Les Pitchounets Kindergarten (T+33 (0)479-090728) in 1650 will keep kids from 18 months entertained.

Best après-ski Skiers from all areas head to **La Santa Forêt** where happy hour entertains the guests with music and special drinks offers.

Bars and clubs Purple Caffe is popular, and there are also two nightclubs, **Les Caves** and **La Grange**, open until 0500, both with huge party atmospheres to go with the huge prices. For something more reasonable check out new bar **Le Milk** (T+33 (0)479-004883).

Hire shop/rental Privilege Ski Hire (T+33 (0)683-515021) will sort out all your ski gear before you arrive. They'll then deliver equipment to wherever you're staying and pick it up again before you leave.

Lift tickets People tend to buy a lift pass that covers the Trois Vallées – if the snow is poor in Courchevel, it doesn't necessarily mean it will be in Val Thorens or Méribel. Available at all main lift points.

Health and wellbeing Make like a WAG and head to **Les Thermes Carlina** (T+33 (0)479-080403) to make use of the pool, hot tub and chiropodist.

Down days with kids Kids will love the floodlit luge and most hotels offer facilities such as the games rooms at the **Annapurna** (T+33 (0)479-080460) and the **Courcheneige** (T+33 (0)479-080259).

⦿ OPENING TIMES
Early Dec to late Apr: 0845-1630

⦿ RESORT PRICES
Week pass: €178 for 6 days/€200 for 7 days

Day pass: €37

Season pass: €790 (€950 Trois Vallées)

⦿ DIRECTORY
Website: courchevel.com

Tourist office: T+33 (0)479-080029

Medical Centre: T+33 (0)479-082640

Taxi: T+33 (0)479-003000

Internet There's free wireless available at each of the tourist offices and most of the hotels offer Wi-Fi for a small fee. If you need a computer, try **Cyber Café** (T+33 (0)479-010953).

Transfer options If you want to visit in style, Courchevel has its own private airport on the slopes: strap on your boots and ski straight to the front door of your hotel. If arriving on train or by bus, there is a regular bus service but check the airport websites for details (gva.ch or chambery-airport.com).

You can also ski here ... La Tania, Méribel, Les Menuires, Val Thorens and St Martin.

If you like this ... try Val d'Isère ▶▶ *p188*, Verbier ▶▶ *p308*.

↘8 Flaine

Town altitude	1600 m	Km of pistes	140 km	Funicular/cable cars	2/1
Km to airport	70 km	Nursery areas	2	Gondolas/chairs	2/9
Airport	Geneva	Blues	19	Drags	13
Highest lift	2500 m	Reds	22	Night skiing	yes
Vertical drop	1100 m	Blacks	4		

Terrain parks	3
Glühwein factor	★★☆
Ski in/ski out	★★★
Environmental rating	★★★★☆

PROS

- ✓ Pedestrianized, so is safe for families.
- ✓ Arguably the best snow coverage in France.

CONS

- ✗ Cheap prices often attract package tour groups on 'benders'.
- ✗ Purpose-built for skiing, Flaine doesn't provide great shopping opportunities.

A work of modern art or a monstrosity? However you see the village, the great skiing is undeniable.

Flaine is a huge snow-sure bowl at the heart of the Grand Massif ski area, the fourth largest ski domain in France. The skiing is extensive and varied, with trees, moguls and sunny motorways. These predominantly north- and northwest-facing runs are very reliable; all levels of skier should find something to suit.

Beginners Novice skiers love the wide, gentle nursery slopes close to the village centre and there are some free beginners' lifts. Cristal and Olivine are a nice way to ease into it.

Intermediate The red slopes in the Flaine bowl are perfect for improving your skills; go to the Serpentine, Faust or Mephisto. The Dolomie leading to the neighbouring resorts follows more challenging, narrow tree-lined trails.

Expert Taxing black runs include the Diamond Noir, Styx and the wooded run down to Samoëns or try the off-piste in the Gers bowl.

Powder Gers bowl and the off-piste surrounds are the best place to get some deep snow. With a guide and some energy for hiking you can find some of the best powder in France!

Moguls If you're into moguls the steeper faces on the Cristal run will test your legs.

Tuition Well-established French ski schools ESF (esf-flaine.com) and SEI (flaine-internationalskischool.com) both offer classes seven days a week. No prior booking is necessary; just go and register in the respective huts.

Kids For more English-speaking instructors and the newest teaching techniques go to SEI. Catherine Pouppeville (T+33 (0)609-266008) is a famous French school which specializes in private tuition for children from 2½ to 12 years old.

Not to miss The monumental works of art throughout the resort: the *Tête de Femme* by Picasso, the *Trois Hexagones* by Vasarely and the *Boqueteau* by Dubuffet.

Remember to avoid Taking your car into the resort. You won't need it and parking costs can be very high.

Relive a famous moment French actor Sebastian Roché and his family often ski in Flaine – try to spot them on their favourite black run Styx, or in the après bars in the village.

Best mountain restaurant Chez la Jeanne on the piste is a lovely pizzeria with local pasta specialities.

☺ LOCALS DO

- ✓ Get defensive when talking about Flaine's infamous architect, Marcel Breuer. He did design the Palais de l'Unesco in Paris and the Whitney Museum in NYC, after all!

☹ LOCALS DON'T

- ✗ Care too much about on-piste fashion. You will see them happily skiing around in a one-piece suit from 1974.
- ✗ Speak great English. Your hotel receptionist will, but the lift operators don't often get further than "Allo".

Practicalities

As with many purpose-built French resorts of the 1960s and 1970s, cosy mountain charm is at a minimum. But don't let Flaine's ugly tag put you off – it's ideal for families with its pedestrianized streets, ski in/ski out accommodation and excellent entertainment facilities. At an average 6 m per year, the area is blessed with one of the best snowfalls in the Alps.

Sleeping Le Vieux Rascard (levieuxrascard.com) is a sweet little B&B in the old town. **Hotel Campagnol** (T+33 (0)125-307191) is friendly, warm, clean and very good value – it's only two star but the Ski guesthouse **La Cascade** is right in the middle of the Azurite piste, while **Mer Montagne Vacances** (T+33 (0)450-908010) has English-speaking staff and family packages. Full or even half board is a great option for those on a tight budget: try **Flaine Forêt** (T+33 (0) 450-908766).

Eating Good choices for basic French fare are **Les Chalets du Michet** (T+33 (0)450-908008), which operates from a converted cowshed on the piste, or **La Perdrix Noire** (lapedrixnoir.com). **Limes Rock Café** has good value meals, and **Chez Daniel** is famous for its mouth-watering crêpe selection.

Au pair/crèche The Garderie les P'tits Loups (T+33 (0)450-908782) welcomes children from six months to three years while MMV club hotels **L'Aujon** and **Le Flaine** (T+33 (0)492-126212) cater for children between 18 months and 14 years.

Bars and clubs Brits flock to Le Diament Noir (T+33 (0)450-908465) with its pool tables and Champions League football showing on certain nights of the week. Go to Le White Bar when you're up for a massive night, The Flying Dutchman if live music is your thing or Le Skifun for some low-key disco action.

Hire shop/rental Flaine Super Ski's two stores are very competitive and conveniently placed (flainesuperski.com); Simond Sports (flainesimondsports.net) supply top-end brands with a personalized service.

Shopping The two shopping arcades, one in Flaine Forêt and another in Flaine Forum, contain most of the resort's shops, where you can buy basic necessities and maybe replace lost gloves and hats.

Health and wellbeing The fitness centre has a gym, sauna, spa and steam room, and there are also daily aerobics and yoga classes.

Down days with the kids There's a natural ice-skating rink for sunny days, while the sports centre's indoor climbing wall and swimming pool and the cinema are bad-weather opions. Try ice-quading and ice-karting with the older kids (T+33 (0)609-453662) – bookings can be made in the tourist office.

Internet Flaine Forêt has a new 'relax lounge' with high-speed internet and Le White Bar has free Wi-Fi (T+33 (0)450-908476).

Transfer options Flaine is close to major airports (Geneva, Annecy, Lyon), train stations (Cluses, Annecy, Annemasse) and the A40 motorway.

You can also ski here ... Grand Massif ski area.

If you like this ... try Avoriaz ▶▶ *p123*, Crans-Montana ▶▶ *p278*.

France Flaine

↘9 La Clusaz

Town altitude	1100 m	Km of pistes	128 km	Funicular/cable cars	0/2	Terrain parks	1

Town altitude 1100 m
Km to airport 50 km
Airport Geneva
Highest lift 2477 m
Vertical drop 1377 m

Km of pistes 128 km
Nursery areas 3
Blues 45
Reds 20
Blacks 7

Funicular/cable cars 0/2
Gondolas/chairs 3/16
Drags 28
Night skiing yes

Terrain parks 1
Glühwein factor ★★☆
Ski in/ski out ★☆☆
Environmental rating ★★★★☆

PROS

- As it's so close to Geneva it offers a great alternative to Chamonix or the Trois Vallées if you've not got long.
- Eating out is really good value and of a very high standard.
- Great for freeskiers.

CONS

- Nightlife not lively compared to others.
- There aren't many challenging runs so unless you like leaving the piste you could get bored.

Quickly becoming regarded as the freestyle skiing capital of Europe, La Clusaz has extensive off-piste and is rarely busy – hurrah!

One of the few ski resorts left in Europe to maintain its traditional French ways, La Clusaz provides all the facilities you would expect from a modern ski resort without being consumed with – well, consumerism.

The relatively small village hides a deceptively large amount of ski terrain. Based over five mountains, there's a wide range to suit everyone, from nursery slopes to some amazing backcountry. La Clusaz also has the world's first Telemix lift combining chair-lift seats with covered gondolas for those slightly more miserable days.

Beginners At the top of the Massif de Beauregard, the beginner's area is easily accessible and has plenty of space in which to find your feet.

Intermediate If you're starting to branch out into reds and some of the easier blacks, most of L'Aiguilles have quiet, steady runs that will allow you to develop your skills without venturing too far out of your comfort zone. Get the lift to the top of the Massif de Balme, Massif de L'Aiguille or the Massif d'Etale and try some of the long red runs back towards town.

Expert Some of the freestyle skiing is pretty intimidating, especially from the younger (slightly more fearless) locals. When you see a lot of advanced skiers just cruising the slopes, they tend to have a young child in tow. The Massif de

☺ LOCALS DO

- Treat visitors like honorary locals.
- Attend all the events that the tourist office puts on.
- Practise their freestyle moves on the Massif de Balme regardless of the weather.

☹ LOCALS DON'T

- Stay out late unless an event has taken place.
- Speak a lot of English – take a phrase book.

Balme, being the highest point in the resort, usually has the best snow.

Powder Although there are only two red runs on the Massif de Balme, the powder possibilities are immense. Even during high season, it's quite common to get fresh tracks a day or so after it has snowed. For the best off-piste, hire a guide who will show you some of the great runs – you might need to hike to reach them.

Moguls The best place to go for moguls is on the black La Mur Edward but check out some of the terrain in the trees off La Motte too.

Kids The **Piou Piou Club** offers a fun area on the slopes for kids aged three to five, while **Club des Mouflets** (T+33 (0)450-326543; laclusaz.fr) is a public childcare centre.

Bad light When the light is poor, head into the trees on the Bois de la Motte. This is mainly off-piste but there are some nice green runs such as La Motte for beginners too.

Not to miss Try the Full Moon events held about three times each season. The bars on the hill stay open till late and the piste is moonlit. Beautiful.

Remember to avoid Getting stuck in Le Fernuy after the last lift. There's not much there and the buses aren't as regular as some of the bigger resorts.

Relive a famous moment Check the jumps made for the Candide Invitational, a famous international freeski event – scary stuff!

Best mountain restaurant Le Bercail (T+33 (0)450-024375; lebercail74.com), situated on the Massif de L'Aiguille, is accessed by skis during the day or a sleigh from the bottom of the slopes at night.

Practicalities

Based in the Haute-Savoie region, La Clusaz is close enough to drive to neighbouring towns St Gervais and Megève. A word of caution – it's often reached by the Col de l'Aravis, an access road with some amazing scenery but one that's also prone to rock falls throughout the year.

Sleeping If it's ski in/ski out you're after, head for the **Hotel Beauregard** (T+33 (0)450-326800; hotel-beauregard. fr). Its sister hotel the **Alpen Roc** (T+33 (0)450-025896; hotel-alpenroc.fr) has similar facilities and both are excellent for children, offering duplex rooms for families. **La Chalets de la Serraz** (T+33 (0)450-024829; laserraz.com) has some great views and the **Carlina** (T+33 (0)450-024348; hotel-carlina.com) is good value.

Eating Try the **Chalet du Lac** for superb local food and a disturbing range of home-brewed liqueurs. **La Table d'UgoH** does a great selection of pizzas, while family-friendly restaurants include **La Scierie** and **La Bergerie**.

Bars and clubs The Irish bar **Salto** is worth a visit and **Les Caves de Paccaly** has a nice relaxed atmosphere. If you're in the mood, **L'Ecluse** has a glass floor over the river and is open till 0500.

Hire shop/rental With over 25 sports shops in the village alone, you'll be spoilt for choice. Try the **Bossonnet Pro Shop** where you can buy outfits to match the local heroes.

Health and wellbeing The **Beauvoir Wellness Institut** (T+33 (0)450-648615; beauvoir-institut.com) offers massage and beauty treatments using mountain plants from the surrounding areas.

Down days with kids You can't miss

the enormous **Aqua Centre** (T+33 (0)450-024301). Many hotels provide the Carte Détente allowing kids free entry to various attractions.

Internet You'll probably notice the distinct lack of internet connections – especially if you haven't brought a laptop. **Sno Académie** has the facilities but watch the erratic opening hours.

Transfer options Easiest access is via Geneva Airport. Hire a car and follow the directions to Chamonix, leaving the motorway at Sallanches, or take a shuttle bus (altibus.com).

You can also ski here ... Chamonix, St Gervais and Les Contamines are all within an hour.

If you like this ... try Grandvalira ▶▶ p40, Vallnord ▶▶ p42, Les Contamines ▶▶ p154.

OPENING TIMES
Late Dec to late Apr: 0900-1630

RESORT PRICES
Week pass: €137.50-149.50

Day pass: €28.50

Season pass: €590

DIRECTORY
Website: laclusaz.com

Tourist office: T+33 (0)450-326500

Medical Centre: T+33 (0)450-455930

Taxi: T+33 (0)450-513238

↘10 La Grave

Town altitude 1450 m	*Grave is not groomed,*	Funicular/cable	Glühwein
Km to airport 77 km	*so figures apply to a*	cars 0/0	factor ★☆☆
Airport Grenoble	*small area of the resort*	Gondolas/chairs 1/0	Ski in/ski out ★☆☆
Highest lift 3550 m	Nursery areas 0	Drags 2	Environmental
Vertical drop 2150 m	Blues 2	Night skiing No	rating n/a
Km of pistes 12 km	Reds Not measured	Terrain parks 0	
90% of the terrain in La	Blacks Not measured		

PROS

- ✓ Wild and raw freeriding – some of the world's best.
- ✓ Provides a unique, unspoiled piece of mountain life.
- ✓ Will push all skiers to the very limits of their capabilities – expect to improve dramatically.

CONS

- ✗ Being north-facing, the mountain can be toe-curlingly cold until March.
- ✗ The mountain is frequently shut down due to bad storms.
- ✗ There can be queues for the gondola, especially on weekends.

A cult destination for hardcore skiers looking for extreme off-piste. One of the world's last remaining true mountain experiences.

La Grave offers some of Europe's most challenging high-altitude skiing, with a vertical drop of around 2200 m. The ski area is unique in that 90% of it is unprepared and unpatrolled, with just 12 km of designated pistes and three ski lifts. The 'piste map' says it all – pick your own route, with care. The retro-style 'pulse' gondola inches up to 3200 m in 30 minutes, pausing at the P1 mid-station. At the top, a short walk brings you to two drag lifts on the glacier. After pretty technical entry points, the two primary descents, Vallons de Chancel and Vallons de la Meije, offer a mixture of steeps, open powder fields and forest. Extreme cliff drops and couloirs await those with a guide, equipment, skill and guts. A few words of serious warning: many of La Grave's extreme ski routes are on glaciers – this means gaping crevasses, falling seracs and extreme avalanche danger. Furthermore, the couloirs are frequently no broader than a ski, are prone to *goulottes* (ice bands formed during the daily springtime freeze/thaw cycles) and offer no other way out other than down.

Beginners If you're a beginner, La Grave is not the place for you.

Intermediate To enjoy skiing here, you'll need to be confident about skiing in powder, on steeps and through (tight) trees. A guide is absolutely essential and will take you down some of the variations on classic Chancel and Meije routes. A steep learning curve!

Expert Your guide will adapt his itinerary to your capabilities but expect to cover the classic routes before tackling more challenging terrain such as La Voute and the Trifides couloirs.

Powder A powder day on La Grave is the holy grail of skiing. If you're lucky

☺ LOCALS DO

✔ Respect the mountain, check the weather and come equipped for all conditions.

✔ Catch up on local gossip over a Pastis with Michou, landlady of Lou Ratel.

✔ Ski, hike, climb, go ski touring, paragliding, kite-skiing, snowshoeing...

✔ Take training for the Derby de la Meije very, very seriously.

☹ LOCALS DON'T

✘ Brag about what they've done that day.

✘ Spend money on ski clothes but save up for newer, fatter skis.

✘ Ignore the advice of the ski patrollers at the base of the gondola.

enough to have more than one, explore some longer itineraries with a guide and plenty of rope. Examples include: the couloirs off the Girose drag lift into the Romanche valley (Maison Neuve, Chirouze, Girose and Orcières); the three Couloirs du Lac on Chancel (Traverse, Banane and the hidden couloir); the Fréaux couloir in the forest; and skiing from Chirouze to St Christophe.

Moguls The whole mountain turns into bumps a few days after a storm as it's not groomed.

Trees The most accessible tree-skiing for bad-light days is from the top of the gondola down to P1 and the valleys on both sides of Chancelle. Explore the Bois de Fréaux in good visibility (with caution).

Book a guide It's essential to book a guide when visiting La Grave. The terrain is unpredictable and riddled with crevasses, seracs, cliffs and drops.

Kids Don't bring your children here, unless they're budding professional freeriders

Not to miss The SwallowMania testing weekend (February) and the Derby de la Meije (March).

Remember to avoid Ducking the rope on the left of the Chancel traverse and disappearing into the Fréaux forest – the huge ice cliffs at the bottom claim lives. Regularly.

Relive a famous moment Take part in the legendary Derby de la Meije. You might not be reliving someone else's moment but you'll relive it with your mates if you win (or just finish).

Best mountain restaurant There are only three mountain restaurants – **Refuge Chancel** arguably does the best food but **Le Haut-Dessus** has delicious cake, pizza and a sun terrace overlooking the glacier. People also return to the village for lunch.

Practicalities

> We don't try to create a product at La Grave, like some ski 'resorts'. Here we share a common spirit and love of the mountains.
>
> *Didier Grillet, La Grave local*

La Grave is a tiny, rugged mountaineering village in the heart of the Massif des Ecrins on the road between Briançon and Le Bourg d'Oisans. The mighty 3982 m La Meije towers above the village – the last great peak of the Alps to be conquered – its blue glaciers and vast crevasses offering a stark reminder that La Grave defies all the stereotypes of ski resorts.

Sleeping The **Edelweiss** (T T+33 (0)476-799093; hotel-edelweiss.com) is a central hotel with sauna and jacuzzi, while the **Castillan** (T+33 (0)476-799004; perso.wanadoo.fr/castillan/) opposite the gondola offers more basic accommodation. **Chalets de la Meije** (T+33 (0)476-799797; chaletdelameije.com) are well-equipped self-catering apartments near the gondola. Alternatively, try **La Chaumine** (T+33 (0)476-799028; hotel-lachaumine.com) just 3 km away in Ventelon or **Le Faranchin** (T+33 (0)476-799001) in Villar d'Arène, also 3 km from La Grave. **Hôtel des Alpes** (T+33 (0)476-110318; skierslodge.com) is La Grave's answer to luxury. Swedish/Turkish husband and wife team Pelle and Ayse have lived in La Grave for 20 years and run the Skiers Lodge, offering half-board packages in the renovated old hotel, including transfers and fully qualified guiding.

Eating Lou Ratel is the only bar and restaurant that stays open all year and is much loved by locals, serving up good food with a dose of gossip from the friendly owner, Michou. The **Edelweiss** has a great set menu and **Bois des Fées** does good basics. La Farenchin in Villar d'Arène is worth the short journey for traditional cuisine. The four-course dinners in the **Hôtel des Alpes** are excellent and accompanied by fine wines. Le Vieux Guide does good traditional food.

Au pair/crèche The ESF in neighbouring Le Chazelet accepts children from four years. Babysitting can be arranged through the tourist office.

Best après-ski La Grave doesn't do loud après action but chilled-out beers are enjoyed at **Bois des Fées** (popular with locals), **Edelweiss** and on the sunny terraces of **Hôtel des Alpes** and **Castillan**.

Bars and clubs Night-time action is generally limited to a good meal and quiet drinks unless you befriend some locals, who throw secret wild house parties. However, the **K2 Bar** in Hôtel des Alpes is popular and **Bois des Fées** often has live music.

Shopping There's an excellent delicatessen, bakery and supermarket. Le Vannoir in Villar d'Arène is a large general store with a pharmacy.

Hire shop/rental Twinner and Objectif Meige stock top-end equipment. **Ski Extreme** is nearer the lift and makes La Grave-branded clothes to prove you were here.

Lift tickets Buy passes at the gondola. **Castillan** and **Hôtel des Alpes** can organize passes for guests.

Health and wellbeing Edelweiss, Castillan, Hôtel des Alpes and Chalets de la Meije have saunas. Meije Massage (T+33 (0)609-646827) in Villar d'Arène offers various types of massage and will come to you.

Internet Edelweiss, Castillan and Hôtel des Alpes (including the K2 bar) have Wi-Fi. There are machines in the Bois des Fées.

Transfer options Take a bus from Grenoble and St Geoirs airport (vfd.fr). From Lyon Saint-Exupéry, get a bus to Grenoble (satobus.com), then take the VDF transfer.

You can also ski here ... Les Deux Alpes is linked with La Grave but not included in the ski pass (although La Grave is included in the Deux Alpes ski pass). Serre Chevalier, Alpe d'Huez and Montgenèvre are under 45 minutes' drive away.

If you like this ... try Chamonix ▶▶ *p126*, Andermatt ▶▶ *p273* and Zinal ▶▶ *p320*.

France La Grave

⊚ **OPENING TIMES**

Mid-Dec to early May: 0900-1650

Ⓢ **RESORT PRICES**

Week pass: €162

Day pass: €34

Season pass: €625

ⓘ **DIRECTORY**

Website: lagrave-lameije.com

Tourist office: T+33 (0)476-799005

Medical Centre: T+33 (0)476-799803

Lifts: T+33 (0)476-799109

Pisteurs: T+33 (0)892-680238

Taxi: T+33 (0)679-534567

SKICLUB.CO.UK

↘11 La Plagne

Town altitude 1250-2100 m	Highest lift 3250 m	Blacks 129	Terrain parks 3
Km to airport 75 km/194 km	Vertical drop 2000 m	Funicular/cable cars 1/3	Glühwein factor ★★☆
	Km of pistes 425 km		Ski in/ski out ★★☆
Airport Chambéry/ Lyon	Nursery areas 12	Gondolas/chairs 13/66	Environmental rating ★★★★☆
	Blues 35	Drags 54	
	Reds 66	Night skiing yes	

PROS

- ✓ Huge area.
- ✓ Uncrowded compared to Les Arcs.
- ✓ Great for beginners.

CONS

- ✗ Architecture leaves something to be desired.
- ✗ Might be too easy for some advanced skiers.

Extensive, uncrowded pistes, high altitude riding and access to the Paradiski area – La Plagne has much going for it (except the architecture).

There's no doubt that the profile of La Plagne has gone through the ceiling since the establishment of the Paradiski ski area. Previously overshadowed by its illustrious neighbour, Les Arcs, the added muscle of the Les Arcs region has hoisted La Plagne right up the ladder. Which is just as well, as La Plagne has long been underrated. Relatively flat topography makes it great for beginners and intermediates, while experts will love those Les Arcs links and some of the less well-known off-piste runs.

Beginners The majority of the runs in La Plagne are suitable for newbies. To start things off, head to the Roche de Mio, one cable car from Plagne Bellecôte. There's a restaurant at the top, and a really long motorway run back down (perfect for finding your feet and building confidence) plus awe-inspiring views to get you all jazzed up.

Intermediate You'll like the slopes and the lack of crowds, especially when compared to some of the busy runs in Les Arcs. Hit the winding tree runs in the Montchavin/Les Coches sector for long, winding pistes. They're great for carving your turns.

Expert The north face of Bellecôte is a known freerider haunt, while the glacier of Col de Nant is an incredible run that winds down to Laissonney and its cross-country tracks, before finishing at Champagny le Haut. Here you can catch the bus back to Champagny.

Powder Wait for the snow, hire a guide and then hit the off-piste runs down to Champagny.

Tuition El Pro Belle Plagne (T+33 (0)479-091162) and **ESF** (T+33 (0)479-090668) are based in Belle Plagne, while **Oxygène** (T+33 (0)479-090399) is the best bet in Plagne Centre.

Kids All ski schools offer kids' programmes, while the big holiday operators also offer kids' lessons in their packages.

Bad light Head over the valley to Peisey Vallandry, which has the best tree runs in the Paradiski area.

France La Plagne

☺ LOCALS DO

- ✓ Hit the moguls under the Bellecôte Bubble on the Roche de Mio glacier.
- ✓ Use the free bus service between all the resorts.

☹ LOCALS DON'T

- ✗ Stray too far off-piste if avalanche risk is high.
- ✗ Miss the last free bus and be forced into a long, cold walk.

Not to miss A visit to the **Tour de Glace** in the nearby Champagny le Haut valley. The 22-m-high ice tower designed for ice-climbing is the only one of its kind in Europe.

Remember to avoid The 1600 queues at the Bellecôte chairlift – make your decision before then, as this is a hideous bottleneck.

Relive a famous moment Hit the bobsleigh track, tackle the mono-bob, hit speeds of 90 kph and win your own gold medal, as occurred here in the 1992 Winter Olympics.

Best mountain restaurant La Mine (T+33 (0)479-090775), with its elegant dining room and open fireplace, is perhaps the best for 'serious' food.

Practicalities

La Plagne actually consists of 10 villages, each linked by roads, lifts and pistes and varying markedly in terms of altitude, attractiveness and services. Sleepy, more traditional villages like Montchavin and Les Coches sit lower down the mountain, while the bigger, more functional and decidedly uglier towns of Plagne Centre, Bellecôte and Aime-la-Plagne are located around 2000 m and provide excellent access to the almost endless terrain.

Sleeping Le Granges du Soleil (cgh-residences.com) is a new MGM four-star hotel offering equal doses of chic and spa comfort, all at 2050 m. A little cheaper is **Le Carlina** (T+33 (0)479-097846; carlina-belleplagne.com), with bright rooms and suites at €130 per person per night for half board in a double room. **Summit View** (T+44 (0)844-557 3118; snowline. co.uk) in Plagne Centre offer large family-friendly chalet rooms with an incredible piste-side location.

Eating Locals swear by **La Grolle** in Plagne Centre for amazing, locally produced and sourced restaurant food. In the charming village of Champagny en Vanoise, **Les Verdons Sud** (T+33 (0)621-543924) offers glacier views, a sun-drenched balcony and slow-cooked traditional cuisine. If you're in Belle Plagne, try the always busy, cheap and cheerful **Le Matafan** (T+33 (0)479-090919).

Au pair/crèche Ski Beat (skibeat.co.uk) offers childcare in the crèche below Chalet Perrier in Plagne 1800.

Bars and clubs Season workers and holidaymakers mix at **No'Bl'm** (No Problem) in Plagne Centre, where bands and DJs pump out cool music every night. **La Luna** is the other bar in the centre to hang out (and drink towers of beer), while in Aime-la-Plage try **La Montana**, a smallish bar with live music, themed evenings and sheepskins on the chairs.

Hire shop/rental Ski shops are abundant in all of the villages, especially on piste. Hit **Oxygène** (T+33 (0)479-090399) and **Ski Republic** (T+33 (0)479-071269) in Plagne Centre, both of which have been in operation for more than 15 years.

Shopping With so many villages there's plenty here from supermarkets to boutiques and speciality wine shops.

Health and wellbeing The **Centre Vita Plagne** (T+33 (0)479-090345) at Plagne Centre boasts a beauty area, physiotherapy, osteotherapy plus saunas, spas and qualified masseurs.

Down days with kids Head for the **Piste Olympic Bobsleigh** (T+33 (0)479-09127), which has a range of automated bobsleigh rides for all ages.

Internet Cyber Café in Plagne Centre by the shuttle bus stop is probably the most well known, but there are also various hot spots around all the resorts.

Transfer options Fly to Chambéry and take a bus (T+33 (0)479-544954), which takes about 75 minutes. Alternatively, fly to Lyon and take a taxi or bus (satobus-alpes.altibus.com) or fly to Grenoble then take a bus (T+33 (0)476-654848). Transfer time from both airports is about 2½ hours.

You can also ski here ... La Plagne is part of the Paradiski ski resort, linked to Les Arcs and Peisey Vallandry, covering an enormous 425 km of pistes.

If you like this ... try Val Thorens ▶▶ *p193*.

ⓘ **OPENING TIMES**

20 Dec to 25 Apr: 0900-1700

Ⓢ **RESORT PRICES (for Paradiski)**

Week pass: €216

Day pass: €47

Season pass: €935

ⓘ **DIRECTORY**

Website: la-plagne.com

Tourist office: T+33 (0)479-090201

Medical centre: T+33 (0)479-090466

Lift company: T+33 (0)479-080246

Taxi: T+33 (0)479-090341

France La Plagne

↘12 La Rosière

Town altitude 1850 m	Funicular/cable
Km to airport 170 km	cars 0/1
Airport Geneva	Gondolas/chairs 0/17
Highest lift 2641 m	Drags 17
Vertical drop 1465 m	Night skiing no
Km of pistes 150 km	Terrain parks 3
Nursery areas 3	Glühwein factor ★☆☆
Blues 30	Ski in/ski out ★★★
Reds 32	Environmental
Blacks 12	rating ★☆☆☆☆

A purpose-built ski village at 1850 m, a snow-sure altitude, La Rosière offers two massive snow bowls to ski – one in France, one in Italy.

La Rosière might lack the charm of a historical Alpine village, but the easy access to the main cable car does make up for this.

La Rosière has a couple of unique selling points that help to explain its enduring popularity. It enjoys glorious views over Mont Blanc and is set over two bowls spanning the border between France and Italy.

Beginners Complete beginners will begin on the nursery lifts in town before progressing to the straightforward blues accessed by the Roches Noire chair.

Intermediate The main La Rosière bowl is pretty much intermediate heaven, with red after red to explore.

Expert If you go over to La Thuile you'll find some more open reds and blues and also some extremely steep blacks that run down through the trees to the village. There's also an interesting off-piste area that is covered by the mountain security but not pisted or bashed in any way. Perfect for the budding extremist.

 OPENING TIMES
Early Dec to late Apr: 0845-1645

RESORT PRICES
Week pass: €161
Day pass: €34
Season pass: €650

DIRECTORY
Website: larosiere.net
Tourist office: T+33 (0)479-068051
Medical centre: T+33 (0)479-068909
Pisteurs: T+33 (0)479-401200
Taxi: T+33 (0)626-459416

Tuition English-speaking ESF (esflarosiere.com) is probably the most convenient school in town.

Kids Kids will love this resort. There are three nursery slopes and the blues are easily accessible.

Bad light Stay on the south-facing slopes and don't venture to the opposite side of the ski area.

Not to miss ESF Ski Show every Monday night. Check out the ski rugby, (almost) naked synchronized skiing and ski freestyle jumping. Free *vin chaud*, hot chocolate and taxis all evening.

Remember to avoid Getting stuck in La Thuile at the end of the day.

Practicalities

Most hotels, guesthouses and chalets are within walking distance. It is mainly geared up for families, although you'll find some nightlife if you search hard enough.

Sleeping Chalet Matsuzaka (T+33 (0)479-075313) is inspired by Japanese ski lodges and chalets and has a zen-like atmosphere. Half-board **Le Relais du Petit San Bernard** (T+33 (0)479-068048; petit-saint-bernard.com) suits medium budgets. Brit-run **Snow Crazy** (snowcrazy.co.uk) offer high-end catered chalets.

Eating The Génépi (T+33 (0)479-075209) is probably the best place to sample the local cuisine with high quality versions of all the French alpine classics on the menu. **Les Marmottes** (T+33 (0)479-401988) is also very good – try the delicious *escaloppe Marguerite*.

Bars and clubs La Rosière isn't set up for major nightlife attractions and is fairly quiet in that respect. However **Bar Fusion** on the main drag has a good atmosphere and **La Grange** and **Kitzbuhel** in Eucherts are fun.

Kids The ESF (esflarosiere.com) offer a 'Baby Club' for ages 18 months to three, as well as dedicated lessons for children.

Transfer options Resort Hoppa (resorthoppa.com) take care of transfers from Bourg and airports further afield. **Airport Transfer Service** (a-t-s.net) is also an old Alpine stalwart.

You can also ski here ... La Rosière is linked to La Thuile, making two countries in one day obligatory!

If you like this ... try Châtel ▶▶ *p131*, Sauze d'Oulx ▶▶ *p240*, Åre ▶▶ *p260*.

↘13 La Tania

Town altitude 1400 m	Funicular/cable
Km to airport 128 km	cars 0/6
Airport Geneva	Gondolas/chairs 33/69
Highest lift 3200 m	Drags 72
Vertical drop 1800 m	Night skiing no
Km of pistes 600 km	Terrain parks 9
Nursery areas 3	Glühwein factor ★★☆
Blues 121	Ski in/ski out ★★★
Reds 114	Environmental
Blacks 33	rating ★☆☆☆☆

La Tania is a great, low-key way to experience the incredible skiing of the Trois Vallées.

Pretty La Tania nestles in the forest between Méribel and Courchevel, yet enjoys quick links to both of them.

La Tania's own pistes are great fun, but it is the links to the Trois Vallées that enable the resort to punch well above its weight. Lifts take you to Méribel and Courchevel with ease should you get bored with what's on offer in the immediate vicinity.

Beginners La Tania is a good place to get to grips with skiing, with a beginners' area in the village and then wide, easy blues to progress to. For the more confident, there are some fun pistes at La Loze. Try to build up to the home run by week's end.

Intermediate Take the lift to the Col de la Loze and head back down towards La Tania for some quick, tree-lined pistes – this is fantastic fun. Later, explore Courchevel's many options.

Expert The front face, underneath the Dou les Lanches chair, has some very challenging terrain if there is fresh snow. Othewise, grab a Trois Vallées lift map and get exploring. The Chanrossa chair near the Saulire is a good place to seek out some steeps.

Tuition Magic Snowsports Academy (magicinmotion.co.uk) is a Trois Vallées stalwart.

Bad light La Tania is the ace up the Trois Vallées' sleeve during bad weather: its low, tree-lined slopes are perfect for retaining visibility.

Not to miss High-speed turns down the main piste at the end of the day, followed by a cold beer outside the ski lodge.

Remember to avoid Getting stuck in the next valley after the lifts close. It's a long taxi ride back to Méribel.

Practicalities

Built to provide accommodation for the 1992 Olympics, subtle development has made it the dark horse of the Trois Vallées area and especially suits families and couples.

Sleeping The **Telemark** (hoteltelemark. com), with its stylish modern rooms, is our favourite hotel, while **Le Montana** (htelelmontana.com) is a solid three-star hotel 100 m from the lift. **Ski Magic** (skimagic.co.uk) offers a range of catered chalets.

Eating **Ski Lodge** (publeskilodge.com) is a perennial favourite for pub grub, although the **Telemark** restaurant offers a gourmet experience. Newcomer **La Taiga** (easytaiga.com) is also popular.

Bars and clubs The **Ski Lodge** is the social hub of La Tania for après-ski and bands. For later nights, head to Méribel and **Dick's Tea Bar**. The **Chrome Bar** is another newcomer attracting the crowds.

Hire shop/rental Trois Vallées specialists **Ski Higher** (skihigher.com) have a shop in town, as well as others in Méribel and Courchevel.

Transfer options Transfers from Geneva and Lyon are easy to come by thanks to the services of a raft of companies. We like long-time local residents **Snowbound Transfers** (snowboundtransfers.com).

You can also ski here ... Full links to the Trois Vallées network.

If you like this ... try Bansko ▶▶ *p104*, Hemsedal ▶▶ *p256*, Ste Foy ▶▶ *p178*.

◉ OPENING TIMES
20 Dec to 17 Apr: 0900-1630/1700

⑤ RESORT PRICES (Trois Vallées)
Week pass: €225
Day pass: €45
Season pass: €970

① DIRECTORY
Website: latania.co.uk
Tourist office: T+33 (0)479-084040
Medical centre: T+33 (0)479-084354
Pisteurs: T+33 (0)479-080409
Taxi: T+33 (0)479-086510

France La Tania

↘14 Les Arcs

Town altitude 800 m (Bourg Saint Maurice) – 2000 m (Arc 2000)	Highest lift 3250 m	Funicular/cable cars 1/3	Glühwein factor ★★☆
Km to airport 75 km/194 km	Vertical drop various	Gondolas/chairs 13/66	Ski in/ski out ★★★
Airport Chambéry/ Lyon	Km of pistes 425 km	Drags 54	Environmental rating ★★★★☆
	Nursery areas 12	Night skiing yes	
	Blues 35	Terrain parks 3	
	Reds 66		
	Blacks 129		

PROS

- ✔ Huge area.
- ✔ Slick infrastructure.
- ✔ Massively varied terrain.

CONS

- ✖ 1950 and 2000 are somewhat isolated from front side of mountain.
- ✖ February is usually ridiculously busy.

Huge amounts of varied terrain, coupled with new investment, means this popular French resort is re-establishing itself as a major player.

Les Arcs consists of several villages, all located at different levels. Starting down the mountain, the valley town of Bourg St Maurice is linked to the mountain via a quick funicular ride and also to the other towns of 1600, 1800, 1950 and 2000. On either side, the villages of Vallandry and Villaroger, plus other small hamlets, make up Les Arcs. The newest resort is 1950, which architecturally appears to have been parachuted in

from Whistler or another Intrawest resort. Still, each resort has its own individual feel, is well serviced and, most importantly, gives easy access to the incredible terrain on offer at Les Arcs.

The link with La Plagne has certainly changed the dynamic of Les Arcs, even if the 2007-08 season was a write-off thanks to technical difficulties with the linking cable car. So how relevant is the new Paradiski for the average skier? The answer really depends on your own personal level. Certainly advanced and adventurous intermediates will find much to enjoy, not least being able to cover some serious ground. For the beginner, the huge amount of accessible terrain is probably of less importance than the large number of quick, comfy chairlifts that have recently been brought into service. It makes learning here something of a pleasure, and is another reason why Les Arcs is considered to be one of France's very best.

Beginner The consensus seems to be that 1800 offers the easiest terrain for complete beginners, and it is true that it is very easy to get to grips here thanks to the simple lift layout. Chantel 2 and Villards 25 should ease you in. Elsewhere, there are simple blues in each of the other villages to get you started. We're also big fans of the large number of mellow blues in the middle valley, especially the meandering Vallée de l'Arc, so build up to this during the week. It is a great long run.

Intermediate In all honesty, Les Arcs is heaven for anyone with a thirst for adventure and some basic techniques under the skis. The area is enormous, well planned and slickly run so grab a map and get exploring.

Expert You'll want to explore the varied terrain off the top of the Aiguille Rouge, which is where you'll find some of the most notable blacks and in-bounds steeps. But for top-level skiers the real draw here is the variety of terrain, as a visit to Peisey and Vallandry will attest. Here you'll find some tight, quick tree runs as well as some other long runs.

Powder Yet again Les Arcs scores, thanks to some well-worked powder runs both in and out of bounds. Probably the easiest to access is the varied terrain

☺LOCALS DO

- ✔ Either live or shop in Bourg – it is far cheaper.
- ✔ Explore La Plagne as well.
- ✔ Hit the mogul hills under the Comborcière chairlift.

☹LOCALS DON'T

- ✖ Drive up to the resort from Bourg – use the funicular.
- ✖ Try going anywhere by road on a Saturday – the traffic can be terrible.
- ✖ Stay in one part of the mountain – they really do know how to use the massive area on offer.

underneath 'Chair 69' as it is known locally. You can pick your line down on the way up.

Trees Definitely head to Peisey and Vallandry in bad light. The tree coverage here is excellent, particularly around chairs 74, 68 and 61. You could easily spend a day exploring these areas.

Moguls While anything marked red or black on the piste map is likely to be mogully a couple of days after a fall, the best moguls are to be found on the Grand Col.

Book a guide ESF Arc 2000 (T+33 (0)479-074752), **Arc Adventures** (T+33 (0)479-042572) and **Spirit 1950** (T+33 (0)479-042572) all have over 30 experienced guides to get you in the best possible position in this huge area.

Tuition The many ski schools offer similarly priced tuition for all levels, with the larger schools more likely to provide English-speaking instructors.

Kids Children under six get a free pass when accompanied by an adult. Check out the Milka forest above 1800 and even the baby jumps in the park!

Bad light If the mountain is closed, head down to Bourg for a wander and a coffee.

Not to miss The Columbia Speed Flying Pro, held in February, is the flagship competition in this revolutionary sport that combines snowsports and flying. Les Arc is one of only three resorts to have a designated area for the sport.

Remember to avoid Anything off the back of the Aiguille Rouge and above Villaroger is National Park. If you're in there without a pisteur, you'll be fined.

Relive a famous moment Les Arcs hosted the final climb of the 1996 Tour de France, when Miguel Indurain snapped for the first time in five years as the Spaniard, seeking a record sixth consecutive win, trailed home by three minutes and lost the race.

Pitstop and sunbathe Locals all seem to point to the **Bar Mont Blanc** in Vallandry. There's a great sunny terrace, and good food and beer. Take the Grizzly lift back to 1800 once you're done.

Best mountain restaurant Former bear-hunting lodge **Belliou La Fumée** (T+33 (0)479-072913), in the valley of Arc 2000, is a favourite establishment for those in the know. A rough slate roof, stone walls and big fireplaces create just the right atmosphere for Jean-Pierre Merie's traditional cooking.

REP IN RESORT # Practicalities

Sleeping Arc 1950, the newest and easiest on the eye of all the resorts, tends to offer the better high-end accommodation. There's a flash new **Radisson Resort** (hotels.radissonsas.com) there, with a pool and ski in/ski out access, while **Le Manoir Savoir** and the **Chalet des Lys** (T+33 (0)479-231000) are two brand new ski-in/ski-out hotels that offer a chic country atmosphere. With over 750 apartments available in 1950, all owned by **HMC hotels** (hmc-hotels.com), there is also no shortage of quality apartments. More affordable accommodation is on offer in the other villages. In 1800, the best bet is the **Grand Hôtel Mercure** (T+33 (0)479-076500), while in Vallandry the **Chalet Himalaya** (T+33 (0)479-041566) is a renovated 17th-century farmhouse that sleeps up to 20 people with seven en-suite bedrooms. The cheapest options are in Bourg Saint Maurice, which is why most *saisonnaires* tend to live and commute from there. **Chillchalet** (chillchalet.com) offers great accommodation in contemporary surroundings, with good food too. At the other end of the spectrum, **Chalet Richermoz** (chaletrichermoz.com) in Peisey Nancroix offers luxury for up to 20 people and has the usual sauna/massage facilities you expect at this price range.

Eating At the top end, cosy **Le Chalet de l'Arcelle** in Arc 1600 is a gastronomic delight, while for those craving seafood the **Bergerie de Raphaël** in Vallandry specializes in crayfish (chose your own from the tank) and Savoyard cuisine. The **Mountain Café** is a Les Arcs favourite, serving good Tex-Mex in a great atmosphere. For a sunny afternoon try **Mamie Crêpe**, while the Italian food at **Casa Mia** in 1800 is a worker favourite. For local specialities we recommend **La Santaline**.

Au pair/crèche SafeHands France (T+33 (0)479-041834) offer crèche services in all of the Les Arc villages.

Best après-ski 1800 tends to get most of the action, with **Le Gabotte, Ambiente** and **Benji's Bar** always full. In 2000 we recommend **Whistler's Dream** and **Red Rock**, both of which do great food.

Bars and clubs **Club ARC 1950** opens till 0400 and hosts the best DJs on the mountain, while **Le Chalet de Luigi** – a restaurant with a cool bar and nightclub, **Le Bachal** – has the potential to keep you off the mountain till quite late the next day.

Hire shop/rental Pretty much every village has a good variety of shop and rental available, with modern equipment and reliable instructors and good local guides.

Lift tickets There is a quite bewildering number of ticket permutations available thanks to the establishment of the Paradiski. Your best bet is to check lesarcs.com before your trip to try and work out which pass will suit you best.

Shopping There are the usual resort facilities in Les Arcs – think pricey souvenir shops – but much more choice and value down in Bourg. Self-caterers should definitely head down the valley to the huge **Super U**.

Health and wellbeing For pampering, head to the **Spas and Beauté Montagne** centre at **Les Granges du Soleil** (cgh-residences.com) which offers personalized treatments and hydro-massage baths.

Down days with kids Take the children for a dogsled ride at Arc 2000. **Arctik Adventures** (T+33 (0)616-032401) let you explore the amazing countryside around Villaroger in the best possible way.

Internet There is Wi-Fi and/or internet points in most hotels (especially in 1950).

Transfer options Fly to Chambéry and take a bus (T+33 (0)479-544954), which takes about 75 minutes. Alternatively, fly to Lyon and take a taxi or bus (satobus-alpes.altibus.com) or fly to Grenoble then take a bus (T+33 (0)476-654848). Transfer time from both airports is about 2½ hours. If travelling from the UK, there is a direct Eurostar (T+44 (0)870-518 6186) connection from Waterloo to Bourg which takes eight hours.

You can also ski here ... Easy access to La Plagne and the Paradiski area, while day trips to Tigne, Val d'Isère and the Trois Vallées are possible.

If you like this ... try Avoriaz ▶▶ *p123*, Serre Chevalier ▶▶ *p180*.

© **OPENING TIMES**

20 Dec to 25 Apr: 0900-1700

⑤ **RESORT PRICES (Paradiski)**

Week pass: €216

Week pass: €47

Week pass: €935

ℹ **DIRECTORY**

Website: lesarcs.com

Medical centre: T+33 (0)479- 070988

Pisteurs: T+33 (0)479-078566

Taxi: T+33 (0)686-242383

↘15 Les Contamines

Town altitude 1200 m	Km of pistes 120 km	Funicular/cable cars 0/0	Terrain parks 3
Km to airport 57 km	Nursery areas 2	Gondolas/chairs 4/9	Glühwein factor ★☆☆
Airport Geneva	Blues 17	Drags 11	Ski in/ski out ☆☆☆
Highest lift 2500 m	Reds 17	Night skiing yes	Environmental rating ★★★☆☆
Vertical drop 1336 m	Blacks 10		

PROS

- ✓ Extremely friendly.
- ✓ Quiet slopes.

CONS

- ✗ The town is spread along a 4-km road so it's probably best to take a car.
- ✗ Speaking French is an advantage.
- ✗ Not great for party animals.

This small, family-friendly resort is often overlooked, but is perfect if you like quiet and don't mind limited entertainment.

⊙ OPENING TIMES

Late Dec to late Apr: 0900-1630

⊛ RESORT PRICES

Week pass: €152.50

Day pass: €30.50

⊙ DIRECTORY

Website: lescontamines.com

Tourist office: T+33 (0)450-470158

Medical centre: T+33 (0)450-470382

Pisteurs: T+33 (0)892-680274

Taxi: T+33 (0)450-780533

Les Contamines hides a surprising amount of ski terrain behind a relatively small village. The majority of visitors come from nearby resorts, so you tend to find a lot of French locals on the slopes rather than holidaying Brits. With the lifts located outside the village, it isn't really ski in/ski out. But you can take the lift system right to the top of the Aiguille Croche, where the views are magnificent, and ski all the way back to the car park. It's also extremely easy to access Hauteluce-les-Contamines on the other side of the mountain, which has some great blue and red runs.

Beginners For absolute beginners, try Dahu and Morgiers in the village. Up the mountain, the long blue Coins from TSD Tierces is wide and not too steep, so build your confidence here.

Intermediate Start at the Montjoie to build your confidence. Advanced intermediates will enjoy exploring the nearby Evasion ski area with its better range of reds and easier blacks.

Expert You'll only truly be able to make the most of the amazing off-piste with a guide. There's some really challenging terrain just off Veleray and Aiguille Croche and most advanced skiers have a field day on black run Liaison-Rebans.

Tuition International ski school (T+33 (0)450-915881; snowsession.com) provides tuition for adults and children.

Bad light Stick to the lower pistes or head to the half-pipe and watch the locals freestyling.

Not to miss The floodlit half-pipe in the village centre hosts various events throughout the year.

Remember to avoid The long cat-track Retour Gorge back to the car park at the La Gorge lift station.

Practicalities ⊙⊙⊘⊞

Sleeping La Ferme du Bon Papa (T+33 (0)450-903328) has pretty rooms and prepares an excellent continental breakfast, while local hotels La Chemenaz (T+33 (0)450-470244) and Le Christiania (T+33 (0)450-470272) welcome families and pets. It might be worth getting in touch with the tourist office before you go as they offer some great all-inclusive packs.

Eating Trendy new eatery L'Oà la Bouche (T+33 (0)450-478167) allows you to mix gastronomic dining and a great wine list with the more traditional cuisine served in Auberge de Columbaz (T+33 (0)450-470150) and L'Air du Temps (T+33 (0)450-470692). For late-night pizza try La Fringale (T+33 (0)450-477729).

Bars and clubs Not much nightlife, but for a change of scenery head to Le Saxo, where they distil their own rum, or Auberge du Télé, which is open till 2300 and has 'aperitif-concerts' on Thursday nights.

Kids La Galipette day-care chalet fulfils all childcare needs – book through the tourist office.

Hire shop/rental Lots of ski shops in town so prices are competitive.

Transfer options Sat Bus (T+33 (0)450-780533; sat-montblanc.com) offer return travel from Geneva airport straight to Les Contamines tourist office.

You can also ski here ... No local partners, but Chamonix, Megève and Courmayeur are close.

If you like this ... try La Clusaz ▶▶ p138.

↘16 Les Carroz

Town altitude 1140 m	Km of pistes 265 km	Funicular/cable	Terrain parks no
Km to airport 55 km	Nursery areas 13	cars 0/1	Glühwein factor ★★☆
Airport Geneva	Blues 41	Gondolas/chairs 1/6	Ski in/ski out ☆☆☆
Highest lift 2500 m	Reds 56	Drags 7	Environmental
Vertical drop 1340 m	Blacks 15	Night skiing yes	rating n/a

This authentic village offers extensive mid-altitude skiing, with Mont Blanc as the backdrop, close to Geneva and Chamonix.

Practicalities

Created in 1936 after the installation of its first drag lift, Les Carroz is a modern resort that has managed to retain its character, with farms, chalets and chapels providing the setting for a relaxed, year-round social scene.

Sleeping Hôtel Arbaron (T+33 (0)450-900267) is family friendly with open fires, while the eight-bedroom **Hôtel les Servages d'Armelle** (T+33 (0)450-900162) offers quiet, Alpine charm. Self-catering rental agencies include **Immobili re Renand** (immorenand. com/), **Agence Altimmo** (altimmo-lescarroz.com) and **Carroz Immobilier** (carroz-immobilier.com), or book accommodation direct through the tourist office.

Eating Like most Haute Savoie resorts, French and Savoyard cuisine dominates. In the town square, the **Agora** (T+33 (0)450-900078) is reasonably priced and popular. **Crêperie Bretonne** (T+33 (0)450-900764) makes exquisite crêpes and cakes. **Les Servages** (T+33 (0)450-900162) is prestigious, with diners making the journey from Geneva, so it's worth booking.

Bars and clubs Aux Petits Oignons has a lounge bar, sun terrace and speed dating! **Carpe Diem** serves cocktails with a side of snooker. **Le Marlow** is a relaxed pub, with lively happy hours. There is also **Le Club** for late nights.

Hire shop/rental It all happens on the Route des Moulins: take your pick from **Abondance Ski Twinner** (T+33 (0)450-902334), **Alex Sport** (T+33 (0)450-900112), **Ambiance Carroz** (T+33 (0)450-536174) and **Carroz Sports** (T+33 (0)450-900025).

Transfer options Buses run from Geneva to the resort – contact the airport (gva.ch) for details. You can also get the train to Cluses (sncf.fr), then a bus (alpbus-fournier.com). Private transfers can be arranged with **easyJet** (easyjet.co.uk), **ATS** (a-t-s.net) and **Rolling Road** (rrtransfers.com).

You can also ski here ... Flaine, Samoëns, Morillon and Sixt-Fer-à-Cheval, plus Chamonix.

If you like this ... try Khutai ▶▶ *p65*, Levi ▶▶ *p252*.

With the whole of the Grand Massif area – the third largest interconnected ski domain in the French Alps – accessible via one chairlift, Les Carroz offers extensive terrain, although we find it most suited to intermediates. The larger ski area gives it added punch, with spectacular powder bowls if you head towards Flaine or Samoëns.

Beginners For long green runs head to the Flaine bowl, or Molliachets is a mellow green that crosses Les Carroz. Take the Moilliets chairlift then either the windy Blanchot run, or the long Sarbotte trail back to the village.

Intermediate For an easy tour, try the blue Lous Darbes Haut and Sarbotte pistes. Red runs Cupoire and Timalets are a bit more challenging.

Expert The Flaine bowl has some spectacular routes, while the mogul hounds should head towards the Diamant Noir.

Tuition ESF (T+33 (0)450-900238) or **Nouvelle Dimension** (T+33 (0)450-903603).

Remember to avoid Leaving it too late to get back from Flaine as it can take two hours, with no shuttles between resorts.

◉ OPENING TIMES
Early Dec to late Apr: 0830-1730
⑤ RESORT PRICES
Week pass: local €154.80/area €187.20
Day pass: local €30/area €38
Season pass: local €510/area €798
① DIRECTORY
Website: lescarroz.com
Tourist office: T+33 (0)450-900004
Medical centre: T+33 (0)450-903843
Police: T+33 (0)450-900041
Taxi: T+33 (0)450-900060

France Les Carroz

↘17 Les Deux Alpes

Town altitude 1650 m	Km of pistes 225 km	Funicular/cable	Terrain parks 2
Km to airport 110 km	Nursery areas 3	cars 1/3	Glühwein factor ★★★
Airport Grenoble	Blues 45	Gondolas/chairs 2/23	Ski in/ski out ★★★
Highest lift 3568 m	Reds 18	Drags 19	Environmental
Vertical drop 2298 m	Blacks 14	Night skiing yes	rating ★★★★☆

PROS

- ✔ Loads of challenging off-piste, a world-class terrain park and complimentary 'Free Respect' avalanche-awareness courses.
- ✔ Large glacier suits all skiing abilities and is snow-secure throughout the season.

CONS

- ✘ The young, predominantly Brit party element won't appeal to everyone.
- ✘ Lift queues (going up and coming down) can be endless, particularly at weekends.
- ✘ Lack of trees for bad-light days.

A great resort for beginners, experts, freestylers and party animals – popular with Brits.

The name Les Deux Alpes reflects the shared history of two sheep-grazing villages (or *alpages*) – Venosc and Mont de Lans. Today the villages are joined as one resort by way of a 2-km strip of hotels, bars and shops that runs along a narrow plateau.

The result is a lively entertainment highway, vaguely reminiscent of towns in the Canary Islands.

Les Deux Alpes has nearly as many black runs as reds, 1400 ha of off-piste terrain with vertical drops of over 2000 m and one of Europe's best terrain parks. Add to this one of Europe's largest glaciers and a link with La Grave and its appeal to expert skiers is obvious. The mountain's also well suited to families and beginners although offers slightly less to intermediate skiers.

Beginners Several short lifts at the base of the village access nursery runs (four lifts are free). There are lots of gentle runs up on the glacier, although less confident novices won't like the busy green down to the village, making a lift down the only option. Pied Montet and La Fée offer gentle, less crowded runs.

Intermediate Tentative intermediates will thrive on the gentle, open glacial slopes but confident intermediates who haven't fully conquered off-piste might find the limited amount of (crowded) terrain disappointing. They should try the red Fée run and the relatively steep Super Diable, which leads into Descente, practise powder technique on the Dôme red on the glacier and learn some tricks in the terrain park.

Expert You're spoiled for choice here. Favourite routes include freeriding down the Clots de Chalance into the Fée bowl, the Vallons Diable itinerary and North Rachas area by Grand Couloir from Tête Moute.

Powder The La Fée bowl offers endless accessible powder hits with different angles. It's often opened late for avalanche sweeping, in which case

warm up with great lines off La Déversoir under the Thuit chair and on the Sapins and L'Y runs into town.

Trees Pretty limited with two red runs down to the small satellite villages of Bons and Mont de Lans.

Moguls The Grand Couloir black under the Bellecombes chair and L'Y into town.

Book a guide As always, it's essential to book a guide when skiing off-piste on a glacier. There are some really challenging itineraries here – skiing across to La Grave or St Christophe are must-dos for experts. Guides love the Pylone Electrique couloir – apparently it's 'electrifying'.

Tuition There are nearly 300 ski instructors and 10 high-mountain guides working for 10 ski schools. British-run **EasiSki**, which caters for small private group lessons (maximum of four people), and **European Ski School** are popular.

Kids The resort caters very well for children, with four free lifts, free skiing for kids under five, three nursery areas, a kids' freestyle park and even an annual week-long children's event in April.

Bad light Given the lack of trees, head for Serre Chevalier.

Not to miss The free **Respect** avalanche awareness and mountain safety programme. There's a free seminar on Monday evenings and daytime guiding on Tuesday.

☺ **LOCALS DO**

☻ Bring their own lunch and eat it on the hill.

☻ Take part in the Mondial du Ski testing weekend.

☻ Use the terrain park.

☹ **LOCALS DON'T**

☒ Sleep late on a powder day.

☒ Advise anyone to ski to La Grave without a guide.

Remember to avoid Skiing over to La Grave if you're not an advanced skier.

Relive a famous moment Joseph Martin invented the ski pass in Les Deux Alpes in 1958 – it cost FR2.50

Pitstop and sunbathe Le Piano Bar at Le Panoramic by Toura kicks off the afternoon with a live DJ, **La Patache** at Les Crêtes has a popular sun terrace and **Les Glaciers** has awesome views.

Best mountain restaurant La Bergerie **Kanata** on Pied Moutet serves colossal

helpings of excellent food. Escape the crowds on the main mountain in **Chalet de la Fée** or nip down to **Le Côte Brune** hotel by the Jandri base station for good food on a sunny terrace.

Practicalities

Venosc, at the southern end, boasts the most character, best hotels, bars and restaurants, and has the least through traffic. It also accesses the Diable gondola. The main Jandri Express gondola is in the centre of town near many of the apartments.

Sleeping If you want to break the bank, Chalet Mounier (T+33 (0)476-805690; chalet-mounier.com) was built by Pierre Balme, a Venosc native, in the late 1870s to attract tourists in the summer. Today the beautifully maintained and extended chalet has large rooms, excellent facilities and is tucked away in a quiet spot in Venosc. Otherwise, there's a bewildering choice of accommodation here – let Peak Retreats (peakretreats.co.uk) or the key tour operators (**Crystal, Inghams**) advise you. Hotel Le Côte Brune (T+33 (0)476-805489; hotel-cotebrune. com) is a three-minute walk from the Jandri gondola, very cosy and does great food. Our pick of apartments is the slick Le Cortina (peakretreats.co.uk).

Eating Visitors to Les Deux Alpes will not go hungry. **Crêpes à Gogo** is lively and does great basics, **La Spaghetteria** is excellent value and **Le Blue Salmon** offers everything from moules to fondue. Le Cellier (Venosc) has a great kids' menu while Smithy's Tavern does fajitas and burgers washed down with racks of vodka. Le P'tit Polyte in Chalet Mounier offers modern French cuisine using local produce accompanied by excellent wines.

The chef at L'Alisier, also in Venosc, adapts his menu to reflect seasonal foods.

Au pair/crèche The Clos des Fonds crèche (6-23 months), Bonhomme de Neige day nursery (2-6 years) and Sports Centre (6-17 years).

Best après-ski Après kicks off at Smokey Joe's by the Jandri, in Crêpes à Gogo and at the Brit hang-outs Smithy's Tavern, The Red Frog and Pub Ours Blanc.

Bars and clubs There are 30 bars packed into the 2-km stretch of Les Deux Alpes and nightlife is boisterous. The bars above continue till late, as do Pub Le Windsor, Le Brésilien and The Secret. L'Avalanche next to Smithy's is the best disco.

Hire shop/rental There's a wide choice of rental shops, with very similar prices. Given that your accommodation will be ski in/ski out, choose one that's most convenient for you.

Lift tickets Buy them at the lift stations.

Shopping There are two good supermarkets either side of town. Le Vieux Chalet is best for local meats, cheeses and wine.

Health and wellbeing The Tanking Centre, open 1500-2000, has a gym, spa, sauna and hammam. The luxurious Le Spa at Chalet Mounier is open to non-residents but you have to make an appointment.

Down days with kids Go as foot passengers on a Croisière Blanche excursion – a tracked minibus that takes you up to 3600 m – and visit the Ice Caves on the way back down.

Internet There's Wi-Fi at the tourist office and Pub Le Windsor and machines at the Rip Curl Café.

Transfer options Fly to Grenoble Isère airport and book a shuttle directly to the resort (route-oisans.com) or transfer to Grenoble coach station by bus and from there by coach (transisere.fr).

You can also ski here ... Alpe d'Huez, La Grave, Serre Chevalier, Puy St Vincent, the Milky Way.

If you like this ... try Mayrhofen ▶▶ *p75*, Sölden ▶▶ *p83*, Flims Laax ▶▶ *p287*.

⊙ OPENING TIMES

End Nov to end Apr: 0900-1700

⑤ RESORT PRICES

Week pass: €172

Day pass: €36.40

Season pass: €700

ⓘ DIRECTORY

Website: les2alpes.com

Tourist office: T+33 (0)476-797501

Medical centre: T+33 (0)476-792896

Lifts: T+33 (0)476-797500

Taxi: T+33 (0)476-800697

↘18 Les Gets

Town altitude	1172 m	Km of pistes	650 km	Funicular/cable cars	0/4	Terrain parks	9
Km to airport	68 km	Nursery areas	2	Gondolas/chairs	9/80	Glühwein factor	★☆☆
Airport	Geneva	Blues	112	Drags	102	Ski in/ski out	★★☆
Highest lift	2002 m	Reds	104	Night skiing	yes	Environmental rating	★★★★★
Vertical drop	830 m	Blacks	28				

PROS

- ✅ Friendly, attractive resort that's ideal for families.
- ✅ Town and slopes are quiet in comparison to other Portes du Soleil resorts.

CONS

- ❌ Access to Portes du Soleil, although feasible, is not particularly easy.
- ❌ Fairly limited expert skiing.
- ❌ Low altitude can mean unreliable snow cover.

A charming village with good local skiing and access to the Portes du Soleil ski area.

☺ **LOCALS DO**

- ✅ Call the Chavannes gondola the 'red egg'.
- ✅ Take the Chavannes Express rather than the Chavannes gondola and de la Crois chair, which is painfully slow.

☹ **LOCALS DON'T**

- ❌ Ski on Chavannes when it's busy.
- ❌ Access the Portes du Soleil area by lift – take the bus.

Les Gets shares its local ski area with Morzine and is divided into two areas: Chavannes (linked to Morzine) and Mont-Chéry. Both areas offer tree-lined blues and reds, although Mont-Chéry is quieter with slightly more challenging terrain. The quickest way to reach the Portes du Soleil ski area is by ski bus to the gondola at Les Prodains, which goes straight to Avoriaz, although you can reach the circuit by lift from Chavannes.

Beginners Take the Chavannes Express to the greens up top and blues into town. The blues off La Rosta and Pointe de la Turche are gentle and sunny. Explore Morzine's blues as well, returning to Les Gets on the long blue Crocus run.

Intermediate Warm up on Chavannes' long blues before tackling the reds and blacks on Mont-Chéry. Les Gets is a great resort in which to build on skills: tree-skiing on La Turche; bumps under the Nauchets Express lift to the skier's right of Ambresalles; carving on the Mont-Chéry reds; and developing stamina on a Portes du Soleil circuit.

Expert There's great tree-skiing, easily accessible off-piste (particularly over towards Nyon) and some challenging blacks (particularly on Mont-Chéry). There are loads of off-piste cut-throughs to find; we particularly like exploring under the little-used Perri res Express up to La Turche.

Powder Les Gets is quieter than other Portes du Soleil resorts, meaning powder doesn't get tracked out as quickly. Head for the Chavannes bowl, where favourite runs include: under the Chavannes gondola; dropping into a small bowl from Ranfoilly into the Tetras red and down to the Charalez Express; and the Combe d'Angolon, accessed from the Chamossière chair.

Moguls The black Yeti and Myrtilles on Chavannes and Mouflon and Chevreuil on Mont-Chéry.

Tuition ESF and 360 International are both good. The British Alpine Ski & Snowboard School (BASS) teaches small groups – book early to get in.

France Les Gets

Kids ESF runs **Jardins des Neiges** (three to five years) and **Club des P'tits Montagnys** (four to 12 years). **Ile des Enfants** teaches kids from three while BASS instructors are all English-speaking.

Bad light You're in a good place – stick to the Rosta, Grains d'Or Express and Ranfoilly Express lifts to access the best tree runs, like Chavanne's blue Violettes and lower La Turche pistes.

Not to miss Coming to Les Gets if your children love skiing as much as you do.

Remember to avoid Missing out on a 10% discount on 6-14 day Les Gets/Morzine ski passes if you're in a group of four or more – buy on sagets.fr before you arrive.

Relive a famous moment The **Ferme de Moudon** chalet in Les Gets (descent.co.uk) featured in the most watched episode of Channel 4's *Grand Designs Abroad*.

Best mountain restaurant They're all good but **Les Lhotty's** has spectacular views and **La Rossetaz** does colossal, affordable baguettes.

France Les Gets

OPENING TIMES

20 Dec to 3 Apr: 0830-1630

RESORT PRICES

Week pass: €216

Day pass: €47

Season pass: €935

DIRECTORY

Website: lesgets.com

Tourist office: T+33 (0)450-758080

Medical centre: T+33 (0)450-758070

Pisteurs: T+33 (0)450-758099

Taxi: T+33 (0)450-757088

Practicalities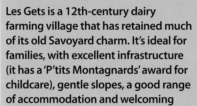

Les Gets is a 12th-century dairy farming village that has retained much of its old Savoyard charm. It's ideal for families, with excellent infrastructure (it has a 'P'tits Montagnards' award for childcare), gentle slopes, a good range of accommodation and welcoming locals.

Sleeping Mid-range accommodation includes **Le Boomerang II** (T+33 (0)450-798065; leboomerang2.com), a lively, Aussie-run hotel with transfer service; **Hôtel Mont-Chéry** (T+33 (0)450-758075; hotelmontchery.com), opposite the lifts and with a pool; and **Chalet Tressud** (T+33 (0)450-758294; tressud.com), which offers flexible packages.

Eating Restaurants are good although there's not much variety in the cuisine – try **Le Flambeau, Le Tourbillon, Le Vieux Chêne** and **Le Tyrol**. **La Tannière**, at the base of the pistes, is also good and the **Irish Bar** serves food till 2200.

Au pair/crèche **Les Fripouilles** (T+33 (0)450-798484) cares for children from six months.

Bars and clubs The **Irish Bar** is cosy and intimate, the **Canadian Bar** (above the Irish Bar) and **Zebra** are slightly trendier, and **Bar Bush** and **Le Boomerang** are popular. The village nightclub is **L'Igloo**.

Hire shop/rental There's a vast choice of rental shops in Les Gets. Several offer online reservation before you arrive – check lesgets.com for details.

Shopping Local shops cater well for Savoyarde delicacies, clothing and gifts.

Health and wellbeing Spa **Sereni Cimes** (Hotel Marmotte) is open to the public and the **Institut Clair Moment** offers beauty treatments.

Down days with kids There's an outdoor ice- rink, tobogganing, a **Mechanical Music Museum** and **Sapaba** (T+33 (0)450- 756507), a ceramic painting workshop.

Internet There's Wi-Fi at the hotels **Alpina, Bel Alpe, Nagano** and **Stella** and **Restaurant l'Op Traken**.

Transfer options Fly to Geneva and take a bus (altibus.com) or shuttle (a.t.s.net).

You can also ski here ... Morzine and the Portes du Soleil.

If you like this ... try Westendorf ▶▶*p91*, Montgenèvre ▶▶*p170*.

⬇19 Les Houches

Town altitude 1000 m	Km of pistes 55 km	Funicular/cable	Terrain parks 1
Km to airport 92 km	Nursery areas 3	cars 0/1	Glühwein factor ★☆☆
Airport Geneva	Blues 5	Gondolas/chairs 1/7	Ski in/ski out ★☆☆
Highest lift 1860 m	Reds 12	Drags 10	Environmental
Vertical drop 860 m	Blacks 1	Night skiing yes	rating n/a

Family-friendly village ideal for beginners and intermediates, just 6 km from Chamonix.

Les Houches is a tiny, quiet mountain town on the old road to Chamonix. It's ideal for families, with gentle local slopes and Chamonix nearby.

It hosts one of the world's most challenging annual downhill races on its only black piste – 'Kandahar' (or 'Le Verte'). Recent investment in new lifts and a terrain park makes it worth a visit for advanced skiers and ideal for beginners and intermediates.

Beginners Start on the village nursery slopes before progressing to the nursery areas on the mountain. The spectacular views and Alpine experience won't fail to inspire.

Intermediate Les Houches is ideal for you, with plenty of gentle, tree-lined cruising runs. Dip into the powder on the sides of the pistes to find your powder feet.

Expert 'Le Verte' might be the only black, but it's a corker. Expert skiers also love the relatively untracked powder and excellent tree-skiing.

Tuition ESF, Evolution2 and Ski Sensations are all good.

Kids ESF runs the Jardin des Neiges for skiers from three.

Not to miss Lunch and hot chocoate at Les Vielles Luges.

Remember to avoid Mistaking 'Le Verte' black piste for a green run.

Practicalities

Sleeping Hotel Slalom (T+33 (0)450-544060; hotelslalom.net) is opposite the cable car while **Hôtel and Chalet du Bois** (T+33 (0)450-545035; hotel-du-bois.com) has rooms and apartments. **Les Granges d'en Haut** (T+33 (0)450-546536; grangesdenhaut. com) comprises 14 new luxury chalets in a mini hamlet.

Eating Le Delice has a good bar, does great food and has a children's menu. **La Ferme des Agapes** offers local dishes. **Hotel Gorges de la Diosaz** (in neighbouring Servoz) serves excellent food, as does **Les Vielles Luges** on the mountain, which takes group bookings for evening meals (T+33 (0)684-423700).

Bars and clubs If you're looking for more than a quiet drink, head for Chamonix. If not, you'll enjoy **Le Delice** and **Slalom Bar**.

Hire shop/rental Cyprien Sports has a large selection and friendly service.

Transfer options Check out chamexpress.com and alpybus.com for shared transfers from Geneva or a.t.s.net for private transfer. Public buses cost around €50 (sat-montblanc.com).

You can also ski here ... Buy a Mont Blanc Unlimited ski pass for access to all Chamonix valley resorts.

If you like this ... try St Foy ▶▶ *p178*, Grimentz ▶▶ *p290*.

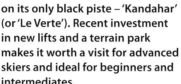

⊙ **OPENING TIMES**

Early Dec to late Apr: 0830-1630

$ **RESORT PRICES**

Week pass: €147.80

Day pass: €30.80

Season pass: €650 (Chamonix le Pass)

ⓘ **DIRECTORY**

Website: leshouches.com

Tourist office: T+33 (0)450-555062

Medical centre: T+33 (0)450-555027

Pisteurs: T+33 (0)450-544032

Taxi: T+33 (0)450-544109

France Les Houches

↘20 Les Menuires

Town altitude	1800 m	Km of pistes	600 km	Funicular/cable cars	0/6	Terrain parks	9

Town altitude 1800 m	Km of pistes 600 km	Funicular/cable	Terrain parks 9
Km to airport 100 km	Nursery areas 3	cars 0/6	Glühwein factor ★☆☆
Airport Chambéry	Blues 121	Gondolas/chairs 33/69	Ski in/ski out ★★★
Highest lift 3200 m	Reds 114	Drags 72	Environmental
Vertical drop 1400 m	Blacks 33	Night skiing yes	rating ★★★★☆

PROS

- ✓ Cheap Trois Vallées base.
- ✓ Extensive snowmaking.
- ✓ Family friendly.

CONS

- ✗ Completely functional appearance.
- ✗ No trees.

Les Menuires mixes Trois Vallées access with modern ski resort infrastructure and is pretty much perfect for families. Just don't mention the architecture ...

Forget the slightly dodgy buildings: the main reason to go to Les Menuires is the snow-sure guarantee this confident resort offers. If 80% or more of the pistes are closed, you're offered money back on your accommodation and lift pass. That said, conditions here are pretty reliable, with pistes topping out at 2850 m and a comprehensive snowmaking system. And then there is the terrain ...

Beginners There are many wide and open pistes for beginners, such as La Violette, which runs from the top of the Roc des 3 Marches lift back into La Croisette. The beginners' areas lies to skier's left of the Montagnettes lift.

Intermediates There are many red runs off the Roc des 3 Marches and Mont de la Chambre lifts. Head up to Val Thorens for higher reds and blues and try the gentle blacks on La Masse if you are game.

Experts For their thrills, experts go to La Masse where there are good, pisted blacks such as Dame Blanche. Experts will love the links up to Val Thorens and over to Méribel as well, particularly the

Bartevelle and Mottaret areas, which are relatively close and have some great steep terrain.

Powder Some say the opportunities for off-piste here are some of the best in the area – try the Vallon du Lou area off the back of La Masse. La Masse itself offers some of the most challenging terrain in the valley.

Moguls Lac Noir over on La Masse gets pretty bumpy.

Tuition There are three ski schools: Ski School, Les Menuires, and Snowbow Internationale Ski School, Reberty, offer lessons in English; ESF also operate in Les Menuires.

Kids Les Menuires is very much a family resort. ESF offer group lessons for over-fours and snowboard lessons for teenagers.

Bad light The resort's altitude counts against it here, meaning there are very few trees in the Les Menuires ski area. St Martin is slightly better if the snow is good enough to warrant the trip.

Not to miss A freshly groomed descent of Dame Blanche before the masses get to it.

Remember to avoid Spending too much time in the tardis-like shopping centre at La Croisette – it's hideous.

Best mountain restaurant You can ski to the good-value L'Etoile at Reberty; it is also walkable from the centre of Les Menuires. Also try the Alpage on the 4 vents piste.

☺ LOCALS DO

- ✓ Get up early for fresh La Masse tracks.
- ✓ Head to Val Thorens for some variety.

☹ LOCALS DON'T

- ✗ Hit the lower slopes in the afternoon – they can be very busy and get slushy easily.

Practicalities

The town of Les Menuires is a classic example of the throw-'em-up-fast architecture of many French ski resorts built in the 1960s and 70s. The resort is essentially divided into three tiers: Reberty, La Croisette and Preyerand, with accommodation at all levels. The ugly architecture is mostly concentrated around the main base of La Croisette, and the resort is shedding its poor image with the creation of smaller, more sympathetic off-shoots such as the chalet-style village of Hameau de Marmottes.

Sleeping Until recently none of the hotels had more than three-star status, but the addition of four-star **Chalet Hotel Kaya** (T+33 (0)479-414200) in the village of Reberty provides a touch of luxury. The best of the rest are the family-oriented three-star **Latitudes** (T+33 (0)479-007510) in Les Bruyères and the ski-in, ski-out two-star **Hôtel du Soleil Pierre Blanche** (T+33 (0)479-013737) in Brelin. For cheap apartments try **Les Côtes d'Or** (T+33 (0)479-306534). If budget is not an issue, **La Montagnettes** (T+33 (0)479-104915) in Reberty is a good option.

Eating All budgets and all tastes are catered for in Les Menuires, from traditional Savoyard to the increasingly traditional (well, in Alpine ski-resort terms) Tex-Mex and Italian. **Le K** (T+33 (0)479-414202) is the restaurant of the Hotel Kaya – it serves high-end lunches and dinner. A short walk from the base of La Croisette is the cosy **L'Etoile** (T+33 (0)479-007558) with tables centred around a giant fireplace. **La Ferme de Reberty** (T+33 (0)479-007701) is one of the best places to eat in Les Menuires, yet prices are still pretty reasonable.

Au pair/crèche The Piou-Piou village run by the **ESF** (esf-lesmenuires.com) in La Croisette has a nursery and children's club for children from 3-30 months, with various activities from snowshoeing to tobogganing.

Bars and clubs **Leeberty** nightclub in Reberty is classic ski-resort cheese and very popular. The **Passport** in La Croisette is the biggest club in the resort. In Preyerand, the lowest part of the resort, is **The Yeti** – if you like banging Dutch aprés-ski this is the place for you.

Hire shop/rental There are local hire shops along with the usual chain ski-hire outfits (Skiset, Twinner etc.) in all three main areas of the resort.

Shopping The truly dreadful shopping centre in the centre of La Croisette has a surprisingly good range of shops including specialist food shops.

Health and wellbeing The sports centre in La Croisette, **SOGEVAB** (sogevab.com), has an outdoor pool (open all year), saunas and jacuzzis as well as a 160-sq-m gym gym with free weights, squash courts and sports hall.

Down days with kids Take them to the funpark at the sports centre where there are trampolines, bouncy castles and a plastic ball pool.

Internet **La Mousse** bar and internet café in La Croisette has PCs and offers printing.

Transfer options The nearest airports are Lyon (2½ hours) and Chambéry (two hours). Bus operator **Altibus** (T+33 (0)820-320368; altibus.com) runs transfers from both airports to Les Menuires. The nearest train station is Moûtiers (Eurostar stops here); take a bus from the train station to the resort (Altibus as before).

You can also ski here ... The entire Trois Vallées region.

If you like this ... try Alpbach ▶▶ *p56*, La Plagne ▶▶ *p146*.

France Les Menuires

⊙ OPENING TIMES
Mid-Dec to late Apr: 0900-1630

⑤ RESORT PRICES
Week pass: €225
Day pass: €45
Season pass: €950

ⓘ DIRECTORY
Website: lesmenuires.com
Tourist office: T+33 (0)479-007300
Medical centre: T+33 (0)479-1542
Pisteurs: T+33 (0)479-6447
Taxi: T+33 (0)479-006954

↘21 Megève

Town altitude 1113 m	Km of pistes 325 km		Funicular/cable		Terrain parks 1
Km to airport 70 km	Nursery areas 2		cars 0/3		Glühwein factor ★★★
Airport Geneva	Blues 56		Gondolas/chairs 7/30		Ski in/ski out ★★★
Highest lift 2350 m	Reds 77		Drags 63		Environmental
Vertical drop 1237 m	Blacks 32		Night skiing yes		rating ★★★★☆

PROS

- ✓ Plenty of events.
- ✓ Close to other major resorts.
- ✓ Short transfer time.

CONS

- ✗ Skiing isn't the priority in Megève, which can be quite frustrating if you want the snow-loving atmosphere.
- ✗ It's not that cheap, especially if you're staying in a chalet.

Megève is heaven for skiers who like a change of scenery each day before being looked after in five-star style every evening.

😊 LOCALS DO

- 😊 Stay in at night.
- 😊 Eat in the mountain restaurants: the standard of food on offer is some of the best in France and better than most places in town.

😠 LOCALS DON'T

- ✗ Like being known as a tourist attraction. They haven't got the best reputation with visitors.
- ✗ Drive – local roads can be poor.
- ✗ Stay on the mountain too long, particularly when the weather is bad.

Megève might not be so popular as it was in its heyday in the 1960s, overshadowed as it is by nearby Chamonix and La Clusaz, but it is still a classic example of a mid-Alps French resort. The centre oozes French charm, with deserted streets wrapped around the quaintest town square you'll ever see, and a predominance of upmarket clothes shops and restaurants. Although it might be a little quiet at times, there's a wealth of events and activities to keep visitors happy.

Megève's proximity to Geneva suggests that you might meet a lot of holidaying Europeans throughout the season but during the week the resort is practically deserted. And it would be very hard to get bored in Megève as the area it covers is enormous, stretching from St Nicolas de Véroce to the small village of La Giettaz. The resort is expected to join the Espace Diamant ski area in the next few years, expanding the available terrain even further.

Beginners There's plenty of room to practise your turns and build confidence on the long greens of Mont d'Arbois. When you're ready head over to Rochebrune and try some of the wide steady blues.

Intermediate Developing skiers will love the long blue and red runs throughout Megève. Lanchettes is a wide red that is usually very quiet. If you're feeling really adventurous, Super Megève is marked as a black but is probably more a red – not that it matters when telling everyone how fast you went down this 'amazing black'. Mont d'Arbois is perfect for immediate skiers, Princesse being the best.

Expert The first run you should try is the Côte 2000 to whet your appetite. There's not an enormous range of choice for advanced skiers but the blacks and more difficult reds that you can access are very good. If you're willing to venture out of the village, try La Giettaz for runs Rhodos and Aigle.

Powder If you're visiting outside peak season, consider yourself lucky. Powder can often still be found up to a week after fresh snow, so find the best in between the Radaz and Lanchettes chairlifts, known locally as 'The Magic Garden'.

Moguls Artificial moguls can be found in the snow park. If you like them a little more 'raw', there are plenty on the runs in and around the Côte 2000, particularly towards the end of the season.

Tuition ESI (T+33 (0)450-587888) are the popular choice. For those who prefer a more upmarket service, **Agence de Ski à Megève** (agencedeski-megeve. com) offer lessons in French, English or Spanish.

Kids For one-on-one, visit independent instructor Mike Beaudet at **Ski Pros Megève** (T+33 (0)681-610615).

Bad light Rochebrune has some of the best tree runs; their size means that – crossed fingers – you won't be mown down by any of the locals.

Not to miss A hot-air balloon ride with **Alpes Montgolfière** (alpes-montgolfiere. fr) Spectacular views and free champagne on arrival – bonus!

Remember to avoid Skiing at the end of the season – the low altitude often results in a lot of the runs being closed.

Relive a famous moment Megève is the only resort in Europe with its own permanent downhill course – the Côte 2000 downhill stadium often hosts training in the run-up to the Alpine World Cup.

Practicalities

Sleeping Four-star **Les Fermes de Marie** (T+33 (0)450-930310; fermesdemarie.com) and **Mont Blanc** (T+33 (0)450-212002; hotelmontblanc. com) head the bill. Closer to town, the **Au Coeur de Megève** (T+33 (0)50-212530; hotel-megeve.com) has cosy rooms and a very good in-house restaurant.

Eating For high quality Savoyard dining, **L'Atelier de la Taverne** (T+33 (0)450-210353) adds a modern twist. **Delicium** (T+33 (0)450-213715) welcomes children and serves a wide range of Italian specialities. If you're visiting on a budget, there's always **McDonald's**!

Bars and clubs Jazz Club **Les 5 Rues** (T+33 (0)450-919069) has live music and a great atmosphere take revellers past midnight before sending them on to nightclub **White Pearl**. Or try **Palo Alto** (T+33 (0)450-918258) where the walls shift according to how many people are there.

Hire shop/rental Atmoski and **Ski Flash** have a wide range of ski and snowboard equipment for sale and hire and offer group discounts.

Health and wellbeing Newly opened Le Cabinet AA (T+33 (0)450-907690) and L'Eau Vive (T+33 (0)628-327294; spaeauvive.com) offer new and old treatments.

Down days with kids The Palais des Sports (T+33 (0)450-211571) is regarded as one of the best sports facilities in France and has a heated indoor pool and ice-rink.

Internet There's not a huge choice of internet connectivity but most bars and cafés around town offer Wi-Fi; if you're still looking, try **Bar des Alpes** (T+33 (0)450-930815).

Transfer options Driving from Geneva airport, follow the directions for Chamonix leaving the motorway at Sallanches. **Autocars SAT** (T+33 (0)450-212518) run a regular bus service to Megève during peak season.

You can also ski here ... In the opionion of **Ski Pros Megève** (skiprosmegeve.com), a true trip to Megève needs to take in day trips to Chamonix and Courmayeur.

If you like this ... try Zell am See ▶▶ *p93*, Val d'Isère ▶▶ *p188*.

OPENING TIMES

Dec to late Apr: 0900-1645

RESORT PRICES

Week pass: €182.50

Day pass: €33

DIRECTORY

Website: megeve.com

Tourist office: T+33 (0)450-212728

Medical centre: T+33 (0)450-473030

Pisteurs: T+33 (0)450-213839

Taxi: T+33 (0)450-930325

France Megève

↘22 Méribel

Town altitude	1450 m	Km of pistes	600 km	Funicular/cable		Terrain parks	9
Km to airport	128 km	Nursery areas	3	cars	0/6	Glühwein factor	★★★
Airport	Geneva	Blues	121	Gondolas/chairs	33/69	Ski in/ski out	★★★
Highest lift	3200 m	Reds	114	Drags	72	Environmental	
Vertical drop	1750 m	Blacks	33	Night skiing	no	rating	★★★★★★

PROS

- ✓ Extremely fluid lift system.
- ✓ Fantastic nightlife.
- ✓ Very 'English' atmosphere.

CONS

- ✗ Very 'English' atmosphere.
- ✗ Ridiculously busy in February – avoid!

Its heavy Brit influence may keep purists away, but the pretty village, strong skiing and legendary partying makes this one of the big French Alp resorts.

Like all such 'big name' resorts, Méribel is a lot more than the sum of its parts. There is an indefinable air about the place, with so much going on, both up the hill and after skiing, that everybody will find something to enjoy here.

Méribel alone is a great, challenging mountain, especially for beginners and intermediates. Once the enormous scope of the Trois Vallées region is also included, it becomes one of the Alps' outstanding resorts. Of course, the same can be said for Courchevel and Val Thorens, but we believe this and the vibrant town lift Méribel into the upper echelon. Although some might argue that Méribel lacks steep terrain, in all honesty there is enough quality terrain here to keep most skiers occupied for their entire skiing career. Plus, the constant upgrading and overhauling of the lift system make this one of the smoothest day's skiing you'll ever experience. In short, Méribel is the model of a modern ski station. Here are our highlights.

Beginners Beginners will want to head to the Altiport area. Here you'll find wide greens and blues serviced by a rapid chair and some easy drag lifts. You can access this area from town by taking the Rhodos lift. Once you've conquered this, take the 'six-man' chair (down from the Rond Point) or the Burgin Saulire to the mid-station.

Intermediate Solid intermediates might have just found their favourite resort. The Burgin Saulire lift takes you to the top of Méribel proper and from there it is an exhilarating, sunny descent back down to Méribel. The Tougnète lifts also access some fantastic, easy terrain leading to Mottaret and the Platières runs. It is possible to ski from here back to Méribel for a long, sweeping descent.

Expert Experts should head for the Olympic Express chair; it was the run used when Méribel hosted the Women's Downhill in 1992 and is usually well groomed and quick in the morning. Other notable blacks include Combe Tougnète and the Bartavelle. To really make the most of this terrain, though, a Trois Vallées pass is a must, especially for the heights of Val Thorens and the steeps of Courchevel.

France Méribel

☺LOCALS DO

- ✓ Party like the world is about to end.
- ✓ Speak English.
- ✓ Still get up early for powder days.

☹LOCALS DON'T

- ✗ Drink the extremely potent local lager *Mutzig* in pints – they stick to a *demi*.
- ✗ Underestimate the avalanche dangers in this deceptively safe resort. It can still be dangerous.

Powder Méribel has some fantastic powder opportunities for adventurous skiers of all levels, from the front face majesty of Mont Vallon, at the head of the valley, to the area located off the top of the Roc de Tougne drag known to locals as 'The Spot'. You'll really need a guide for this though. Other easy powder routes for those getting to grips include the runs accessed off the Loze chair, along the Col de la Loze cat track, and the steep, open faces off the Chanrossa chair in Courchevel.

Trees Again, there are some fantastic itineraries. From the Olympic Express chair, there are a number of routes down to Le Raffort and even Les Allues. From Saulire mid-station, it is also possible to head down through the route aptly named 'Christmas Trees'. Again, a guide is probably best here.

Moguls Le Face is usually filled with knee-high bumps by mid-afternoon, while Les Bosses ('the bumps') is a must for those with bionic knees.

Book a guide Sensations 3 Valleys (ski-sensations.com) are noted local guides, although we really prefer **Magic** (magicfr.com), who cater for English-speaking visitors, providing high-level guiding and coaching for expert skiers.

Tuition Magic are again fantastic, but other options include **Parallel Lines** (parallel-lines.com), predominantly French-speaking **ESF Méribel** (esf-meribel.com) and **New Generation** (skinewgen.com).

Kids We like the **Kids Etc Snow Club** (kidsetc.co.uk), which takes care of children while parents enjoy a stress-free ski.

Bad light The La Tania tree runs are good fun – take the Loze chair over and navigate your way down. In Mottaret, the Table Vert chair is also a favourite with locals looking to find some definition.

Not to miss Using the Rond Point as a base from which to lap the Adret chair in the sunshine. It is the quintessential Méribel ski experience.

Remember to avoid Mistakenly following the Méribel Village signs thinking you're on your way back to the centre of Méribel.

Relive a famous moment Take on Le Face run and relive the 1992 Olympics.

Pitstop and sunbathe Either **Le Rond Point** for a mid-afternoon pitcher of beer or, if you're in town, the pool by **Evolution**.

Best mountain Les Rhododendrons restaurant at the top of the Altiport and the Rhodos lift is a really convenient meeting place for skiers of all standards.

OPENING TIMES
20 Dec to 17 Apr: 0900-1630/1700

RESORT PRICES
Week pass: €225
Day pass: €45
Season pass: €970

DIRECTORY
Website: meribel.net
Tourist office: T+33 (0)479-005000
Medical centre: T+33 (0)479-086540
Pisteurs: T+33 (0)479-086532
Taxi: meribel-taxi.com

Practicalities

Méribel has long had the reputation as an Alpine party stronghold. Some romantics reckon toffee vodka, that staple of the ski-week booze-up, was invented here one fateful season. Certainly, a holiday in Méribel wouldn't be complete without necking a bottle of said loopy juice while dancing around in your ski boots to a covers band at the Rond Point. Yet the stereotype doesn't do full justice to the strengths of this resort.

Sleeping Méribel has grown hugely over the years but the centre is still where most people stay. That said, families and those after some peace and quiet should head for Méribel Village, a few kilometres out of town on the road to Courchevel. **Les Fermes de Méribel** (residences-mgm.com) is a four-star chalet close to the linking chair. In town, central **Grand Coeur** (grandcoeur.com) takes care of the four-star/spa bracket. Those here for the partying might want to look at the cheap and cheerful **Hotel Le Roc** (hotelleroc.com) or the **Chaudanne** (chaudanne.com) complex of hotels, chalets and restaurants with enviable access to the lifts. The Belvedere area, up near the Rond Point, is the exclusive part of town. We like **The Lodge** (supertravel.co.uk), which sleeps 16, is next to the Georges Maduit piste and has a sauna and jacuzzi.

Eating Where to begin? Lunch at the **Rond Point** (T+33 (0)479-003751; rondpointmeribel.com) is a must, while **Evolution** (T+33 (0)479-004426) does great aprés snacks, fry-ups and roasts, and **Pizza Express** provides, as ever, some of the best pizzas in town. For local cuisine, **La Kouisena**, in the Chaudanne area, and **Le Fromagerie**, in town, are very popular. Other favourites include **Le**

Plantin and **La Gallette**, while gourmet heaven has to be **Chez Kiki**, in the Morel area, a local institution – and that's just the eponymous chef Kiki. The beef is legendary, as is the Savoyard fondue.

Au pair/crèche Méribel is such a popular resort for families that there are plenty of options. **Les Farfadets** (lesfarfadets.com) is a professional English-speaking nannying service, while **Kids Etc** (kidsetc.co.uk) is an independent nannying and snow-club service.

Best après-ski Now we're talking. The **Rond Point** is probably one of the most famous après bars in the Alps, with live bands, dancing on tables and a brilliant atmosphere. In town, **Evolution** and **Jack's Bar** are lively and close to the base lifts.

Bars and clubs One of the main reasons for Méribel's enduring popularity is the frenzied nightlife. In the town centre, **The Pub**, **Scott's Bar** and the **Taverne** are always packed, while **Jack's Bar** shows the football and has DJs and pool tables. While old Méribel hands still lament the loss of the old Capricorne, **Le Poste de Secours** now sits in the same spot and is the town's 'chic' bar. When these places close, head to either **Dick's Tea Bar** or the **Loft** down at the Chaudanne.

Hire shop/rental Options wherever you're staying, including the long-standing **Georges Maduit** and **Intersport** in the centre, **Sports Méribel Village** in Méribel Village and numerous options in Morel, 1600 and Rond Point areas.

Lift tickets It can get complicated – you can buy a Méribel-only pass, a Méribel-Mottaret pass or a Trois Vallées

pass. There are also beginner-only options, so make sure you check the Méribel-Alpina website (meribel-alpina.com) for all the permutations.

Shopping Food shopping is far cheaper down in Moûtiers but in Méribel there is a large **Spar in Mussilon**. The town centre has plenty of boutique ski shops such as **Fat Face** and **White Stuff**.

Health and wellbeing The impressive **La Chaudanne Olympic Park** has been substantially upgraded and has a wellness area including pool, ice-rink and sauna, jacuzzi and hot tubs. **Le Grand Coeur** (legrandcoeur.com) also has a spa and fitness centre. There are also great physio facilities in Méribel 1600 run by British doctors (ski-physio.com).

Down days with kids Take them to the **Olympic Park** for a day swimming and ice-skating. There is also a cinema in town that shows up to date films – just make sure it is a 'VO' showing.

Internet The **Cybar** downstairs in the **Taverne** is the best spot in the centre, but we prefer **Evolution** for its Wi-Fi access and general laid-back atmosphere.

Transfer options Many options, but try **Three Vallee Transfers** (3vt.co.uk), **Alpine Ski Transfers** (alpineskitransfers.com) and **Snowbound Airport Transfers** (snowboundtransfers.co.uk).

You can also ski here ... A Trois Vallées pass allows you to ski Val Thorens, Les Menuires, St Martin, Courchevel and La Tania. The pass also offers day passes in nearby resorts such as Tignes and Val d'Isère, but check with the lift company for full details.

If you like this ... try St Anton ▶▶*p85*, Cortina ▶▶*p222*, Verbier ▶▶*p308*.

↘23 Montgenèvre

Town altitude 1860 m	Km of pistes 100 km	Funicular/cable	Terrain parks 1
Km to airport 100 km	Nursery areas 3	cars 0/0	Glühwein factor ★★★
Airport Turin	Blues 12	Gondolas/chairs 2/11	Ski in/ski out ★★★
Highest lift 2630 m	Reds 7	Drags 17	Environmental
Vertical drop 770 m	Blacks 7	Night skiing yes	rating ★★★★★

The only French resort linked to the Milky Way ski area – and the snowiest.

⊘ **OPENING TIMES**

Early Dec to end Apr: 0900-1630

Ⓢ **RESORT PRICES**

Week pass: €93.50

Day pass: €25.50

Season pass: €490

ⓘ **DIRECTORY**

Website: montgenevre.com

Tourist office: T+33 (0)492-215252

Medical centre: T+33 (0)492-219120

Pisteurs: T+33 (0)492-219173

Taxi: T+33 (0)607-067998

Montgenèvre is a family-friendly, inexpensive village set on a pass between France and Italy.

There's skiing on both sides of Montgenèvre, on Les Gondrans (north-facing and linked to Claviere) and the smaller Le Chalvet. Terrain

is best suited to beginners and intermediates although it's a high-altitude snow pocket with good, quiet off-piste.

Beginners Nursery slopes are accessed from the village and there are plenty of blues to progress to. Best of all is the green from the top of Gondrans into the village, giving a real sense of achievement.

Intermediate Plenty of varied cruising terrain here and across the Milky Way. Our favourite run is the (easy) black 4 from Le Chalvet, which leads into red 3.

Expert Stick to the bowl on Gondrans and Rocher de l'Aigle (you can drop off the back into Italy). Visit Serre Chevalier and La Grave.

Tuition ESF is friendly, while **A Peak** is small with English-speaking instructors.

Kids ESF runs **Club Piou Piou** (T+33 (0)492-219046) for three to five year-olds.

Not to miss An evening Skidoo Safari and dinner in Claviere – ask the tourist office for details.

Remember to avoid Missing the last Tremplin chair from Claviere to Montgenèvre at 1630.

Practicalities

Accommodation is close to the pistes and/or lifts, which are at either end of the village.

Sleeping Hotel le Chalet Blanc (T+33 (0)492-442702; hotellechaletblanc.com) styles itself as Montgenèvre's 'finest luxury ski hotel', with ski in/ski out facilities and a spa. **Hotel Alpis Cottia** (T+33 (0)492-215000; hotelalpiscottia.com) is on the slopes. **Neilson** (T+44 (0)870-333 3356; neilson.co.uk) operates two ski in/ski out chalets.

Eating Le Jamy does French food, Le Refuge *raclette* and Le Capitaine pizza. Skiers generally lunch in the village – try **Outside Burger** and **Le Petit Creux**.

Au pair/crèche Les Sourires Children's Club (T+33 (0)492-215250) offers non-skiing day care (six months to six years).

Bars and clubs Nightlife is subdued, with action focusing on **Le Graal**, **Pub Chaberton**, **Le Tourmandre** and **Les Rois Mages**. The **Blue Night** is the disco.

Transfer options Take a train from Turin to Briançon (sncf.com) and bus (autocars.resalp.free.fr) or taxi (T+33 (0)607-067998) from there.

You can also ski here ... The Milky Way.

If you like this ... try Kühtai ▶▶ *p65*, La Tania ▶▶ *p149*, Les Gets ▶▶ *p159*.

↘24 Mottaret

Town altitude	1450 m	Funicular/cable	
Km to airport	128 km	cars	0/6
Airport	Geneva	Gondolas/chairs	33/69
Highest lift	3200 m	Drags	72
Vertical drop	1750 m	Night skiing	no
Km of pistes	600 km	Terrain parks	9
Nursery areas	3	Glühwein factor	★★★
Blues	121	Ski in/ski out	★★★
Reds	114	Environmental	
Blacks	33	rating	n/a

Méribel's sister resort sits slightly higher up the valley and offers more complete ski in/ski out accommodation.

Mottaret is a purpose-built village designed to offer visitors complete ski in/ski out access. It is also quieter than Méribel, making it slightly better for families or those not attracted to the frenetic nightlife available in that resort. The two are linked by a winding road and by the flat Truite piste.

Although Mottaret has the Pas du Lac lift linking it to the Saulire side of the Méribel valley, the great advantage of a stay here is the easy access to the higher slopes of the valley. The Platières lift leads up to the Côte Brune and Mont Vallon areas, and there are the trees of Table Verte should the weather close in.

Beginners Pretty much perfect, as the pistes in Mottaret are essentially flat. The Ramées lift offers some gentle slopes for those with a few days under their skis.

Intermediate The Tougnète and Platières areas are intermediate heaven. Aim for Mont Vallon by the end of the week.

Expert Côte Brune has some of the steeper terrain in the valley and leads easily into Val Thorens.

Tuition Snow Systems (snow-systems.com) are based in Mottaret, as are ESF (esf-meribel.com) and Méribel legends Magic (magicfr.com).

Bad light The Table Verte area has some of the easiest and most accessible tree cover in the entire valley. It is where the locals flock during a cloudy day.

Not to miss Heading to the summit of Mont Vallon, the highest point (2952 m) in the Méribel valley.

Remember to avoid Skiing down to Méribel at the end of the day, rather than making it back to Mottaret. You'll need to catch the bus back.

◉ OPENING TIMES

20 Dec to 26 Apr: 0900-1630/1700

◉ RESORT PRICES (Trois Vallées)

Week pass: €225

Day pass: €45

Season pass: €970

◉ DIRECTORY

Website: meribel.net

Tourist office: T+33 (0)479-005000

Medical centre: T+33 (0)479-086540

Pisteurs: T+33 (0)479-086532

Taxi: meribel-taxi.com

Practicalities

Sleeping Almost all accommodation in Mottaret is self-catering studio style, with **Residence Le Hameau** and **Residences MGM** typical – book through meribel.net. That said, there are a few larger hotels, including three-star **Alpen Ruitor** (alpenruitor.com), **Mont Vallon** (hotel-montvallon.com) and **Le Mottaret** (hotellemottaret.com).

Eating Au Temps Perdu (T+33 (0)479-003664) for superior local nosh, **Zig Zag** (T+33 (0)479-004740) for cheaper eats and **Côte Brune** (T+33 (0)479-004097) for a busy lunchtime experience. **Pizzeria du Mottaret** also takes care of the obvious.

Bars and clubs For real partying, head down the valley to Méribel. In Mottare there are a few options, with **Le Rastro, Downtown Bar, Piano Bar** and **Le Privilege** all popular.

Hire shop/rental Ski Evasion (ski-evasion.sport2000.fr) and **Skiset** (meribel-mottaret.skiset.co.uk) are both central and good options for hiring kit.

Transfer options As with Méribel, we like **Three Vallee Transfers** (3vt.co.uk), **Alpine Ski Transfers** (alpineskitransfers.com) and **Snowbound Airport Transfers** (snowboundtransfers.co.uk).

You can also ski here … A Trois Vallées pass means you can ski Val Thorens, Les Menuires, St Martin, Courchevel and La Tania. The pass also offers day passes in nearby resorts such as Tignes and Val d'Is re, but check with the lift company for full details.

If you like this … try Flaine ▶▶*p136*, La Tania ▶▶*p149*, Canazei ▶▶*p214*.

↘25 Morzine

Town altitude	1000 m	Km of pistes	650 km	Funicular/cable	
Km to airport	70 km	Nursery areas	2	cars	0/4
Airport	Geneva	Blues	112	Gondolas/chairs	9/80
Highest lift	2466 m	Reds	104	Drags	102
Vertical drop	1466 m	Blacks	28	Night skiing	yes

Terrain parks	9
Glühwein factor	★★★
Ski in/ski out	☆☆☆
Environmental rating	★★★★☆☆

PROS

- ✔ Enormous area.
- ✔ Fantastic nightlife.
- ✔ Vibrant town.

CONS

- ✖ Sprawling town means some accommodation far from lifts.
- ✖ Extremely busy during February.

Chamonix-style valley town plugged into one of Europe's largest linked ski areas.

For our money, Morzine is the best base from which to explore the enormous Portes du Soleil area. It combines the bustle of a busy, vibrant town with some of the finest skiing in Europe, and as such is hugely popular with British skiers. Even better, it is extremely picturesque, thanks to a lovely location along the dramatic River Dranse, and its northerly location (only an hour or so from Geneva) makes it great for short transfers and self-drive trips. Perhaps the only drawback is the size of the place.

Run the numbers and the sheer size of this area becomes apparent –

12 resorts in 2 countries, 650 km of pistes and a whopping 80 chairlifts. That said, it is likely that, unless you're very intrepid indeed, you'll spend most of your time in Avoriaz (via the Super Morzine lift) and on the Pleney side, over towards Les Gets. Although Super Morzine accesses a larger area, there can be large queues so Pleney is a welcome, easy alternative during busy times.

Beginners Two obvious options are to take the Super Morzine lift and then spend the day lapping the east blues accessed via the Zore, Baron and Seraussaix lifts.

Or take the Pleney lift and explore the blues from the Belvedera chair. Complete beginners will probably find it best to stick to the nursery slopes in Morzine.

Intermediate You'll want to spend most of your time in Avoriaz. If Super Morzine is too busy, it might be worth taking the bus to Les Prodains and getting the big lift up to Avoriaz. From there, you have many options. The Grandes Combes, Lac Intrets, Prolays and Lindarets all offer varied reds that should keep most skiers occupied for the season, let alone the week. You might also want to explore Les Lindarets if Avoriaz is too crowded. Get the bus from Morzine to Ardent and take the lift from there.

Expert You've probably already heard of 'The Wall', the infamous run that links Avoriaz to Switzerland. Make your way to the Chavanette area if you want to test yourself on this most famous of Alpine runs. Elsewhere, there are a number of blacks coming off the Grandes Combes chair, and a renowned black off the top of the Chamossière chair.

Powder For an easy hike and some basic off-piste turns, look for the Satellite

run in the Lindarets area. You'll also find plenty of easy turns off Le Fornet chair if you're just getting to grips with powder.

Moguls As 'The Wall' is probably one of the most famous mogul runs in the Alps, it's the logical place to head.

Trees Make for the Les Prodains area and drop into some of the trees higher up there. As it is quite low, people usually head there at the end of the day so it can be a good, uncrowded spot to try.

Book a guide Mountain Tracks (mountaintracks.co.uk) run specialized

performance clinics each winter, while new outfit **The Snow School** (the-snow-school.com) run an impressive array of individual and group guided lessons.

Tuition As you might expect, there's a bewildering choice but we're highlighting **The Snow Institute** (thesnowinstitute. com), **Morzine Ski Schools** (morzineskischools.com), the **British Alpine Ski and Snowboard Schools** (britishskischool.com) and the ubiquitous **ESF** (esf-morzine.com) as our picks.

Kids Morzine is a 'Family +' resort, which means there is a programme of special events and activities for families with young children. Check morzine.com for more information.

Bad light Cloud shouldn't stop play here (try the Prodain trees or the Montriand area), but if it does take your pick from one of the many guided tours or activities laid on by the tourist board.

Not to miss The Wall! It is a rite-of-passage for many skiers.

Remember to avoid Missing the last lifts back to the resort while exploring the Swiss parts of the Portes du Soleil. It'll be an expensive taxi ride back.

Relive a famous moment Morzine has long been a stage finish on the Tour de France, with Lance Armstrong suffering on the Col de Joux-Plane climb back in 2000.

Pitstop and sunbathe Try the ever-popular **Changabang** in Avoriaz for a coffee and brownie.

Best mountain restaurant It's a bit of a mission, but **La Rossetaz** in Les Gets, by La Rosta chair, is fantastic. Brilliant views of Mont Blanc complement the great food perfectly.

France Morzine

☺ **LOCALS DO**

✔ Use the Les Prodains and Ardent lifts when Super Morzine is busy.

✔ Ride Les Gets for some variety.

☹ **LOCALS DON'T**

✘ Risk any of the Swiss resorts after 1500 – it takes too long to get back.

✘ Drive into town.

Practicalities

As it follows a valley, Morzine's perpetual growth means that if you're staying at the far end of town you'll probably have to catch a bus to get to the lifts. Some might also find the centre, which in some respects resembles a boozy summer resort rather than a pretty Alpine town, something of a turn-off. But really, this comes with the territory when you're dealing with a resort of this size and the pros here definitely outweigh the cons.

Sleeping Self-catering, chalets, hotels – Morzine has it all and plenty more besides. If you are set on breaking the bank, **La Vieille Ferme** (alpineaddictsmorzine.com), in nearby La Côte d'Arbroz, is a converted 250 year-old farmhouse with a beautiful standard of accommodation, sleeping up to 14 with an outdoor hot tub. **Chalet Mustang** (chaletmustang.com), in the heart of town 100 m from the Avoriaz cable car, is also likely to make you gasp once your credit card statement comes through. Otherwise, for the fully catered option, we like **Mountain Mavericks** (mountainmavericks.com), a family-run operation with a different take on the chalet holiday. **The Lodge Morzine** (thelodgemorzine.com) is great for modern self-catering and has a wellness area and a lovely bijou bar in the basement. On the other side of town, over the river, **Chalet Philibert** (chalet-philibert.com) is more of an old style, three-star French hotel. **Rude Chalets** (rudechalets.com) offer a cheeky take on the chalet experience.

Eating Morzine is a large town with many options. Some firm favourites include the **Rhodos Hotel** (T+33 (0)450-791985), Morzine's take on the Alpine gastro pub/roast dinner/

full-English trend, and **La Flamme** for unpretentious and fairly priced local nosh. **L'Etale** (T+33 (0)450-790929) is universally regarded as the best mid-price place in town and is usually packed as a result. **Le Clin d'Oeil** (T+33 (0)450-790310) is also recommended. Further up the scale, **La Chamade** (T+33 (0)450-791391; lachamade.com), run by husband and wife team Thierry and Valerie Thorens, specializes in sophisticated French cuisine. Booking is essential.

Au pair/crèche Nursery L'Outa (outa-morzine.com) takes kids aged three months to five years, while **Powder Babies** (powderbabies.co.uk) and **Cheeky Monkeys Childcare** (cheekymonkeysmorzine.com) offer English-speaking alternatives.

Best après-ski Either **Bar Robinson** to try legendary local lager *Mutzig* (be warned, it is very strong so stick to the halves) or the **Cavern** for some mellow acoustic guitar sessions.

Bars and clubs Morzine has a bewildering number of bars. For raucous band nights and local flavour, **Le Garage** has a cult following, while in town **Dixie Bar** is always packed, as is the **Cavern**, which wouldn't be out of place in Benidorm or Blackpool.

Shopping Independent shops rub shoulders with larger, established brands in Morzine. Indeed, the local supermarkets have their own website! **Shopi** and **Champion** are in the centre, while **Promocash** is a little farther out of town.

Hire shop/rental Being such a large town, Morzine has a high number of hire shops so you'll be better off finding out which one is closest to your accommodation.

Lift tickets There is a ticket office next to the Super Morzine lift but be warned: there

is usually an enormous queue both for tickets and the lift itself, so try to buy tickets before the morning you need them. Book online at morzine.com and pick them up at the Pleney cable car to save time.

Health and wellbeing There are two great spa facilities in town, **Un Cocon au Pays des Flocons** (uncoconaupaysdesflocons.com) and **Spa Massage du Monde** (spamassagedumonde.com).

Down days with kids Take them to Annecy, a captivating medieval French town by the beautiful Lake Annecy, just over an hour's drive away.

Internet **Monty's Bar**, on the main drag, or **Rhodos Hotel** have Wi-Fi.

Transfer options Morzine is so close to Geneva airport that transfers are very straightforward – try **Morzine Taxi** (morzine-taxi.com) or **Ski Transfer** (skitransfers.com). If money is tight, **Alpy Bus** (alpybus.com) is cheap and cheerful and runs bespoke services.

You can also ski here ... The entire Portes du Soleil region.

If you like this ... try Chamonix ▶▶ *p126*, Zermatt ▶▶ *p316*.

⊘ OPENING TIMES		
End 20 Dec to 3 Apr: 0830-1730		
ⓢ RESORT PRICES		
Week pass: €200		
Day pass: €39		
Season pass: €760		
ⓘ DIRECTORY		
Website: morzine.com		
Tourist office: T+33 (0)450-747272		
Medical centre: T+33 (0)450-759917		
Taxi: T+33 (0)620-719844		

↘26 Risoul

Town altitude	1850 m	Funicular/cable	
Km to airport	150 km	cars	0/1
Airport	Grenoble	Gondolas/chairs	1/15
Highest lift	2750 m	Drags	36
Vertical drop	1100 m	Night skiing	yes
Km of pistes	180 km	Terrain parks	2
Nursery areas	2	Glühwein factor	★★☆
Blues	57	Ski in/ski out	★★★
Reds	37	Environmental	
Blacks	10	rating	★☆☆☆☆

Purpose-built French suntrap, perfect for groups.

Risoul's big attraction is its proximity to the slopes. And what slopes! The Forêt Blanche ski region, linking Risoul's lift system with neighbouring Vars, is one of the most picturesque skiing areas in Europe. With 180 km of pistes it is easily big enough to entertain the most ardent of skiers, and because of the remote location – and limited clientele – you can expect plenty of room. Risoul's relative cheapness, combined with its large area, means it has become popular with Eastern European skiers looking for an authentic French holiday. The area was bestowed a French government award for its family-friendly leanings (it incorporates the Vigeoski system, where parents can track the movements of their children's ski pass at all times).

Beginners 'Le White Park' in Risoul is a perfect beginner area, featuring some interesting, gentle objects to challenge the learner skier.

Intermediate The Forêt Blanche is absolutely made for intermediate skiers, with wide, open, tree-lined runs stretching as far as the eye can see.

Expert Risoul's difficult runs are said to be given their 'black' status due to the fact that they are infrequently pisted rather than because they are steep. That said, there are some decent challenges in the forest, plus Risoul is rightly famous for Surfland – one of the best funparks and halfpipes in France.

Ski school/Tuition The ubiquitous ESF (T+33 (0)492-461922) is number one.

Kids Le Garderie (T+33 (0)492-460260) and Les Pitchouns (T+33 (0)492-462937) both take children from six months to six years.

Bad light There is an outside ice-rink (T+33 (0)670-717736), which is perfect for a down day.

Not to miss A go on the speed-skiing course to practise that tuck.

Remember to avoid If you don't like long transfers. Risoul isn't close to an airport, and can frequently find its road links closed due to adverse weather conditions.

ⓘ **OPENING TIMES**
Early Dec to mid-Apr: 0830-1630

$ **RESORT PRICES**
Week pass: €149.50
Day pass: €25

ⓘ **DIRECTORY**
Website: risoul.com
Tourist office: T+33 (0)492-460260
Medical centre: T+33 (0)492-462545
Pisteurs: T+33 (0)492-460751
Taxi: T+33 (0)492-452202

Practicalities

Risoul has much going for it: great tree runs, fantastic views, an out-of-the-way mountain, and – being so far south – long skiing days. What it doesn't have is pretty accommodation. The majority of buildings were built in 1970, though reinvestment since 2003 has resulted in a few wooden chalets springing up. Overall though, at 1850 m Risoul is perfect for ski-in/ski-out, brilliant for groups, and is an award-winning family centre.

Sleeping Sara Residences (T+33 (0)492-460347; sara-residences.com) offer upmarket apartments for weekly rental in Les Balcons de Sirius plus a range of cheap and cheerful self-catering apartments. La Bonne Auberge, (T+33 (0)492-450240; labonneauberge-risoul.com) is a two-star hotel in town.

Eating For fondue, *raclette* and *pierre chaude*, La Dalle en Pente (T+33 (0)492-460540) can't be beaten. Otherwise, the Snowboard Café (don't be put off by the name!) is busy, friendly and has the cheapest eats in town.

Bars and clubs All the bars in town have great après-ski owing to their location on the slopes. For a really late night, Le Morgan is pretty much the only place in town.

Transfer options Grenoble is the nearest airport, but many take the transfer from Lyon (over four hours).

You can also ski here ... Vars – Risoul's partner in the Forêt Blanche.

If you like this ... Try Avoriaz ▶▶ *p123*, Flaine ▶▶ *p136*.

France Risoul

↘27 St Gervais

Town altitude 810 m	Funicular/cable cars 2/3
Km to airport 95 km	Gondolas/chairs 10/35
Airport Geneva	Drags 64
Highest lift 2350 m	Night skiing yes
Vertical drop 1540 m	Terrain parks 2
Km of pistes 445 km	Glühwein factor ★☆☆
Nursery areas 2	Ski in/ski out ★★☆
Blues 63	Environmental
Reds 84	rating n/a
Blacks 33	

Old-school spa town with similar architecture and views to its famous resort neighbour Chamonix.

Describing St Gervais as a cheaper, more family-orientated version of nearby Megève – as most guidebooks seem to do – does a great disservice to the town. An old-fashioned spa town first popular in the early 1800s, Saint-Gervais-les-Bains – to give the place its full name – boasts classic stone buildings, ironwork and sculptures reminiscent of the Paris Métro, some beautiful bridges, a working, rustic funicular and a stunning gorge location. In any other country it would be a major resort; in France it is overshadowed by neighbouring Chamonix and Megève.

The Evasion Mont-Blanc area is beginner and intermediate heaven, with a huge variety of slopes and incredible views towards Mt Blanc and down the valley towards Sallanches. Expect slushy, mainly south-facing pistes, tree-lined runs and picturesque cowsheds to ski past.

Beginners The gentle slopes of Les Contamines are a perfect introduction to skiing.

Intermediate Take the funicular rack-and-pinion train (built in 1904) to Les Houches for an unforgettable day's skiing – this is how sophisticated skiing once was.

Expert Good skiers will find much to entertain them in the St Gervais and Les Contamines areas, though it's probably best to head for Megève to be truly satisfied.

Tuition ESF (T+33 (0)450-477621) operate here.

Kids ESF runs the 'Snow Garden' – two lifts and fun obstacles for kids to learn to ski on (€27 for 2½ hours, or €99 for a week's ticket).

Bad light The local spa, Les Thermes de Saint-Gervais-les-Bains (T+33 (0)450-475457; thermes-st-gervais.com), is an absolute must visit. First built to treat ailments over 200 years ago (it still advertises its healing properties), it is now a pamper zone of some repute.

Not to miss A trip up the funicular to see the views over Mont Blanc.

Remember to avoid If you want hedonistic nightlife or snow on the ground. At just over 800 m, this is a low ski resort, with snow in town a rarity.

Practicalities

Sleeping At the top end, La Ferme de Cupelin (T+33 (0)450-934730; ferme-de-cupelin.com) has rustic charm in spades. Chalet hotel La Maison Blanche (T+33 (0)450-477581) is a two-star, traditional hotel while La Grand Panorama (T+33 (0)450-586760; eurogroup-vacances.com) is a fantastic self-catering option.

Eating Good food can be found at the Star of County Down, a tea room in town.

Bars and clubs There are no clubs in St Gervais (nearby Megève has plenty), but the Yucatan Café and the Lounge Bar both have great atmosphere.

Transfer options Geneva airport is close and linked by motorway or super-efficient TGV train via nearby town Le Fayet.

You can also ski here ... The 'Evasion Mont-Blanc' pass entitles you to ski at Megève, St Nicolas de Véroce, Combloux, Les Contamines and Les Houches. The 'Skipass Mont-Blanc' gives access to the entire Chamonix valley.

If you like this ... try Les Contamines ▶▶ p154, Ste Foy ▶▶ p178, Peisey-Nancroix (France).

⊙ OPENING TIMES

Early Dec to mid-Apr: 0830-1630

⊙ RESORT PRICES

Week pass: €162
Day pass: €33.50

⊙ DIRECTORY

Website: st-gervais.net
Tourist office: T+33 (0)450-477608
Medical centre: T+33 (0)450-935178
Pisteurs: T+33 (0)450-931187
Taxi: T+33 (0)450-471753

↘28 St Martin de Belleville

Town altitude 1450 m	Funicular/cable
Km to airport 180	cars 0/6
km/100 km	Gondolas/
Airport Lyon/	chairs 33/69
Chambéry	Drags 72
Highest lift 3200 m	Night skiing no
Vertical drop 1750 m	Terrain parks 9
Km of pistes 600 km	Glühwein
Nursery areas 1	factor ★☆☆
Blues 121	Ski in/ski out ★☆☆
Reds 114	Environmental
Blacks 33	rating ★★★★★☆

A traditional French village with access to the Trois Vallées ski area, the resort is a realistic, laid-back alternative to the big-hitters Courchevel and Val Thorens.

St Martin's unique selling point is its link to the vast 600-km Trois Vallées ski area. By taking the gondola (St Martin 1) and the super-fast four-man quad (St Martin 2) you can access Les Menuires on one side and Méribel on the other. There is beautiful off-piste skiing under the Jerusalem chair – refer to the Trois Vallées off-piste guide (ask at the tourist office) for more itineraries and maps. The skiing in St Martin alone goes up to 3200 m and in case of poor snow there are 270 snow cannons in place to keep the resort snow in skiable condition.

Beginners There are gentle blues all the way from the top of the St Martin quad back to the village – the return to St Martin is particularly quiet and picturesque.

Intermediates The nearest reds in St Martin are Teppes and Pramint. Head over to Les Menuires for more variety and a greater challenge.

Advanced The area accessible from St Martin is vast, with great expanses of challenging terrain. Add to this a purpose built snowcross track, complete with berms and rolling jumps, in Les Menuires and the terrain parks of Méribel (above Arpasson on the Tougnète side of Mottaret) and Courchevel and you have it all. La Masse, up near Les Menuires, is a huge off-piste playground, even if there is a bit of a traverse.

Ski school/Tuition ESF offer ski, snowboard and snowshoeing.

Practicalities

Sleeping At the luxury end is La Bouitte (T+33 (0)479-089677; la-bouitte.com) with its Michelin-starred restaurant. Cheaper alternatives are the three-star Alp Hôtel (T+33 (0)470-089282; alphotel.fr) and Edelweiss (T+33 (0)479-089667; hotel-edelweiss73.com). Brewski's (T+33 (0)479-006234;brewskis.fr) offers good quality budget accommodation.

Eating St Martin is very proud of its traditional fare. La Ferme Chantacoucou (T+33 (0)479-089195) is a working farm that doubles as a restaurant. La Voûte (T+33 (0)479-089148) serves value-for-money salads and pizzas. Chez Bidou in Les Granges is a local favourite serving Savoyard dishes.

Bars and clubs The choice is limited to a few bars. Pourquoi Pas is a cosy piano bar set in an old wine cellar. Yukon at Hotel L'Altitude has Guinness on tap and British staff. If you're looking for the action head to Brewski's – a British/New Zealand-run bar serving pies and burgers by day and with live bands by night.

Hire shop/rental There are six ski shops that rent equipment.

Transfer options The nearest airports are Lyon (2½ hours) and Chambéry (two hours). Buses operate from both airports to St Martin (T+33 (0)820-320368; altibus.com).

You can also ski here ... Les Trois Vallées.

If you like this ... try Ste Foy ▶▶ *p178.*

⊙ OPENING TIMES
13 Dec to 26 Apr: 0900-1630

Ⓢ RESORT PRICES
Week pass: (Les Menuires–St Martin/ Trois Vallées) €172/€225

Day pass: €35.50/€45

Season pass: €759/€950

ⓘ DIRECTORY
Website: st-martin-belleville.com

Tourist office: T+33 (0)479-002000

Medical centre: T+33 (0)479-001542

Pisteurs: T+33 (0)479-002000

Taxi: T+33 (0)479-006954

Bad light Stick to the runs through the trees on the return to the village.

Not to miss Skiing off-piste to Michelin-starred La Bouitte for lunch.

Remember to avoid Missing the last lift back from Méribel; it's a long taxi ride back and very expensive.

↓29 Ste Foy

Town altitude 1550 m	Funicular/cable
Km to airport 160 km	cars 0/0
Airport Geneva	Gondolas/chairs 0/4
Highest lift 2620 m	Drags 0
Vertical drop 1070 m	Night skiing no
Km of pistes 25 km	Terrain parks 1
Nursery areas 2	Glühwein factor ★☆☆
Blues 4	Ski in/ski out ★★☆
Reds 8	Environmental
Blacks 3	rating ★★★★☆

The perennial bridesmaid to the Espace Killy bride, Ste Foy deserves the 'best kept secret in the Alps' tag.

Situated 12 km from Val d'Isère, Sainte Foy is the ideal resort for experienced skiers and beginners alike. It's relatively quiet, without much nightlife, so it is great for families and groups who are looking for a bit of escapism. Probably due to the lack of clubs and bars this is a less populated resort, which means relatively short waits for lifts and plenty of room on the slopes.

It is difficult to pinpoint why the place is so good – after all, there are only four chairs and 15 runs. But the fantastic terrain (there are two dedicated 'freeride off-piste areas') and the lack of crowds make it something of a gem for advanced and intermediates looking to stretch their wings in a true Alpine environment.

Beginners Complete beginners should take the Grand Plan chair and acquaint themselves with the Plan Bois run. Once confidence is up, there are a good number of blues.

Intermediate Eight reds should keep you busy. They snake over the entire resort and encompass every type of terrain.

Expert For experts this resort is a delight, and if you're lucky enough to get fresh snow you'll be in hog heaven. Take the L'Aiguille chair and head both ways into the sanctioned off-piste zones. Or hire a guide and get exploring.

Tuition You won't go far wrong with the local ESF (T+33 (0)479-069676).

Bad light Again, Ste Foy scores highly thanks to great tree cover, but stay on the L'Arpettaz and Grand Plan lifts.

Not to miss If high-grade, uncrowded pistes are a priority.

Remember to avoid If nightlife is a priority.

Practicalities

Sleeping Snowology (snowology. com) run great all-in chalet holidays, **Auberge Le Perce Neige** (T+33 (0)479-069747) is a bijou guesthouse just out of town, while **Le Monal** (le-monal.com) is an old-fashioned stopover providing old-style hospitality and modern amenities.

Eating We're big fans of the fondue at **La Maison à Colonnes** (T+33 (0)479-069480), while **La Bergerie** (T+33 (0)479-062551) takes care of local Savoyard fayre in fine old surroundings, as does **La Grange** (T+33 (0)479-069730).

Bars and clubs Ste Foy isn't a nightlife hotspot, but there are a few options, with the **Piano Bar** probably the liveliest. English-run **Chez Alison** also has a loyal clientele.

Hire shop/rental Most people seem to rate **Zig Zags** (zigzags.fr) although there is also a branch of the ubiquitous **Skiset** (T+33 (0)479-069995).

Transfer options One of the easiest resorts to access in the Alps, thanks to the Eurostar terminal at nearby Bourg-St-Maurice (sncf.com). Taxi transfers from the closest airport can be arranged through **Taxi Papillon** (T+33 (0)608-999396).

You can also ski here ... Tignes, Val d'Isère, La Rosière, Les Arcs, La Plagne are all within half an hour.

If you like this ... try Baqueira-Beret ▶▶ *p44*, Canazei ▶▶ *p214*, Leysin ▶▶ *p298*.

⊙ OPENING TIMES

Mid-Dec to mid-Apr: 0930-1630

⊙ RESORT PRICES

Week pass: €126

Day pass: €23

Season pass: €397

⊙ DIRECTORY

Website: saintefoy-tarentaise.com

Tourist office: T+33 (0)479-069519

Medical centre: T+33 (0)479-069222

Taxi: T+33 (0)608-999396

⬊30 Samoëns

Town altitude 720 km	Funicular/cable
Km to airport 45 km	cars 0/1
Airport Geneva	Gondolas/chairs 5/28
Highest lift 2500 m	Drags 8
Vertical drop 1780 m	Night skiing no
Km of pistes 265 km	Terrain parks 3
Nursery areas 15	Glühwein factor ★★☆
Blues 53	Ski in/ski out ☆☆☆
Reds 51	Environmental
Blacks 14	rating n/a

Samoëns is one of the more challenging of the five Grand Massif mountain range resorts, with stunning views and virtually no queues.

Part of the larger Grand Massif area, Samoëns' trump card is the high number of north-facing slopes – 80% according to the tourist board. It means there is abundant, regular snow. Terrain-wise it is equally good news, with plenty of blacks balanced by some mellow intermediate terrain.

Beginners Assuming you've outgrown the Samoëns 1600 nursery area, there are plenty of blue runs in the immediate Samoëns vicinity; once you include the Grand Massif area the options are many. Start with the easy options off the Chariande lifts, before progressing to the Gouilles.

Intermediate You'll want to explore the wider Grand Massif. Top of the list must be the Les Cascades run from the summit of the Grandes Platières. It's a long, long descent so stop for a break in Sixt before getting the bus back to town.

Expert For a challenge go to the 800-m drop of the Combe de Gers or the mogul slopes from the Tête des Saix.

Practicalities

Samoëns has grown and expanded recently but still retains plenty of old-school French charm. Known chiefly for its stonemasons, this listed village boasts medieval fountains, rustic old buildings and an ancient church.

Sleeping The Neige et Roc (neigeetroc.com) is a homely three-star hotel, with a great restaurant and a relaxation and wellness centre. **Peak Retreats** (peakretreats.co.uk) has an extensive range of self-catering accommodation, while **Alps Accommodation** (alpsaccommodation.com) offers catered chalets.

Eating La Louisiane (T+33 (0)450-344283) is famed for wood-fired pizzas, but for cosy local French Savoyard dishes **La Tornalta** (T+33 (0)450-349868) is well priced with lots of cheese. **La Table de Fifine** (T+33 (0)450-341029) is more upmarket, while on the slopes **Restaurant l'Epicea** is a gem with a sun terrace.

Bars and clubs La Clarine has Alpine decor and is popular with locals, while **Covey's Irish Pub** is open until late. For cocktails and an open fire go to **La Bois de Lune**.

Hire shop/rental You'll find the usual suspects, including **Intersport 1600** (intersport.com), **Sport 2000** (passionglisse.sport2000.fr) and local outfit **Samoëns Sports** (samoens-sports.fr).

Transfer options Local outfits **Go Massif** (gomassif.com) and **Ski Transfers** (skitransfers.com) offer rides to and from Geneva, Chambéry and Grenoble airports.

You can also ski here ... The nearby Vallée Blanche, in the Mont Blanc region, boasts 24-km of pistes with panoramic views.

If you like this ... try Les Contamines ▶▶ p154, Campitello ▶▶ p212.

⊕ OPENING TIMES
Early Dec to late Apr: 0900-1730

⊛ RESORT PRICES
Week pass: €187.20
Day pass: € 38
Season pass: €798
Website: samoens.com
Tourist office: T+33 (0)450-908001
Medical centre: T+33 (0)450-908142
Taxi: T+33 (0)450-908335

Tuition 360 International (ecoledeski360.com) or **Zig Zag** (zigzagski.com).

Not to miss A dogsled ride across the Haut Giffre valley (T+33 (0)450-341379).

Remember to avoid The summit if you're a beginner: stick to the specially made lower slopes.

France Samoëns

↘31 Serre Chevalier

Town altitude	Vertical drop 1630 m	Blacks 15	Terrain parks 1
1200-1500 m	Km of pistes 250 km	Funicular/cable cars 0/3	Glühwein factor ★★☆
Km to airport 180 km	Nursery areas 3	Gondolas/chairs 6/21	Ski in/ski out ★★☆
Airport Turin	Blues 58	Drags 32	Environmental
Highest lift 2830 m	Reds 42	Night skiing yes	rating ★★★★☆

PROS

- Exceptionally friendly and welcoming locals, with plenty of English spoken.
- Caters for skiers of all abilities.
- Generally uncrowded by European standards.
- Plenty to do for families, party-animals, food-lovers and hardcore freeriders.

CONS

- Travel between the villages can be tricky, particularly as shuttles stop at 1900.
- Fills up during French school holidays – avoid if possible!

'France's largest unknown resort' – family-friendly, with awesome freeriding and empty slopes (at the right times).

Serre Chevalier's main appeal is that it's freeride heaven. There are plenty of accessible off-piste spots stretching from Briançon to Monêtier. Seek and you will find!

Ash Strain, High Rock Chalet proprietor

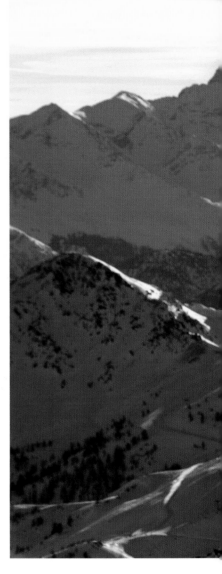

Serre Chevalier has 250 km of pistes, excellent off-piste opportunities and probably more trees than any resort in Europe, making it freeride heaven. It's also perfect for intermediates breaking into off-piste, with short powder hits and an avalanche transceiver training park. Like the village, the mountain has distinct areas, but they're well linked by lifts so it's easy to roam the area.

Beginners Find your feet on Monêtier's nursery area before heading to Serre Ratier's nursery slopes on the mountain. Cruise the blues on Grand Serre before the long greens down to Villeneuve from Aravet and Casse du Boeuf.

Intermediate Most of the mountain is your playground. Not to miss are the long Cucumelle red to Fréjus and the Aiguilette and Col de la Ricelle areas. Confident intermediates will enjoy the steeper Yret and Cibouït slopes, learning to ski powder on Clot Gauthier and the trees above Monêtier.

Expert Villeneuve and Chantemerle are best for accessing the resort's black runs, while Monêtier is the best starting point for freeriders. Pisted highlights are Isolée off l'Eychauda, Casse du Boeuf, Super Draye under Clot Gauthier, and Creux de Loup by Cucumelle. There's stacks of

accessible off-piste around Cucumelle, with good hits down from the Couloir de la Balme.

Powder Warm up on the Face des Neyzets under the Yret chair before dropping off Pic de l'Yret into the Vallon de la Montagnole, which brings you round onto the black Tabuc run. Also from the top of Yret, follow Voie Jackson down to Cucumelle. A short climb from the Cucumelle chair up Col de l'Eychauda will get you onto the Vallon des Corneilles, which drop into trees and a narrow canyon to Monêtier.

Moguls Face des Neyzets, Luc Alphand into Chantemerle and Rocher de l'Enfer from Serre Chevalier down to the Clot Gauthier chair.

Trees There's tree-skiing for all levels from wide greens and blues to narrow blacks. Favourites include the red Aiguilette and the black Casse du Boeuf and Tabuc runs.

Book a guide Confident intermediates will benefit from a guide here, gaining confidence in the trees and powder. Expert skiers should consider a day's

guiding in the freeriding mecca, La Grave (30 minutes away).

Tuition Serre Chevalier's four **ESF** ski schools have 500 instructors, making it the largest in France. **Ski Evasion**, based in Chantemerle, is a small school dedicated to families and British-run **EurekaSki** guarantees small classes and offers one-day avalanche awareness courses.

Kids Skiing is free for under fives. Monêtier's nursery slopes are easily accessible at the base station whereas the Serre Ratier area above Chantemerle is on the mountain.

Bad light Serre Chevalier is probably the best resort in Europe to be on a bad-light day, with two-thirds of the resort in the trees. Alternatively, visit Briançon to explore the ancient ramparts, old town and shops.

Not to miss Having lunch at **Pi Maï** before meandering back to Villeneuve on the gentle, tree-lined Refuge de Fréjus slope.

Remember to avoid Freeriding without avalanche safety gear – the area is prone to avalanche.

Relive a famous moment Local man Eric Bobrowicz (aka Bob) designed the world's first twin tips. Buy or rent from Bob's own ski line at his **Ride Doctor** shop in Villeneuve.

Pitstop and sunbathe Café Soleil at Serre Ratier has a large sun terrace, **Chalet de Serre Blanc** near the top of Prorel has great views, while **Pi Maï** in the hamlet of Fréjus is the cosiest spot on the mountain.

Best mountain restaurant For gourmet heaven on the slopes, you can't beat **Le Bivouac**'s 'first class' restaurant above the Casse Boeuf chair, although the less expensive **Tatou** is also popular. **Pra Long** on Brian on combines food and views and, for a truly authentic experience, join the locals in **Peyra-Juana** on Monêtier.

😊 LOCALS DO

✅ Get an early start at Monêtier on powder days.

✅ Have early lunch and late afternoon beers at Peyra-Juana on Monêtier.

✅ Ski in La Grave on weekdays.

😠 LOCALS DON'T

❌ Ski off-piste without avalanche gear.

❌ Share their secret powder stashes with anyone!

❌ Forget to bring a camera – the views are spectacular.

Practicalities

Serre Chevalier is the collective name for 13 villages stretching 15 km along the Guisane valley to Briançon (France's highest Alpine town). The main ski stations are Briançon (1200 m), Chantemerle (1350 m), Villeneuve (1400 m) and Monêtier (1500 m). Each has a distinctive character, so choose carefully before you book. We recommend Briançon for non-skiers and townies, Chantemerle for families, Villeneuve for party animals and Monêtier for mountain-loving freeriders and romantic couples.

Sleeping Most visitors stay in chalets or apartments – visit serre-chevalier-reservation.com for a directory and miquelhols.co.uk for affordable packages in Monêtier. There are plenty of comfortable, family-run hotels like **Plein Sud** (T+33 (0)492-241701; hotelpleinsud.com) in Chantemerle and **Le Christiania** (T+33 (0)492-247633; hotel-lechristiania.com) in Villeneuve. If you are pushing the boat out, **Hôtel Alliey** in Monêtier (T+33 (0)492-244002; alliey.com) is small and welcoming with excellent food, spa facilities and apartments. The five-star chalet **Chez Bear** (T+33 (0)492-211170; chezbear. com) near Briançon sleeps 10-12. Find more luxury accommodation through chalet-prestige.com.

Eating In Briançon, foodies head for **Le PasséSimple** (T+33 (0)492-213743), which recreates ancient local recipes. In Chantermerle, **Le Crystal** (T+33 (0)492-240309) is the gourmet's choice, while **Le Petit Chalet** (T+33 (0)492-240579) and **Le Triptyque** (T+33 (0)492-241494) are both popular. In Villeneuve, tiny and atmospheric **La Marotte** (T+33 (0)492-247723) serves up local cuisine, as does **La Pastorale** (T+33 (0)492-247547),

while **La Grotte du Yetti** is the place for fry-ups and burgers. In Monêtier, first choice for locals is **Hotel Alliey's** restaurant, **Caribou** does traditional Savoyard food, and **Pizzaria des Neiges** (T+33 (0)492-244382) is ideal for families.

Au pair/crèche La Garderie des Eterlous (T+33 (0)492-244575) takes kids from six months to nine years. The tourist office holds a list of accredited nannies (T+33 (0)492-249899).

Best après-ski La Grotte du Yetti and Le Frog in Villeneuve, **Extreme Bar** in Chantemerle and **Alpen Bar** and **Rif Blanc** in Monêtier are the liveliest bars for après. Alternatively, test the ice-driving circuit near Monêtier or soak in the Bains du Monêtier.

Bars and clubs The bars above are popular later in the evening as well as **Mojos** in Villeneuve, **L'Escapade** in Chantemerle, **Central Bar** and **Eden** in Briançon. Villeneuve's **La Baita** is the best nightclub.

Shopping Each village has good food and rental shops in large commercial centres.

Hire shop/rental With 33 rental shops to chose from, pick what's most convenient for you. The **Ride Doctor** in Villeneuve rents and sells unique twin tips. If you're feeling flash, visit Monêtier's **Stawug Sport**.

Health and wellbeing Relax in the natural hot springs and spa facilities at **Les Bains du Monêtier**. The **Plein Sud** in Chantemerle has a spa and **Spa Montagne** (Hotel Alliey) offers beauty treatments and massages.

Down days with kids Guided nature walks teach kids about animals, basic orientation and how to build an igloo

(T+33 (0)492-247590). **Le Triptyque** (T+33 (0)492-241494) runs children's cookery courses during school holidays.

Internet Le Frog in Villeneuve, **Extreme Bar** in Chantemerle and **Alpen** in Monêtier have Wi-Fi (among others). There are machines at the tourist office.

Transfer options There's a shuttle service from Turin airport (turin-airport. com) to Brian on on Saturdays. **ATS** (a-t-s.net) offer shared transfers from Lyon, Turin and Grenoble airports. The **TGV** (raileurope.com) goes from Paris to Oulx in Italy, from where there are regular buses to Serre Chevalier.

You can also ski here ... Les Deux Alpes, Montgenèvre, Puy-St-Vincent and Alpe d'Huez.

If you like this ... try Alpe d'Huez ▶▶ p120, Mayrhofen ▶▶ p75, Engelberg ▶▶ p284.

France Serre Chevalier

☺ **OPENING TIMES**

Early Dec to late Apr: 0900-1645

💲 **RESORT PRICES**

Week pass: €181

Day pass: €38

Season pass: €745

ⓘ **DIRECTORY**

Website: serre-chevalier.com

Tourist office: T+33 (0)492-249898

Medical centre: T+33 (0)492-244254

Pisteurs: T+33 (0)492-255500

Taxi: T+33 (0)492-240558

↘32 Tignes

Town altitude 2100 m	Nursery areas 4	Funicular/cable	Terrain parks 1
Km to airport 173 km/ 132 km	Blues 40	cars 2/4	Glühwein factor ★★☆
Airport Geneva/ Chambéry	Reds 16	Gondolas/chairs 4/49	Ski in/ski out ☆☆☆
Highest lift 3456 m	Blacks 10	Drags 41	Environmental
	Km of pistes 150 km	Night skiing no	rating ★★★★★★
Vertical drop 1900 m			

PROS

- ☺ If you take your piste time seriously, you'll find plenty of like-minded individuals.
- ☺ Accommodation is much more reasonably priced than in neighbouring Val d'Isère.
- ☺ Area is connected to Val d'Isère extremely well so venturing out isn't a problem.

CONS

- ☒ There's not a lot to do in the evenings if you like your après-ski.
- ☒ Having to fight for the best snow, which gets old pretty quickly.
- ☒ The place is ugly. The beautiful scenery is seriously let down by the architecture.

For the serious snow enthusiast, Tignes has it all. Take advantage of the amazing L'Espace Killy terrain before relaxing in the local bars and restaurants.

Tignes shares the Espace Killy with nearby Val d'Isère, so wherever you're staying you'll have access to a whopping 320 km of trails. Unlike a lot of French ski areas, Tignes is open year round, with visitors coming to mix glacier skiing with afternoons on the shore of the lake. The population is doubled during the winter by the seasonaires, primarily young British males attracted to the huge range of on- and off-piste action. Although the high altitude prevents any tree-skiing, it does mean that Tignes' snow-sure factor is one of the highest in France. The resort does its best to cater for as many skiers as possible and on the whole succeeds in doing so. Where pistes are marked as 'Tranquil' zones, a strict speed limit is observed for beginners. At the other extreme, 'Naturide' areas (a new category of black run popping up all over Europe) are off-piste areas patrolled and avalanche protected, but not groomed – heaven for advanced off-pisters.

Beginners Lavachet in Val Claret is one of the best beginners' slopes in the resort and is surrounded by some great bars and restaurants if you're feeling defeated. When you're ready to venture further up the hill, try the blues Lac and Anemone on L'Aiguille Percée or take the Tovière chair and cruise the greens on the border between Tignes and Val d'Isère.

Intermediate One of the biggest drawbacks to the resort is the crowds. In peak season try to avoid the Double M underneath Les Lanches chairlift. Although it's a great run, the crowds make it very hard to get any sort of speed up. If you head up the other side of the valley, the blue and red runs from Chardonnet and Palafour are quiet enough for you to let rip.

Expert There are some pretty horrific blacks and it's those skiers who are after some challenging terrain who will truly make the most of Tignes. Notorious La Face, the Olympic piste from the summit of La Bellevarde to Val d'Isère, is a must-do for adrenalin junkies, but try to go first thing in the morning as later in the day it's crazy busy. In the afternoon, hang out in the Naturide zone (marked Le Spot on the piste map).

Powder The Naturide area has never seen a piste-basher so offers a whole slope of off-piste – so to speak. When there's new snow, most advanced skiers will head here, although you'll be able to find fresh tracks for a few days after. Be warned, you'll probably have to fight the locals for the best powder.

Moguls The first stage of the 2007-08 Mogul World Cup was held in Tignes, so make like the pros and check out Sache towards Les Brévières.

Trees Because of the high altitude, there aren't many options for tree-skiing. When the light's bad, you can try Pavot or Sache down into Les Brévières, which takes the altitude down to 1550, but most tend to head back into town to try again the next day.

☺ LOCALS DO

- ☺ Avoid the Brits and take shelter in the Embuscade hotel bar.
- ☺ Take their skiing very seriously and see early nights and early mornings as a way of life.
- ☺ Avoid the crowds on the Face piste in the afternoon.

☺ LOCALS DON'T

- ☒ Travel on a Saturday – like Val d'Isère, transfer day is a nightmare on the road from Bourg St Maurice.
- ☒ Eat in the mountain restaurants, which can get quite pricey especially if you end up in Val d'Isère – most will take a packed lunch instead.

espace **killy**

le plus bel espace de ski du monde

Book a guide The **Bureau des Guides de Tignes** (T+33 (0)479-064276) will show you where to go for some of the best off-piste you'll ever ski.

Tuition **Snocool** (T+33 (0)479-063992; snocool.com) cater for skiing and snowboarding at every level and will customize the training sessions to suit you.

Kids **Les Marmottons** (T+33 (0)479-063712; marmottons-tignes.com) have offices in Val Claret and Le Lac and will look after kids from 2½ months to six years.

Bad light If the light's bad, you're out of luck. The lowest altitude available is

Practicalities

Compared to its neighbour Val d'Isère, sport comes first here and you're more likely to find visitors staying on the slopes as long as possible rather than partying the night away. The actual resort is split between Val Claret, Le Lac and Le Lavachet, although most visitors tend to move between each of the villages. They take the protection of their environment very seriously and are one of the first ski resorts in the world to introduce measures such as replacing salt with gravel on the roads and having an ongoing programme to replace several different lifts with just one. Like Val d'Isère, the resort is a favourite with British seasonaires, but you'll find a different type of skier from those down the road: stopping for lunch is considered a weakness!

Sleeping You'll save money by staying here rather than in Val d'Isère. Top-end chalets in the resort such as 'Moonstone' and 'Mosaic Agate' provided by **Alps Executive Class** (T+33 (0)450-882195;

aec-collection.com) are just as good accommodation-wise as in Val d'Isère but nowhere near as expensive. **Village Montana** (T+33 (0)479-400144; vmontana.com) is by far the nicest place (this is where the French football team stays during their summer training camps), but **Hôtel Le Pâquis** (T+33 (0)479-063733) and **Hôtel L'Arbina** (T+33 (0)479-063478) are two other good-value *residences* that impress. For its incredible location, **Hôtel Le Levanna** (T+33 (0)479-063294) should also be highly recommended.

Eating Upstairs in L'Arbina (T+33 (0)479-064683), in Le Lac, is generally regarded as the hang-out for the more affluent types in the area. It serves superb seafood dishes – try the oysters or *foie gras*. **Clin d'Oeil** (T+33 (0)479-065910), also in Le Lac, cook locally sourced Savoyard food in a cosy setting, prices starting at €35 a head for a three-course meal. The majority of restaurants in the resort are excellent value, such as **Restaurant la Poutrerie** (T+33 (0)479-063264), who serve

enormous steaks with cocktails, and **L'Indochine** (T+33 (0)479-060807), for an all-you-can-eat Chinese buffet, both in Val Claret

Au pair/crèche Situated next to Le Lagon, **Kids Club/Youth Club** (T+33 (0)479-400440) provide entertainment for kids from six to 16. Prices start at €130 for a week's package. Note that the tourist office advises that Tignes isn't the best place to bring children under two due to the high altitude.

Best après-ski Especially for the battered beginners, Le Lavachet and Val Claret hold most of the après-ski action, in particular **Scotty's** just off the Lavachet piste. Most skiers prefer to stay up on the mountain rather than starting their après early, but you can still enjoy the late afternoon sunshine and a beer in **Grizzly's** or **Le Kfe Lounge**, where they do an amazing chocolate fondue for €12.

Bars and clubs For live music and Fisherman's Friend-flavoured shots, **Couloir** is the place to be in Val Claret.

Tignes Les Brévières at 1550 m where you'll find some trees in the area above the village but remember that everyone else will be thinking the same thing. Perhaps better to head over to Val d'Isère and start the après-ski early.

Not to miss Even if you only do it once, get up early and fight the seasonaires for the new snow if there's heavy ground coverage overnight. Get to Guerlain Chicherit in the Naturide area and you'll see why Tignes is one of the best resorts in France for off-piste.

Remember to avoid Bringing a car if you can do without one – the tourist board are very conscious about cars blotting the scenery (have they seen some of the buildings?) and insist on underground parking for all, which you'll need to pay for.

Relive a famous moment For six weeks between the winter and summer seasons the resort shuts down and becomes a training camp for the French football team.

Pit-stop and sunbathe What? You want to stop? Well, I suppose everyone deserves a rest and the chance to get fresh legs, so put your feet up outside **Escale Blanche** (T+33 (0)479-064550)

and enjoy a beer and a slice of home-made pizza.

Best mountain restaurant
Panoramic (T+33 (0)479-066011) has a great table-service menu and is good value for money but try to avoid their self-service options. If you're in the mood for splashing out, **Lo Solis** (T+33 (0)479-060742), halfway down the corniche, serves excellent Italian food (especially pasta). For a quick bite, burgers and chips are served by the bowlful in the bars along the Lavachet beginners' area. **TC's** (T+33 (0)479-064646) is one of the best.

Presumed to be considerably tamer than Val d'Isère, Tignes stands its ground with great bars such as Le Lac's **Grotte du Yeti** and Val Claret's **Fish Tank**. The local snowboarders hang at out at **Crowded House** in Val Claret before heading on to local nightclub **Blue Girl**, famous for its 'theme' nights.

Shopping Those visiting Tignes certainly don't go there for the shopping. Most shops tend to offer ski and boarding wear such as the **Quiksilver Boardriders Club** for freestyle gear or **Snow Tec** (T+33 (0)479-064246) for a professional boot-fitting service.

Hire shop/rental Snowfun (T+33 (0)479-062224; snowfun.com) have 12 shops throughout Tignes, with 10% off if you arrange equipment hire online through tignes.co.uk – can't say fairer than that!

Health and wellbeing The best place for pampering is **Les Campanules** (T+33 (0)479-063436/; campanules.com) where treatments include hydrotherapy, massage and reflexology.

Lift tickets It's good value to buy a lift ticket that also covers nearby Val d'Isère – it's only a fraction more than a ticket for Tignes.

Down days with kids Le Lagon (T+33 (0)479-402995) is definitely worth a visit – it has water slides, kids' pool and spa, as well as free entry for under-fives. **Evolution 2** (T+33 (0)479-064378) organize 'ski joring' where you can attend beginners' classes in being pulled on skis by a horse. Alternatively, you'll find most kids are happy to be on the beginners' slopes with a hired sledge while the grown-ups enjoy the après-ski.

Internet TC's (T+33 (0)479-064646) provides free Wi-Fi and internet terminals to accompany a late-night menu serving chips and kebabs.

Transfer options A bus runs every day between Geneva airport and Tignes (call T+33 (0)419-571500 for times). You don't really need a car as the villages are serviced by a 24-hour bus link, but if you are driving, follow the directions from Geneva to Bourg St Maurice and on to Tignes from there.

You can also ski here ... Val d'Isère, 30 minutes away on skis, extends the available terrain to 320 km. If you want a challenge, try the 10-km run from the top of L'Aiguille Percée right down into Tignes Brévières – phew!

If you like this ... try Les Deux Alpes ▶▶*p156*, Val Thorens ▶▶*p193*.

▶▶*p156*, Val Thorens ▶▶*p193*.

France Tignes

◉ **OPENING TIMES**

Dec to early May: 0800-1700

💲 **RESORT PRICES**

Week pass: €202.50 for 6 days/€231 for 7 days

Day pass: €42

Season pass: €980

ⓘ **DIRECTORY**

Website: tignes.net

Tourist office: T+33 (0)479-400440

Medical centre: T+33 (0)479-065964

Taxi: T+33 (0)609-436090

↘33 Val d'Isère

Town altitude 1850 m	Km of pistes 150 km	Funicular/cable	Terrain parks 1
Km to airport 175 km	Nursery areas 2	cars 2/4	Glühwein factor ★★★
Airport Geneva	Blues 24	Gondolas/chairs 4/45	Ski in/ski out ★★☆
Highest lift 3450 m	Reds 19	Drags 24	Environmental
Vertical drop 1700 m	Blacks 12	Night skiing no	rating ★★☆☆☆

PROS

- ✅ Among the best nights out in the Alps.
- ✅ Everyone speaks English. Mainly because everyone is English.
- ✅ Access to the huge Espace Killy area means you'll never exhaust the possibilities.

CONS

- ❌ Too hectic for some.
- ❌ Very English, so not suitable for those looking for a classic French resort.
- ❌ Expensive.

Val d'Isère attracts Europe's biggest poseurs, to see and be seen on some of its superb terrain and to party the night away in its first-class bars and restaurants.

Compared to the cool subtlety of ultra-rich Courchevel (perhaps its closest rival), Val d'Isère can come across as somewhat nouveau riche. But the skiing is amazing, and the close proximity of Tignes allows you to venture out to quieter climes if it all gets a bit much. It's easy to see why so many Brits are attracted to the area, with its crazy nightlife and the wide variety of entertainment on offer. As long as your perfect holiday doesn't include tranquillity and relaxation, it's hard not to have a good time!

Combined with Tignes, L'Espace Killy has more skiable terrain than Whistler or nearly anywhere else in Europe. This means that there's plenty of room to practise although you'll find most skiers tend to remain on the central runs in Solaise and on the Bellavarde. To make the most of Val d'Isère you need to know where to go, so hiring a guide is well worthwhile – especially if you're a powder seeker.

Beginners Beginners need to head as high as possible (try some of the greens from the Borset Express) as many of the pistes back into town or further down the valley can get pretty steep. Val d'Isère probably isn't ideal for absolute beginners as the slopes can get very busy but quieter Le Fornet allows you to practise in peace.

Intermediate Again, if crowds scare you, try to avoid Solaise or Rocher de Bellevarde and explore the edges of the

piste map. For some challenging terrain that keeps you within your comfort zone, the Tommeuses lift takes you over to Tignes where the mix of blues and reds will keep you busy.

Expert Val gets busy, so you'll be fighting for the best off-piste. But the high altitude means there are a lot of freeriding possibilities, especially off the runs back down into the village. Germain Mattis, piste A and piste M are all quite tricky, but undoubtedly the best is Face on the Rocher de Bellavarde.

Powder One of the best places to head for fresh snow is Tignes, but if you prefer to stay on this side of the valley you've still got a huge amount of off-piste at your disposal. Venture off St Jacques or Arcelle for some of the best powder in Europe.

Moguls With this amount of off-piste, it's inevitable you're going to encounter moguls, particularly towards the end of the season. Face and L'Epaule are bumpy for most of the season thanks to their high amount of ride time.

Trees Check out Le Fornet trees, at the far end of the valley. It might be busy but it's the biggest expanse of greenery in the valley.

Book a guide Although the off-piste is amazing, it brings with it an increased avalanche risk and deaths can and do occur. **Top Ski** (T+33 (0)479-061480; topskival.com) specializes in off-piste and freestyle.

Tuition Tuition doesn't come cheap but **Alpine Experience** (alpineexperience.com) is good value and designer junkies will love being instructed by the **DC School** (dc-school.com).

Kids British company **New Generation** (skinewgen.com) have won awards for

the quality of their instruction. They provide kids' tuition between the ages of six and 12 and reward everyone with badges and certificates at the end of the week.

Bad light Locals rate the trees off the Super L off the Solaise as a good flat-light alternative.

Not to miss Even if you're only visiting for a week, try and make it over to

Tignes – it offers a refreshing change from all the crowds and posing.

Remember to avoid Skiing back into the village at the end of the day – the pistes are so busy that you'll be much happier having another run up the mountain and getting the gondola back down.

Relive a famous moment L'Espace Killy is named after skiing legend Jean-Claude Killy – his sports shops dominate Val d'Isère and he's generally regarded as the Daddy of élite French skiing.

Pit-stop and sunbathe Bar de l'Ouillette (T+33 (0)479-419474) on Solaise is only small but the outdoor barbecue is perfect for those sunny moments. Put your feet up in one of the deckchairs, grab your shades and congratulate yourself on avoiding the self-service and saving some cash ...

Best mountain restaurant It's no secret how good **Edelweiss** (T+33 (0)610-287064) on the Mangard is. If you forget to book, try **La Tanière** (T+33 (0)479-061129), which serves traditional Savoyard lunches and dinners, or self-styled 'Ibiza in the Mountains' **La Folie Douce** (T+33 (0)479-060147), where from 1500 the live DJ entertains guests in the sunshine at the outdoor bar.

☺ LOCALS DO

☑ Wait till midweek to travel. The road to Val d'Is re is narrow and windy and a nightmare on transfer day (Saturday).

☑ Self cater and buy their supplies in Bourg St Maurice rather than paying a fortune in the village centre.

☑ Head over to Tignes for the day to escape the crowds of noisy tourists.

☹ LOCALS DON'T

☒ Hang around long at the end of the day – the pistes can become very congested as everyone tries to get back into town.

☒ Get stuck in Tignes-les-Brévières after the last lift – it's a long way back to town.

Practicalities

Sleeping

One of the biggest problems in the village is the accommodation gap between the nice and not so nice hotels – there's very little middle ground. At the luxury end, **Le Chardon Mountain Lodges** (lechardonvaldisere.com) provide accommodation for up to 20 guests who come back year after year for the five-star service, which includes champagne receptions, a driver service, a free nanny and a private hot tub. If you want to splash out without, hopefully, breaking the bank, **Le Blizzard**, with its outdoor pool and free parking, and **L'Aigle des Neiges** (T+33 (0)479-061888; pv-holidays.com) are two of the best; or you could try **Les Chalets du Laissant** (T+33 (0)892-350680) for some serious ski in/ski out. Val d'Isère in general is quite expensive, but **La Savoyarde** (T+33 (0)479-060155; la-savoyarde.com) and family-friendly **Odalys** (T+33 (0)825-562562; odalys-vacances.com) offer good value for money.

Eating

La Grand Ourse (T+33 (0)479-060019) is considered one of the best and most fashionable places to go for 'gastronomique' but can be quite pricey. For a similar standard, **La Perdrix Blanche** (T+33 (0)479-061209) is slightly cheaper. **Pier Paul Jack** (T+33 (0)479-062108; pierpauljack.com) is spread across three levels, each serving a different menu. Pull up a bean bag,

order the white-chocolate *foie gras* and relax with the live jazz pianist.

Au pair/crèche

Lift passes are free for the under-fives but if you want them in ski-school, they can attend from the age of three. Contact the tourist office for a list of registered babysitters or try **Le Village des Enfants** (valdisere-levillagedesenfants.com).

Best après-ski

Where to begin? Après-ski starts early at the **Moris Pub** (morispub.com) or head to **Taverne d'Alsace** (T+33 (0)479-064849) where a slightly older crowd enjoy the relaxed atmosphere. New bar **Saloon** (T+33 (0)479-400761) is where the seasonaires chill before a big night or **Victors** (T+33 (0)479-060652) for the dangerous range of 2-4-1 cocktails.

Bars and clubs

Join the season workers in legendary **Dicks Tea Bar** or try something a little more down to earth. New bar **Warm Up** or **Bananas** are good places to start the night before everyone heads to **Le Graal** nightclub.

Shopping

You'll find most of the big names in Val d'Isère and a lot of kit shops. There are two reasonably sized **Spar** shops in the village centre – stock up on your basics here.

Hire shop/rental

If you want something a bit special, **Oxygène** (T+33 (0)479-419958; oxygene-ski.com) have English-speaking boot-fitters and offer special kids' packs at good rates.

Lift tickets

Lift tickets are quite expensive but only a few euros more for access to Tignes as well – definitely worth the money for almost doubling your available piste.

Health and wellbeing

La Savoie (T+33 (0)479-000115; lesavoie.com) is

one of the best, with access to the pool and jacuzzi etc included with every one-hour treatment.

Down days with kids

For something a bit different, try 'air boarding' on the Font de Neige. It's a bit like tobogganing on a short, fat lilo.

Internet

The tourist office has six terminals, available during opening hours, or try the **Powder Monkey Café**.

Transfer options

It's a bit of a trek from Geneva airport. If you can, try to bag a flight using Chambéry. Alternatively, jump on the train and head for Bourg St Maurice, then take the bus – it's worth it just for the view. **Altibus** (T+33 (0)479-410125; altibus.com) run frequent services.

You can also ski here ...

Head over the hill and try Tignes: it's a bit quieter and they take their snow sports very seriously but it's well worth paying an extra few euros for the access.

If you like this ...

try Chamonix ▶▶ *p126*, Verbier ▶▶ *p308*

◉ OPENING TIMES

Early Dec to early May: 0930-1630

⑤ RESORT PRICES

Week pass: €202.50 for 6 days/€231 for 7 days

Day pass: €42

Season pass: €980

ⓘ DIRECTORY

Website: valdisere.com

Tourist office: T+33 (0)479-060660

Medical centre: T+33 (0)479-402680

Pisteurs: T+33 (0)479-061866

Taxi: T+33 (0)479-410125

France Val d'Isère

↘34 Valmorel

Town altitude	1400 m	Funicular/cable cars	0/0
Km to airport	125 km	Gondolas/chairs	2/17
Airport	Geneva	Drags	30
Highest lift	2550 m	Night skiing	no
Vertical drop	1150 m	Terrain parks	2
Km of pistes	150 km	Glühwein factor	★★☆
Nursery areas	22	Ski in/ski out	★★☆
Blues	38	Environmental	
Reds	17	rating	★★★★☆
Blacks	8		

A picturesque French-speaking enclave in the middle of the Tarantaise, Valmorel is part of the Grand Domaine region.

For British skiers, Valmorel has slipped somewhat mystifyingly through the net, although those adherents who have discovered its time capsule charms tend to be fanatical about returning.

Valmorel's links to Saint Francois Longchamps greatly increase the amount of skiable terrain on offer. Its position at the 'head' of the Tarantaise also means it seems to get more snow than other areas, and the mix of north and south facing slopes gives a good mix of sunny and shaded slopes, so fresh snow tends to last.

Beginners There are dedicated beginner areas in Valmorel ('mini domaine') and nearby Doucy. In Valmorel you'll find some easy, easy blues off the Creve Coeur lift and the Cote Soleil lift.

Intermediates For confident intermediates, Valmorel offers a lot of challenges. The obvious place to start is the Col du Mottet, with its many reds, while a long range excursion to St Francois will take up a jolly day and test your legs.

Experts Valmorel doesn't immediately strike you as the most challenging area in the world, but there are some good steeps here, with Mottet, Biollene and Col du Gollet where you'll find the majority of reds and blacks.

Tuition The ESF (esf-valmorel.com) are a safe bet and run the **Piou-Piou Club** for the little ones.

Bad light Much of the lower terrain is in the trees, but experts might struggle if the snow does come in.

Not to miss The lovely atmosphere of this unique village when compared to some of its party-mad neighbours.

Remember to avoid If nightlife is a must. You'll be better off up in nearby Méribel.

Practicalities

Valmorel's village atmosphere sets it apart from the other main Tarantaise resorts, and the low buildings covered in local stone and wood give it a certain charm.

Sleeping Hôtel du Bourg (+33 (0)479 099288) is slap bang in the middle of town on the main street. A cosy lounge with fireplace make it a local's favourite. For slightly out of town living, **Hôtel les Marmottons** (+33 (0)479 096670), in the small village of La Charmette, is reachable on skis and has a nice bar and restaurant. You can also book other options through the valmorel.com website.

Eating Our man in Valmorel picks out **Le Petit Prince** (+33 (0)479 098171), while you'll either love or hate **La Marmite** (+33 (0)479 098319) and its Savoyarde fondue, **L'Aigle Blanc** is a unique location just out of town with an eccentric owner – and not just because he doesn't accept credit cards.

Bars and Clubs La Cordée attracts the foreign après ski crowd, while **L'Annexe** is a nice bar and lounge. Local skiers frequent **Le Café de la Gare** in an attempt to escape the hordes at **Le Perce Neige**. After, head to – well, **l'After** for dancing.

Hire shop/rental Plenty of choice, but local emporium **Valmosports** (valmosports.com) offers rentals and new equipment in a friendly, English-speaking environment.

Transfer options You'll likely fly into Geneva, and it is about two hours transfer. Local specialists **Alpine Cab** are a good bet – alpinecab.com.

You can also ski here ... the Grand Domaine area is made up of Valmorel, Doucy Combelouviere and Satin Francois Longchamp.

If you like this, try ... Châtel ▶▶ *p131*, Champéry ▶▶ *p277*.

⊛ OPENING TIMES
19 Dec-18 Apr: 0915-1630

⑤ RESORT PRICES
Week pass: €180

Day pass: €35.50

◐ DIRECTORY
Website: valmorel.com

Tourist office: T+33 (0)479-098026

Medical Centre: T+33 (0)479-098045

Pisteurs: T+33 (0)479-098026

Taxi: T+33 (0)621 527739

↘35 Val Thorens

Town altitude 1800 m	Km of pistes 600 km	Funicular/cable cars 0/6	Terrain parks 9
Km to airport 159 km	Nursery areas 3	Gondolas/chair	Glühwein factor ★★★
Airport Geneva	Blues 121	lifts 33/69	Ski in/ski out ★★☆
Highest lift 3200 m	Reds 114	Drags 72	Environmental
Vertical drop 2130 m	Blacks 33	Night skiing no	rating ★★★★☆

PROS

- ✅ High-altitude, snow-sure destination with great access to the Trois Vallées.
- ✅ Excellent intermediate terrain.
- ✅ Car-free village.

CONS

- ❌ When the weather comes in there is no skiing to be had.
- ❌ High winds can leave the pistes rock hard.
- ❌ Some crowded pistes in the centre of the resort.

The highest resort in Europe, with access to the Trois Vallées, it's a good bet for early and late season skiing. A lively, cheaper alternative to its neighbours.

Val Thorens is all about altitude. With the highest lifts in the Trois Vallées, skiers can expect to find some of the most challenging terrain here. There seems to be something about the height of the place that gives the nightlife a somewhat frenzied air as well: expect to rub shoulders with party-happy Scandinavians in addition to the French and English. There's a friendly vibe here, even if it doesn't extend to the somewhat questionable architecture.

Val T's height can be something of a double-edged sword early on in the winter. While snow conditions are all but guaranteed, there's a risk of bad weather and the fact that it is entirely above the treeline means there isn't much in reserve once cloud rolls in. Trois Vallées access, via Méribel's Côte Brune area, is relatively simple, but we think everyone bar the most intrepid will spend most of their time in the Belleville valley (Val Thorens, Les Menuires and St Martin de Belleville).

Beginners There are lots of gentle green runs near the village and even a magic carpet for those struggling with the lifts. To progress onto the longer blue runs take the Moraine or Moutière chairlifts. Beginners may be put off by the bleakness of the resort on bad-weather days.

Intermediates Les Trois Vallées is an intermediate skier's wonderland. There are plenty of blues and red runs around the village that offer some excellent skiing. Push yourself by taking the steep red run off the Col lift, which is fabulous, especially when just groomed. The Funitel Péclet cable car opens up some great reds, which lead back down to the resort.

Expert Experts need to explore the area to make the most of the terrain. There are some challenging, though not steep, blacks and reds off the Cime de Caron cable car. Off the back of this peak is a nice black that leads into the lesser known 'fourth valley' of Orelle, which is so often overlooked. The Pierre Lory pass is a good place to start testing the powder skis. It requires a short traverse from the top of the Col chairlift. Fast skiers can make it over to Courchevel in just over an hour.

Powder There is masses of off-piste terrain in Val Thorens and, thanks to the high altitude, the powder usually holds up for a few days. The Cime de Caron cable car gives access to the huge Lac

du Lou area, which usually has good snow until late season. To really get away from the crowds, take one of the numerous routes down to Orelle.

Moguls Head for the black off the Cascades chair. The red runs from the top of the Funitel Grand Fond (Variante, Chamois, Falaise) get bumpy too.

Trees The Achilles' heel of this very good resort is that there are no trees in Val Thorens. None at all! The nearest are in Méribel Mottaret around the Combes chairlift. If you venture as far as Courchevel there are masses, especially around La Praz.

Book a guide Ski schools **ESF** and **ESI Prosneige** both have high-altitude mountain guides who are also ski instructors.

Tuition ESF (T+33 (0)689-292336) and **ESI Prosneige** (T+33 (0)479-010700) organize group and individual lessons.

Kids Both ski schools offer lessons for kids. ESI Prosneige only takes over-fives. There is a ski area for children (Espace Junior) accessed from the 2 Lac chair.

Bad light This is the downside to what is otherwise a great resort. In a Val Thorens white-out, you could be on the moon. If you can, get over to Méribel Mottaret, where the trees offer some solace.

Not to miss A 'John's Favourite' burger from **John's** restaurant.

Remember to avoid Early season if you're a beginner even slightly worried about the weather.

Relive a famous moment Imitate local hero, Adrien Théaux, junior French Super G, Downhill and Combination champion, as you get up speed on the slopes.

Pitstop and sunbathe The **Frog and Roastbeef** has a sunny terrace that is perfect for apr s-ski refuelling. **Chalet de la Marine** on the Dallas piste has DJs in the afternoons from 1500 until the lifts close.

Best mountain restaurant Etape 3200 at the top of the Cime de Caron has stunning views. **Chalet de la Marine** does (expensive) à la carte but also has a self-service restaurant with pizzas, pastas and sandwiches. The Moutière, nearby, is more reasonable. **Chalet des 2 Lacs**, off the 2 Lacs or Moutière lift, reportedly does a good potato pie.

☺ LOCALS DO	☹ LOCALS DON'T
✓ Explore the Orelle valley to get away from the crowds.	✗ Find themselves in the main resort at peak times.
✓ Stick to the French bars – it's a multicultural place.	✗ Go out in a white-out. It's just not worth it.

Practicalities

While not as bad as neighbouring Les Menuires, Val Thorens lacks the picturesque appeal of Méribel or even St Martin. Still, for party-hungry, budget-conscious skiers looking for instant access to the slopes, it ticks a lot of boxes.

Sleeping There is a wide range of catered and self-catering accommodation in both the lower and higher part of the car-free village. The four-star **Fitz Roy** (T+33 (0)479-000478; hotelfitzroy.com) is part of the Luxury Mountain Hotels Group, which says it all, and there is also a **Club Med** (T+33 (0)479-000483; valthorens.com) right on the slopes. Good three-star hotels include **Le Sherpa** (T+33 (0)479-000070; lesherpa.com), where the food is excellent, and the ski-in/ski-out **Le Val Thorens** (T+33 (0)479-000433; levalthorens.com). For higher-end self-catering, try **Residence Village Montana** (T+33 (0)479-002101; snow-line.co.uk). For the cheapest do-it-yourself options, try the **Altineige** or the **Maeva Le Gypate** (T0825-888544; valthorens.com).

Eating With over 70 restaurants and bars, Val T caters for every taste and budget. Perennial Footprint favourite **L'Oxalys** (T+33 (0)479-001200; loxalys.com) is the top place to eat in the resort. The restaurant of the Oxalys serviced apartments is expensive but well worth it. For pub grub try the **Frog and Roastbeef**, a British outpost and allegedly the highest pub in Europe. The name also reveals much about Val Thorens! **John's** (T+33 (0)479-000515) is well known for its burgers, **Vieux Chalet** (T+33 (0)479-000793) and **Chamière** (T+33 (0)479-000879) both do excellent Savoyard fare, while **La Joyeuse Fondue** (T+33 (0)479-000388) does what it says on the tin.

Au pair/crèche The ESF (esf-valthorens.com) runs a crèche for babies from three months old. There are ski lessons for the over-twos. Every Friday during the season there are children's shows.

Best après-ski For Swedish après-ski go to **Tango** where it gets lively when the lifts shut. The Brits tend to hang out at the **Frog and Roastbeef**. The **Rhum Box** is a tiny bar tucked away on the edge of the Galerie Péclet where the home-flavoured rum can be intoxicating.

Bars and clubs There is no shortage of bars. **Le Viking** is surprisingly not a Swedish bar and attracts lots of Brits – it has a large screen for showing sports as well as free pool and internet access. L'**Eclipse** bar in the Galerie Caron is open late. The resort is a little short on clubs: **Malaysia** tries to create an urban club vibe, the **Underground** is more of a dive dirty and **Beach Mountain** attracts the money crowd.

Shopping The two shopping areas are situated at either end of the resort: Galerie Caron at the lower end, Galerie Péclet at the top end. Neither is very pretty to look at but you can buy just about anything you could need here. You will also find supermarkets such as Sherpa.

Hire shop/rental It's worth shopping around for your ski hire. There are many hire shops, including the usual **Twinner**, **Skiset** and **Intersport**. Hotels and *résidences* sometimes have preferential rates.

Lift tickets These can be bought in advance online at least 10 days before the first day of your holiday (valthorens.com). The resort is starting to offer a recharge service on hands-free passes bought the previous year.

Health and wellbeing The 7500-sq-m **Aquaclub** offers every activity under the sun: a 50-m pool, saunas, jacuzzis and steam rooms, a fitness centre, squash, table tennis and indoor tennis courts. Some of the hotels and apartments, such as the Espace Yin Yang at the **Residence Village Montana**, have their own in-house spas.

Down days with kids It's a long ride back down the mountain so staying in the resort is preferential. The sports centre has enough to keep the little ones amused – there are trampolines and, occasionally, a bouncy castle. The resort also has a bowling alley and a cinema.

Internet The tourist office has internet access, while **Le Viking** bar has Wi-Fi.

Transfer options The nearest airports are Lyon (3½ hours) and Geneva (3 hours) – **Altibus** (altibus.com) operates transfers from both of them. The Eurostar stops at Moûtiers (37 km away) from where you can take a bus up the mountain – again, try Altibus.

You can also ski here ... The Trois Vallées.

If you like this ... try La Plagne ▶▶ *p146*, Les Arcs ▶▶ *p150*.

If you like this ... try La Plagne ▶▶ *p146*, Les Arcs ▶▶ *p150*.

⊚ OPENING TIMES

22 Nov to 3 May: 0900-1645

⊙ RESORT PRICES

Week pass: (20 Dec to 17 Apr) €225
Day pass: (20 Dec to 17 Apr) €45.50
Season pass: (from opening day) €970

ⓘ DIRECTORY

Website: valthorens.com
Tourist office: T+44 (0)479-000808
Medical centre: T+ 44 (0)479 000037
Pisteurs: T+ 44 (0)479-006341
Taxi: T+ 44 (0)479-006944

France Val Thorens

↘36 Vars

Town altitude 1850 m	Km of pistes 180 km	Funicular/cable	Terrain parks 2
Km to airport	Nursery areas 1	cars 0/0	Glühwein factor ★☆☆
154/250 km	Blues 46	Gondolas/chairs 18	Ski in/ski out ★★☆
Airport Turin/Marseille	Reds 40	Drags 33	Environmental
Highest lift 2750 m	Blacks 11	Night skiing no	rating ★★★★☆☆
Vertical drop 1650 m			

One of the most southerly in France, Vars combines the authenticity and charm of a traditional French village with the facilities of a modern resort.

With a long season (the beginning of December until late April), Vars and neighbouring Risoul are scenic resorts with a good snow record. The Domaine de la Forêt Blanche lift pass offers skiers 180 km of pistes that are particularly good for beginners and families, with green and blue runs allowing access to the whole area. The skiing is split over two main sectors: the west-facing Peynier area and the east-facing bowl beneath Pic de Chabriéres.

Beginners Vars is perfect for beginners. There is a beginners' area close to the centre of Les Claux. After mastering the basics take the Crevoux lift to access the long, sweeping forested runs (Escondus is particularly noteworthy) back to the resort.

Intermediates Mid-level skiers will be able to access the entire Forêt Blanche region straight away; there are lots of blues and many easy reds throughout the main bowl, and there are gentle blues such as Vallon Blue leading down into the Risoul sector. For a more challenging run try the reds off the La Mayt and Razis lifts.

Expert There are 11 black runs for advanced skiers but little else on-piste to challenge experts.

Powder There can be some good off-piste in the Risoul area and there are some difficult gullies off the Pic de Chabrières, although taking a guide is highly recommended and safety equipment is essential.

Moguls Try the bumps off the Pic de Chabrières leading back to the resort.

Tuition There are two ski schools, **ESF** (esf-vars.fr) and **ESI** (Eysinna New School), which offers lessons in freestyle as well as group and individual on-piste lessons.

Kids The **ESF** run a kids' club for children over two years; the over-twos can have ski lessons. There is also a ski nursery.

Bad light Stick to the forested slopes on Peynier for some scenic tree runs.

Not to miss The Olympic red run from the top of La Mayt to Ste Marie – expect some heart-in-mouth moments during a vertical descent of almost 1000 m.

Remember to avoid Missing the last lift back over the mountain from Risoul and having to pay for a taxi.

Relive a famous moment Nearby Col du Vars is a Tour de France hotspot – at the last count the famous race had passed through 33 times.

Best mountain restaurants Refuge Napoléon (take the Peynier lift) does good mountain specialities. There is also **Les Balcon** and **L'Horizon**. Many skiers head down the mountain for lunch.

Practicalities

Made up of four hamlets spread out along the Routes des Grandes Alpes, the oldest of which, St Marcellin, dates from around the 11th century, Vars was developed as a ski resort in the 1960s. The centre, Les Claux, is purpose-built but the low-rise, chalet-style buildings are less of an eyesore than in other French resorts of the same era. There is accommodation in all four villages but most skiers stay in Les Claux. Linked to the neighbouring resort of Risoul, the Forêt Blanche ski area is the largest in the southern Alps. There is a distinct Provençal feel to the area, thanks to the wooded, über-sunny slopes.

Sleeping Hotels are limited to two-star but there are some good options. Family-run **La Mayt** in Sainte Marie has a good restaurant and rustic rooms (T+33 (0)492-465007; vars-lamayt.com). **L'Ecureuil** (T+33 (0)492-465072) is a chalet-style hotel with 19 rooms located at the heart of Les Claux (Vars 1850), 150 m from the main base station. For basic apartments, try two-star **Résidence de Tourisme** (T+33 (0)492-450946) or for higher end four-star apartments try the newer **Résidence de l'Albane** (T+33 (0)492-206670).

Eating Among the usual raft of pizza joints, fondue places and mountain restaurants there are a couple of gems. **Rocky Mountain** in Les Claux does pizza, crêpes and mountain specialities. **Chez Plumot** specializes in traditional French cuisine and is our pick.

Au pair/crèche The ESF (esf-vars.fr) runs a ski nursery for children over three months.

Bars and clubs The number of bars and clubs is limited. Après-ski tends to take place straight after the lifts have closed. Try **Le Kha**, a favourite of seasonaires, or **Le Lynx** in **Le Club Hôtel Les Claux**.

Shopping There are four shopping areas, the largest in Les Claux, with a range of clothing, food and gift shops.

Hire shop/rental **Skiset**, **Sport 2000** and **Dominique Sports** hire skis on a daily or weekly basis. All can be found in Les Claux.

Health and wellbeing The main village boasts a gym and sports centre offering saunas, massage, steam rooms and fitness centre. Enquire at the tourist office.

Down days with kids There is a 2 km-long sledging area open on Tuesdays and Thursdays.

Internet Wi-Fi available at the tourist office from the 2008-09 season.

Transfer options The nearest airport is Turin (two hours). Bus transfers operate to the resort (**Navettes Blanche**, T+33 (0)491-466467). By train, travel to Marseille via Paris and then take a local train to Gare de Montdauphin-Guillestre, 18 km from Vars, where you can pick up a bus transfer from **Autocars Imbert** (T+33 (0)492-451811).

You can also ski here ... Risoul, part of the Forêt Blanche ski region.

If you like this ... try Isola (France).

OPENING TIMES
Early Dec to late Apr: 0900-1650

RESORT PRICES
Week pass: (La Forêt Blanche) €153.50
Day pass: €32.00
Season pass: €608

DIRECTORY
Website: vars.com
Tourist office: T+33 (0)492-465131
Medical centre: T+33 (0)492-450103
Pisteurs: T+33 (0)492-465104
Taxi: T+33 (0)624-032723

Italy

Italy
Value for money
★★★★★
Nightlife
★★★☆☆
Off-piste
★★★☆☆
Family
★★★★☆

LAAX
Chur
AUSTRIA
Brenner Pass
Hochfeiler (3510 m)
SWITZERLAND
Pusteria Valley
⬂ 9
⬂ 17
⬂ 20
Simplon Tunnel
St Moritz
Pernina (4049 m)
Ortles (3905 m)
⬂ 13
⬂ 14
Bolzano
✈ BZO
Martigny ⬂ 6
Zermatt
Chiavenno
Venosta Valley
Dolomiti Mountains
FRANCE ⬂ 10
Domodossola
Lugano
Lake Como
Cevedale (3757 m)
⬂ 4
⬂ 5
Matterhorn (3738 m) Mount Rosa (4634 m)
Pennine Alps
Lake Maggiore
Orobie Alps ⬂ 15
Trento
⬂ 2
Brenta
Mt Blanc (4808 m)
Aosta
⬂ 7
⬂ 11
Varese
Como
Frejus Tunnel
⬂ 12
⬂ 1
⬂ 16
Gran Paradiso (4061 m)
Novara
Ticino
✈ MXP
Milan
✈ BGY
Bergamo
Lake Iseo
Lake Garda
✈ TSF
Treviso
⬂ 3
Susa Valley
Turin
Asti
✈ TRN
ITALY
✈ VBS
Brescia
✈ VRN
Verona
Venice
Bardonecchia ⬂ 18
⬂ 8
Sestriere
⬂ 19
Viso (3841 m)
Alessandria
Tortona
Piacenza
Po
Po Valley
Adige
Delta of Po
Cottian Alps
Po
Tanaro
Taro
Taro
Enza
Reno
Cuneo
Genoa
Maggiorasca (1799 m)
Piacenza
Maritime Alps
Savona
Succiso (2017 m)
FRANCE
La Spezia
Appennino Modenese
Apuane Alps
Cimone (2165 m)
MONACO

N
20 km
20 miles

✈ Airport codes...
BGY = Bergamo
BZO = Bolzano
MXP = Milan
TRN = Turin
TSF = Treviso
VBS = Brescia
VRN = Verona

Amiata (1738 m)
Bolsena Lake
Tiber

The Italian heritage that the British have so long admired – incredibly varied architecture, landscapes and traditions – applies of course to the country's mountainous regions, the Dolomites and the Alps. At times it seems that each Italian resort has its own individual charm and lifestyle. Take the Aosta valley. The predominant language might be French, but on any given trip you're likely to hear people speaking a dialect of German in the towns of Gressoney and Alagna.

Yet if there is one thing that unites these occasionally disparate regions, it is the incredible food. It remains a major draw when planning a ski trip to Italy. After all, where better to sample your favourite pasta than on top of a mountain in the country where it originated?

There are other definite advantages of booking a trip to Italy. As a general rule, ski holidays in Italy are less expensive than in the neighbouring countries of France, Austria and Switzerland – without compromising standards. The Italian Alps are just as beautiful as the rest of the range and the less well-known Dolomites are equally stunning with steeper and craggier peaks dominating the skyline. The snow is just as white, the locals friendlier, the lift queues smaller and the fun times are, like everywhere, what you make them. For the serious European skier, used to the obvious Austrian, French and Swiss choices, a trip to sample the charms of our Italian neighbours really is a must.

Skiing Italy

The Dolomites in northeast Italy are home to the famous SuperDolomiti and Milky Way ski resorts, offering hundreds of kilometres of linked slopes. Formed 200 million years ago and reaching a height of more than 3000 m, this section of the Alps was named after Déodat de Dolomieu (1750-1801), who defined their unique rock composition.

Over in the northwest, Italy can boast the two highest peaks in the Alps located above the Aosta valley on the borders of France and Switzerland. Skiing here is a remarkable experience without the free-for-all lift queues of other European resorts. The runs are wide, open and well groomed and if you catch a fresh snowfall, the snowy bowls are brimming with soft powder. The ticket sharing between resorts in the Aosta valley and their close proximity to each other means that you can easily experience three or four different ski areas in one holiday.

For a lot of Italians, skiing is not the most important activity on a ski holiday. Sunbathing, eating long lunches and general relaxation are also pretty high on the list. This laid-back atmosphere undoubtedly adds to the charm of an Italian ski holiday.

On a final note, we would like to dispel a lingering reputation – Italian ski lifts are not as bad as they are made out to be. Plus, with new lifts being installed all the time and the older ones being systematically renovated or replaced, the infrastructure is catching up with France and Switzerland. You won't find yourself fearing for your life in windy conditions!

Conditions

Italy's mountains are pretty high so it can be very cold in January and February. The weather can sweep down from the north very quickly, meaning mountain-top links can close

without warning leaving you stranded in the wrong valley with a long taxi ride back to your hotel. However, being situated in the southern part of the Alps, it is usually slightly warmer than other Alpine countries – perfect for those of you who like to sunbathe at lunchtime. The treeline can be over 2000 m in some resorts making them good in cloudy conditions.

When To Go
The best snow is in January and February with March, April and late December offering respectable conditions. Do not consider going in May. Most of the resorts will be closed and any fresh snow melts within a day or two.

Off-Piste Policy
Although it is actually illegal to ski off-piste in Italy, we found that the guides actively encouraged it and the heli-ski companies seem to have immunity. Although we would never encourage anyone to engage in illegal activities, it seems to be a law that is seldom enforced. It goes without saying that any off-piste activity requires transceiver, probe and shovel, as well as the ability to use this equipment.

PROS

Not as busy as other European areas.

Locals are relaxed and friendly.

Heli-skiing is legal.

Off-piste is world renowned and little used.

Less expensive than other countries.

Delicious and varied cuisine.

Easy airport transfers.

Good ticket-sharing opportunities.

CONS

Warmer weather means fresh snow melts quickly towards the end of the season.

Some resort towns can be pretty ugly.

Be aware of the Italians' love of posing and high fashion.

Some antiquated lifts, although the worst have been replaced.

Off-piste policy makes *some* areas illegal to ski.

The nightlife, in general, is not as busy as other countries.

Essentials

Getting there

In the northwest, in or around the Aosta valley, you can fly to numerous airports including Turin, Milan, Bergamo, Geneva or Grenoble. The small local airport in Aosta itself is rumoured to be extending its runway to receive larger aeroplanes, so in a few years' time transfers to the Aosta valley resorts could be some of the easiest in Europe. The Dolomites are best accessed by Bolzano airport. However, it's a small airport and its services change regularly. There's a downloadable list of carriers and times at abd-airport.it. Alternatively, Venice has Treviso airport (trevisoairport.it) which **Ryan Air** (ryanair.com) fly to, while **easyJet** (easyjet.com) is serviced by Marco Polo airport, which is a little further from the mountains and closer to the city of Venice. Alternatively, the Dolomites can be reached via Innsbruck airport.

Italy also has fantastic road links to France, Switzerland, Austria and Croatia, although it is advisable to check that the mountain passes are open. Most, including the Brenner Pass, the Mont Blanc Tunnel, and the Fréjus Pass are motorway trade routes for lorries, which means they are unlikely to be shut unless a serious accident or severe weather has hit.

Red Tape

There's a no-smoking policy in all public places and that's about it.

Getting Around

Being an EU country, a valid driving licence from your home country is enough to get you on the road. Italy has a reputation for aggressive drivers but if you're used to driving in big cities you should have no problems. Keep your change out as there are tolls for the motorways, mountain passes and tunnels. Italy's motorways are reliable, safe and direct.

Car Hire Most major hire car companies (easycar.com, hertz.com, avis.com etc.) have offices in airports and cities. Usual age restrictions apply.

Public Transport Italian trains are divided into Eurostar, Intercity, Interregionale and Regionale services. All are complicated, have unnecessary validation stamping on tickets and have huge price fluctuations depending on seasons and times of day. To use the trains you will need patience and have your wits about you. The national rail website trenitalia.com is translatable into English.

Going green

Italy's Alta Badia has been investing in environmental solutions since before the current climate-change debate began. The resort is home to the most eco-friendly ski lift in the Alps. It consists of a long rope that skiers hold on to and a sledge powered by a pair of horses. Not only does this lift use a fraction of the raw materials and energy usually required to build modern lifts, but its impact on the mountain is tiny as well. It also runs on hay and fodder!

Fact File

Currency Euro €

Time Zone GMT +1

Country Code +39

Emergency Numbers

Ambulance T118

Police T113

Fire T115

General emergency T112

The Pan-European emergency number T112 works in any EU country from any telephone. It's also the number to call for any emergency services if you're using a mobile.

Opening Hours and Traditions

Depending on where you go, you may encounter shops closed for siesta or bars with a tradition of staying open until the last customer leaves. Generally, though, shops have long opening hours, restaurants are open well into the night, and most clubbing goes on very late.

Eating

One of the highlights of any trip to Italy is the food, especially the many regional variations. In the Alps and Dolomites there is a lot of culinary influence from central Europe and you may find yourself tucking into fondue or the odd *bratwurst*. Each region in Italy (each valley, sometimes) has its own version of classic Italian dishes or a regional speciality. Try traditional Walser dishes if you are staying in the northeastern valleys of the Aosta region. If you are closer to the Austrian border, you have to try the traditional farmers' winter warmer – a small pot of cooked bacon fat with crusty bread.

If you are vegetarian you will have plenty of choice on the menu, with many local specialities meat free. Typically you will find dishes with asparagus, peas and other garden vegetables and it's worth noting that the emphasis in genuine Italian cuisine is on freshness and health.

Language

Italian. English is spoken by many of the younger generation, and many of the ski areas use French and German as a second language so you shouldn't have too many problems. A smattering of basic Italian sayings will be handy for politeness and a bit of fun.

Top Tips

1 **Try** to use the odd word in Italian when conversing with the locals.
2 **Never** miss an opportunity to have a coffee, gesticulate, or say "ciao".
3 **Always** try the local food dishes. They're often the best and most reasonably priced.
4 **Lunch** is very important in Italy so pick a good mountain restaurant and relax.
5 **Mountain** roads are beautiful but slow. Take the motorways if you are in a hurry.

Crime and Safety

Like most resorts, you are unlikely to have your skis pinched from outside a mountain restaurant but don't leave them anywhere accessible overnight in the bigger resorts.

Health

Italy is a member of the European Union. Health insurance is recommended, and EU citizens should carry a European Health Insurance Card (EHIC), which replaces the old E1-11 form. Go to ehic.org.uk to apply for one.

↘1 Alagna

Town altitude 1212 m	Km of pistes 180 km	Funicular/cable cars 0/2	Terrain parks 1
Km to airport 160 km/120 km	Nursery areas 6	Gondolas/chairs 5/12	Glühwein factor ★☆☆
Airport Turin/Milan	Blues 19	Drags/conveyors 1/0	Ski in/ski out ★★☆
Highest lift 2971 m	Reds 40	Night skiing no	Environmental
Vertical drop 1759 m	Blacks 6		rating ★★☆☆☆

A sleepy and romantic village with ski-in access. Popular with experts due to the close proximity of masses of heli-skiing and off-piste.

Probably the smallest and sleepiest of the three villages that have direct access to the Monte Rosa resort, Alagna oozes romantic charm. It's situated right at the top of the craggy Valsesia valley where the river is still just a stream.

With the Col d'Olen and the other off-piste areas on your doorstep, experts will be thrilled. There's also heli-skiing and, of course, access to the massive Monte Rosa resort which has wide open runs for all levels.

Beginners If you're a true beginner it'll be hard for you here as the easy runs are on the other side of the resort. You can always go to the mini-resort down the valley at Bielcuicken.

Intermediate The Frachey and Champoluc side of the resort is best. It's a bit of a trek over there, but the lovely views on your way and the great runs when you arrive will make up for that.

Expert Hire a guide and enjoy the powder. You can generally find untracked areas up to a week after a snowfall. It's the perfect place to try out heli-skiing – inexpensive and professional companies work from here.

Tuition Enquire with your hotel. Discounts and recommendations change each year.

Bad light You don't want to get stuck in the wrong valley so stick to Alagna-side where there is plenty of coverage.

Not to miss The off-piste madness that everyone comes here for.

Remember to avoid Trying to ski over to Champoluc until you're experienced enough. Some of the runs over are very steep.

Practicalities 🛏💡🚌

Being a quiet village, Alagna is perfect for families and die-hard skiers who don't want late nights or social temptations.

Sleeping There are two hotels within 100 m of the lifts. The three-star **Hotel Monte Rosa** (hotelmonterosa-alagna.it) has a charming dining room and an après-ski bar in part of the same building. The **Hotel Cristallo** (hotelcristalloalagna. com) is four star, has a spa, a drinks lounge that gets fairly lively some evenings and a traditional restaurant.

Eating Dir und Don is a stylish and intimate restaurant that serves typical 'Walser' dishes. **Caffè del Centro Luisa** offers fresh brioche with your morning coffee. Loads of snacks and a good glass of wine can be found in the **Caffè delle Guide.**

Bars and clubs Not much on offer, however there's always some lively après-ski in **Caffè delle Guide** and **Caffè del Centro.**

Hire shop/rental Sport Haus Centro **Burton**, at the entrance to the village, has kit to rent and to buy.

Transfer options The best option is to hire a car or book a taxi. Public transport is limited.

You can also ski here ... Champoluc ▶▶ *p218* and the Aosta valley resorts, Gressoney ▶▶ *p228*.

⊛ **OPENING TIMES**

Early Dec to mid-Apr: 0845-1700

💲 **RESORT PRICES**

Week pass: €185

Day pass: €36

Season pass: €700

ⓘ **DIRECTORY**

Websites: alagna.it/atlvalsesiavercelli.it

Tourist office: T+39 (0)163-564404

Medical centre: T+39 (0)163-203111

Pisteurs: T118 or T+39 (0)163-51633

Taxi: T+39 (0)163-92293

↘2 Alta Badia

Town altitude	Vertical drop 653m	Funicular/cable	Terrain parks 1
Corvara 1568 m,	Km of pistes 130 km	cars 1/1	Glühwein factor ★★☆
Colfosco 1645 m	Nursery areas 6	Gondolas/chairs 8/29	Ski in/ski out ★★☆
Km to airport 60 km	Blues 44	Drags 13	Environmental
Airport Bolzano	Reds 23	Night skiing yes	rating ★★★★☆☆
Highest lift 2778 m	Blacks 4		

PROS

- ✔ Probably the best resort in the world for foodies.
- ✔ Great for families.
- ✔ Very relaxed atmosphere and attitude to skiing.

CONS

- ✘ Very little for expert skiers.
- ✘ Limited snow after February.
- ✘ Slopes and the Sella Ronda circuit get very crowded.

Five sophisticated villages with acres of gentle skiing in the heart of the Dolomites.

Skiing in Alta Badia involves gentle cruising surrounded by arguably Europe's most beautiful mountains; access to the vast Sella Ronda ski area and famous Sella Ronda circuit; and excellent food. The attitude towards skiing is very relaxed – people are here to enjoy the mountains, sun and food.

Beginners There are nursery slopes at Corvara and La Villa. Once you've found your feet, explore the rest of the area – most slopes are wide, gentle blues.

Intermediate By starting early and keeping pitstops to a minimum, fit intermediates can complete the 26-km Sella Ronda circuit – circumnavigating the stunning Sella massif – in a day. A visit to Falzarego is worth it.

Expert On-piste is limited – some good lines on Lagazuoi, under La Villa's Piz La Ila gondola and under the Vallon chair. Further afield, Marmolada and Arabba will entertain. Take a guide to explore Val Mezdi, Sassolungo and Passo Pordoi.

Powder Book a guide for Val Mezdi.

Moguls People are too relaxed to make moguls – we couldn't find any!

Tuition There are six schools, with at least one in each village. **Ski School Ladinia** (Corvara) has English-speaking instructors, **Ski School La Villa** is popular with families.

Kids **Ski School La Villa** works with local childcare centre La Bimbo to offer **Ski Miniclub** – care for children up to 11 years with ski instruction from three years.

Bad light Head for the trees under the Bamby chair, above Corvara towards Passo Campolongo and on the runs down into La Villa.

Not to miss Sipping Jimmy's grappa on the sun terrace admiring the Sella massif.

Remember to avoid Attempting the Sella Ronda circuit on Fridays and Sundays when it's busiest.

☺ LOCALS DO

- ✔ Drink Enzian grappa and Bombardinos (hot Advocaat, whisky and cream).
- ✔ Go green – the village uses biomass heating and produces bioenergy from kitchen waste.

☹ LOCALS DON'T

- ✘ Ski during the Christmas holidays when slopes are crowded.
- ✘ Ever seem to leave Alta Badia.

Relive a famous moment George Clooney was so enthralled by Corvara while motoring through on his Harley, he stopped for an all-nighter in the Rosa Alpina restaurant.

Best mountain restaurant Basically, you can't go wrong. Highlights include **Jimmy's Hütte** at the top of the Frara gondola, **Club Moritzino** at the top of Piz La Ila for fresh seafood and **Las Vegas Lodge** at the top of the Ciampi chair.

Practicalities 🛏🍴🚌

Alta Badia encompasses five villages (Colfosco, Corvara, La Villa, San Cassiano and Pedraces) in the heart of the Dolomites. It in turn forms the largest corner of the Sella Ronda ski area, which is part of the vast Dolomiti Superski area. The largest, liveliest villages are Corvara and Colfosco, which also access the most skiing.

Sleeping In Corvara, the luxurious **Hotel La Perla** (T+39 (0)471-831000; hotel-laperla.it) has a beautiful spa and excellent food while three-star **Marmolada** (T+39 (0)471-836139; marmolada.org) is close to the lifts. Family-owned **Hotel Melodia del Bosco** (T+39 (0)471-839620; melodiadelbosco) in Pedraces is blissfully quiet and San Cassiano's **Hotel Diamant** (T+39 (0)471-849499; hoteldiamant.com) is popular with families. Sleep on the mountain in **Las Vegas Lodge** (T+39 (0)471-840138; lasvegasonline.it) – rooms are modern and views unbeatable.

Eating Alta Badia is a gourmet gem with no fewer than three Michelin-starred restaurants, notably Hotel La Perla's **Stüa de Mikil**. Menus combine authentic Italian and Tyrolean dishes as well as local Ladin specialities, which you must try at the 19th-century **Runch Farm** in Pedraces.

Au pair/crèche Ski Miniclub (T+39 (0)471-847258) in La Villa offers non-skiing childcare for kids from six months.

Bars and clubs Start on the mountain at **Club Moritzino** and **Las Vegas Lodge**, then move to the rustic **L Murin** opposite La Perla and **Toccami** by the Hotel Marmalada (Corovara). There's a wine bar in **Hotel La Majun** (La Villa)

and disco action in **Hotel Posta Zirm's Taverna** (Corvara).

Hire shop/rental Each village has a handful of rental shops. **Kostner** in Corvara is the largest.

Health and wellbeing Hotel Posta Zirm (postazirm.com) in Corvara has a **Wellness Farm** and San Cassiano's **Hotel Fanes** (hotelfanes.it) has a 2000-sq-m spa.

Down days with kids There's a public pool in La Villa and sledging into San Cassiano.

Internet The tourist offices in Corvara and Colfosco and library in La Villa all have internet facilities.

Transfer options Fly to Bolzano and hire a car. Alternatively, fly to Milan, Venice (Treviso or Marco Polo), Verano or Innsbruck and take a bus (terravision.eu).

You can also ski here ... The Sella Ronda and the Dolomiti Superski areas.

If you like this ... try Cortina ▶▶ *p222*, Val Gardena ▶▶ *p243*.

ⓦ **OPENING TIMES**

End Nov to end Apr: 0830-1700

ⓢ **RESORT PRICES (for Val Gardena ski pass/Dolomiti Superski pass)**

Week pass: €201/209
Day pass: €40/42
Season pass: €460/590

ⓘ **DIRECTORY**

Website: altabadia.org
Tourist office: T+39 (0)471-836176
Medical Centre: T+39 (0)471-849300
Pisteurs: T+39 (0)471-836176
Taxi: T+39 329-227 1991
Alta Badia night shuttle: T+39 335-6114441

↘3 Bardonecchia

Town altitude 1300 m	Funicular/cable	Terrain parks 2	
Km to airport 90 km	cars 0/0	Glühwein factor ★☆☆	
Airport Turin	Gondolas/chairs 1/9	Ski in/ski out ★☆☆	
Highest lift 2694 m	Drags 11	Environmental	
Vertical drop 1344 m	Night skiing yes	rating ★★★☆☆	
Km of pistes 100 km			
Nursery areas 2			
Blues 10			
Reds 18			
Blacks 5			

PROS

- ✓ Very family-friendly resort.
- ✓ Easily accessible and a good base for exploring Trois Vallées and Milky Way.
- ✓ Very quiet with queues a rarity.

CONS

- ✗ Lacks classic ski resort atmosphere.
- ✗ Limited advanced skiing.
- ✗ Patchy snow record and relatively short season.

Friendly, quiet historical town with a relatively large ski area and easy access to nearby resorts.

Bardonecchia's ski area consists of two mountains on either side of the town, linked by free (although erratic) buses. Campo Smith is the larger of the two, made up of Colomion, Les Arnauds and Melezet base areas. Lower slopes are large, sunny and surrounded by larch forest with the steeper Vallon Cros area rising above tree level. Jafferau is more exposed, with fantastic views and good off-piste skiing.

Beginners Learn the basics on the Campo Smith and Mezelet nursery areas and the short blue down from Pian del Sole. Confident beginners will enjoy the mountain experience offered by Jafferau, without taking drag lifts.

Intermediate A great area for intermediates with varied terrain and long red runs. Take some lessons and learn how to ski powder.

Expert With only one black run, experts will need good conditions to keep themselves entertained in the trees on Campo Smith and off-piste on Punta della Mulattiera and Jafferau.

Powder If visibility is good, head for Jafferau. If not, stick to Melezet for the lines off Cresta Seba and Punta della Mulattiera.

Tuition There are four ski schools, all with bases at Campo Smith. **Spazio Neve** is the biggest with lots of English-speaking instructors while **Nord Ovest** is popular with youngsters.

Kids All four ski schools offer kids' programmes. There's snowtubing at Campo Smith and the magic carpet is open until 1900 on Saturdays.

Bad light Stick to the trees on Campo Smith – you won't get bored!

☺ LOCALS DO

- ✓ Ski on weekdays when it's quiet.
- ✓ Go straight for the Mezelet lift for fresh tracks on a powder day.
- ✓ Ski and snowboard – the resort is fantastic for boarding.

☹ LOCALS DON'T

- ✗ Ski on Jafferau in bad weather – it gets seriously cold.
- ✗ Expect buses to run on time.
- ✗ Hit 'rush hour' at Campo Smith between 1000 and 1030.

Not to miss The views from the top of Jafferau on a clear day.

Remember to avoid The queues for lift tickets at the kiosks on weekends – buy them from the train station instead.

Relive a famous moment Bardonnechia hosted the 2006 Olympic snowboard parallel giant slalom and snowboard cross events – if you've never tried snowboarding, why not do it here?

Best mountain restaurant **Punta Colomion** does great food with views, **La Grangia** at Pian del Sole is cosy and has delicious cakes while **Hotel Jafferau** offers efficient self-service.

Practicalities 🏨🍴🚌

Bardonecchia is located in a wide basin in western Piemont by the Fréjus tunnel, which takes drivers through to France. It's more working town than ski resort but is very popular with Italians, who visit on weekends from Turin, when the nightlife picks up. Via Medail, the street where the restaurants and shops are found, is about 15 minutes' walk from Campo Smith, the main ski area.

Sleeping The large **Campo Rivé Hotel** (T+39 (0)122-909233; hotelrive.it) dominates Campo Smith ski base, offering rooms and apartments on the slopes. Two good, less expensive hotels are **I Larici** (T+39 (0)122-902490; hotelilarici.com) and **La Quiete** (T+39 (0)122-999859; hotellaquiete.it) – both are family-owned and centrally located. Foodies will like **Hotel Villa Myosotis** (T+39 (0)122-999883; villamyosotis.it).

Eating Families love ordering pizza by the metre at **Sotta Sopra**. **Stella Alpina** on Via Medail is popular with locals, as is **Il Sole e la Luna** by the Melezet chairlift. For authentic local dining, book the tiny agricultural B&B **Alla Buona** (T+39 (0)122-901799) in Les Arnauds or the **III Alpini** refuge (T+39 (0)122-902071) in Valle Stretta.

Au pair/crèche There's a crèche at Campo Smith.

Bars and clubs Nights are quiet during the week but **Colomion di Cipo** at the base of Campo Smith is popular for après-ski. **Lalimentari Multicafé**, five minutes from Campo Smith, is good for drinks and light snacks, as is **Bar Medail**. There's a disco in the Olympic village on the road between town and Campo Smith.

Shopping There's plenty here from supermarkets to boutiques and speciality wine shops.

Hire shop/rental Most shops are at Campo Smith – **Spazio Neve** has knowledgeable, English-speaking staff.

Health and wellbeing There's a public swimming pool at Campo Smith. **Campo Rivé** has a sauna, Turkish bath and gym.

Down days with kids Visit the local museums or head to Turin for the day.

Internet There are internet points at **Informagic** on Via Callet and Wi-Fi at **Campo Rivé**.

Transfer options Fly to Turin and take a train (trenitalia.it) or reserve cheap seats on a shuttle service 24 hours ahead (extraservice.it/buscharter).

You can also ski here ... The Trois Vallées and Milky Way resorts are nearby, although not included in the ski pass.

If you like this ... try Serre Chevalier ▶▶ p180.

⊙ OPENING TIMES

Early Dec to mid-Apr: 0900-1700

⑨ RESORT PRICES

Week pass: €137

Day pass: €27

Season pass: €590

ⓘ DIRECTORY

Website: bardonecchiaski.com

Tourist office: T+39 (0)122-99032

Medical centre: T+39 (0)122-901833

Lift company: T+39 (0)122-99137

Taxi: T+39 (0)122-999177

↘4 Campitello

Town altitude 1440 m	Km of pistes 1200 km		Funicular/cable cars 0/1		Terrain parks 1
Km to airport 180 km	Nursery areas 1		Gondolas/chairs 1/5		Glühwein factor ★★☆
Airport Verona	Blues 1		Drags 3		Ski in/ski out ☆☆☆
Highest lift 2485 m	Reds 10		Night skiing yes		Environmental
Vertical drop 1045 m	Blacks 0				rating ★★★★☆

A low-key town in Val di Fassa which has good restaurants and lively après. A good option for intermediates who like to stay away from the crowds.

Although relatively tiny compared to some of the other resorts in this book, Campitello benefits from links to the huge Sella Ronda area and some incredible views. Use it as a base and start exploring.

Beginners For total beginners the nursery slope in Campitello is better than the alternative red option at the top of the cable car. Canazei bowl, which can be accessed using the ski bus, is more for beginners.

Intermediate The runs out of Campitello towards Canazei (green Sella Ronda route) or Val Gardena (orange Sella Ronda route) are ideal for intermediates. Corvara, Colfosco, Ortesei and Alpe di Susi are just some of the intermediate havens accessed from the Sella Ronda.

Expert The World Cup run in Val Gardena: Saslong and the giant slalom at La Villa are options for adrenaline seekers.

Tuition Scuola di Sci Campitello is situated in the main piazza.

Bad light Head over to Plan di Gralba towards the trees.

Not to miss Tuesday night's ski school show on the nursery slope in town with free hot wine supplied.

Remember to avoid Being in town during the siesta period as everything closes.

Practicalities

Campitello is the small town in Val di Fassa before Canazei. It is self-contained with bars, restaurants and places to stay. The Col Rodella cable car leads up to a bowl area and into the Sella Ronda. The Canazei ski area is also easily skied to.

Sleeping Immobiliare Ladina (T+39 (0)462-750238; ladina.net) arrange self-catering apartments for all budgets. Union Hotels (T+39 (0)462-601033; monica@uhc.it) own a chain of hotels in Val di Fassa. Campitello hotels include the **Soreghes** (T+39 (0)462-750060), **Diamant** (T+39 (0)462-750440) and **Rubino** (T+39 (0)462-601033).

Eating Snow Bar is good for slices of pizza and beers. The **Rosticceria da Fiorenzo** is also a good stop for takeaway food. **La Cantinetta** serves pizzas, pasta and steaks. And the **Mini Restaurant** is a real find – booking recommended.

Bars and clubs Da Guilio has a good après and evening atmosphere. **Evita Bar** serves snacks, cocktails, beers and tea. **Tomato Club** is an excellent hangout.

Hire shop/rental Sporting 2000 is central while **Noleggio dei Maestri** (skirent.net) is next to the ski school.

Transfer options It's 2½ hours from Verona airport, which most people use, three hours from Brescia and four from Bergamo. Ryan Air flights into Brescia and Bergamo link with Saturday shuttle buses to the resort.

You can also ski here ... Pera, Predazzo.

◉ OPENING TIMES
Early Dec to late Apr: 0830-1630

⑤ RESORT PRICES
Week pass: (6 days) €184-209
Day pass: €37-42.
Season pass: €415

◉ DIRECTORY
Website: valdifassa.com
Tourist office: T+39 (0)84-0000
Medical Centre: T+39 (0)462-620140
Pisteurs: T118
Taxi: T+39 336-352881
Local radio: Latmiele, Radio Dolomiti

↘5 Canazei

Town altitude	1460 m	Km of pistes	1200 km	Funicular/cable	
Km to airport	182 km	Nursery areas	1	cars	0/1
Airport	Verona	Blues	4	Gondolas/chairs	3/7
Highest lift	2395 m	Reds	10	Drags	2
Vertical drop	935 m	Blacks	0	Night skiing	yes

Terrain parks	2
Glühwein factor	★★☆
Ski in/ski out	☆☆☆
Environmental rating	★★★☆☆

PROS

- ✓ Extensive ski area with skiing for all abilities.
- ✓ Sufficient terrain to ski different slopes for a week.
- ✓ A week's holiday will definitely not exhaust the potential here.

CONS

- ✗ Not much expert skiing.

Intermediate Italian ski heaven: great food, easy skiing, plenty of ski and friendly locals.

The slopes at Canazei are reached by taking the Belvedere from the town, and it's fair to say that the town is due an upgrade. The main slopes above the town are universally known as 'the Bowl' and link to the wider Dolomiti Superski area.

Beginners Canazei bowl is ideal for beginners or the first few runs for intermediates. The lift from Pecol is now a gondola to take you into the bowl for easy blues. Once there, two chairs serving both sides of the bowl access red runs.

Intermediate From the Canazei bowl head along the orange Sella Ronda route, which is a great day out. This naturally leads into Val Gardena which also has wide red runs. In the opposite direction from the top of the Canazei bowl, Sas Becé has red runs on offer which is a good start for intermediates in this area.

Expert The area around Arabba has the steepest runs on the Sella Ronda. Head to the Marmolada glacier: the three consecutive cable cars take you up to 3250 m where skiing is more challenging with some excellent off-piste opportunities. There is also some riskier off-piste skiing from the Passo Pordoi which is generally considered to be the best off-piste in the area. It is very dependent on snow conditions and you're advised to take a guide.

☺ LOCALS DO

- ✓ The grappa ronda not the Sella Ronda.
- ✓ Use the Lupo Bianco and Canazei home run to get back to resort.
- ✓ Speak Ladin.

☹ LOCALS DON'T

- ✗ Care what they wear up the mountain.
- ✗ Go out until after midnight.
- ✗ Have area lift passes.

Moguls The Lupo Bianco and the home run into Canazei gets chopped up during the course of the day. The area around Arraba has steep moguls at the end of the day, both on and at the sides off-piste.

Tuition Marmolada Ski School.

Kids The **Marmolada Ski School** has a **Kinderland** which also has a crèche with English-speaking staff.

Bad light Head to Rosengarten and take advantage of the tree areas. This can be accessed via Alba or the free ski bus from Canazei to Pera.

Not to miss A day out to the Sottaguda gorge, a less commercial version of the Hidden Valley found at the bottom of the Marmolada glacier.

Remember to avoid The Danish school holidays.

Relive a famous moment The film crew and stuntmen stayed here while filming the 2003 version of *The Italian Job*, which has impressive scenes around the Passo Pordoi and Fedaia.

Best mountain restaurant **Rifugio Fodom** has the best quality and good value burgers and its deckchair area is perfectly positioned to enjoy views of the Passo Pordoi.

Practicalities

Canazei is growing in popularity and building work is catching up with demand. Thankfully, all the buildings so far are in keeping with the setting and the time-capsule feel of yesteryear is still present: this is a great place for one-piece ski suits with matching bum bags.

Sleeping The Rosengarten (T+39 (0)462-602221), situated at the bottom of the home run in the old part of town, has low-cost rooms with shared bathrooms and a great breakfast. The **Fiordiliso** is a good family-run hotel with sauna facilities and a minibus service. **La Perla Hotel** (T+39 (0)462-602453; hotellaperla.net) is at the top end of the scale and has lu xurious wellness facilities and excellent cuisine.

Eating The **Montanara** pub serves wholesome evening meals. **Pizza Italia**, across the road from the Montanara, serves pasta and pizza dishes in a cosy atmosphere. The **Rosengarten** has a selection of burgers and fast food. **L'Osteria** has has large pizzas and goblets of wine served in front of a roaring log fire. **Kaiser Stube** welcomes families and has a children's menu. **Wine and Dine** above **Husky Bar** has a good à la carte menu and is ideal for a special occasion.

Au pair/crèche **Kinderland** next to the ski school organize crèche faciles for children of all ages.

Bars and clubs The **Montanara** serves draught beer, Guinness, house wine and potent Red Bull mixes to a rowdy après crowd straight after skiing. Sometimes there is live music; there is always a great atmosphere.

Shopping There are two supermarkets in Canazei: **Spar** and the cheaper **Co-op**. In the centre of town, a few boutiques can be found alongside ordinary high street shops and the usual souvenir shops. **Detomas**, on the road towards the Belvedere, has a good selection of male and female ski gear.

Hire shop/rental Sport Walter, on the main drag, is the cheapest and has the most up-to-date equipment. **Northland** is good for free-ride skis.

Health and wellbeing The Eghes Wellness Centre (T+39 (0)462-601348) is independent from hotels. Swimming hats are compulsory in the pool, but swimming costumes are not allowed in the wellness centre.

Down days with kids Snow-tubing along the road from Canazei to Alba and ice-skating in Alba are two options.

Internet Inside the **Scuola di Snowboard** office, along the main road, is an internet café, €6 per hour. Most of the three- and four-star hotels have Wi-Fi. The **Hotel Astoria** has a private area with internet access.

Transfer options Ryanair (ryanair.com) flights into Brescia and Bergamo link with Saturday shuttle buses to the resort.

You can also ski here ... Predazzo and Obereggen.

⊚ **OPENING TIMES**

Late Nov to mid-Apr: 0900-1630

⊚ **RESORT PRICES**

Week pass: (6 days) €184-209

Day pass: €37-42

Season pass: €415

⊚ **DIRECTORY**

Website: valdifassa.com

Tourist office: T+39 (0)84-0000

Medical Centre: T+39 (0)462-620140

Pisteurs: T118

Taxi: T+39 336-352881

Local radio: Latmiele, Radio Dolomiti

↘6 Cervinia

Town altitude 2050 m	Km of pistes 350 km	Funicular/cable	Terrain parks 1
Km to airport 140 km	Nursery areas 2	cars 0/0	Glühwein factor ★★★
Airport Turin	Blues 17	Gondolas/chairs 7/13	Ski in/ski out ★★☆
Highest lift 3899 m	Reds 31	Drags 12	Environmental
Vertical drop 1849 m	Blacks 7	Night skiing yes	rating ★★☆☆☆

PROS

- ✅ Lots of cheap package and late deals available due to the number of tour operators in the resort.

CONS

- ❌ Wind and limitations on lift pass make this a frustrating resort at times.
- ❌ Long T-bar lifts back from Zermatt are compulsory if the cable car is closed.

A great week away with a combination of partying and a few days' skiing in Zermatt.

Cervinia sits above the treeline at just over 2000 m with the famous Cervino (or Matterhorn, as the Swiss call it) dominating the scenery. Intermediate skiers with an international pass can take advantage of skiing in Zermatt without having to pay the high prices for accommodation in Switzerland.

Three interlinked valleys give a wide range of terrain, with plenty to suit all levels of ability. Choose from tree runs in the lower area of Valtournenche, Goillet's off-piste, or the perfectly groomed slopes up on the glacier, all overlooked by the distinctive outline of the Cervino.

Beginners Plan Maison is an excellent area for beginners, but getting to the lift station in ski boots and with equipment can be tiring. Hiring lockers at Plan Maison or at the ski-hire shop **Genzinella** next to the main gondola lift helps massively in getting to ski school on time as this is where group lessons leave from. Alternatively go for private lessons and ask to meet at the

😊 LOCALS DO

- ✅ Ski with passports/ID when skiing to Zermatt.
- ✅ Have a face mask for the T-bar lifts on the glacier.
- ✅ Pay for lunch by credit card in Zermatt.

😠 LOCALS DON'T

- ❌ Walk to Plan Maison in ski boots.
- ❌ Shop in Cervinia.
- ❌ Ever appear to suffer from hangovers.

Practicalities 🛏🍴🚌

Most of the hotels are only accessible on foot which means coach/taxi drop-offs are from a central point.

Sleeping For apartments, contact **Il Cervino** (T+39 (0)166-949510) rental agent who have a selection. The **Hotel Astoria** (info@astoriacervinia.com) has different types of room, some renovated, but the real bonus of this hotel is the location, right next to the lift. In town and nearer the Crétaz lift, **Grivola** (T+39 (0)166-948287) and the four-star **Punta Maquignaz** (T+39 (0)166-949145) are good value.

Eating Cervinia's cuisine is one of the main reasons for visiting. **Copa Pan** (T+39 (0)166-940084) has a stylish downstairs restaurant with a fusion-filled menu and a good selection of house and local wines. It is perfect for a romantic meal. The restaurant of the **Punta Maquignaz** boasts an open grill and has delicious lamb chops. The **Tea Rooms** are a divine find – like Bettys of Harrogate meeting ski-resort chic, with sandwiches, gorgeous cakes, hot chocolate and sweets eaten with candlelight and good music.

Au pair/crèche The Baby-Club Bianca Neve takes children from nine months to eight years. Contact the **Centro Sociale Sportivo** of Breuil Cervinia (info@ansed. com) for more information.

Bars and clubs All of the bars in Cervinia seriously turn the heating up. The **Copapan** is a great place to head for before hitting the **Bianconiglio**. **Gasoline** is another late-night drinking option, an alternative to the trendy bars.

Shopping There is a small **Crai** supermarket surrounded by a couple of shops selling ski gear.

Hire shop/rental Genzianella (genzianella.it) have two shops, one in town and one near the lift-pass office and main lift.

Health and wellbeing The **Punta Maquinaz** has a good wellness centre with sauna, steam room and relax areas. Massages can be booked in advance from hotel reception.

Down days with kids There is a natural ice rink in the centre at **Lino's**, which also serves pizzas. The bowling alley is a good walk up the hill.

Internet There is no email café but internet can be found at the **Yeti Bar**. Most of the hotels have Wi-Fi.

Transfer options Two hours from Turin.

You can also ski here ... the whole of the Aosta with a local pass, Zermatt with an international pass.

If you like this ... try Avoriaz ▶▶ *p123*.

⊚ OPENING TIMES

End Oct to end Apr. (Summer skiing on the glacier starts 4 July.)

⑤ RESORT PRICES

Week pass: (6 days) €148-185, intenational €192-240.

Day pass: €32-34.

❶ DIRECTORY

Website: cervinia.it

Tourist office: info@breuil-cervinia.it

Medical Centre: T+39 (0)166-949120

Pisteurs: T113

Taxi: T+39 (0)166-62220/3355-653189

Italy Cervinia

Crétaz lift – as a starting point this is ideal for accommodation in the town. The blue 5 using the Plan Torette lift above the Crétaz is a lovely long home run.

Intermediates Cervinia is a great place to ease into reds. Intermediates should head to Plateau Rosa, which has some good sweeping runs to warm up on, and the quiet pistes of Valtournenche are an ideal way to prepare before heading down to Zermatt. Intermediates cannot be disappointed in this resort.

Experts Cervinia is not an experts' resort but there are seven pisted blacks and challenging runs over in Zermatt. Adrenaline seekers should contact the Breuil School who can provide information about heli-skiing and freeriding.

Moguls Can be found at the top of the Fornet/Bardoney lift and on the long run down towards the Hotel Petit Palais.

Tuition Breuil School (T+39 (0)166-940960) or Scoula di Sci del Cervino (T+39 (0)166-948744).

Bad light Tree runs can be found at Cielo Alto which will save a bad-light day.

Remember to avoid Sunday traffic jams!

Relive a famous moment Cervinia was developed during the times of Mussolini.

Best mountain restaurant Chalet Etoile (T+39 (0)166-940220), accessible from the easy blue pistes above Plan Maison and under the Rocce chairlift, has top-notch food with waiter service.

↘7 Champoluc

Town altitude 1564 m	Vertical drop 1759 m	Blacks 6	Terrain parks 1
Km to airport	Km of pistes 180 km	Funicular/cable cars 0/2	Glühwein factor ★☆☆
104 km/160 km	Nursery areas 6	Gondolas/chairs 5/12	Ski in/ski out ★★☆
Airport Turin/Milan	Blues 19	Drags 1	Environmental rating
Highest lift 2971 m	Reds 40	Night skiing no	☆☆☆☆☆☆

PROS

- ✔ Hardly any lift queues and empty slopes.
- ✔ Huge ski area and amazing off-piste.
- ✔ Heli-skiing.

CONS

- ✘ Not much for the absolute beginner.
- ✘ No hard-core nightlife.
- ✘ Limited non-mountain activities.

A lively little base for the Monte Rosa region. Champoluc is a beautiful town with direct access to wide open pistes and practically no lift queues.

Acting as a frontier between Italy and Switzerland, the peaks surrounding Champoluc have the greatest average height of any resort in Europe and include Punta Dufour, the second highest peak in Europe at 4634 m. Enthusiasts come from all over the world for the off-piste, which increases the 180 km of pisted runs by a huge amount. On piste, the three deep valleys that make up the area give you huge, empty, wide runs that seem to go on forever.

Beginners Ski schools meet at Crest or Mont Ros. There are blues and easy reds here to get you going.

Intermediate The on-piste runs are all superb for intermediates. There are a couple of fairly easy groomed blacks to challenge you as well. Try some easy off-piste as you can hop off the edge of nearly every run to make your own fresh tracks in the powder.

Expert The Col d'Olen over by Passo Salati is massively popular with off-pisters. Hire a guide to show you some areas where you won't see anyone and you can soak up the majesty of the mountains around you. The new lift to Cresta Rossa (due to open for the 2009-10 season) will open up a huge off-piste area with a 2400 m vertical descent to Alagna.

Powder The amount of off-piste means you can find untracked territory up to a week after snowfall.

Moguls The pistes are all groomed so look out for sections in the off-piste that have got bumpy.

Tuition There's a choice of schools offering tuition in different languages.

Champoluc is my home town and where I was born. I've been skiing all over the world but I like Monte Rosa because it is a big ski resort with great off-piste skiing and the panorama is amazing.
Simone Origone, speed skier, current world record holder (251.4 kph!)

Kids Under-12 passes are half price and those under six travel free on all lifts.

Bad light Stick to the wide pistes and don't venture into the other valleys. Alternatively, book yourself in at the Breithorn.

Not to miss All the other mountain activities including inexpensive heli-skiing.

Remember to avoid The expensive taxi ride home if you get stuck in the

Alagna valley after the lifts close or in bad weather.

Relive a famous moment Make sure you get a photo of yourself with the three highest peaks in Europe in the background.

Best mountain restaurant Rifugio Guglielmina (T+39 (0)163-91444; rifugioguglielmina.com), with its amazing views – choose a sunny day and make sure you book.

Practicalities 🛏️🍴🚌

This relatively unknown (to the British) ski town has seen a lot of growth over the last few years. There are now around 800 beds at varying prices, several very good restaurants and a couple of lively bars, all with the charm and friendliness of the Italian Aosta valley. The old part of town is small but perfectly formed with winding cobbled pathways leading you up the south-facing slope of the valley.

Sleeping Le Vieux Rascard (levieuxrascard.com) is a sweet little B&B in the old town. **Hotel Campagnol** (T+39 (0)125-307191) is friendly, warm, clean and very good value – it's only two star but the quality of food here is four star. For a high-end hotel experience stay at the **Breithorn Hotel** (breithornhotel.com) or its little refugee sister up the mountain, the **Hotellerie de Mascognaz**, where Richard Branson is known to stay.

Eating By far the best restaurant is the **Breithorn Hotel** restaurant – the lamb is sublime. At the other end of the scale there are snack bars up the slopes and in the town. There are plenty of other places to eat so take your pick from pizzas to traditionally cooked local dishes.

Bars and clubs You'll always find something going on for après-ski – the **Atelier Gourmand** next to the gondola in the village has a sun terrace. Just up the road towards Frachey is the **Hotel California** where they put on karaoke evenings and there are pool tables and a DJ. For dancing there's **Pachamama**, which really gets going on Tuesdays and Fridays.

Shopping Be sure to sample some of the local cuisine to take home – Fontina cheese, Mocetta cured meat and Génépi liqueur.

Hire shop/rental Plenty, with two right next to the main lift.

Health and wellbeing Most hotels have saunas, with the **Breithorn** having holistic and Ayurvedic massage facilities.

Down days with kids A walk up the valley through Frachey to visit the church in Saint Jacques or a trip to Aosta.

Internet No public access point, but the main hotels have Wi-Fi.

Transfer options From Turin/Milan you can get the train to Verrès (trenitalia. com) and then the bus (VITA, T+39 (0)125-966546) up the valley to the town.

You can also ski here ... Gressoney, Alagna and the Aosta valley resorts.

If you like this ... try La Rosière ▶▶ p148, Montgenèvre ▶▶ p170.

Italy Champoluc

⊙ OPENING TIMES
Early Dec to mid-Apr: 0845-1700

⊙ RESORT PRICES
Week pass: €185

Day pass: €36

Season pass: €700

⊙ DIRECTORY
Website: monterosa-ski.com

Tourist office: T+39 (0)125-307113

Medical Centre: T+39 (0)125-307466

Pisteurs: T+39 (0)125-303111

Taxi: T+39 339-5033525

↘8 Claviere

Town altitude 1760 m	Km of pistes 33 km	Funicular/cable	Terrain parks 1
Km to airport 97 km	Nursery areas 1	cars 0/0	Glühwein factor ★★☆
Airport Turin	Blues 5	Gondolas/chairs 0/6	Ski in/ski out ★★★
Highest lift 2823 m	Reds 10	Drags 6	Environmental
Vertical drop 1473 m	Blacks 4	Night skiing yes	rating ★☆☆☆☆

A cosy village with some of the best snow in the extensive Milky Way ski area.

A small village on the Italian side of the Italy-France border and one of Italy's first resorts, Claviere is well connected to 400 km of pistes.

This high shoulder on the border with France is extremely snow-sure, and benefited from the regeneration of the area for the 2006 Turin Winter Olympics. Given the size of the village, the ski area is surprisingly good.

Practicalities

The mixture of old and new buildings isn't without critics. It's best for beginners and intermediates who fancy a calm and relaxed holiday.

Sleeping Two-star **Miramonti** (T+39 (0)122-878804) is clean and friendly, or try **Hotel Bes** (T+39 (0)122 878735) for their gallery of Picasso paintings. The **Sagnalonga Sporthotel** (T+39 (0)122-878085) is up on the mountain – who cares if it's basic when first tracks are yours?

Eating Many of the hotels have excellent Italian food (try the **Gran Bouc**) or head 3 km over to Montgenèvre for French cuisine. **Montanina** is the best of the mountain huts – friendly and atmospheric.

Bars and clubs There are 14 bars in this tiny village, which tend towards cosy rather than rowdy. **Gran Bouc** is lively, and **Gallo Cedrone** has karaoke. Montgenèvre is only a 20-minute walk away: for a late one head to the **Blue Night** disco and get a taxi home.

Hire shop/rental Rent and Go is in the village.

Transfer options Fly to Turin and get the train to Oulx and the bus up from there, or if you want to approach from the French side, Grenoble is the closest airport, and trains run to Briançon.

You can also ski here … Montgenèvre area over the border in France, and Sauze, Sestriere, Sansicario and Cesana on the Italian side, but take care to buy the right ticket – there's currently some confusion.

If you like this … try Peisey-Nancroix (France).

Beginners Claviere has its own nursery slope, a bit steeper than some, but the good snow and lack of crowds make up for it. A wide, long blue run accessed by the Nuova Coche is ideal for getting braver on.

Intermediate The runs from Pian del Sole to the village are enjoyably narrow, and the reds down from Collet Vert are just right. Don't shy away from the black runs – they're ideal for intermediates.

Expert Not very much for experts in Claviere or in Montgenèvre – black runs here would be reds elsewhere. Go off-piste – between La Montanina and Sagnalonga there's some great powder.

Tuition Sculoa Italiana Sci has a base in Claviere.

Bad light Try the runs off Pian del Sole – narrow and through dense trees, they stay a bit clearer than anything above the treeline.

Not to miss Historic Briançon is beautiful if you need a day off the slopes.

Remember to avoid Buying a pass for the whole Milky Way area without checking that the Sagnalonga pistes are open – it's a long lift up and down otherwise.

◎ OPENING TIMES

Early Dec to mid-Apr: 0900-1700

◉ RESORT PRICES

Week pass: €126

Day pass: €24

Season pass: €750

◐ DIRECTORY

Website: claviere.it

Tourist office: T+39 (0)122-878856

Medical Centre: T+39 (0)492-219120

Taxi: T+39 335-233467

↘9 Cortina

Town altitude 1224 m	Km of pistes 140 km	Funicular/cable	Terrain parks 1
Km to airport 126 km	Nursery areas 2	cars 0/6	Glühwein factor ★★☆
Airport Treviso	Blues 33	Gondolas/chairs 0/31	Ski in/ski out ☆☆☆
Highest lift 2939 m	Reds 63	Drags 10	Environmental
Vertical drop 1715 m	Blacks 5	Night skiing no	rating ★☆☆☆☆

A glimpse of what ski resorts were like 20 years ago: antiquated cable cars, wild mountains, some seriously steep slopes and grand architecture.

When you arrive in Cortina, it's hard to take your eyes off the magnificent granite amphitheatre that towers above the little town. Cortina's skiing is divided into four very distinct areas, linked by (erratic and frequently overcrowded) ski buses: Faloria-Cristallo-Mietres, Tofana-Socrepes, Cinque Torri and Lagazuoi. The areas are very different in terms of terrain, aspect and elevation, enabling visitors to experience varied skiing.

Beginners Head for Socrepes with its nursery slopes and acres of gentle, uncrowded, tree-lined blues. There's more of the same at Mietres.

Intermediate You've essentially got 140 km of pistes to play on, with only the Forcella Rossa black on Tofana to worry you (go slowly or take the gondola down). Follow the sun (Italian-style) and stick to Tofana in the morning and Faloria in the afternoon. A day trip to Cinque Torri is a must – for the breathtaking views and excellent restaurants as well as skiing – as is a visit to Lagazuoi.

Expert Expert terrain here is about quality, not quantity. Two of the best blacks are Canalone Staunies, the steepest piste in the Dolomites, and Forcella Rossa on Tofana, which squeezes you through a narrow gully.

Powder The Cristallo bowl is great in powder, when the top chair opens. Cinque Torri has gentle powder fields which expert and intermediate powder skiers will enjoy.

Moguls The blacks on Falloria get bumped out when it hasn't snowed.

Trees Plenty on the lower slopes of Tofana.

Book a guide For those in the know, Cortina boasts some hardcore off-piste. Book a guide (guidecortina.com) to negotiate steep, dramatic routes like Canalino del Prete, Creste Bianche and Sci 18. Mountain lovers should consider ski touring – stay at the plush **Malga Pezie de Paru** refuge (T+39 338-9245718).

Tuition All four ski schools offer similarly priced tuition for all levels. English-speaking instructors aren't guaranteed, so request in advance if necessary.

Kids If you buy Dolomiti Superski passes, under eights ski and sleep free – check dolomitisuperski.com for details.

Bad light You could spend the day skiing under wet trees or tearing through them on a zip wire and past them in a bobsled at the **Adrenalin Center**

😊 LOCALS DO

✅ Wear fur for the ritual *passeggiata* (evening stroll) – lots of fur.

✅ Catch up with mates outside La Cooperativa and in Enoteca.

😠 LOCALS DON'T

❌ Forget to book a table for lunch.

❌ Ski for more than a few hours each day and definitely don't go off-piste.

❌ Spend less than two hours over lunch – take advantage of the empty slopes!

(T+39 (0)436-860808; adrenalincenter. it) – we know what we'd do.

Not to miss A day ski touring or snowshoeing in the jaw-droppingly beautiful Natural Park of the Ampezzo Dolomites with Cortina's **Gruppo Guide Alpine** (guidecortina.com).

Remember to avoid Arriving by car without having asked for directions to your hotel and reserved parking – signposts are erratic, the one-way system confusing and locals drive like maniacs.

Relive a famous moment Sip Campari on the sun terrace of the **Miramonti Hotel**, where Peter Sellers and David Niven filmed *The Pink Panther* (1963) and Roger Moore filmed *For Your Eyes Only* (1981).

Pitstop and sunbathe Rifugio Scoiattoli (Cinque Torri) is home to the Scoiattoli of Cortina – pioneers of Italian alpinism. **Rifugio Faloria**'s large sun terrace is lively and **Rifugio Lagazuoi** has 360° views.

Best mountain restaurant If you queue anywhere in Cortina, it will be for lunch. It's essential to book a table or turn up early. Worth waiting (and paying) for are: **Rifugio Averau** (T+39 (0)436-4660) in Cinque Torri, **Rifugio Scotoni** (T+39 (0)436-847330) towards Lagazuoi, **Capanna Tondi** on Faloria (T+39 (0)436-5775) and **Rifugio Duca d'Aosta** (T+39 (0)436-2780) on Tofana.

Practicalities

There's a stubborn streak to Cortina and its residents. A frontier town, it has retained a strong sense of independence through countless foreign occupations and many locals still speak the ancient language of Ladin. They appear impervious to the pressure on ski resorts to renovate dated hotels and replace ancient lift systems, barely seeming to embrace modern skiing at all. However, as you stroll past the elegant boutiques that line Cortina's Corso Italia at dusk, watching highly animated, furry Italians greeting each other beneath the green and white church tower – you won't really care either.

Sleeping Cortina's two five-star hotels are the **Palace Hotel & Spa Cristallo** (T+39 (0)436-881111; cristallo.it) and **Miramonti Majestic Grand Hotel** (T+39 (0)436-4201; geturhotels.com). However, they're both out of town – we'd rather stay central to soak up the atmosphere and splash out on food. The hotels are virtually all affordable. We like Ernest Hemingway's old favourite, **Hotel de la Poste** (T+39 (0)436-4271; delaposte.it); the quirkily designed **Hotel Ancora** (T+39 (0)436-3261; hotelancoracortina.com); and family-owned **Victoria Parc Hotel** (T+39 (0)436-3246; hotelvictoriacortina. com). Good, central B&Bs (Hotels Meublé) include the four-star **Ambra** (T+39 (0)436-867344; hotelambracortina. it), large **Royal** (T+39 (0)436-867045; hotelroyalcortina.it), cosy **Villa Alpina** (T+39 (0)436-2418; villaalpina.it) and **Olimpia** (T+39 (0)436-3256; hotelolimpiacortina.com) – basic but walking distance from the Faloria lift.

Eating At the top of the range, Michelin-starred **Tivoli** should also get stars for its views over Cortina while **El Toulá** offers divine food in a converted

hay barn – prices are less rustic. The food at Hotel Ancora's **Petit Fleur** restaurant vies for your attention over the décor. **Zamvor**, next to the Impero, does modern Italian while the informal **Ariston**, opposite the bus stop, does Cortina's best pizza. **Leone e Anna** is a tiny, romantic Sardinian restaurant on the road towards Passe Trégochi.

Au pair/crèche Gulliver Park (T+39 340-0558399) takes kids from three months to 12 years. Ask the tourist office for babysitters.

Best après-ski Despite its proximity to Austria, don't expect Austrian-style après-ski. Only a few bars attract younger, ski-suited visitors, like **Clipper** and **Bar Sporte**. By 1700, people are showered, changed and sipping coffee in Hotel Ancora's **Terrezza Viennese** or wine in one of Cortina's many wine bars – **Gerry's Enoteca** behind the ski school, **Villa Sandi**, **Brio di Vino** and **LP26** are favourites.

Bars and clubs The wine bars fill up as people nibble on local cheese and meats before dinner. Things perk up again after 2300, when the discos open (there are six): **VIP Club** in Hotel Europa, **Ciarlis** and **Bilbò Club** are popular.

Shopping La Cooperativa on Corso Italia sells everything from groceries to local crafts and is a major social hub.

Hire shop/rental Snow Service has two shops in town and one near Socrepes. **Socrepes Sports Rental** has an outlet and depot at the Tofana base station and shop in town.

Health and wellbeing There's a public pool at Guargnè. **Corte Spa** (cortespa.it) – 10 minutes from town – is excellent.

Down days with kids Head for the **Adrenalin Center & Adventure Park**

(T+39 (0)436-860808; adrenalincenter. it) for bobsledding (from 16 years) and the **Junior Park** – an outdoor aerial adventure park open from February.

Internet Wi-Fi and/or internet points in most hotels. The **Multimedia Centre** next to Hotel Alaska has computers.

Transfer options Some hotels offer a free or discounted weekend shuttle service from Venice's Marco Polo and Treviso airports (cortina.dolomiti.org). Alternatively, take a train (trenitalia.it) to Calalzo di Cadore and a bus from there – cheap but time-consuming. Don't forget Innsbruck airport – check oebb.at for train timetables.

You can also ski here ... the Dolomiti Superski area.

If you like this ... try Kitzbühel ▶▶ *p70*, Megève ▶▶ *p164*, Courmayeur ▶▶ *p225*, St Moritz ▶▶ *p304*.

⊙ OPENING TIMES

End Nov to mid-Apr: 0845-1600

⊙ RESORT PRICES

Week pass: €193
Day pass: €38
Season pass: €570

⊙ DIRECTORY

Website: cortina.dolomiti.org
Tourist office: T+39 (0)436-866252
Medical Centre: T+39 (0)436-883111
Pisteurs: T+39 (0)436-862171
Taxi: T+39 (0)436-2839

↘10 Courmayeur

Town altitude 1224 m	Vertical drop 1099 m	Blacks 4	Terrain parks 1
Km to airport 150 km/	Km of pistes 70 km	Funicular/cable cars 0/4	Glühwein rating ★★☆
106 km	Nursery areas 3	Gondolas/chairs 3/8	Ski in/ski out ★☆☆
Airport Turin/Geneva	Blues 6	Drags 5	Environmental
Highest lift 2755 m	Reds 14	Night skiing no	rating ★☆☆☆☆

PROS

- ✔ Dramatic scenery.
- ✔ Huge choice of gastronomic restaurants.
- ✔ Access to loads of off-piste.

CONS

- ✖ Not a ski-in resort.
- ✖ On piste not particularly challenging for experts.
- ✖ Relatively small ski area.

Nestling on the southeastern slope of the Mont Blanc massif, Courmayeur's dramatic Alpine scenery has 14 peaks over 4000 m.

Six years ago I moved to Courmayeur because I love Mont Blanc. In my opinion it is the most fantastic mountain and gives to Courmayeur every kind of outdoor pursuit you could want. I love the cut-off mountain village feeling of the town – knowing that I am not far from a major city and airport.

Anna Torretta, former World Ice Climbing Champion

😊 LOCALS DO

- ✔ Get to Arp early and miss the queues for safer off-piste.
- ✔ Eat hog roast at Petit Mont Blanc.

☹ LOCALS DON'T

- ✖ Vallée Blanche at weekends.
- ✖ Checrouit on a warm afternoon – slush!

Italy Courmayeur

Founded in the 17th century as a spa town located at the very top of the Aosta valley, Courmayeur has world-famous charm. Nearly every rooftop is made of huge slabs of chunky slate hewn from Europe's highest mountain. In fact almost every building, street and fountain in the town is either made from or built into the mountain. The cobbled streets that trickle off the Via Roma in the old town boast some of the best restaurants in the Alps and also some of the highest Italian fashion.

Looking at the piste map, an expert may be put off by the lack of black runs. However, if you get right up to the highest point of the ski area, the Cresta d'Arp, you'll find a whole array of challenging off-piste options. For beginners and intermediates, the reds and blues are actually fairly steep compared to some resorts and you'll definitely be pushing your boundaries. All the runs are located on the two sides of a ridge. The morning sun shines on the Checrouit side accessed from the Courmayeur and Dolonne lifts. Here, the runs are wide open slopes perfect for practising your carving. In the afternoon the sun hits the Val Veny side, which comprises picturesque runs through trees with Mont Blanc and its glaciers towering above you.

Beginners A great resort for newbies. The 'Baby Bowl' beside the Tzaly lift is fun and so is the Pra Neyron. Make sure you get over to the Val Veny side in the afternoons for the best snow conditions. The blues get very slushy in Checrouit. Use the runs down from the Zerotta lift. Good final runs are the Pra Neyron and the Chiecco.

Intermediate More than half of the runs in this resort are red, so you intermediates will get a lot out of this resort. Around the Col Checrouit there's a whole array of reds and some are actually pretty steep. Try Le Greye – a good short run that's relatively unused. The Cresta Youla (2624 m) is the highest point that your ability will allow you to ski. From here you can use a series of red runs, ending in Zerotta at 1525 m – a drop of about 1100 m. You can also get to grips with some easy off-piste around the top of the Gabba lift.

Expert Three French words – La Vallée Blanche. You have to experience possibly the most breathtaking mountain view of your life. Booking a guide for this trip is essential so plan well in advance. Pack a good picnic lunch and your camera and the day starts early. Highlights are: La Mer de Glace, an ice plateau with an almost imperceptible slope that will carry you along at jogging speed, giving you the chance to take in the horseshoe of mountain peaks all around you; the crevasse field where your guide is indispensable as he takes you on a twisting route through crevasses and deep blue ice shards jutting out into the sky; a giant beer in Chamonix, France, before you jump on the bus home.

Powder Most people head straight for Arp after fresh snow. If you're not up for the Arp, concentrate on the Gabba area. The terrain between the two runs and the lift is skiable and doesn't often get tracked out until after lunch.

Moguls Being an Italian resort, the piste-bashers work overtime. You'll have to search around for challenges here.

Trees Get to Gabba. There's a really steep section down under the lift or just interesting wooded areas between the runs.

Book a guide Societa Guide Alpina (T+39 (0)165-842064).

Tuition There are a number of ski schools offering tuition in different languages.

Kids The 'Baby Bowl' is perfect with little conveyor belts and button lifts.

Bad light Stick to the Val Veny side. The trees will keep the clouds off.

Not to miss Vallée Blanche – even if you can't ski it you can get some snowshoes on and experience it on foot.

Remember to avoid Going out for dinner after 1930 without booking a table.

Relive a famous moment Get yourself on the World Cup downhill run and ski like Tomba.

Pitstop and sunbathe Da Geremia (near the Zerotta lift base) has a sun terrace and, if you're lucky, some live music. The game sausages cooked on the barbecue grill are delicious.

Best mountain restaurant La Petite Mont Blanc at the bottom of Zerotta lift. Several Sardinian suckling pigs are spit-roasted here every afternoon on a massive outdoor barbecue on the sun terrace. You can smell the crackling on the way down the slope!

Practicalities

The Courmayeur resort is split into three main areas or towns: Courmayeur, on a south-facing ridge; Dolonne, just over the river in the valley; and Entrèves, a little way up the valley from Dolonne. Each has its own lift to the resort ski area.

Sleeping For those prepared to break the bank, try the pretty little **Hotel Gran Baita** (T+34 (0)165-844040; sogliahotels.com), about 1 km out of town. It has the usual excellent in-house restaurant and wellness centre. Close to the cable car in Courmayeur are the high-end **Hotel Pavillion** and three-star **Hotel Triolet** (T+39 (0)165-846822). If you're on a budget, go for **Hotel Tavernier** (T+39 (0)165-230015) in Dolonne – a great location, just a couple of minutes' walk from the Dolonne lift and a 10-minute walk up the hill to Courmayeur old town. It has a wellness spa and is right on the edge of the river.

Eating The restaurants in Courmayeur are top quality but they are also top dollar and there are over 40 to choose from. Gourmet heaven must be restaurant **La Maison de Filippo** in Entrèves (T+39 (0)165-846873) where you can order a 30-course dinner extravaganza. If you finish everything, they roll you home for free! Rather more down to earth is the lively café bar **Petit Bistro** (6 Via G. Marconi off Via Roma) which serves real alpine farmer's fayre. With all this on offer, though, our advice is to get up the mountain. That's where you'll find the best cooking by locals who give you good value for money.

Au pair/crèche Many hotels offer day care, but the **Kinderheim** (T+39 (0)165-842477) at Plan Chercrouit take care of kids under four all day.

Best après-ski **Bar Roma** on the Via Roma has a free buffet for après-ski clients. It can get pretty wild as all the ski bums hang out here to take advantage of the free grub.

Bars and clubs Surprisingly, for such a big town, nightlife is limited. For after-dinner drinks with a bit of life and youth go to the **American Bar** or **Poppy's Bar**. For dancing get over to **Jimmy's Night Café** in Entrèves – don't worry about falling into a ditch getting back to your hotel either as Jimmy runs a free shuttle service to get his punters home safely.

Hire shop/rental Plenty of choice, but the rootsy **4810 Sport** (4180sport.com) has been open since 1818!

Health and wellbeing There's a wellness centre at the **Forum Sport Center** (T+39 (0)165-842666).

Down days with kids The huge Courmayeur **Forum Sport Center** (T+39 (0)165-847898) is in Dolonne and should keep them busy.

Internet There are five internet locations – free at the library and Villa Cameron.

Transfer options Fly to three different airports: Turin, Milan or Geneva. With Geneva (108 km) and Turin (150 km), go to a-t-s.com for taxi prices. Alternatively, get the train from Turin to Pré-Saint-Didier, changing at Aosta, and then a bus or taxi.

You can also ski here ... Chamonix and the Aosta valley resorts, although they are not linked.

If you like this ... try Ischgl ▶▶ *p66*, Les Arcs ▶▶ *p150*.

Italy Courmayeur

⊚ **OPENING TIMES**

Early Dec to mid-Apr: 0820-1630

⊛ **RESORT PRICES**

Week pass: €199

Day pass: €41

Season pass: €750

ⓘ **DIRECTORY**

Website: aiat-monte-bianco.com/regione.vda.it/turismo

Tourist office: T+39 (0)165-842060

Medical Centre: T+39 (0)165-844684

Pisteurs: T+39 (0)165-846658

Taxi: T+39 (0)165-842960

↘11 Gressoney

Town altitude 1637 m	Km of pistes 180 km	Funicular/cable	Terrain parks 1
Km to airport	Nursery areas 6	cars 0/2	Glühwein factor ★☆☆
110 km/170 km	Blues 19	Gondolas/chairs 5/12	Ski in/ski out ★☆☆
Airport Turin/Milan	Reds 40	Drags 1	Environmental
Highest lift 2971 m	Blacks 6	Night skiing no	rating ☆☆☆☆☆
Vertical drop 1759 m			

Situated in the central valley of the Monte Rosa ski region, Gressoney is perfect if you want to make use of the wide open runs over the whole area.

Italy Gressoney

The Monte Rosa is a fantastic ski area encompassing some world-renowned off-piste. In the three deep valleys you'll find long, wide and empty runs at all levels. The lifts are efficient, rarely with queues. The scenery is outstanding with the peaks of the Monte Rosa massif surrounding you.

Beginners Get over to the Champoluc side. You'll find a huge array of blues and easy reds between Frachey and Champoluc.

Intermediate Again, over by Frachey and Champoluc is best, but you can brave the black down to Gressoney

towards the end of the week if you're feeling brave.

Expert Our advice is to work on your off-piste skills. You've got so much on offer, especially when they open the new lift to Cresta Rossa in the 2009-10 season.

Tuition There are plenty of ski schools to choose from, so make your choice depending on which part of the town you're staying in.

Bad light Stay in the Gressoney valley and use the west-facing slops.

Not to miss The long red all the way down from Passo Salati into Gressoney.

Remember to avoid Using the other valleys if the weather is bad. Lifts tend to get closed down.

Practicalities

Gressoney is actually split into three parts. Gressoney-Saint-Jean, a 20-minute bus journey from the lift station, is the largest but it's quiet and very pretty. Gressoney-La-Trinité is 15 minutes further up the valley and has a two-person chairlift that will take you up to the ski area. Stafal, the third part, is at the base of the main gondolas that take you up to the slopes.

Sleeping The Hotel Jolanda Sport (hoteljolandasport.com) in Gressoney-La-Trinité has mid-range prices for the area, a pool and wellness centre, and is situated right next to the Punta Jolanda chairlift. The mid-range **Lyshaus Hotel** (lyshaus.com) in G-St-J is clean with friendly staff, good food and a huge wine list.

Eating You can generally find a three-course meal for about €20 or pasta for under €10 at a number of places dotted around the town. The **Ristorante Nordkapp** (nordkapprestaurant.com) in G-St-J is a charming place for a romantic dinner or to warm up next to the stove in the bar.

Bars and clubs Gressoney is pretty tame. G-St-J, the liveliest place to stay, has three or four bars and a nightclub. You can get a very good draught beer at **Hirsch Stube** in G-La-T.

Hire shop/rental Use the ski-hire shop next to the main lift station.

Transfer options For public transport your best option is the twice-daily bus from Turin airport to Pont Saint Martin, then the hourly bus up the valley to Gressoney.

You can also ski here ... Alagna, Champoluc and the Aosta valley resorts.

OPENING TIMES
Early Dec to mid-Apr: 0845-1700

RESORT PRICES
Week pass: €185
Day pass: €36
Season pass: €700

DIRECTORY
Website: gressoneymonterosa.it/ aiatmonterosawalser.it
Tourist office: T+39 (0)125-356670
Medical Centre: T+39 (0)125-355192
Pisteurs: T+39 (0)125-367111
Taxi: T+39 (0)125-355957

↘12 La Thuile

Town altitude	1441 m	Vertical drop	1465 m	Blacks	12
Km to airport	150 km/	Km of pistes	150 km	Funicular/cable cars	0/1
	130 km	Nursery areas	4	Gondolas/chairs	0/17
Airport	Turin/Geneva	Blues	30	Drags	20
Highest lift	2641 m	Reds	32	Night skiing	no

Terrain parks	3
Glühwein rating	★★☆
Ski in/ski out	★★☆
Environmental rating	★☆☆☆☆

PROS

- ✔ Non-existent queues.
- ✔ Heli-skiing.
- ✔ Large ski-in family resort.

CONS

- ✘ Not very pretty town.
- ✘ Lots of school groups.
- ✘ Limited nightlife.

La Thuile, a family resort, gives you access to 150 km of pistes ranging over the Petit San Bernardo Pass and into France.

Linked with La Rosière in France and sharing with it the Espace San Bernardo, La Thuile is best for beginners and intermediates. With 30 reds and 32 blues, there are challenges-a-plenty and you'll find it hard to get bored here. There are two areas, one in Italy, one in France, and a lovely wide bowl with challenging runs and and snowy hillocks in between.

Beginners Use the Chalet Express and Chaz Dura lifts to access the numerous blues in this area – enough to keep you amused for hours. There are also the easy reds down through the trees into the village.

Intermediate At Col de la Traversette on the La Rosière side you can play snakes and ladders on the 9 or 10 red runs flowing down from the top of this ridge. On your way back to La Thuile, use Piccollo San Bernardo Express and Fourclaz Express to enjoy the lovely empty reds in this sunny valley between the two main areas. The longest run in the resort will take you 11 km all the way back to La Thuile from here.

Expert This is not a great resort for experts. However, there are numerous black runs down to the town, some of them almost vertical, and lots of off-piste. Have a play around in the snow cross area on the La Rosière side. It's designated as part of the pisteurs'"safe' area so there's no fear of avalanches and you don't need a guide.

Powder Get to the snow cross area on the La Rosière side. It's also possible to organize a very cheap day heli-skiing here with a company such as **Heli Ski Valgrisenche** (heliskivalgrisenche.it).

Moguls Again, the snow cross area is best, plus a few areas between runs on the La Rosière side.

Tuition **Interski** offer adult beginner classes, adult group lessons, private

Italy La Thuile

Practicalities 🛏🍴🚌

In a few years' time La Thuile will most probably have much more charm and atmosphere but the continued building and renovating currently visible from every aspect may spoil it for some years to come. That aside, the resort itself punches above its weight. Families and school groups will find it more suitable than party animals, but partying does take place in certain bars.

Sleeping Stay in Entrèves or Arly as they are the areas nearest the lifts. Hôtel du Glacier (hotelduglacier.it) is close to the lifts and freshly renovated. Even closer to the lifts are the **Planibel Apartments** (T+39 (0)165-884541), a range of self-catering apartments of varying sizes and a hotel in a large complex with ski shops, restaurants and gyms.

Eating La Fordze (T+39 (0)165-884800) is the winner of several Italian pizza awards. For a carnivorous treat, go to **La Taverna Coppapan** (T+39 (0)165-884797) and order the châteaubriand (€28 per person) – you can choose from over 300 wines to accompany your steak.

Bars and clubs Don't expect anything too exciting but you can drink until the early hours in **La Bricolette Pub** or dance into the early hours in **La Bricole Disco Bar**, where they occasionally put on live music. **La Buvette** is great for après.

Hire shop/rental Try the shops in Planibel complex. It's very close to the lift and nursery area.

Health and wellbeing The thermal spa at Pré-St-Didier (termedipre.it) will be an experience you won't forget. Don't forget to book, especially at weekends.

Down days with kids Not that much to choose from, but a visit to the chocolate shop will always excite.

Internet Available at the library, where there's a €5 one-off charge.

Transfer options Your best bet is a taxi transfer from either Geneva, Turin or Milan Malpensa – try **Autonoleggio Laura** (T+39 (0)335-6757386).

You can also ski here ... the other Aosta valley resorts.

If you like this ... try La Plagne ▶▶ *p146*, Engelberg ▶▶ *p284*.

⊙ OPENING TIMES

Early Dec to mid-Apr: 0845-1645

Ⓢ RESORT PRICES

Week pass: €185

Day pass: €34

Season pass: €660

Ⓒ DIRECTORY

Website: lathuile.it

Tourist office: T+39 (0)165-884179

Medical Centre: T+39 (0)165-884041

Pisteurs: T+39 (0)165-884563

Taxi: T+39 335-6757386

tuition by the hour, 'learn to ski' weeks and a junior ski school for 7- to 16-year-olds.

Kids There's a nursery slope down in the village near the ticket office where kids under six go free.

Bad light Get into the trees on the village runs down from Les Suches.

Not to miss Heli-skiing, the thermal spa at Pré-St-Didier and the chocolate shop.

Remember to avoid Getting stuck in the wrong country when the lifts close!

Relive a famous moment If you go to La Rosière for the day you'll have to take the Petit San Bernardo Pass. It is thought that Hannibal led his elephants through this pass on his way over the Alps in 219 BC.

Best mountain restaurant Restaurant Berthod, on the red 28 run, is a cosy Himalaya-themed sanctuary complete with Nepalese rugs and slippers issued to diners.

↘13 Livigno

Town altitude	1816 m	Km of pistes	115 km	Funicular/cable cars	0/0	Terrain parks	10

Town altitude 1816 m
Km to airport 190 km
Airport Bergamo
Highest lift 2800 m
Vertical drop 984 m

Km of pistes 115 km
Nursery areas 2
Blues 26
Reds 36
Blacks 4

Funicular/cable cars 0/0
Gondolas/chairs 4/14
Drags 13
Night skiing yes

Terrain parks 10
Glühwein factor ★★☆
Ski in/ski out ★★☆
Environmental rating ★☆☆☆☆

PROS
- Cheap compared to other high-altitude resorts.
- Duty-free shops mean you can treat yourself to new kit.
- Excellent for beginners.

CONS
- Getting to the resort can be a bit of a mission.
- The piste map is pretty useless, as is on-piste signage.
- Gets busy during holidays.

Europe's remotest resort, complete with duty-free shopping.

Thanks to its high altitude, Livigno doesn't have to worry about lack of snow, although it does get very cold. There are three key ski areas – Carosello, Costaccia and Mottolino – which provide varied terrain for beginners and intermediates but little for expert skiers.

Beginners There are nursery slopes dotted all along the lower part of Costaccia and Carosello. Slopes nearest to San Antonio tend to be busiest and those towards Santa Maria are slightly steeper. Progress to the gentle blues higher up on both areas.

Intermediate Warm up on Carosello and Costaccia before trying the steeper runs on Mottolino – the long red under the gondola is great for carving.

Confident intermediates will be able to tackle the blacks with relative ease. Build up freeriding confidence on the Livigno Fun Courses, patrolled off-piste areas full of natural obstacles.

Expert Limited to the point of being non-existent. Most black runs should be red and off-piste skiing is banned. However, Livigno does have some of Europe's best terrain parks, so freestylers will be happy.

☺ LOCALS DO
- Kick off après-ski at the Tea del Vidal.
- Expect the ski bus drivers to know where they're going.

☹ LOCALS DON'T
- Forget to wrap up warm – it gets seriously cold.
- Get caught skiing off-piste – there's an €80 fee.

Moguls The black slope from Carosello past Tea da Borch gets bumped out (and icy).

Tuition There are seven ski schools. Scuola Sci Top Club Mottolino is small and teaches 'new school' skiing, which appeals to youngsters.

Kids Scuola Sci Top Club Mottolino offers Miniclub (4-13 years) and has a dedicated play area. Ski School Inverno Estate runs the Ali Baba kindergarten (6-11 years).

Bad light Trees are limited due to the altitude, so hit the shops or visit Bormio.

Not to miss The end of season sales – seriously cheap kit.

Remember to avoid Driving to the resort without snow chains or without checking the opening schedule of the Munt La Schera tunnel.

Relive a famous moment Italians call Livigno 'Little Tibet in Italy' because of the cold and snow. Fancy seven years here?

Best mountain restaurant It's hard to go wrong here – favourites include La Costaccia, Passo d'Eira and Tea da Borch.

Practicalities 🛏🍴🚌

Set high up at the end of the Valtellina valley, Livigno's isolation hasn't prevented it from becoming a lively mountain community. It's essentially three small villages (San Antonio, Santa Maria and San Rocco) dotted along a valley that have joined to become one long resort. Ski lifts access mountains on both sides of the valley and free buses provide relatively reliable access.

Sleeping Most accommodation in Livigno is ski in/ski out. **Inghams** has a good selection of hotels and apartments, including the luxurious four-star **Lac Salin Spa & Mountain Resort** (lungolivigno.com) and small, family-run **Hotel San Giovanni** (T+39 342-970515; stgiovanni.com). **Hotel Spöl** (T+39 342-996105; hotelspol.it) is central with a good spa and **Hotel Concordia** (T+39 342-990100; lungolivigno.com) is popular with foodies.

Eating There's plenty of good, affordable food here. **La Rusticana** and **Bellavista** do pizza and local dishes, while **Chalet Mattias** and **La Piöda** are more formal, offering excellent local food and wines.

Au pair/crèche Per i bimbi (T+39 342-970711) takes kids from 18 months to three years. Contact the tourist office for babysitters.

Bars and clubs Après kicks off at **Tea del Vidal** (base of Mottolino), **Stalet Bar** (base of Carosello) and **Caffé della Posta** in town. Action starts later at **Echo** (Europe's highest brewery), **Galli's Pub** and **Kuhstall** in **Hotel Bivio**. **Kokodi** disco keeps going till late.

Shopping The Austro-Hungarian Empire gave Livigno freedom from purchase tax in the 1840s, an anomaly which still exists today. Stock up on ski kit, cameras and designer clothes.

Hire shop/rental There's a vast choice of rental shops – choose one that's close to your hotel.

Health and wellbeing Most hotels have spa facilities. The **Bagni di Bormio** (bagnidibormio.it) spa and wellness centre is worth a visit for its extensive facilities and breathtaking views.

Down days with kids Visit the public swimming pool in Bormio or go dogsledding or horse riding (ask at the tourist office for more information).

Internet Wi-Fi is rare. There are internet points at the public library, **Bar Jpioca** and **Roxy** bar.

Transfer options Fly to Milan or Bergamo and take a transfer bus – buses run four days a week (mtbus.it). The journey takes about four hours.

You can also ski here ... Bormio and Santa Caterina. A six-day pass gives you a discount on a day in St Moritz.

If you like this ... try Avoriaz ▶▶ *p123*, Les Deux Alpes ▶▶ *p156*, Flims-Laax ▶▶ *p287*.

⊚ OPENING TIMES

Early Dec to mid-Apr: 0900-1700

⑤ RESORT PRICES

Week pass: €177

Day pass: €36

Season pass: €558

ⓘ DIRECTORY

Website: livigno.eu

Tourist office: T+39 342-052200

Medical Centre: T+39 342-978107

Pisteurs: T+39 342-996915

Taxi: T+39 342-997400

↘14 Madonna di Campiglio

Town altitude	1550 m	Km of pistes	150 km	Funicular/cable		Terrain parks	2
Km to airport	127 km	Nursery areas	2	cars	0/1	Glÿhwein factor	★★★
Airport	Brescia	Blues	17	Gondolas/chairs	4/12	Ski in/ski out	★★☆
Highest lift	2580 m	Reds	13	Drags	5	Environmental	
Vertical drop	1030 m	Blacks	5	Night skiing	no	rating	★★★★☆

PROS

- ✓ High for an Italian resort, with a good snow record and eight out of ten days of sun.
- ✓ Party town, Italian style.

CONS

- ✗ Expensive by Italian standards.
- ✗ Relatively inaccessible.
- ✗ Limited advanced skiing.

Stylish and supremely Italian, yet with quiet charm, this resort offers sunny, snow-sure conditions and lashings of la dolce vita – at a price.

Italians take eating, shopping and strolling at least as seriously as skiing, so Campiglio's tree-lined slopes are rarely busy – and by late afternoon they're virtually empty. Italians also like to look good on the hill and Campiglio's beautifully manicured, gentle slopes help do exactly that. The ski area can be divided into four: Passo Grosté and Monte Spinale on one side of the village and Pradalago and Pancugolo on the other side.

Beginners Start at the Campo Carlo Mango nursery slopes (a short bus ride from town) before graduating to the blues on Grosté and long blue from Pradalago into town.

Intermediate Perfect your carving on the blues on Grosté and Pradalago before tackling the steeper slopes on Monte Spinale and Pancugolo. Get some miles under your ski belt exploring Pinzolo and Folgarida-Marilleva.

Expert While the 3 Tre, Amazzonia and Spinale blacks will entertain experts and the terrain park will keep freestylers busy, Campiglio is limiting for advanced skiers.

Powder Fortunately most visitors aren't here for powder, so get fresh tracks under the Patascoss lift.

Moguls Apparently require too much effort – moguls don't seem to exist here.

Tuition There are seven ski schools, all offering similarly priced packages. Scuola Italiana Sci Rainalter's instructors are almost infallibly friendly.

Kids Scuola Italiana Sci Rainalter has a 'Baby Camp' children's area in the centre of Campiglio. The rest of the kids action happens on Campo Carlo Mango's nursery slopes.

Bad light Plenty of tree-lined slopes, particularly the glades off Mont Spinale. Alternatively, work on your safety skills at the **Madonna di Campiglio Avalanche Training Centre** (T+39 349-8692508).

Not to miss Joining the locals for Sunday morning coffee and pastries in Suisse Bar or La Posta.

Remember to avoid The valley floor Grosté/Pradalago crossover in the middle of the day: hectic with families meeting up for lunch.

Relive a famous moment Visit Campiglio during the classic car Winter Marathon and you're likely to spot Michael Schumacher and other famous Ferrari and Ducati celebs.

Best mountain restaurant Cascina Zeledria on Pradalago, **Malga Montagnoli** on Monte Spinale and **Giorgio Graffer** on Grosté do the best food.

☺ LOCALS DO

- ✓ Ski in the afternoon, when the slopes are quieter.
- ✓ Party late – clubs close at 0600.

☹ LOCALS DON'T

- ✗ Abbreviate to 'Madonna' – it's 'Campiglio'.
- ✗ Ski over Christmas or Easter, when it's super-busy.

Practicalities 🛏🍴🚌

Tucked into a secluded nook in Val Rendena, with slopes tumbling down into town from both sides of the valley, Campiglio's pedestrianized village has an intimate atmosphere. Exclusive, but understated rather than ostentatious, it's popular with wealthy Italian families, fairly well known outside Italy and a proper party town. That said, it feels crowded only at Easter, Christmas and New Year, thanks to its relative isolation when compared to other Dolomite resorts.

Sleeping Hotel Garni la Montanara (T+39 (0)465-441105) is one of Campiglio's oldest buildings. Family-owned since 1880, it's ski-in and a five-minute walk to the lifts. **Hotel St Hubertus** (T+39 (0)465-441144; valrendena.it) is dated but atmospheric and central. **Hotel Golf** (T+39 (0)465-441003; atahotels.it/golfhotel) is popular with families for its quiet location by the Campo Carlo Magno lifts.

⊙ OPENING TIMES

Mid-Dec to late Apr: 0900-1630

⑤ RESORT PRICES (Madonna di Campiglio ski pass/Superskirama pass)

Week pass: €175/208

Day pass: €36/39

Season pass: €580/660

① DIRECTORY

Website: campiglio.to

Tourist office: T+39 (0)465-447501

Medical Centre: T+39 (0)465-322702

Pisteurs: T+39 (0)465-447744

Taxi: T+39 337-838115

Eating Everywhere is good but favourites include **Da Afiero** and Hotel Bertelli's **Gallo Cedrone** restaurant for fine dining and **Antico Focolare** for local dishes. Ride up to the **Cascina Zeledria** mountain refuge by snowcat for local chef Artini's specialities.

Au pair/cr che The larger hotels often have childcare – check when you book.

Bars and clubs Après-ski kicks off at Bar Suisse, La Cantina del Suisse and Franz Josef's Stube. Enjoy cocktails at Pasticceria Pasquini, Cliffhanger and Ober-One. But it's just a warm-up for Zangola – one of Europe's classic ski discos located in an old dairy (you'll need transport to get there).

Shopping Famiglia Cooperativa stocks basics and local produce, while **La Bottega** is a tempting delicatessen.

Hire shop/rental Rent & Go has two well-equipped shops in town.

Health and wellbeing Most hotels have spa facilities. **Bio-Hotel Hermitage** (T+39 (0)465-441618; biohotelhermitage. it), just out of town, has extensive spa facilities.

Down days with kids Learn how to mush – Maurizio offers a day-long dogsledding course (T+39 333-1328490).

Internet There are computers in the library – bring ID.

Transfer options There's an affordable shuttle service from Trento rail station and from Bergamo, Bolzano, Brescia, Milan, Venice and Verona airports (campiglio.to).

You can also ski here ... Folgarida-Marilleva and Pinzolo. Access to a further six resorts with a Superskirama ski pass.

If you like this ... try Ischgl ▶▶ *p66*, Saalbach ▶▶ *p80*, Cortina ▶▶ *p222*.

↘15 Passo Tonale

Town altitude	1800 m	Funicular/ cable cars	3/0
Km to airport	160 km		
Airport	Bergamo/ Brescia	Gondolas/chairs	2/8
		Drags	3
Highest lift	3025 m	Night skiing	yes
Vertical drop	1225 m	Terrain parks	1
Km of pistes	87	Glühwein	
Nursery areas	2	factor	★★☆
Blues	15	Ski in/ski out	☆☆☆
Reds	12	Environmental	
Blacks	5	rating	★☆☆☆☆☆

Excellent for beginners with linked ski areas for intermediate and advanced skiing.

Italy Passo Tonale

Passo Tonale can seem quite barren at first, but a closer inspection reveals more than initially meets the eye. It is excellent for beginners and especially cheap for families. Mountain restaurants on blue runs and the glacier make it an easy place for mixed-ability families or groups to enjoy lunches together up the mountain.

Beginners The central beginner slopes in Tonale are serviced by drag lifts staggered in steepness. Either side of these are easy, wide blue runs with chairlifts. A good long blue is accessed from the Valbiolo lift. From here it is a natural progression to the reds above it.

Intermediate The easy blue and nursery slopes can be used to get high enough to traverse across the entire resort, making the link to the more challenging reds on the left side of Tonale easier than walking. The reds Blies and Alpino are good pistes to get started

Practicalities 🛏🍴🎷

Sleeping All accommodation is within easy reach of the slopes. **Top Residence** (T+39 364-903772; tonaletop@tiscali.it) has low-budget apartments that can sleep up to five. Most hotels are half board although full board and bed and breakfast can be arranged in advance. The **Hotel Miramonti** (T+39 364-900502; info@miramonti.com) is a four-star option which has an excellent location and all the benefits of a four-star hotel. The more economical **Hotel Dolomiti** (T+39 364-900251; hoteldolomiti@pontedilegno.it) also has an excellent location and a good restaurant.

Eating The hotel **La Torretta** serves excellent pizzas from the wood fire. **Il Focolare** is a great place for steaks and home-cooked food. **La Mirandola** is located slightly out of town on the mountain and is ideal for a special occasion.

Bars and clubs **El Bait**, on the road towards the Vabiolo lift, is a cool late place for drinks and sandwiches. **Cantuccio's** shows football games and is a good place for after-dinner drinks. **Snowbreak** and **Magic Bar** are good meeting places at the bottom of the beginner's slopes which serve fast food.

Hire shop/rental **Bimaestri** has a shop in the centre near **Heaven** and

another one near the Vabiolo lift which is quieter; both have good equipment. Skiset.com is linked to the shop **Cinto Sport** which gives good discounts for booking online in advance.

Transfer options It's three hours from Bergamo and Brescia; shuttle buses linked with Ryan Air flights run from both airports.

You can also ski here ... Ponte di Legno, Temu, Marilleva, Folgarida, Madonna di Campiglio.

If you like this ... try Prato Nevoso (Italy), Livingo ▶▶ *p232*.

⊚ OPENING TIMES
End Nov to end Apr: 0900-1700

⑤ RESORT PRICES
Week pass: €160-184

Day pass: €33

Season pass: €545

① DIRECTORY
Website: valdisole.net

Tourist office: T+39 364-903838

Medical Centre: T+39 335-8240262

Pisteurs: T118

Taxi: T+39 338-5072743

Local radio: Radio Number 1

on and from here you are perfectly placed to head down to Ponte di Legno and Temu which are red and black pistes only with some interesting tree areas.

Expert Tonale is definitely not an expert's paradise. Having said that, there are some options to keep advanced skiers entertained. The Presena glacier, found on the opposite side of the road from the main ski area, has black runs while on the back of the glacier are the Pisgana, Sgualdrina Cantiere and Alveo Presena. Behind the main ski areas are Lunarally and Vescasa. All of these are marked on the piste map with a red dotted line.

Tuition There are two ski schools in Tonale: **Tonale Presena** and the **Ponte Tonale**. Learn-to-ski packages can be booked and savings made through British tour operators.

Bad light The local bus from Tonale ties in with the train to Malé from where you can take a beautiful train journey through fields of apple and other fruit trees to the town of Trento.

Not to miss A trip up to the Presena glacier. The T-bars at the top are a fun challenge and there is a decent long black run down to the road.

Remember to avoid The beginner slopes on a Friday morning – it's ski school race day!

Best mountain restaurant Albiolo lift serves snacks and sandwiches as well as an excellent self-serve restaurant.

↓16 Pila

Town altitude	1814 m	Funicular/cable	
Km to airport	80 km	cars	0/0
Airport	Turin	Gondolas/chairs	3/8
Highest lift	2752 m	Drags	0
Vertical drop	938 m	Night skiing	no
Km of pistes	70 km	Terrain parks	2
Nursery areas	2	Glühwein factor	★★☆
Blues	3	Ski in/ski out	☆☆☆
Reds	20	Environmental	
Blacks	3	rating	★☆☆☆☆

This small but perfectly-formed Italian resort is packed with cultural attractions – but may leave expert skiers unsatisfied.

Pila is small but seems to punch well above its weight thanks to a highest lift that tops out at 2752 m. It means there is an above average chance of snow. Experts might struggle due to a dearth of black runs.

Beginners Beginners will find Pila, with its predominantly mellow terrain, to their liking. Stick to the obvious blues until confidence is rising. Then the entire resort is yours to explore.

⊚ OPENING TIMES

Dec to Apr: 0800-1700

Ⓢ RESORT PRICES

Week pass: €153-173
Day pass: €31
Season pass: €620

ⓘ DIRECTORY

Website: pila.it
Tourist office: T+39 (0)165-521055
Medical Centre: T+39 (0)165-521014
Pisteurs: T118
Taxi: T+39 (0)165-262010

Intermediate With 20 red runs out of 26, intermediates might just have found their perfect resort. Really, everything is on but you'll find yourself returning again and again to the Leisse chair.

Expert There are only four blacks, but there is some surprisingly challenging off-piste if you take the time to explore. Really high standard skiers might prefer the challenges of Courmayeur or La Thuile though.

Tuition It's worth pointing out that private tuition here is half the price of some of the A-list resorts in France and Switzerland. If you're staying with Interski, group tuition will be included in your package.

Bad light It's a small resort and there are plenty of reds winding in and out of trees. Avoid the high lifts, especially Couis 1.

Not to miss Light-aircraft flights up the valley from Aosta airport offer amazing views all the way up to Mont Blanc and back.

Remember to avoid Gondola queues at 0900. Big school groups!

Practicalities 🛏🍴🚌

Aosta is the regional capital and the centre of cultural life in the valley. Although at first sight an ordinary Italian town, it has a strong cultural and historical heritage as well as plenty of shops, bars, restaurants and sporting activities to explore. Stay here and use it as a base.

Sleeping Hotel Europe (ethotels.com) is where all the dignitaries and the Italian It-crowd stay. If you are going budget then try La Belle Epoque (hotelbelleepoque.it) just off the pedestrianized area in the old town. Interski (interski.co.uk) are the UK Aosta experts.

Eating The Bataclan (bataclan.it; T+39 (0)165-363921) is very popular with the locals so make sure you book. Ristorante Vecchia (vecchiaosta.it) is an excellent restaurant built between two Roman arches. Trattoria degli Artisti (T+39 (0)165-40960) is also recommended.

Bars and clubs Gekoo, on the beautiful Piazza Chanoux, has a projector for sporting events while Jive kicks off on Wednesdays and Saturdays..

Hire shop/rental Try Ski Set (aosta.skiset.co.uk) for the usual hire solutions.

Transfer options You can get a train directly to Aosta from Turin Porta Nuove railway station (trenitalia.com) and there are regular buses from Torino Caselle airport to the station. Alternatively you can get a taxi transfer (a-t-s.net) or you can fly up the valley to Aosta airport (airvallee.it).

You can also ski here ... An Aosta valley pass means you can ski in Pila's neighbouring resorts.

If you like this ... try Plan de Corones ▶▶*p239*, Klosters ▶▶*p294*.

↘17 Plan de Corones

Town altitude 786-1650 m	Funicular/cable cars 0/0
Km to airport 70 km	Gondolas/chairs 20/6
Airport Innsbruck	Drags 6
Highest lift 2275 m	Night skiing yes
Vertical drop 1295 m	Terrain parks 1
Km of pistes 105 km	Glühwein
Nursery areas 3	factor ★★☆
Blues 25	Ski in/ski out ★☆☆
Reds 13	Environmental
Blacks 6	rating n/a

Large ski area that's virtually unknown in England.

Kronplatz – German for Plan de Corones – mountain towers above the resort's villages like a giant panettone with lifts ascending from Reischach, Olang and San Vigilio to the summit (Concordia).

Beginners San Vigilio has sheltered nursery slopes and a brilliant long blue from the Miara gondola.

Practicalities 🛏🍴🚌

The resort of Plan de Corones encompasses a mountain of the same name, 13 villages and the town of Bruneck.It has excellent family facilities and the world's most modern gondola network.

Sleeping Bruneck: Hotel Post (T+39 (0)474-555127; hotelpost-bruneck. com). Olang for ski in/ski out: **Hotel Mirabell** (T+39 (0)474-496191; mirabell.it). San Vigilio for charm: **Hotel Corona** (T+39 (0)474-501038; hotelcorona.net).

Eating Bruneck: **Weisses Lamb** for traditional, **Zum Goldener Löwen** for international. San Vigilio: **Fana Ladina** for local specialities. Mountain huts: **Huberalm**, **Geiselberghütte** and **Oberegger Alm**.

Bars and clubs Olang, San Vigilio and the Kronplatz base station (Reischach) offer après-ski in **K1**, **Tenne**, **Gigger** and **Igloo** bar. Bruneck has trendy lounge-bars like **Bar Hintergasse** and **Café Mojito**.

Hire shop/rental Rent-a-sport Italy rental and depot at Reischach.

Transfer options Fly to Innsbruck, take the train to Pustertal (trenitalia. it) followed by bus. Alternatively, fly to Venice and take a shuttle bus (bustransfers.it).

You can also ski here ... Alta Badia and the Dolomiti Superski area.

If you like this ... try Zell am See ▶▶*p93*, Bardonecchia ▶▶*p210*.

Intermediate Enjoy the runs off Concordia before taking the long red into San Vigilio from the top of the Pre da Peres gondola. Then go up to Piz de Plaies for quiet reds into Piccolino.

Expert Limited, with just six black pistes. Take a ski bus to Alta Badia for a day.

Tuition Sculoa Italiana Sci has bases in Olang and Reischach and runs Croniworld, which cares for skiing and non-skiing kids (three to eight years), at Concordia.

Bad light Explore Bruneck, the beautiful village of Valle di Caseis or soak in the Kron 4 wellness centre near Reischach.

Not to miss Watching the sun go down from the Biwacco mountain hut.

Remember to avoid Drinking too many Zirm Schnapps at Biwako before skiing home.

☺ OPENING TIMES

Early Dec to late Apr: 0830-1630

⊙ RESORT PRICES

Week pass: €194

Day pass: €38

Season pass: €470

ⓘ DIRECTORY

Website: kronplatz.com

Tourist office: T+39 (0)474-555447

Medical Centre: T+39 (0)474-496131

Pisteurs: T+39 (0)474-555447

Taxi: T+39 335-5959660

Italy Plan de Corones

↘18 Sauze d'Oulx

Town altitude	1509 m	Km of pistes	400 km	Funicular/cable cars	0/0
Km to airport	95 km	Nursery areas	4	Gondolas/chairs	5/38
Airport	Turin	Blues	42	Drags	45
Highest lift	2823 m	Reds	102	Night skiing	yes
Vertical drop	1314 m	Blacks	21		

Terrain parks	1	
Glühwein factor	★★☆	
Ski in/ski out	★☆☆	
Environmental rating	★★★★☆	

PROS

- ✔ English is widely spoken, so no language barrier.
- ✔ Good value.
- ✔ A great introduction to tree-skiing and powder for intermediate skiers.

CONS

- ✘ Boisterous nightlife will put some people off.
- ✘ Poor piste map and on-piste markings.
- ✘ Getting to the ski lifts requires either walking or waiting for buses (not free).

Pretty, lively village with good intermediate skiing on the Milky Way ski area.

Pronounced 'Sau-zee doox,' this resort is located high in the Susa valley with larch forests reaching down to it from the surrounding mountains. Known in the 1980s as Ibiza-on-snow, Sauze remains popular with young party-goers and Brits looking for affordable skiing breaks.

Sauze is ideal for intermediate skiers, offering open terrain, long cruisers and attractive wooded slopes. However, it suffers from unreliable snow cover (particularly towards the end of the season) and antiquated lifts, causing peak-time queues and frequent lift closures.

Beginners Many red runs here should be classified blue, opening up more of the mountain to beginners than an initial piste-map inspection might suggest. However, the location of the nursery area up on the mountain and lack of easy runs into the village can be off-putting.

Intermediate Sauze offers intermediates plenty of opportunities to gain confidence and learn new skills. Improve technique on the slopes round Pian della Rocca, get to grips with powder and tree-skiing and build up to the steeper slopes of Rio Nere. Try to ski over to Montgen vre – a full day but worth it.

Expert The most challenging slopes are located far left and far right of Sauze d'Oulx, accessed by steep drag lifts on Genevris and Fraiteve respectively. Moncros also offers some off-piste opportunities.

Powder Hit Rio Nere under Fraiteve for some long descents down to Jouvenceaux. Then head back towards Clotes taking in some short runs on Moncros to end the day on Genevris. Newcomers to powder will enjoy short, open runs on Pian della Rocca and Roche Nere.

Moguls Few and far between – the blacks on Bourget and Vallone develop into moguls.

Tuition The **Scuola Sci Sauze d'Oulx** and **Sportinia** have more English-speaking instructors than the smaller **Sauze Project** but it's very popular with children.

Kids Children up to eight years ski free. The ski schools meet at the top of the Sportinia chairlift where there's a sunny, sheltered nursery area.

Bad light Stick to the tree-lined runs under the Pian della Rocca chair and around Sportinia.

Not to miss Exploring the beautiful old town with its narrow cobbled streets.

Remember to avoid Packing heavy bags if you're coming by bus – all buses stop at the tourist office and unless you're in the Torre it's a long, uphill walk to your hotel.

Relive a famous moment Piero Gros, Olympic gold medallist slalom skier, was born in Sauze and learned to ski here.

Best mountain restaurant **Bar Marmotte** at the top of the Triplex lift has the best views, **Bar Clotes** and **Restaurant Sosta** in Clotes do good local food, while **Ciao Pais** off the red 2000 piste down to Clotes is a real getaway.

Practicalities 🍴🚠

Sleeping Inghams and Crystal offer packages to most hotels – **Relais des Alpes**, **Derby Hotel** and **Hotel Sauze** are all central. The four-star **Grand Hotel La Torre** (T+39 (0)122-859812; grandhotellatorre.it) is the smartest address in town while the secluded **Ciao Pais** (T+39 (0)122-850280; ciaopais.it) is on the slopes.

Eating Sugo's Bruschette & Spaghetteria does delicious, great value fresh pasta and pizza. The more expensive **Ristorante del Borgo** and **Ristorante del Falco** do pizza and 'skiers menus'. **Albergo Assietta**'s bar snacks at 1800 are popular.

Au pair/crèche Dumbo Kindergarten in the centre of town takes kids up to six years. Ask the tourist office for babysitters.

Bars and clubs Perennial favourites include **Paddy McGinty's**, the **New Scotch Bar** and **Enoteca Il Lampione** wine bar for early doors. Move on to **Osteria dei Vagabondi**, **Cotton Club** and **La Grotta di Bourud** till late.

Shopping Try the **Alpine Zoological Centre** farm shop for fresh local produce.

Hire shop/rental Besson on the Piazza Assietta stocks good equipment and has a separate clothing shop.

Health and wellbeing The **Grand Hotel La Torre** has spa facilities ranging from hydrotherapy treatments to facials.

Down days with kids Check out the **Adventure Park** in Grand Villar (T+39 (0)122-858500) or visit the Alpine Zoological Centre to see local animals and plants.

Internet NonSoloGiochi next to the Derby Hotel has computers.

Transfer options Fly into Turin (turinairport.com) and get a shuttle bus directly to Sauze or take a train to Oulx then a bus (trenitalia.it; sapav.it).

You can also ski here ... the Milky Way (Via Lattea): Sestriere, Sansicario, Cesana, Claviere and Montgenèvre.

If you like this ... try Sölden ▶▶ *p83*, Sestriere ▶▶ *p242*.

Italy Sauze d'Oulx

◉ OPENING TIMES
Early Dec to mid-Apr: 0900-1700

⑤ RESORT PRICES (Milky Way pass)
Week pass: €155

Day pass: €39

Season pass: €750

ⓘ DIRECTORY
Website: comune.sauzedoulx.to.it

Tourist office: T+39 (0)122-858009

Medical Centre: T+39 (0)122-858159

Pisteurs: T+39 (0)122-799411

Taxi: T+39 360-595558

↘19 Sestriere

Town altitude	2035 m	Funicular/cable	
Km to airport	90 km	cars	0/0
Airport	Turin	Gondolas/chairs	5/38
Highest lift	2823 m	Drags	45
Vertical drop	1000 m	Night skiing	yes
Km of pistes	400 km	Terrain parks	1
Nursery areas	4	Glühwein factor	★☆☆
Blues	42	Ski in/ski out	★★☆
Reds	102	Environmental	
Blacks	21	rating	★☆☆☆☆

High-altitude resort popular with Brits exploring the Milky Way ski area.

Sestriere's high, northwest-facing slopes make it more snow-secure than its neighbours and the terrain is more challenging than other Milky Way resorts. Lifts from town access three key areas: Sises, Motta and Fraiteve, which leads into Sauze d'Oulx.

Beginners Gentle meadows flank Sestriere, creating good nursery slopes and rolling blues.

Intermediate Build confidence on Sises before trying the relatively steep reds on Motta and skiing to Sauze.

Expert There are some short steeps off the two drag lifts at the top of Motta and Sises and towards Fraiteve. The trees also offer some fun but experts should explore the Milky Way.

Tuition There are four schools. **Scuola Nazionale Sci Sestriere** is good for kids but check that instructors speak English.

Not to miss Practising your carving on the Olympic giant slalom Col de Sises black.

Remember to avoid If you want to escape fellow Brits.

☺ OPENING TIMES

Early Dec to mid-Apr: 0900-1700

Ⓢ RESORT PRICES (Milky Way pass)

Week pass: €155

Day pass: €39

Season pass: €750

ⓘ DIRECTORY

Website: sestriere.it

Tourist office: T+39 (0)122-755444

Medical Centre: T141

Practicalities

Sestriere, built by Fiat founder Giovanni Agnelli in 1934, was Europe's first purpose-built ski resort. Located at 2035 m at the foot of Mt Sises, the resort sadly has less style than the cars. Accommodation is located in four separate 'housing areas' – choose yours carefully as shuttles stop at 1800.

Sleeping Four-star **Hotel Cristallo** (T+39 (0)122-750190; newlinehotels. com) is close to the pistes. Mid-range **Hotel Savoy Edelweiss** (T+39 (0)122-77040; hotelsavoysestriere. com) is welcoming with Wi-Fi and spa facilities. **Hotel du Col** (T+39 (0)122-76990; gestioniabe.it) is on the slopes. Contact the tourist office for apartments.

Eating **Pinky's Pizzeria & Bar** is popular, **Il Ritrivo** does hearty mountain food and **Tre Rubinetti** has good wines.

Bars and clubs **Pinky's**, **Prestige** and the **Hotel du Col** bar are both popular. **Kandahar Wine Bar** is good for pre-dinner drinks, **Irish Igloo** for later.

Hire shop/rental All shops adopt the same pricing strategy. **Marcellin Sport** next to Hotel Cristallo is large with on-piste storage.

Transfer options Fly to Turin and take a train (trenitalia.it) or bus (sapav.com).

You can also ski here ... the Milky Way (Via Lattea): Sauze d'Oulx, Sansicario, Cesana, Claviere and Montgenèvre.

If you like this ... try Avoriaz ►►*p123*, Sauze d'Oulx ►►*p240*.

Italy Sestriere

↘20 Val Gardena

Town altitude 1236-1563 m	Funicular/cable cars 0/2
Km to airport 40 km	Gondolas/chairs 7/45
Airport Bolzano	Drags 28
Highest lift 2518 m	Night skiing no
Vertical drop 1282 m	Terrain parks 5
Km of pistes 175 km	Glühwein
Nursery areas 3	factor ★☆☆
Blues 32	Ski in/ski out ★★☆
Reds 23	Environmental
Blacks 3	rating ★★☆☆☆

A luxurious combination of German efficiency and Italian cooking.

Val Gardena is part of the Sella Ronda and Dolomiti Superski areas in addition to having 175 km of its own pistes. Skiing is mostly gentle, wide open cruising and best suited for beginners and intermediates.

Beginners   Each village has its own nursery area. Build up to the long blues on Alpe di Siuse above Ortisei.

⊙ OPENING TIMES

End Nov to mid-Apr: 0900-1700

Ⓢ RESORT PRICES (Val Gardena ski pass/Dolomiti Superski pass)

Week pass: €155/209
Day pass: €31/42
Season pass: €479/590

ⓘ DIRECTORY

Website: valgardena.it
Tourist office: T+39 (0)471-777777
Medical Centre: T+39 (0)471-794266
Pisteurs: T+39 (0)471-777702
Taxi: T+39 (0)471-796888

Intermediate   Miles of cruising here for you. Confident intermediates can complete the Sella Ronda circuit.

Expert   The Ciampinoi/Sassolungo area between Selva and S. Cristina has the toughest on-piste skiing. Book a guide to show you the off-piste.

Tuition   Two schools in each village, with uniform prices.

Not to miss   The 'Great War ski tour' around the Col di Lana.

Remember to avoid   The Sella Ronda circuit on a Sunday.

Practicalities

Val Gardena encompasses three villages in the Dolomites – Ortisei, S. Cristina and Selva. Locals speak German, Italian and Ladin (the native language) and towns have both German and Ladin names. With three five-star and 30 four-star hotels between them and excellent restaurants, comfort is key.

Sleeping   Ortisei is largest and most convenient, with a lively atmosphere. We recommend **Hotel Madonna** (T+39 (0)471-796207; hotel-madonna.com) and **Cavallino Bianco** (T+39 (0)471-783333; cavallino-bianco.com). Selva's **Hotel Sun Valley** (T+39 (0)471-795152; hotelsunvalley.it) is family-friendly.

Eating   Ortisei: **Tubladl** for traditional and **Hotel Gardena's Anna Stuben** for Michelin-starred gourmet. Selva: **Gérard Chalet** for lunch and views. S. Cristina: **L Fudlé** for local specialities.

Bars and clubs   Oom-pah-pah après at **Piz Secteur** (Plan de Gralba), **Seceda** (Ortisei base station), **Crazy Pub** (S. Cristina) and **Luislkeller** (Selva). Later, head for Hotel Adler's **Siglu Bar** and **Mauriz** (Ortisei) and **La Stüa**, **Umbrella Bar** and **Heustadl** (Selva).

Hire shop/rental   Ortisei Ski School combines tuition with rental at the **Olympic** shops. **Dolomiti Adventures** (Selva) combines rental and guiding.

Transfer options   Fly to Bolzano, Venice, Verona or Innsbruck. Visit flytovalgardena.com for transfer options.

You can also ski here ...   Sella Ronda and Dolomiti Superski.

If you like this ...   try Champéry ▶▶*p277.*

Italy Val Gardena

Scandinavia

Scandinavia
Value for money
★☆☆☆☆
Nightlife
★★★☆☆
Off-piste
★★★☆☆
Family
★★★☆☆

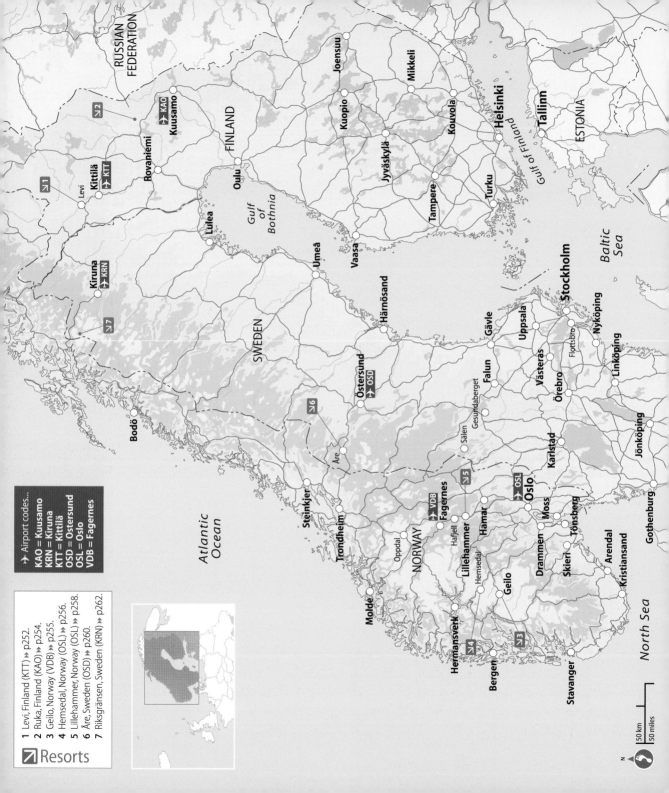

RUSSIAN FEDERATION

✈ KAO

Kuusamo

Rovaniemi

FINLAND

Kittilä
✈ KTT

Levi

⤴1

⤵2

Oulu

Luleå

Gulf of Bothnia

Umeå

Vaasa

Tampere

Joensuu

Kuopio

Mikkeli

Jyväskylä

Kouvola

Turku

Helsinki

Tallinn

ESTONIA

Gulf of Finland

Baltic Sea

Härnösand

Kiruna
✈ KRN

⤴7

SWEDEN

Bodö

Östersund
✈ OSD

⤶6

Åre

Gävle

Falun

Uppsala

Flottsbro

Nyköping

Linköping

Stockholm

Västerås

Örebro

Karlstad

Gesundaberget

Sälen

⤵5

Oslo
✈ OSL

Jönköping

Steinkjer

Trondheim

Oppdal

NORWAY

Fagernes
✈ VDB

Hafjell

Hemsedal

Lillehammer

Hamar

Geilo

Moss

Drammen

Tönsberg

Skien

Arendal

Kristiansand

Gothenburg

Molde

Hermansverk

Bergen

⤵4

⤵3

Stavanger

Atlantic Ocean

North Sea

Airport codes...

KAO = Kuusamo
KRN = Kiruna
KTT = Kittilä
OSD = Östersund
OSL = Oslo
VDB = Fagernes

1 Levi, Finland (KTT) ▸▸ p252.
2 Ruka, Finland (KAO) ▸▸ p254.
3 Geilo, Norway (VDB) ▸▸ p255.
4 Hemsedal, Norway (OSL) ▸▸ p256.
5 Lillehammer, Norway (OSL) ▸▸ p258.
6 Åre, Sweden (OSD) ▸▸ p260.
7 Riksgränsen, Sweden (KRN) ▸▸ p262.

⤴ Resorts

50 km
50 miles

N

Scandinavia occupies a peculiar place in the snow-sports directory. There probably isn't another skiing and snowboarding region on the planet so full of paradoxes. It has produced many of the world's best skiers and snowboarders and has one of the world's highest population to snow users ratios, yet the mountains are relatively small (compared to the Alps at least), the population centres are few and far between, and throughout much of the winter there is very little day time in which to actually use the mountains.

A lot of this is obviously to do with the fact that Scandinavia has a very strong winter-sports culture. Skiing is thought to have originated in Norway; kids learn ski jumping at school; *langlauf* (cross-country skiing) is a very common activity; and Scandinavia's youth are all hugely into sporty pursuits such as skateboarding, ice-skating, ice hockey and football. They rightly see their mountains as a fantastic playground, and regularly make the most from what natural terrain they have been given.

So look beyond the fact that the mountains are relatively flat and lack the grandeur of the Rockies and the Alps. The parks and facilities are great, and in reality it's not *that* much more expensive than what most westerners are used to. Add to that the chance to see the fabled Northern Lights, to meet some of the friendliest locals in the world, and to ski or snowboard while wearing a *lusekofte* sweater (the traditional knitwear of Norway and Sweden), and the makings of a fantastic holiday are complete.

Skiing Scandinavia

For people used to the steeps of Switzerland, the scale of France or the powder of Canada, Scandinavia isn't the most obvious place to go on a winter holiday. But when you actually sit down and look at the facts it's puzzling why this should be so. Finland, Norway and Sweden all have a long tradition of alpine sports; each country has long, harsh winters; and each country has produced some of the best skiers and snowboarders the world has ever seen. And here's the point: if Scandinavia has a stronghold on the sports on an international level, then surely it must have some good places to go sliding around the mountains? Well, yes. And while it's often said that the only reason the Finns, Norwegians and Swedes are so good at the shorter descents (such as slalom skiing

or halfpipe snowboarding) is because they don't have any decent mountains to ride, it's simply not true. This is a myth that anyone who has been to Riksgränsen or Hemsedal will be able to quickly dispel. True, they're low, and neither of them can even come near the vertical drop of most of the Alpine resorts, but their northerly latitudes mean they enjoy high snowfall and a low snowline, and there are some unexpectedly large areas with some surprisingly fun terrain. Think of it like this: would you prefer one or two truly leg-burning runs in a day's skiing (for example, a top-to-bottom ride in Tignes), or would you instead like to have several, pleasant descents in a day?

Conditions

Scandinavia experiences long, harsh winters, but since the majority of resorts span a large longitudinal distance there are correspondingly big regional variations in weather. The main factor here is the daylight – during midwinter, sunlight is a scarce commodity and many people find this off-putting. As Volcom team manager Jan Proust points out, during the deep midwinters, "Scandos are used to flat light and icy conditions; anything better than that is a bonus."

When To Go

Unfortunately it's the dark months of midwinter when Scandinavia gets the best snow, but if you like skiing or snowboarding in the slushy, spring conditions, then a trip to Scandinavia will be right up your street. Spring is an ideal time to visit – the smaller resorts and funparks begin to come into their own, and there are long hours of daylight, particularly in far northerly resorts such as Riksgränsen. In actual fact, if you go late enough (from the end of April onwards), you'll be able to ski under the midnight sun, a fantastic boast in itself!

Off-Piste Policy

Refreshingly for anyone used to the restrictive policies of Canadian or North American resorts, you can pretty much go where you want here. You're on your own if you venture off the beaten track though – make sure you're prepared with all the relevant safety equipment, and know how to use it.

Secret Spots

Most of the resorts are comparatively small, with a large number of very good skiers and snowboarders, so competition to get to the secret stashes of scarce powder can be high. Some people – particularly the younger skiers and snowboarders – can become a bit testy on occasion, though you'll also meet people who can't wait to show you around. It's the old tried and tested formula: be nice to people, and you'll reap the rewards.

PROS

Beautiful scenery.

Great vibes, welcoming people and a great party scene.

If you're serious about getting better at freestyle skiing or snowboarding this is the place. Just look at the average Scandinavian shredder to see what we mean.

It's different up there – whether it's the light, the latitude or the high suicide rate, there is a different pace of life.

Almost everyone speaks English.

CONS

Very expensive.

It can get cold. *Very* cold.

Mountains lack the scale of the Alps.

Long journey times to some resorts.

Short daylight hours in winter. Though this counts as a plus in May at Riksgränsen when the reverse is true.

Essentials

Getting there

Finland's major airport is Helsinki. Carriers to Helsinki include **SAS** (flysas.co.uk), **British Airways** (ba.com), **Finnair** (finnair.com) and **KLM** (klm.com). Levi is around 15 km from Kittila airport, so fly to Helsinki then get an internal flight from **Finnair**. There are also charter flights direct from the UK available from ski-flights.com.

Oslo is Norway's major airport, and Lillehammer and Geilo are both nearby. Carriers include **Lufthansa** (lufthansa.com), **British Airways** (ba.com), **British Midland** (flybmi.com), **SAS** (flysas.com), **KLM** (klm.com) and **Ryanair** (ryanair.com). There are also charter flights direct to Fagernes (around 100 km from Geilo) from the UK available from ski-flights.com. There's a daily bus service from Oslo to Stryn called the 'Moreekspressen', run by **Fjord1** (fjord1.no), which takes about five hours. Bergen is the nearest airport to Hemsedal – **SAS** fly direct from the UK, or you can get a domestic flight from Oslo.

Sweden's major airports are Stockholm and Gothenburg, and carriers include **SAS** (flysas.com), **Air France** (airfrance.com), **British Airways** (ba.com), **KLM** (klm.com) and **Ryanair** (ryanair.com). Riksgransen is in the far north of Sweden so you can either fly to Kiruna airport, or take the overnight train from Stockholm or Gothenburg. This is run by **Connex** (connex.se) and goes direct to Riksgransen. Ostersund airport is 81 km from Åre, and you can get internal flights from **SAS** (flysas.com) or charter flights direct from the UK from ski-flights.com. See skistar.com for details of transfers to the resort. There are also trains from Gothenburg and Stockholm which run direct to Åre – visit sj.se for details.

Red Tape

Norway is the only country of the three to remain outside the EU (though funnily enough it has adopted more EU legislation into domestic law than any other EU country besides Denmark). In most cases (European and North American countries) a valid passport is all that's required to enter Norway, Finland or Sweden for stays of up to three months.

Getting Around

Car hire is easy enough to organize but can be expensive. Each of these countries takes drink driving very seriously and there are harsh prison sentences for offenders – be warned. Legal limits are lower than in Western Europe. Other points of note are that headlights are mandatory at all times of the day in all three countries, and snow tyres are required by law during the months of winter. Beware of collisions with elk and reindeer!

Car Hire Most major hire car companies (easycar.com, hertz.com, avis.com) have offices in airports and cities. Usual age restrictions apply.

Public Transport Public transport is comfortable and well organized throughout Scandinavia, though it's also pretty expensive. Finland has a good network of trains (vr.fi) and buses (matkahuolto.fi). Internal flights are good but costly. Thanks to Norway's craggy coastline, roads and trains can be quite slow so internal flights are a good option. They're reasonably priced by Norwegian standards, which for the rest of the world means they're still pretty costly. Norway also has a good network of trains (nsb.no) and buses (nbe.no; timekspressen.no) connecting major towns and cities. Public transport in Sweden is excellent, particularly the trains. Planning any travel is easy here – there's a national public transport authority with an online timetable called Resplus (resplus.se). You can buy a Scanrail card (scanrail.com) for cheap rail travel throughout Scandinavia.

Fact file

Finland	Norway	Sweden
Currency Euro €	**Currency** Kroner (NOK)	**Currency** Swedish Krona (SEK)
Time Zone GMT +2	**Time Zone** GMT +1	**Time Zone** GMT +1
Country Code +358	**Country Code** +47	**Country Code** +46
Emergency Numbers	**Emergency Numbers**	**Emergency Numbers**
Ambulance T112	Ambulance T113	Ambulance T112
Police T112	Police T112	Police T112
Fire T112	Fire T110	Fire T112

Opening Hours and Traditions

Shops in Norway generally open from 1000-1700 on weekdays, and from 1000-1500 on Saturdays. Food stores are normally open from 0900-2000 or even 2100. Larger shopping centres tend to open until 2000 on weekdays, and 1800 on Saturdays. Most towns have late shopping on Thursday when the shops stay open until 1900. Shops are closed on Sundays.

Shops in Finland and Sweden share a common 0900-1800 opening on weekdays, and 0900-1300/1600 on Saturday (generally 1500 in Finland). Some larger Swedish department stores stay open until 2000/2200 and open on Sundays from 1200-1600. Finish supermarkets tend to open 0900-2100 on weekdays, closing at 1800 on Saturdays.

Most shops are closed on Sundays, though many smaller grocery shops remain open.

Eating

Scandinavian cuisine tends to make very creative use of potatoes, and has more focus on that which can be trapped, shot or hauled out of the sea. Game (elk, reindeer and fowl) and fish (herring, sardines, salmon, cod and mackerel) are typical Scandinavian ingredients, with smoked salmon being Norway's most notable contribution to dinner tables around the world.

To brighten up the otherwise heavy cuisine, the Swedish often use traditional conserves such as lingonberry and cloudberry jam. The former will be familiar to anyone who has eaten *köttbullar* (Swedish meatballs).

Breads, cheeses and jams are typical breakfast items, with *knäckebröd* (a kind of crisp, flat bread) being very common in Sweden. Yoghurt and fermented milk (such as the Swedish *filmjölk*) are also likely to be at hand. If you're in Finland then expect to eat lots of the delicious *ruisleipä* (a dark, traditional rye bread).

The attitude to drinking is markedly different in these three countries to the rest of Europe. Aside from licensed premises like pubs and restaurants, sales of alcohol are monopolized by government-owned enterprises – in Sweden it's *Systembolaget*, in Finland *Alko* and in Norway *Vinmonopolet*. Other retailers are allowed to sell very weak alcoholic drinks such as certain beer or cider (i.e. in Sweden you can buy beer of up to 3.5% alcohol in shops).

Scandinavians absolutely love drinking coffee, and rank amongst the biggest coffee drinkers in the world. Tipping is not customary – usually, a small service charge is automatically added to hotel or restaurant bills. And bizarrely for a country renowned the world over for being expensive, mountain restaurants in Norway are in fact cheaper than they are in France. Though perhaps this says more about France than it does about Norway.

Language

Thanks to an excellent education system, most Norwegians and Swedes speak a very high standard of English (and often French and German too), so it's easy for most foreigners to

---

Top Tips

1 **Time** your visit carefully. Remember that it's so far north that there aren't many hours of daylight during midwinter.
2 **Bring** your own booze. Lots of it. It's very, very expensive here, particularly in Norway.
3 **Carry** ID if you're going out. Many bars and clubs will ask for it.
4 **Recycle** everything. You'll get money back on bottles and crates.
5 **Talk** to people. Scandinavians tend to be very open and forthright, so they're more approachable than many other nationalities. A little bit of friendliness goes a long way.

---

get by. Though Finland is officially bilingual (in Swedish and Finnish), the vast majority of the population (around 93%) count Finnish as their mother tongue. Unlike Swedish and Norwegian, it is difficult to learn. But don't worry – as in the rest of Scandinavia, the overwhelming majority of Finns speak English remarkably well.

Crime and Safety

Scandinavia must rank as one of the safest and most crime-free areas of the world to visit. Petty crime such as pickpocketing does occur, though on a much smaller scale than the rest of Europe. As ever, the risk increases in busier areas in the larger cities, particularly during the tourist-heavy summer months.

Health

The Scandinavian standard of healthcare is very high, particularly in Norway. EU citizens should obtain a European Health Insurance Card (EHIC), which entitles them to emergency medical treatment on the same terms as Finnish, Norwegian or Swedish nationals. This doesn't cover non-urgent medical treatment or repatriation so having additional comprehensive medical insurance is highly recommended.

Going green

Tack an extra day either side of your trip and consider taking the train between resorts and airports. Although it is a lengthier way to travel, it is surprisingly straightforward and is the best way of exploring the incredible scenery of this achingly beautiful European peninsula. Try scandinavianrail.com for details on passes and itineraries. An overnight transfer from Stockholm to Riksgränsen is one of the most romantic rail journeys in Europe.

↘1 Levi, Finland

Town altitude 206 m	Km of pistes not measured	Blacks 4	Terrain parks 2
Km to airport 15 km		Funicular/cable cars 0	Glühwein factor ★★★
Airport Kitillä	Nursery areas 10	Gondolas/chairs 2/1	Ski in/ski out ★★★
Highest lift 531 m	Blues 18	Drags 24	Environmental
Vertical drop 325 m	Reds 22	Night skiing yes	rating ★☆☆☆☆☆

PROS

- ✔ Unique Lapland culture.
- ✔ Great snow due to the cold.
- ✔ Cheap lift passes and a unique nightlife.

CONS

- ✘ Mostly drag lifts (there's one chair).
- ✘ Small area.
- ✘ No open powder runs.

Super-friendly mountain destination. The perfect resort for those wishing to see the Northern Lights – or Santa Claus.

Levi isn't the most demanding resort in the world in terms of steep, epic skiing, but with 45 well-groomed pistes (15 of them floodlit), a park and a pipe for the freestylers and plenty of forests to explore, it's easy to see why this is one of Finland's best ski areas. With low temperatures throughout much of the year, and with crazy sunshine patterns, this isn't a resort for everyone, but if you want a genuine 'winter' feel – and of course a guaranteed white Christmas – this is the place to come.

Beginners With no chairlifts and a great big T-bar taking you up the beginner slope, Levi isn't ideal for complete first-timers. Those liking turns will enjoy the resort's wide, well-groomed pistes though. Being so small, the place is pretty easy to negotiate, so a good day would be spent making your way over to the eastern pistes at the back of the slope, before taking the meandering green run that leads back down to the village.

Intermediate Levi is great for intermediates, with wide, perfectly groomed runs leading in all directions, and relatively empty slopes during the week. For intermediate skiers, we suggest taking a run through the funpark (you don't have to do the jumps if you don't

want to, there are plenty of banks and fun, sculptured mounds to explore) then head down to the gondola. At the top, head towards the eastern pistes and cut off the sides of the slope for some mellow powder gradients.

Expert Expect to be pleasantly surprised by the actual skiing to be had here, especially if you like crisp, well-groomed snow, and love to carve your skis on empty slopes. There isn't a ridiculous amount of challenging terrain, but there is a World Cup run by the gondola that is steep, icy and will challenge any serious skier.

Powder Those seeking epic powder runs will be sadly disappointed. However, go night skiing when it's snowing and you'll be pleasantly surprised at how similar to off-piste the resort's runs feel.

Moguls Those looking for bumps to ski should head elsewhere. Levi prides itself on grooming the slopes to perfection virtually every night.

Tuition The **Levi Ski School** (T+358 (0)207-960211) has a monopoly on instruction.

Kids For kids under seven who can already ski, the entire resort is free as long as they're skiing with a parent and wearing a helmet. For younger, less experienced children, **Kid's Land** is perfect. In between, there are 10 free kids' lifts.

Practicalities ⬛🍴🚌

Although too small to really be called a town, its claim to be the home of Santa Claus and a fantastic place to see the Northern Lights give it a unique atmosphere. As with many northerly Scandinavian resorts, Levi is essentially a group of buildings clustered around the lifts, although the facilities and infrastructure put many sprawling Western European resorts to shame.

Sleeping Try leviski.fi. Their central booking office has a wide range of accommodation across the resort. Packages remain the easiest way for most people to reach Levi, and UK carrier **Inghams** (inghams.co.uk) is worth looking at as one of the easiest and cheapest ways to sort accommodation in Levi. The four-star **Hotel Levitunturi** (hotellilevitunturi. fi) has plenty of facilities and comfortable rooms right near the hill.

Eating The Arran Bar and Restaurant (T+358 (0)16-641888; arran.fi) has some great local dishes, although if you want to head slightly upmarket the Lappish feast at **Kammi** (hulluporo.fi) is fantastic. Take care of fast-food fixes at the **Kebab Shop** or **Mega Burger** in the Levitunturi Hotel.

Au pair/crèche Levi's Kids Land (T+358 (0)207-960212) have qualified child minders and organize a weekly calendar of free events. **Tenavatokka Childcare** (T+358 (0)207-960212) have a sliding scale of childcare charges depending on age, from €10 per hour for under two to €5 per hour for over six.

Bars and clubs Start at the **Panimo** for darts, local ale and a welcome from the well-oiled locals. Then head to the **Cantina** before ending the night at the legendary **Hullu Pollo (Crazy Reindeer) Club**.

Hire shop/rental Zero Point is part of the cluster of buildings that make up the town centre, while **South Piste Rental** specializes in ski gear for kids.

Shopping Levi suffers somewhat from its purpose-built feel here, although there are three supermarkets, a liquor store and a post office, all in the centre of this small town.

Health and wellbeing Head 10 minutes out of town to **Taivaanvalkeat** for a *kota sauna* – the classic Finnish sauna followed by an ice swim.

Down days with kids There's a lot of traditional Lappish fun to have on flat-light days. Try snowmobiling with arcticsafaris.fi or dogsledding with **Wingren's Farm** (nic. fi/-wingren/). Highly recommended.

Internet The Levitunturi has an internet café with laptop points, Wi-Fi and terminals.

Transfer options Levi is only 15 km from Kitillä airport. Shuttle buses run from the airport to meet the daily flights – check finnair.fi for flights and levi.fi for bus times.

You can also ski here ... No local partners.

If you like this ... try Bansko ▶▶ *p104*.

⏰ OPENING TIMES
Nov to end Apr: 1000-2000

💲 RESORT PRICES
Week pass: €125
Day pass: €30
Season pass: €340

ℹ DIRECTORY
Website: levi.fi
Tourist office: T+358 (0)16-641246
Medical Centre: T+358 (0)16-648630
Pisteurs: T+358 (0)16-641246
Taxi: T+358 (0)16-106441

Bad light Even in heavy snowfall Levi remains skiable due to the fantastic floodlights on many of the main runs. Make sure you have a clear lens to make the most of it.

Not to miss The natural gully on skier's right of the main park is a real must-do, with its snake-like quality and follow-the-leader fun.

Relive a famous moment Challenging the pro skiers' times on that downhill run.

Remember to avoid Then again, that World Cup run will give beginners nightmares. Avoid at all costs unless very confident.

Best mountain restaurant Restaurant **Tuikki** at the top provides some excellent views if the light is right.

↘2 Ruka, Finland

Town altitude 291 m	Funicular/cable
Km to airport 25 km	cars 0/0
Airport Kuusamo	Gondolas/chairs 0/5
Highest lift 496 m	Drags 14
Vertical drop 201 m	Night skiing yes
Km of pistes 20 km	Terrain parks 2
Nursery areas 2	Glühwein
Blues 11	factor ★☆☆
Reds 9	Ski in/ski out ★★☆
Blacks 5	Environmental
	rating ★☆☆☆☆☆

Small resort that's ideal for families with one of Europe's longest ski seasons.

A visit to Ruka isn't just about skiing, it's a full-on Arctic experience. Located in Lapland, near the Russian border, it's a mini Winter Wonderland complete with cosy log cabins, reindeer, huskies and snow-clad pines. Although Ruka gets bitterly cold (particularly in January and February) and lacks long runs, beginners and intermediates love its empty, tree-lined, immaculately groomed slopes, lack of lift queues and magical setting in arctic fells. Floodlighting is required in midwinter but by June the sun literally never sets on the slopes.

Beginners Head over for the blues on Vuoselli before taking on the resort's (easy) reds.

Intermediate All slopes are ideal for you, with the bonus of being virtually deserted. Explore the area, particularly the reds on Masto.

Expert Fairly limited with some fun blacks and good tree-skiing.

Tuition Ruka Ski School is excellent.

Kids Ruka is perfect for children with a kindergarten next to the main ski lift and **Kaltiolampi Kids** area next door, which is free for kids accompanied by their parents.

Bad light Ruka does suffer from freezing fog. If you've had enough, visit the reindeer farm and get your reindeer driving licence.

Not to miss Night-skiing until 2300 under the midnight sun.

Remember to avoid Getting in the way of the Finnish Freestyle team during training – they're not called Flying Finns for nothing.

Practicalities

Sleeping There are only four hotels in Ruka, our favourite being **Chalet Ruka Peak** (T+358 (0)8-868 4100; rukapeak.fi), so many visitors stay in nearby Kuusamo (linked by free bus). Book secluded, self-catering cottages in Ruka through the tourist office.

Eating Vanha Karhu and Hotel Royal Ruka serve good food in fairly plush surroundings. The **Riipinen Game Restaurant** is a simple house in woods that serves local game. Good mountain restaurants include **SkiBistro**, **HillSide Grill** and **Freestyle Café**.

Bars and clubs There's traditional après-ski at **SkiBistro** and **Restaurant Piste**. Enjoy quiet drinks at **KarhuBar** (Hotel Rukahovi) and dancing in **After Safari Restaurant Zone** and **Night Club Tellu**.

Hire shop/rental Ruka Rental Shop is friendly with excellent equipment.

Transfer options Fly to Kuusamo and take a bus. **Inghams**, **Crystal** and **Thomson** organize packages with transfers.

You can also ski here ... No local partners.

If you like this ... try Geilo ▶▶ *p255*.

⊙ OPENING TIMES
Early Oct to early May: 0900-1900

⊙ RESORT PRICES
Week pass: €150
Day pass: €33
Season pass: €420

⊙ DIRECTORY
Website: ruka.fi
Tourist office: T+358 (0)8-8600 200
Medical Centre: T+358 (0)40-707 7123
Pisteurs: T+358 (0)8-8600 200
Taxi: T+358 (0)1-0084 200

⬊3 Geilo, Norway

Town altitude 800 m	Funicular/cable
Km to airport 105 km	cars 0/0
Airport Fagernes	Gondolas/chairs 0/14
Highest lift 1178 m	Drags 6
Vertical drop 380 m	Night skiing yes
Km of pistes 33 km	Terrain parks 3
Nursery areas 4	Glühwein
Blues 9	factor ★☆☆
Reds 15	Ski in/ski out ★★☆
Blacks 5	Environmental
	rating ★★★★☆

Family-friendly village known as the 'Gateway to Norway's roof'.

⊙ OPENING TIMES

Late Nov to early May:
0930-1530/1700

⑤ RESORT PRICES

Week pass: NOK1350

Day pass: NOK325

Season pass: NOK3930

① DIRECTORY

Website: geilo.no

Tourist office: T+47 3209 5900

Medical Centre: T+47 3209 2250

Pisteurs: T+47 3209 5920

Taxi: T+47 3209 1000

Geilo is located on the shores of a fjord, overlooked by the Hallingskarvet mountain range and bordered by Hardangervidda, Northern Europe's largest mountain plateau. It's one of Norway's oldest ski resorts and offers numerous winter activities in addition to skiing. Geilo's slopes are on both sides of town, with access to lifts with a free ski bus. Slopes are wide, immaculately groomed and serviced by fast, modern lifts. Terrain on Vestilia and Geilo Fjellandsby are ideal for beginners while the Slaatta, Taubanen, Geiloheisen and Halstengård slopes suit intermediates.

Beginners Find your feet on the Slaatta Skisenter nursery slopes before heading to the other side of town and enjoying Fjellandsby's long green 51 and gentle blues.

Intermediate Warm up on Vestilia and Fjellandsby before exploring the reds and blacks from town.

Expert Limited with only a handful of black pistes and little scope for off-piste.

Tuition Geilo Skiskole based at Slaatta Skisenter is great for kids while **Geilolia Ski School** does rental as well.

Not to miss Twice-weekly skiing at sunrise (0700) followed by breakfast at **Taubanekroa**. Places are limited, so book ahead!

Remember to avoid Not checking out **Dr Holms Hotel** – it's a Norwegian institution.

Practicalities

🛏️ 🍴 🚌

Sleeping Ustedalen Hotell Geilo (T+47 3209 6700; ustedalen.no) is good for families, **Dr Holms Hotel** (T+47 3209 5700; drholms.no) and **Vestlia Resort** (vestlia.no) are both top-end. **Neilsons** (neilsons.co.uk) offers packages with self-catering chalets.

Eating Dr Holms Hotel does a vast buffet banquet, **Restaurant Hallingstuene** serves good local dishes while **Smiu Biffverksted** is less expensive. Eating on the mountain is no gourmet experience – pack a sandwich or head back to the village.

Bars and clubs Nightlife is sedate. Try **Skibaren** piano bar and **Recepten Pub** (both in Dr Holms Hotel). **Barock'n Orkesterbar** offers dancing and live music.

Hire shop/rental Intersport Geilo is one of Norway's largest Intersports.

Kids Geilo is perfect for families, with a kindergarten at Geilolia ski centre, tobogganing and family slalom competitions.

Transfer options Fly to Fagernes and take a public bus or take a direct transfer bus from Oslo (skigeilo.no).

You can also ski here ... No local partners.

If you like this ... try Ruka ▶▶ *p254*.

↘4 Hemsedal, Norway

Town altitude 625 m	Km of pistes 43 km	Funicular/cable cars 0/0	Terrain parks 3
Km to airport 225 km	Nursery areas 1	Gondolas/chairs 0/6	Glühwein factor ★★★
Airport Oslo	Blues 19	Drags 16	Ski in/ski out ★★☆
Highest lift 1920 m	Reds 21	Night skiing yes	Environmental
Vertical drop 1295 m	Blacks 8		rating ★★★★★★

PROS

- ✔ Friendly.
- ✔ Extremely beautiful part of the world.

CONS

- ✖ Sometimes icy.
- ✖ Not brilliant for the powder hounds.

Beautiful, progressive Norwegian ski resort with much to offer skiers of all levels. Just remember to take out a bank loan beforehand ...

Hemsedal is one beautiful ski resort. This being Scandinavia, the light is spectacular so be prepared for some incredible sunsets. The mountain is based around three main peaks, and has been very carefully laid out, making it great for groups. Most of the runs tend to congregate in the same place, so it is relatively simple for beginners, intermediates and experts to head off for the day and arrange an easy meeting point.

Beginners Complete beginners should use the short drag at the base. Those with some experience will want to head up to the long green run accessed by the chair. At 4 km in length, it's a great confidence booster.

Intermediate Take your pick. The whole resort could have been made for intermediates. The Tinden area has some lovely mellow powder runs if you're lucky enough to get fresh snow. Alternatively, head to nearby Solheisen to ride the drags there. It is usually much quieter.

Expert Hemsedal once again delivers. Much of the steeper terrain is to be found up on the Tinden area , although the Rogjin summit also has some steeper, easily accessible off-piste terrain. And if you've ever thought about trying your hand at jumps, you're in the right place – Hemsedal has up to three funparks!

Powder The Totten Bowl, near the summit, is an obvious place to head in fresh snow.

Moguls There are two mogul runs on which to test your bump skills.

Tuition Hemsedal Ski School does it all – groups, kids, even – whisper it – snowboarding lessons.

Kids Children under six ride for free – nice touch. Then there's an on-slope kindergarten (**Trollia**) and special Family Weeks – check the site.

Bad light Another very good area is the Totten Skogen (forest) with some sweet tree runs.

Relive a famous moment Famous polar explorer Fridtjof Nansen was a fan of Hemsedal.

Remember to avoid Bankrupting yourself by going out every night. Save it for the last night.

Best mountain restaurant Separate from the main resort, **Skarsnuten** has some great facilities.

Practicalities

Hemsedal is one of Scandinavia's most well-rounded ski resorts. Although it isn't the steepest resort in the world, it has a few aces up its sleeve – a brilliant snow record (when the rest of Europe suffers, Hemsedal usually gets the goods), sublime scenery and a diverse mountain that should see everybody going home happy. There is a 'but' though – the price of skiing and living in Norway generally. If you're defined by a budget, it probably isn't for you. But if you're prepared to swallow the sometimes eye-watering bar prices, Hemsedal is a rewarding ski destination.

Sleeping The easiest way is to use an independent operator. We like **Ski Norway** (ski-norway.co.uk) who provide a bespoke service for groups depending on size and travel arrangements. If you're going it alone, the cheapest bet is **Moen Cabins and Camping** (moencamping. com) with their cabins and camping. **Skarsnuten Hotel** (dvgl.no) takes care of the boutique option, while a nice mid-ranger is the **Hemsedal Café Skier's Lodge** (gohemsedal.no).

☺ OPENING TIMES

Mid-Nov to early Feb: 0900-1530; early Feb to early May 0900-1630

⑤ RESORT PRICES

Week pass: NOK4595

Day pass: NOK3450

① DIRECTORY

Website: hemsedal.com

Tourist office: T+47 3205 5030

Medical Centre: T+47 3140 8900

Pisteurs: T+47 3205 5300

Taxi: T+47 3206 2112

Eating You'll find a range of options. **Hemsedal Oxen Bar and Grill** (T+47 3205 5410) is a great steakhouse. **Experten Sportsbar** (T+47 3205 5410) has a kids discount and relatively cheap buffets throughout the day. **Hemsedal Café** in the village has some cheap bar snacks and lunch options. For the full fusion option, the restaurant in the **Skarsnuten Hotel** is also worth splashing out on.

Au pair/crèche There is a great crèche located at the ski centre, at the base of the resort.

Bars and clubs There's a large après-ski scene in Norway, so take your pick from **Hemsedal Café**, **Garasjen** and **Skarsnuten Hotel**. For clubs, try **The Edge** and **Bar (t)**.

Shopping Self-caterers should acquaint themselves with **Spar** and **Co-op**. There is also a wide range of sports and souvenir shops.

Hire shop/rental Two solid options in Hemsedal are **Hemsedal Ski Rental** (T+47 3205 5322) and **Hemsedal**

Skishop (T+47 3205 9999). There's also one a little bit further afield in nearby Solheisen.

Health and wellbeing There is a spa at the lavish **Skogstad Hotel** (skogstadhotell.no).

Down days with kids Each Saturday the resort hosts a day of activities especially for children, while dogsledding, horse riding and family treasure hunts should keep them happy the rest of the time.

Internet Check your mail at **Hemsedal Café** (gohemsedal.com) downtown. Wi-Fi is also available at the tourist office, **Experten Sportsbar** and the **Welcome Centre**.

Transfer options Transfers from any airport can be arranged through ski-norway.co.uk.

You can also ski here ... Hemsedal is a Ski Star resort, who also run Salen, Vemdalen, Trysil and Åre.

If you like this ... try La Clusaz ▶▶ *p138*.

Scandinavia Hemsedal, Norway

↘5 Lillehammer, Norway

Town altitude 200 m	Km of pistes 39 km	Gondolas/chairs 1/3	Ski in/ski out ☆☆☆
Km to airport 190 km	Nursery areas 1	Drags 8	Environmental
Airport Oslo	Blues 18	Night skiing yes	rating ☆☆☆☆☆
Highest lift 1030 m	Reds 6	Terrain parks 1	
Vertical drop 835 m	Blacks 4	Glühwein factor ★★☆	

PROS

- ✅ Impressive parks.
- ✅ Unbelievably quiet.
- ✅ Reliable snow and a long season.

CONS

- ❌ If you don't like to ski in and ski out this is not the place to base yourself.

The Olympic town is a perfect base for exploring the nearby snow centres of Hafjell and Kvitfjell.

The two resorts, Hafjell and Kvitfjell (*fjell* means mountain) are both outside of Lillehammer. Hafjell, the bigger resort, is a 20-minute trip from the town and Kvitfjell is around 45 minutes. The combined resorts have 40 lifts and 80 runs.

Beginners In Hafjell there are long winding trails that meander down the mountain from the Hafjellheis III chair (at the highest lift). There is also a separate beginner area to the left of the main lift, the Hafjellheis I. In Kvitfjell stick to the west side.

Intermediate Intermediates are well catered for in both resorts. In Hafjell wide, tree-lined trails in the Svergardøypa area, like Skivei fra Gaiastova, are perfect for cruising. In Kvitfjell – the site of the 1994 Olympic downhill skiing events – there are more tree-lined runs. Try Skiveien, a long gentle red run.

Experts In Hafjell there are a couple of wide black runs or you could head to the snow park. Kvitfjell claims to have the best expert terrain in Norway with 6 km of runs and an 847-m vertical drop.

Tuition Ski schools in both resorts.

Kids The **Children's Park** at Hafjell has childcare for children aged two to seven and a fenced skiing area for young learners. In Kvitfjell, there is a new children's ski area on the west side and tired tiny skiers can watch films, play or read in the 'Bamsebo' cabin.

Bad light Much of the Hafjell ski area is below the treeline. In Kvitfjell stick to the trees below the Kvitfjell plaza.

Not to miss The 900-m Hafjell Snowboard Park.

Remember to avoid Paying Norwegian prices for your après-ski beer.

Best mountain restaurant In Hafjell try the **Pavilion**, in its glass conservatory, at the top of the gondola. **Tyri-Hans Ski-café** is situated on the west side of Kvitfjell serving pizza, coffee and cakes.

☺ LOCALS DO

- ✅ Keep skiing when the sun goes down under the floodlights in Hafjell – there is night skiing three times a week under extensive floodlights on 7 km of runs.

☹ LOCALS DON'T

- ❌ Stick to the trails – with powder likened to that of North America, there is a whole world off-piste to explore.

Practicalities

This picture-perfect Norwegian town is a winter wonderland set on the northern banks of Lake Mjøsa. Lillehammer is not a ski resort – the nearest downhill runs are 14 km away – but it is a buzzing market town surrounded by snow-capped mountains. Shoppers from all over Norway come to the famous Christmas markets and to stroll through the historic streets and alleys of the town; the Storgata pedestrian area has even won awards for its design.

Sleeping The 95-room **Hammer Hotel** (T+47 6126 7373; choicehotels.no) is centrally located on Storgata Street. **First Hotel Breiseth** (T+47 6124 7777; firsthotels.no/breisethirst) is right next to the bus and railway station from where the winter bus shuttles leave for Hafjell. For bargains, head to **GjesteBu Overnatting** (T+47 6125 4321) or **Mary's Guest House** (T+47 6124 8700).

Eating Choices range from traditional to fusion. **Blåmann Restaurant**, on the river, does Mexican/Norwegian – try the reindeer burritos and quesadillas. For a

relaxed atmosphere try **Café Banken**, while **Svare & Berg** is recommended by locals.

Bars and clubs In the Hafjell ski area, **Woody's** is a British-style pub selling pints for about the same price as in London. In Lillehammer try **Nikkers** or **Bingon** for après ski. **Brenneriet** and **Lille Blå** are nightclubs. **Blå Rock** is one of the most popular spots, with DJs and the occasional live band.

Hire shops and rentals There are rental shops in both ski centres. Equipment can be stored overnight in Hafjell.

Health and wellbeing The Jorekstad swimming pool (T+47 6105 7060; jorekstad.no) – think waterslides, sauna and steam rooms as well as

swimming – is 6 km from Lillehammer. Take the public bus from the bus station to get there. The **Håkons Hall Sports Centre** (T+47 6105 4200; olympiaparken. no) in the Olympic Park has squash courts, weights room and an indoor golf centre complete with simulator.

Internet The public library in has internet access, as do most hotels.

Transfer options The train from Oslo to Lillehammer takes around 2½ hours – there are departures every hour (T+47 8150 0888; nsb.no). Driving to Oslo takes around two hours.

You can also ski here ... No local partners.

If you like this ... try Geilo ▶▶ p255.

☺ OPENING TIMES

End Nov to late Apr: 0930-1630

⏱ RESORT PRICES

Week pass: NOK1315

Day pass: NOK325

Season pass: NOK3900

ⓘ DIRECTORY

Website: lillehammerturist.no

Tourist office: T+47 6128 9800

Medical Centre (Hafjell): T+47 6127 7901 (after 1500, T+47 6127 7901)

Pisteurs: T+47 6127 4711

Taxi: T+47 6127 8980

⬎6 Åre, Sweden

Town altitude 327 m	Km of pistes 101 km	Funicular/cable	Terrain parks 3
Km to airport 100 km	Nursery areas 6	cars 1/1	Glühwein factor ★★☆
Airport Ostersund	Blues 51	Gondolas/chairs 1/6	Ski in/ski out ★★☆
Highest lift 2900 m	Reds 42	Drags 32	Environmental
Vertical drop 853 m	Blacks 5	Night skiing yes	rating ★★★★☆

PROS
- ✔ Very friendly resort.
- ✔ Very good infrastructure for all types of people and families.
- ✔ Wide variety of terrain for all levels.

CONS
- ✘ Can get very windswept.
- ✘ Slight 'identikit' resort feel.
- ✘ You must have ID to purchase any form of alcohol. They are strict.

Sweden's main resort is more akin to a French or Italian resort than somewhere like Riksgränsen thanks to a versatile mountain and a friendly, fun centre.

The most unusual thing about Åre is that it is, in essence, a 'side on' mountain, with lifts very much lined up next to each other. It means that if you want to explore the entire resort, you'll be doing a lot of traversing. Depending on your proclivity, this can be a good or bad thing, but it does mean a day skiing Åre feels more like an adventure than at other resorts, where skiers often tend to stick to one area they're familiar with. The terrain is more undulating than epically steep, but then it is primarily a family ski resort. There is some steeper terrain on offer, but you'll have to seek it out yourself or use a local guide, which is always a good way of finding out exactly what a resort has on offer.

Beginners Beginners will need to choose carefully, as the way Åre is set up means that the steeper routes tend to be nearer the bottom. Head for the right-hand side, using the Tottliften, where there are some good green and blues. Avoid the large gondola until confident.

Intermediate The best tactic is to head straight to the top via the Kabinbana cable car. Here you'll find a lot of red runs. The Bergbanan in central Åre also accesses some solid intermediate terrain. Essentially, the whole mountain is perfect for a week of intermediate exploring.

Expert If you are feeling adventurous, cut left down the Traningsbacken run. To your left you will see wide and steep open fields full of good terrain. The further you traverse, the steeper the terrain. Then there are tight turns and gullies in the trees below Areomradet which will test your legs. And be sure to try the night skiing – it takes place for two hours each evening, and is so well floodlit it makes for a brilliant experience. An Åre must-do.

Tuition Åre Ski School (skistar.com/english/ski_school) offers carving clinics, children's lessons and general group classes.

Kids The Bjornen area has been planned with kids in mind, with family

barbecue area, funparks and inflatable animals to provide ample distractions.

Bad light The Holiday Club (holidayclub.se) is a hub of entertainment with a waterpark, bowling alley and games centre.

Not to miss The beautiful frozen waterfall, just outside town.

Remember to avoid The end of February as schools are on holiday and the resort gets very busy.

Relive a famous moment Tomas Brolin, Mel C and the Swedish royal family are among the stellar celebs to regularly visit Åre.

Best mountain restaurant If the weather is good, walk to the small cottage at the very top of the mountain, accessible by the Kabinbanan gondola, where they serve coffee in front of stunning views of the valley.

☺ LOCALS DO
- ✔ Party at Bygget on Tuesday nights.
- ✔ Go night skiing as it's less crowded.
- ✔ Welcome visitors.

☹ LOCALS DON'T
- ✘ Go to après-ski.
- ✘ Go out on Wednesdays.

Practicalities

Åre is Sweden's largest resort, comprising three villages along the shores of the Åresjon lake. Although this means the place is spread out (essentially, it is one long line), it manages to retain the feeling of a centralized resort thanks to a well-thought-out village centre. The three villages each have a different character, with Åre the buzzy, busy centre, Duved a little mellower and Bjornen designed with kids and families in mind.

Sleeping Perhaps the easiest way to arrange accommodation is through the **Ski Star** website (skistar.com). It has an extremely simple means of navigation and different options for different budgets. The **Hotel Diplomat** (diplomathotel.com) is good for those with more to splash, while the **Tott Hotel** has ski in/ski out accommodation and a luxury spa.

Eating In Åre village, all the best restaurants are located in and around the main village square. For a gourmet experience with traditional feel, try **Dahlboms** or **Twins**, or for a cafe experience, hit the cosy **Lok & Latte** located in the former railway station. In addition, **Hotell Diplomat** boats two good quality restaurants. On the mountain, **Hotel Fjällgården** is a perfect restaurant for a lunch break (and an after ski beer) and is located right in the central ski area.

Au pair/crèche You'll find the main crèche **Barnens Hus** at the Åre Bjornen area where you can leave the kids while you nip off to enjoy the slopes.

Bars and clubs Tuesday is the big local night at **Bygget** nightclub. On Thursdays visit the sophisticated booths of **Dippan**, part of the Diplomat Ski Lodge. Check out the **Broken Bar** for laid-back beers, while the **Wersens** is also worth a look-in.

Shopping The main **ICA Åre** supermarket is up a flight of stairs off the main Åre square. There is a cashpoint just below the stairs.

Hire shop/rental Again, the Swedes have it all worked out: there are an astonishing seven branches of **Skidakarna** rental shop dotted through the resort.

Health and wellbeing **Tott Hoel** has a day spa for guests and non-guests alike.

Down days with kids It's time to take the little ones dogsledding. We recommend **Åre Sled Dog Adventures** (aresleddog.se) or **Camp Åre** (campare. se). **Camp Åre** also offer zip-lining, snowmobiling and sundry other attractions.

Internet Wi-Fi is available in practically all of the apartments and hotels. Otherwise the **Telia** on Åre square or **Zebra Café** both have access.

Transfer options You can take a taxi, or check out skistar.com for details of transfers from nearby Ostersund airport. Trains (sj.se) from Gothenburg and Stockholm run direct to Åre and are a great way to travel.

You can also ski here ... Åre is twinned with other Ski Star resorts such as Salen and Trysil.

If you like this ... try Méribel ▶▶ *p166*, Hemsedal ▶▶ *p256*, Leysin ▶▶ *p298*.

⊚ **OPENING TIMES**

End Nov to early May:
0900-1500/1600

⦿ **RESORT PRICES**

Week pass: SEK1675

Day pass: SEK340

Season pass: SEK3950

⦿ **DIRECTORY**

Website: skistar.com

Tourist office: T+46 (0)647-17712

Medical Centre: T+46 (0)647-16600

Taxi: T+46 (0)647-10022

↘7 Riksgränsen, Sweden

Town altitude 504 m	Km of pistes 19 km	Funicular/cable	Terrain parks 1
Km to airport 137 km	Nursery areas 1	cars 0/0	Glühwein factor ★☆☆
Airport Kiruna	Blues 4	Gondolas/chairs 0/2	Ski in/ski out ★★★
Highest lift 909 m	Reds 12	Drags 4	Environmental
Vertical drop 300 m	Blacks 1	Night skiing yes	rating ★★★☆☆

Located 300 km north of the Arctic Circle, Riksgränsen is the most northerly resort in the world. Ski under the midnight sun in July, or the Northern Lights in winter.

On paper, Riksgränsen is tiny when compared to most of the other resorts in this guide. But it really is a different skiing experience thanks to the enormous wilderness that surrounds the complex. Beginners and intermediates will find the undulating pistes good fun, while adventurous, advanced skiers will find the place enthralling. And then there are the views, the fantastic snow conditions, the unusual daylight hours ...

Beginners The best area for beginners is at the top of the mountain. So take the chair and then find the Blabarsbacken blue to the Nordalsliften where it opens up nicely.

Intermediate You'll probably find yourself riding the Ovre Stolliften chairlift most of the time, although the entire resort is perfect intermediate territory. Go adventuring! The Apelsinklyftan is a mellow blue run that heads to Katterjakk. To get home, hop on the train for one stop.

Expert Take the Ovre Stolliften chairlift to the top and ski down the backside of the Riksgransfjallet. There's a half-hour hike up the Nordalsfjall face but you are virtually assured fresh lines and steeper terrain.

Powder One nice route if there is fresh snow is to bear right from the top of Ovre Stolliften, where there are usually some open fields to explore. It's a short walk back along the train tracks to the bottom chair.

Moguls They develop, but Riksgränsen isn't really the place for bump lovers.

Tuition There is a great ski school on site, check at the hotel.

Kids There is a tiny kids' area cordoned off next to Solliften poma lift. Kids can learn as they glide through the little animal slalom gates.

Bad light Hit the spa or go for a day trip to visit the fjords of Narvik only an hour away by train. There are no trees this far north!

Not to miss Hire a snowmobile and head off with a guide to get some fresh tracks away in the remote wilderness. As ever, hotel reception can book everything for you.

Remember to avoid Going there in February – it's pitch black. Head there in June and it's 24-hour sunshine. Pick your dates carefully!

Relive a famous moment The nearby Ice Hotel (icehotel.com) enjoys a far-flung renown.

Best mountain restaurant Probably Lappi's Café. Again, Riksgränsen isn't really a pitstop-and-sunbathe type of resort.

Practicalities ⬛🍴🚌

Sitting at the end of a train line that links it to Stockholm and the rest of the country, Riksgränsen is more a cluster of buildings than a fully fledged town. As a tiny northern settlement sitting amid outcrops of rock and scrub-like Arctic tundra, it has a remote, rugged feel, although this isolation also makes it one of the friendliest places you'll ever ski in.

Sleeping There's only one hotel here, the Riksgränsen Ski and Spa resort (riksgransen.nu), which is also the largest building in town. The standard of accommodation is high, and you choose between a standard room or self-catering apartments.

Eating Although the scope is limited, what is on offer is generally very good. The Ski and Spa hotel's own restaurant, the Laplandia, serves traditional Swedish cuisine – expect to sample reindeer at least once. For smaller snacks, go to the hotel bar and club, the Matsal. Lappi's Café does bar snacks, pizzas and the like.

Bars and clubs Matsal is surprisingly big and hosts live music. Be aware – it is reputed to be the fourth most expensive club in Sweden, which is quite a claim. The MTR Ski Lodge also has a small bar.

Hire shop/rental With the only trade at this outpost being skiers and snowboarders, unsurprisingly there is a good hire and sports shop on site. Email sportshop@riksgransen.nu for more details.

Health and wellbeing The Riksgränsen Alpine Spa is fully kitted out and has outdoor hot tubs from which to try and espy the Northern Lights. They also do a 'Lappish Zen' treatment for those wanting to get in touch with their Sami side.

Down days with kids Probably not the best spot to be stranded with kids, nevertheless there are dogsledding, fjord trips and whale-watching options nearby. Our advice is to take the kids during the summer.

Internet Wi-Fi access in the rooms and a few terminals in the lobby coffee shop. Beware though, it gets expensive.

Transfer options Renting a car from Kiruna airport gives you a lot of versatility but a better option is taking the overnight train from Stockholm or Gothenburg which goes direct to Riksgränsen and is a holiday in itself (connex.se).

You can also ski here ... An Arctic ski pass is available which give you access to partnering resorts of Narvik, Björkliden, Abisko and the Nuolia backcountry. Speak to reception about the details, as you'll need a guide for many of the excursions.

If you like this ... try Ste Foy ▶▶ *p178*, Levi ▶▶ *p252*.

☺ **OPENING TIMES**

Mid-Feb to late Jun: 0900-1600; midnight sun skiing late May to late Jun 2000-0030

💲 **RESORT PRICES**

Week pass: SEK1455

Day pass: SEK310

Season pass: SEK3395

ⓘ **DIRECTORY**

Tourist office: T+46 (0)980-40200

Medical Centre: T+46 (0)980-73000

Pisteurs: T+46 (0)980-40080

Taxi: T+46 (0)980-18600

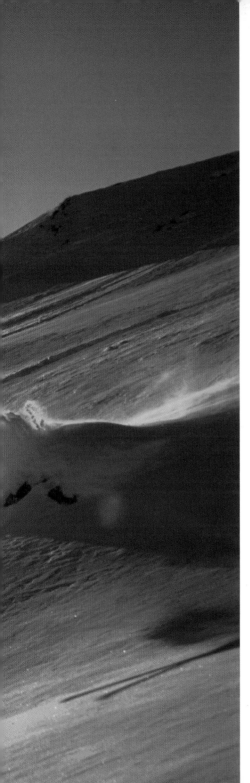

Switzerland

Switzerland
Value for money
★★★☆☆
Nightlife
★★★☆☆
Off-piste
★★★★★
Family
★★★★☆

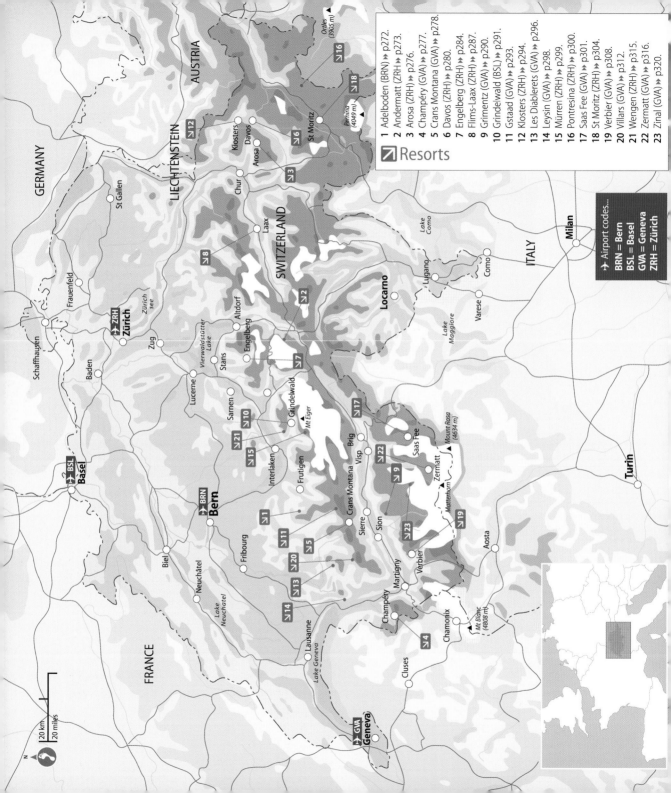

Switzerland – it's a name that conjures up images straight out of a picture book: dramatic, snow-peaked mountains, charming little villages, dinky red mountain trains winding their way through spectacular valleys and pale brown cows with vast bells dangling round their necks. And large private bank accounts.

Fortunately, the Swiss remain conservative mountain people at heart and the immense wealth reaped from their international banking and watchmaking industries hasn't resulted in an excess of flamboyant ski resorts that cater exclusively for the über-wealthy. Instead, Switzerland boasts some of the most diverse, accessible and exciting resorts in the world.

Visitors to this tiny country in the heart of the Alps will discover that the 'Heidi country' superlatives used so frequently to describe it are well deserved – it is breathtakingly beautiful. They also find reliable public transport and excellent hotels, food and service.

For skiers, there are even more plus points: Swiss resorts are easily accessible by plane, train and automobile; they're high – you'll find Europe's largest glaciers and more mountains over 4000 m than in any other European country; and they're attractive, family-friendly and offer a wide range of accommodation. While its reputation for being wildly expensive is partly deserved, particularly in glitzy resorts such as St Moritz and Klosters, on the whole accommodation, food and lift passes are entirely competitive with, if not cheaper, than major French and Austrian resorts.

Skiing Switzerland

One of the great things about skiing in Switzerland is that it offers both the glitz and glamour of major, internationally recognized resorts such as Davos-Klosters, Zermatt and St Moritz and the simple serenity of small, traditional lesser-known resorts like Andermatt, Les Diablerets and Grimentz/Zinal. This enables skiers to find resorts that meet a diverse range of needs, safe in the knowledge that they all provide exceptional accommodation and services.

Many skiers who have tired of 'factory skiing' on crowded French slopes with purpose-built towns are turning to authentic Swiss resorts, which are relatively uncrowded in comparison. They're often surprised to find that many of the resorts are virtually as large as their French counterparts and that the freeriding rates among some of the best in Europe.

Party animals might find some of the smaller Swiss resorts disappointing for après-ski, but if they head for Engelberg, Verbier, Zermatt, St Moritz or Saas Fee they're sure to find enough going on there.

Conditions
Switzerland is dotted with resorts, most of them curving along an imaginary meridian that links the east, south and southwest of the country. Two main weather fronts bring snow to the area, from either the north or the west. North fronts tend to predominate in the earlier part of the season, while west fronts, largely affecting the southern part of the Swiss Alps, begin to take precedence from February onwards.

When To Go

In common with their French and Austrian neighbours, the Swiss usually have their resorts in full swing by early December. It's a good time to visit if you're prepared to gamble on the depth of the snow base and don't mind sacrificing old skis to potential rocks. January and February are snow-sure yet cold, so if you want powder and a goggle tan March is probably the best month to visit – even if it is correspondingly expensive and more crowded. If you're keen on a trip out at the beginning of April, check conditions and book last minute. Most Swiss resorts close by mid-April, although some resorts (Andermatt, Engelberg, Zermatt) with higher slopes remain open later, with the glaciers staying open well into the summer (Saas Fee, Les Diablerets).

Off-Piste Policy

Along with their central European cousins, Switzerland has a pretty laid-back approach to bypassing the resort boundaries. That said, some resorts (Engelberg is one example) enforce nature areas in the resort – ride here and you might get your pass pulled or a fine issued. Check the status with lift operators if in doubt. Check slf.ch for details of any avalanche danger and meteoschweiz.ch for weather info.

PROS

Direct flights to Geneva and Zürich combined with a super-efficient public transport systems, meaning virtually all resorts are quick and easy to reach.

Switzerland has some of Europe's best freeriding terrain in large ski resorts.

The scenery is ridiculously picturesque, with skiing at the base of three of the world's most iconic mountains.

You benefit from Swiss efficiency in the running of ski lifts, public transport and hotels and French and Italian culinary influences.

Good green credentials with eco-friendly resorts.

Has a virtually unparalleled diversity of resorts that cater for various skiing abilities, families and glacier skiing.

CONS

Larger, better-known resorts are undeniably expensive.

The season ends early, meaning it can be all over by early April.

Although there are some party strongholds, Switzerland is generally quieter than its neighbours.

Essentials

Getting there

Switzerland's skiing is concentrated in fairly distinct regions but airports are relatively near each one and public transport is so painless and scenic, the transfer is virtually a pleasure! Most skiers take advantage of direct flights to Geneva, from where resorts such as Villars, Verbier and Les Diablerets are under two hours' drive. Carriers to Geneva (gva.ch) include **SWISS** (swiss.com), **easyJet** (easyjet.com), **British Airways** (ba.com), **Aer Lingus** (aerlingus.com), **KLM** (klm.com), **Alitalia** (alitalia.com), **Lufthansa** (lufthansa.com) and **BMI** (flybmi.com). Zürich airport (zurich-airport.com) is the better choice for resorts in German-speaking Switzerland such as Engelberg, Flims-Laax and Saas Fee. Carriers to Zürich include **SWISS** (swiss.com), **British Airways** (ba.com), **easyJet** (easyjet.com), **KLM** (klm.com), **Aer Lingus** (aerlingus.com), **Lufthansa** (lufthansa.com) and **BMI** (flybmi.com).

Red Tape

Although Switzerland isn't a member of the EU, visitors from EU countries do not require a visa. Other foreigners who don't intend to work or study there can stay for three months without a residence permit.

Getting Around

Although we recommend using the Swiss Travel System for day-to-day travelling (see below), a car is probably the better option if you're planning a longer, multi-resort road trip. The Swiss drive on the right, and a valid UK, EU/EEA or driving licence from your own country is fine. International Driving Permits are not required. People in Switzerland follow all regulations and the police enforce the law fairly strictly – particularly when it comes to the *vignette* road tax.

Fact File

Currency Swiss France (CHF)

Time Zone GMT +1

Country Code +41

Emergency Numbers

Ambulance T144

Police T117

Fire T118

Mountain rescue T144

General emergency T112

The Pan-European emergency number T112 works in any EU country from any telephone. It's also the number to call for any emergency services if you're using a mobile.

Mountain Passes

If you're planning any major midwinter drives, check tcs.ch and mct.sbb.ch for up-to-date information on the status of local mountain passes.

Car Hire

Most major hire car companies (easycar.com, hertz.com, avis.com) have offices in airports and cities. Usual age restrictions apply. If you're flying into Geneva, make sure you hire a car from the Swiss side of the city and not the French side – it will make your life considerably easier!

Public Transport

Switzerland has one of Europe's most efficient, comfortable and affordable integrated transport systems that has you off the plane, bundled into a train and rolling through breathtakingly beautiful scenery to your resort. If travelling from the UK, you can book train tickets in advance at the Swiss Travel Centre (stc.co.uk). We recommend getting a Swiss Travel System pass – a 4-, 8-, 15-, 22-day or one-month pass gives unlimited travel on trains, buses and boats. The system covers 37 cities with 50% off mountain summit trains, cable cars and funiculars. There are other options – for further information visit MySwitzerland.com/rail. For train and bus timetables visit sbb.ch, although you'll find more bus information on postbus.ch.

Opening Hours and Traditions

In mountain areas, shops close on Sundays and can also shut between 1200 and 1400 on weekdays, although it depends on the size of the town or city you're in.

Eating

Even if you haven't been to Switzerland, you'll know that key Swiss contributions to the culinary world involve melted cheese – either in the form of fondue (dipping bread cubes into melted cheese) or *raclette* (cheese is melted in front of an open fire or broiler, scraped onto a plate and served with potatoes and pickled onions) – and chocolate. Both cheese dishes have their roots in Swiss dairy farming, one of the country's main industries, and it makes sense in this context that the national dish is filling, unpretentious and takes advantage of its range of over 200 cheeses. The result is that they're both ubiquitous throughout the country and it's virtually obligatory to sample some when you visit. For non-cheese-eaters, there are two types of meat fondue: *bourguignon*, where you cook your small pieces of meat in hot oil, and *chinoise*, where you cook thin slices of beef in a broth served with oriental sauces.

Breakfast in Switzerland is generally the classic continental mix of bread rolls, cheese, ham, boiled eggs, *birchermüesli* (a filling, nutritious variation of dried muesli), strong coffee and juice. Fill up while you can, as Swiss mountain restaurants are pretty expensive, although you do generally get what you pay for – many of the world's best mountain restaurants can be found in the Swiss Alps, with a concentration in Zermatt. If you're on a budget, stock up at the local supermarkets and make sandwiches to eat on the hill – Migros is a fantastic supermarket that stocks high-quality food and household items at decent prices that remain the same whether you're in a city or mountain village.

In the evening, expect hot cheese and plenty of meat (predominantly veal, pork and sausages) served with potatoes (another classic Swiss dish is *rösti* – grated potato baked in little patties) and vegetables. Generally speaking, you'll find the usual mix of Western fusion food in most places although vegetarians might struggle to find much variety, with cheese, pasta and dumplings being staples.

Finally, you can't possibly come to Switzerland without trying some genuine Swiss chocolate. Some 93,500 tonnes of chocolate were consumed in Switzerland in 2007, implying that the Swiss eat 12.3 kg of chocolate each year – more than any other nation in the world.

Language

For such a small country, the language situation in Switzerland is surprisingly complex. Swiss-German is a dialect of German spoken mainly in the eastern part of the country. In the west, standard French is spoken (not 'Swiss-French', which doesn't exist). Then there is Ticino in the south, where Italian is the official language, and the tiny 2% of the population living in the canton of Grisons in the southeastern corner of the country who speak the obscure Romansch (a sort of modern-day Latin). In identifying the border where Swiss-German becomes French, the Swiss speak about the 'Rösti Graben' – an imaginary border representing the change from one language to another, as well as the many cultural differences this represents.

Crime and Safety

Switzerland is one of Europe's safest, most civil countries, although danger obviously increases in the major cities. In most places, it's safe to leave skis on balconies and restaurant terraces but thefts do occur, particularly in bigger resorts such as Verbier or Flims-Laax. The Swiss police are fair, although drivers must be aware that any travel on Swiss roads requires Swiss car tax (vignette), which can be bought at the border or at newsagents. Checkpoints are frequent and large fines are common.

Health

As part of the EU, Switzerland is governed by European health standards. Health insurance is recommended and EU citizens should carry a European Health Insurance Card (EHIC).

Top Tips

1 **Choose** a resort according to what sort of ski holiday you want – that way, you get the most out of the variety of resorts on offer: Verbier for nightlife, Zermatt for food, Saas Fee for families, Engelberg for off-piste …
2 **Driving**? Buy a *vignette*. You will get fined without one.
3 **Get** your head round the currency conversion rate – while it's not cheap, you might be surprised at how competitively priced a lot of things are.
4 **Try** the Swiss white wine, *Fendant* – it's light, affordable and goes with virtually everything!
5 **If** you're hiring a car from Geneva, make sure you get one from the Swiss rental outlets rather than the French ones in order to save yourself considerable hassle.

Going green

Travelling green couldn't be easier in Switzerland. In addition to having clean, comfortable, efficient trains that run like (Swiss) clockwork, there's also the excellent 'Fly-Rail Baggage' service which enables you to check in your baggage at any airport around the world through to your end destination when you fly via Zürich or Geneva airport. Once you arrive in Switzerland, go straight through customs, hop on a train unencumbered by heavy luggage carrying just your hand-luggage safe while your baggage is forwarded to the nearest railway station to your ski resort, where you can pick it up at given times. Being Switzerland, the nearest station is invariably IN your resort as is the case with Adelboden, Arosa, Davos, Engelberg, Grindelwald, Klosters, Mürren, Saas-Fee, St. Moritz, Wengen and Zermatt. The cost of the service is a mere CHF20 per bag. For more information, contact the Swiss Travel System (swisstravelsystem.com).

↘1 Adelboden

Town altitude	1353 m	Km of pistes	185 km	Funicular/cable		Terrain parks	3
Km to airport	61 km	Nursery areas	5	cars	0/3	Glühwein factor	★☆☆
Airport	Berne	Blues	35	Gondolas/chairs	7/10	Ski in/ski out	☆☆☆
Highest lift	2362 m	Reds	44	Drags	36	Environmental	
Vertical drop	398 m	Blacks	6	Night skiing	yes	rating	★★★★☆

Mid-range Swiss resort that was also home of the first ski package holidays.

Adelboden sits at the end of the Engstligenalp valley, right in the middle of the Bernese Oberland and as such is unspoiled and pristine. With nightlife non-existent, it is probably best suited to families and early riders looking to get some miles under their skis.

With 56 different lifts and 185 km of piste, Adelboden-Lenk is one of the largest ski resorts in Switzerland. In addition to the main ski area between the two villages, there are five other areas for great skiing: Elsigen-Metsch, TschentenAlp, Engstligenalp, Betelberg and Kandersteg. Typically Swiss mountain restaurants and bars dot the landscape throughout.

Beginners Beginners should start off at the ski school at Geils; from there, once they've found their ski legs, there are plenty of blue runs down from Hahnenmoos either back to Geils or down towards Bühlberg in the Lenk ski area.

Intermediate Intermediates are really well catered for in Adelboden-Lenk. From Geils, take the higher lifts to Luegli and Lavey or jump on the bus from Adelboden to Engstligenalp. Both these areas offer a good mix of blue and red runs, so families can spend the day skiing together, but at different levels. And if you're looking to grab a few hours' skiing on your last day, head for TschentenAlp: it may have lift access direct from the heart of the village, but it's usually quiet and has a host of red runs.

Expert There are black runs leading down to Geils from Luegli and Lavey, but those who really want to test their skills will want to head for the World Cup slope at Chuenisbärgli. And there is plenty of off-piste activity when conditions are safe.

Tuition There are three ski schools in Adelboden; the **Adelboden Snowsport School** comes highly recommended (skischule-adelboden.ch).

⊙ OPENING TIMES

Mid-Nov to mid-Apr: 0900-1700

⑤ RESORT PRICES

Week pass: CHF286
Day pass: CHF57
Season pass: CHF805

ⓘ DIRECTORY

Website: adelboden.ch
Tourist office: T+41 (0)33-673 8080
Medical centre: T+41 (0)33-673 2626
Pisteurs: T+41 (0)33 673 3500
Taxi: T+41 (0)33-673 2848

Practicalities

Sleeping New kid on the block **Solís Cambrian Hotel & Spa** (T+41 (0)33-673 8383; solisadelboden.com,) has brought contemporary luxury accommodation to Adelboden, while at the mid price level **Hotel Bären** (baeren-adelboden. ch, T+41 (0)33-673 2151) is a 14-room traditional chalet-style hotel bang in the heart of the village. Those on tighter budgets should look at **Adelbed.ch** (adelbed.ch), a cosy B&B just minutes from the World Cup course.

Eating It's a car or taxi ride away on the other side of the valley but **Hohliebe-Stübli** (hohliebestuebli.ch) is well worth a visit both for the food and the sophisticated rustic charm; alternatively, try **Hotel Bären** for traditional fondues and *raclettes* or **Solís Cambrian Hotel & Spa** if you're craving good Italian.

Bars and clubs Hotel Sport Adler (adleradelboden.ch) has a fantastic terrace for enjoying a late afternoon après-ski drink or two but the place to be at the end of the evening is **Arte Bar + Kunst**, a gallery, shop and bar all under one roof.

Hire shop/rental There are several ski-rental shops, the largest being **Oester Sport** (T+41 (0)33-673 1625; oestersport.ch).

Transfer options We recommend the train from Berne airport, which takes about two hours to Frutigen. From there, take the 30-minute Postbus to Adelboden.

You can also ski here ... During the 2007-08 seasons, those in possession of a four-day Adelboden-Lenk pass can spend the day skiing in Gstaad Mountain Rides, Alpes Vaudoises, Jaunpass and Kandersteg for just CHF10 per day. Check the site for these deals.

If you like this try ... Flachauwinkl (Austria) or Seegrube/Nordpark (Austria).

↘2 Andermatt

Town altitude 1444 m	**Km of pistes** 140 km	**Funicular/cable**		**Terrain parks** 2	
Km to airport 100 km	**Nursery areas** 2	**cars** 1/2		**Glühwein factor** ★☆☆	
Airport Zürich	**Blues** 9	**Gondolas/chairs** 0/8		**Ski in/ski out** ★★☆	
Highest lift 2963 m	**Reds** 23	**Drags** 12		**Environmental**	
Vertical drop 1519 m	**Blacks** 10	**Night skiing** no		**rating** n/a	

PROS

- ✓ Excellent for expert skiers in search of steep, deep powder that's uncrowded in comparison to St Anton, Engelberg and Chamonix.
- ✓ The town has a charming, unspoiled atmosphere (pre-development).

CONS

- ✕ Can get busy at weekends with day visitors from Zürich.
- ✕ Limited activities for bad-light days.
- ✕ Uncertainty about the future nature of the resort in light of major development.

A simple mountain town loved by adventurous families and extreme skiers for its epic freeriding.

Andermatt's skiing is split across three mountains linked by ski buses: Gemstock (high, steep with acres of off-piste); Nätschen (good for families and beginners); and Winterhorn (good for intermediates and off-piste). Sedrun, reached by a 20-minute ride on the Matterhorn Gotthard train, is also part of the ski area. Due to its proximity to Zürich, Andermatt fills up on weekends, resulting in queues for Gemstock in particular. However, the cable car opens 30 minutes early on Saturdays (0800), giving locals a headstart.

Beginners Start on the gently winding 6-km Nätschen blue, which is a road in summer. Progress to the upper half of the mountain, Gütsch, before tackling the blues on Gemstock. You'll have to download from Gemstock's mid-station as the only piste down is black.

Intermediate Find your feet on Gütsch and Winterhorn and spend a day cruising Sedrun's reds before taking on steeper terrain on Gemstock. Once there, practise short turns on the red by Lutersee and dip into the powder just off it. The black piste into town is tricky, so best not attempted at the end of a long day.

Expert Andermatt is your playground. From the top of Gemstock there are two marked pistes – a tough red and the famous Bernard Russi-designed black – that bring you down two glaciers, St Anna and Gurschen respectively. The long black into the village is a delight in good conditions. There's a yellow 'freeride route', which is fantastic if you hit it early, but essentially the entire mountain can be skied. Longer routes include dropping into Guspis about a third of the way down the St Anna glacier red or into Felsental about halfway down it. Guspis takes you right over to Hospental, the base of Winterhorn, and you can either cut back towards Andermatt from Felsental (a short walk to the cable car) or head for Hospental. Winterhorn is quieter than Gemstock and popular with local freeriders.

Powder Start early for first tracks. A favourite run for experts with a guide drops off the back of Gemstock, coming back round to Unteralp via Geissberg. Winterhorn is excellent but again, get there early.

Trees In a word: none. The few trees that survive the altitude are protected and off-limits. Locals perfect the art of 'bush-skiing' on the lower half of Gemstock.

Moguls The short black parallel to Gemstock's Bernard Russi run and Winterhorn's blacks. The freeride runs on both mountains develop into moguls.

Book a guide There are more guiding outfits than ski schools in Andermatt, which says a lot about its clientele. Ask for Sepp, director of the Ski School and Andermatt born and bred. If your group is strong enough, you'll cover all three mountains in a day (a cumulative descent of 10,000 m).

Tuition Schneesport Schule Andermatt is the only official ski school, with multi-national instructors, small classes and competitive prices.

Kids Schneesport Schule Andermatt teaches children from 4½. Kids thrive on the gentle Nätschen blue and Snowpark Valtgeva at Sedrun.

Bad light Take the train to Sedrun and soak in the **Bogn Aqua Wellness Centre** (T+41 (0)81 949-1432; bognsedrun.ch), where you get a 20% discount with your ski pass.

Not to miss A powder day in Andermatt – on a par with La Grave and a deserted Chamonix.

Remember to avoid The queues for the Gemstock cable car between 0900 and 1000 on Saturdays by taking the 0800 lift.

Pitstop and sunbathe Gadä Bar by the Lutersee on Gemstock is a cowshed in summer and atmospheric sun trap in winter. The views from **Stöcklibar** at the top of Gütsch are breathtaking.

Relive a famous moment The Bond movie *Goldfinger* (1964) was filmed in Andermatt – cast and crew stayed in the **Bergidyll Hotel**.

Best mountain restaurant Gemstock's **Bergrestaurant Gurschen** isn't beautiful but the food and views are excellent. **Bergrestaurant Nätschen-Gütsch** and **Lückli** on Winterhorn offer affordable food with a lively atmosphere.

🙂 LOCALS DO	🙁 LOCALS DON'T
✔ Ski on super-wide, super-cool custom-made Birdos skis, handmade in Andermatt (birdos. com).	✘ Drive to the ski lift but use the ski shuttle.
✔ Eat at Gasthof Ochsen.	✘ Ski through the protected forests and get fined CHF150 for doing so.

Practicalities

Andermatt is a small town wedged high in the Swiss mountains where the Swiss army carries out its winter training. A small river flows through the heart of the village, which consists of one main street dotted with hotels and bars leading up the Gemstock cable car. Andermatt has long been popular with hardcore skiers yet remains relatively unknown as an international resort. However, that's about to change: construction of a luxury resort complete with seven hotels and golf course is scheduled to start in 2009 on the outskirts of the village. The project will transform Andermatt – a change welcomed more by locals than regular visitors.

Sleeping There's budget accommodation towards the train station and more upmarket hotels in the centre of town. If you want to push the boat out, **The River House** (T+41 (0)41-887 0025; theriverhouse. ch) is a lovingly renovated 250 year-old house run by Swiss owners Sarah and Kevin. Each of the eight rooms combines high-tech amenities with handmade furniture and traditional charm. Three-star **Kronen Hotel** (T+41 (0)41-887 0088; kronenhotel.ch) is also good. We can also recommend the beautiful, central **Hotel Sonne** (T+41 (0)41-887 1226; hotelsonneandermatt. ch), **Hotel Schweizerhof** (T+41 (0)41-887 1189; schweizerhof-andermatt.ch) and **Gasthaus Sternen** (T+41 (0)41-887 1130; gasthaussternen.com). Family-friendly **Gasthaus Ski-Club** (T+41 (0)41-887 0330; gasthaus-skiclub.ch), by Gemstock is good value.

Eating At the top end, the **River House** restaurant recreates ancient Swiss recipes served with local wines, while the **Kronen Hotel** offers a seven-course seasonal menu. Locals enjoy hearty Swiss dishes at **Gasthaus Ochse** and **Gasthof Sonne**. Trendy **Tautone** does Mediterranean food and **Spycher**'s Italian is popular, particularly on weekends.

Au pair/crèche Ursina Portmann-Zingg runs the informal **Elternzirkel** babysitting network. Call T+41 (0)41-887 0605 or find her at the Meyers Sport Shop in town.

Best après-ski Après starts at the umbrella bar at the top of Gurschen. In town, **Postillion**, **Spycher** and **Di Alt Apothek** are lively, particularly at weekends.

Bars and clubs The bars above continue to be lively after dinner before action moves to **Pinte**, **Bar La Curva** and **Pub Piccadilly**. Dancing **Gotthard** disco warms up at weekends.

Hire shop/rental All four rental shops have the same pricing structure. **Meyers** has outlets at the train station, in town and by Gemstock.

Lift tickets Buy at the base stations and train station.

Shopping **Café Bar 61** (opposite Postillion) sells groceries, rents toboggans and organizes ski touring.

Health and wellbeing Kronen Hotel has a spa and wellness scheme – Alpine Health & Harmony (andermatt-wellness.ch).

Down days with kids Hire a toboggan from **Café Bar 61** and go to Nätschen. Alternatively, take the train to Sedrun and go snowtubing or swimming in the **Bogn Centre**.

Internet There's Wi-Fi in **Di Alt Apothek** bar and computers at **Café Bar 61**.

Transfer options Fly to Zürich and grab a train (rhb.ch) – it takes about two hours. **Genial Shuttle Tours** (T+41 (0)79-229 8280) do airport transfers.

You can also ski here … The Gotthard Oberalp Arena (Gemstock, Nätschen, Winterhorn and Sedrun)

If you like this … try St Anton ▶▶ *p85*, Chamonix ▶▶ *p126*, La Grave ▶▶ *p140*, Engelberg ▶▶ *p284*.

⊙ OPENING TIMES

Gemstock: end Nov to end Apr: 0830-1630. Rest of resort: end Dec to end Mar: 0830-1630

⑤ RESORT PRICES (for Gotthard Oberalp Arena pass)

Week pass: CHF239

Day pass: CHF54

Season pass: CHF665

① DIRECTORY

Website: andermatt.ch

Tourist office: T+41 (0)41-887 1454

Medical centre: T+41 (0)41-887 1977

Pisteurs: T+41 (0)41-887 0181

Taxi: T+41 (0)79-229 8280

↘3 Arosa

Town altitude	1800 m	Funicular/cable cars	0/2
Km to airport	163 km	Gondolas/chairs	1/6
Airport	Zürich	Drags	4
Highest lift	2653 m	Night skiing	yes
Vertical drop	914 m	Terrain parks	1
Km of pistes	100 km	Glühwein factor	★★☆
Nursery areas	3	Ski in/ski out	★★☆
Blues	15	Environmental	
Reds	12	rating	★★★★★
Blacks	2		

Quiet, quintessentially Swiss resort popular with families.

Arosa ticks most ski resort boxes: it's high, picturesque, family-friendly and offers various other winter sports. Inner-Arosa is the old centre, with chocolate-box pretty ski in/ski out chalets while Arosa's buildings are larger, dating to the 1980s. Efficient ski buses link the two with lifts.

Arosa's slopes pour down into the village from three peaks – Hörnli, Weisshorn and Brüggerhorn – which form a large, open bowl. Skiing is above tree-level and suitable for beginners and intermediates.

Beginners Start at Prätschli before progressing to the busier slopes on Tschuggen and Hörnli.

Intermediate Lots of cruising, some steeper reds on Weisshorn. The black down to Carmennahütte is steep – approach with caution.

Expert There are only two black pistes but gentle off-piste on Brüggerhorn and more challenging routes on Weisshorn and Hörnli. Book a guide to ski to Davos and Lenzerheide.

Tuition Both schools – **Swiss** and **ABC** – get busy, so book ahead.

Kids Arosa's **Mickey Mouse Alpine Club** incorporates 12 hotels, several restaurants, tuition, kindergarten and playgrounds.

Bad light Trees are rare, so go sledging, ice-skating, swimming in the public pool or check out **Arosa Kulm's Spa**.

Not to miss The long blue from Brüggerhorn to Obersee: true Winter Wonderland stuff.

Remember to avoid Driving to Arosa – parking is banned, with expensive garages your only option.

Practicalities

Sleeping Options include the five-star **Arosa Kulm Hotel & Alpin Spa** (T+41 (0)81-378 8888; arosakulm.ch); mid-range **Hotel Cristallo** (T+41 (0)81-378 6868; cristalloarosa.ch), which is central (Arosa), friendly and has large rooms; and **G'span** (T+41 (0)81-377 1494; gspan.ch), a small inexpensive hotel in Inner-Arosa.

Eating Hotel Cristallo's 'Le Bistro' offers fine dining. **Pizzeria Grottino** and **Brüggerstuba** are popular Italian restaurants, while traditional **Prätschlistall** does Swiss specialities. On the mountain **Tschuggenhütte** is popular but **Weisshorngipfel** has the best views.

Bars and clubs Après at G'span, Brüggli Bar and Prätschlistall. Sitting Bull, Old Indian Bar and Im Gada (Hotel Carmenna) are good for later. **Nuts** is the disco.

Transfer options Fly to Zürich and take a spectacular train ride into town (rhb.ch).

You can also ski here ... No partners currently but (long-awaited) plans to link the resort with Lenzerheide.

If you like this ... try Kühtai ▶▶ *p65*, Stubai ▶▶*p90*, Saas Fee ▶▶ *p301*.

☺ OPENING TIMES

Early Dec to mid-Apr: 0830-1630

ⓈRESORT PRICES

Week pass: CHF259

Day pass: CHF56

Season pass: CHF869

ⓒ DIRECTORY

Website: arosa.ch

Tourist office: T+41 (0)81-378 7020

Medical centre: T+41 (0)81-377 2728

Pisteurs: T+41 (0)81-378 8450

Taxi: T+41 (0)81-377 1133

↘4 Champéry

Town altitude	1050 m	Km of pistes	650 km	Funicular/cable	Terrain parks	7
Km to airport	130 km	Nursery areas	8	cars 0/4	Glühwein factor ★★☆
Airport	Geneva	Blues	11	Gondolas/chairs 10/83	Ski in/ski out ★☆☆
Highest lift	3200 m	Reds	108	Drags 107	Environmental
Vertical drop	2200 m	Blacks	28	Night skiing yes	rating n/a

Gorgeous village at the foot of the Dents du Midi, with access to Portes du Soleil skiing.

Champéry combines the best of both worlds – it's a quaint little mountain village that provides relatively easy access to the vast Portes du Soleil ski area.

Two lifts operate out of Champéry to Planachaux, where the Portes du Soleil area starts. There's only one in-resort run (a long red to Grand

☺ OPENING TIMES
Mid-Dec to early Apr: 0830-1700

Ⓢ RESORT PRICES (for Portes du Soleil pass)
Week pass: CHF275

Day pass: CHF54

Season pass: CHF1047

ⓘ DIRECTORY
Website: champery.ch

Tourist office: T+41 (0)24-479 2020

Medical centre: T+41 (0)24-473 1731

Pisteurs: T+41 (0)45-073 3254

Taxi: T+41 (0)79-430 1515

Paradis), which means beginners have to download. However, once on the slopes, there's varied terrain for everyone.

Beginners Stick to the blues on Planachaux and Les Crosets.

Intermediate Explore the whole Portes du Soleil but beware: spare your legs for the long journey home! Highlights: the long blue to Morgins, the Grand Paradis red and skiing to Les Lindarets for lunch.

Expert Highlights: 'The Stash' wooded freeride park, Avoriaz's World Cup downhill black, Chavanette (the Swiss Wall) and Col du Fornet for off-piste and bumps.

Tuition There are three: Swiss, Red Carpet ('VIP service' and good excursions) and Freeride (New School).

Bad light Head for Châtel and Morgins for trees.

Not to miss Having lunch at Coquoz at Planachaux – ask nicely for a snowmobile ride back up the hill afterwards.

Remember to avoid Weekend queues for the Champéry cable car by taking the (five-minute) bus to the Grand Paradis chair.

Practicalities

Sleeping At the top end are **Hotel Beau-Séjour** (T+41 (0)24-479 5858; bo-sejour.com) and **The Lodge** (scottdunn.com) apartments. For mid-range options, ask for a balcony at **Hotel National** (T+41 (0)24-479 1130; lenational.ch) or opt for the seclusion of **Auberge de Grand Paradis** (T+41 (0)24-479 1167; grandparadis.ch).

Eating L'Atelier and Café du Centre have reasonably priced gourmet food, **Le Gueullhi** and **Hotel National** are popular with locals and **Le Vieux Chalet** does French food.

Bars and clubs Après-ski at **Auberge de Grand Paradis**, **Mitchell's** and **Bar des Guides** in town. **Café du Centre** picks up later, before **La Crevasse**, **La Mine** and **Avalanche**.

Transfer options Fly to Geneva, take a train to Aigle (sbb.ch) and the scenic train from there (tpc.ch).

You can also ski here ... The Portes du Soleil ski area.

If you like this ... try Westendorf ▶▶ *p91*, Sauze d'Oulx ▶▶*p240*.

Switzerland Champéry

↘5 Crans Montana

Town altitude	1500 m	Km of pistes	140 km	Funicular/cable cars	1/2
Km to airport	142 km	Nursery areas	3	Gondolas/chairs	4/6
Airport	Geneva	Blues	20	Drags	21
Highest lift	3000 m	Reds	28	Night skiing	yes
Vertical drop	1500 m	Blacks	2		

Terrain parks	1
Glühwein factor	★★☆
Ski in/ski out	★★☆
Environmental rating	★★★★☆

PROS

- ✓ Very sunny.
- ✓ Beautiful views.
- ✓ Intermediate stronghold.

CONS

- ✗ The sun can affect fresh snow.
- ✗ Not many options for experts.

High-end Swiss resort popular with families and sun worshipers.

This is unashamedly intermediate territory, with only one black run to speak of. The whole area sits on a plateau overlooking the Rhône valley and receives incredible sunshine. Roughly speaking, there are four main areas – Crans, Montana, Bazzettes and Aminona – as well as a glacier looming over all.

Beginners The debutante areas (which double as a golf course in the summer, indicating how flat they are) are fantastic for first timers. Once you gain in confidence, you can start to explore from there. Cry d'Err is a good place to start.

Intermediate Wow – where not to go? The whole resort is perfect for intermediate skiers, although most seem to head to Cry d'Err, which is the most obvious starting point. As a result, it can get crowded, so if this doesn't appeal try taking the bus to Aminona and from there the gondola to Pt Mont Borvin, which is usually less crowded. For an adventure, try skiing to Anzère down the summer track.

Expert Aminona has some steeper terrain around La Toula lift, although CM isn't really the best option for out-and-out experts looking to dice with death. Instead, you'll find yourself exploring the entire resort and choosing your favourite area. Good job it's cruising central.

Powder The sun changes the snow conditions here faster than

in most resorts. If it's powder you're looking for, try **Air Glacier** (T+41 (0)27-329 1415) who offer heli-skiing on the nearby peaks.

Moguls La Toula has the only really notable pitch in the resort, and is probably the main spot to check out if you're interested in testing your knee ligaments.

Tuition Swiss Snowsports School in Crans (T+41 (0)27-485 9370) does exactly what is says on the tin.

Kids The **Crans Ski School** kindergarten (T+41 (0)27-485 9370) is recommended.

Bad light CM's slopes are mostly within the treeline; avoid the glacial north side and you'll be fine.

Not to miss The sunsets over the Rhône can be spectacular. Apparently, Turner loved the light here.

Remember to avoid Driving up the hill. The road can get congested and the funicular is incredibly picturesque.

Relive a famous moment Roger Moore bought a chalet in Crans after filming *For Your Eyes Only* in 1980. This fact epitomizes the resort.

Best mountain restaurant Plenty to choose from, with **Cabane de la Tieche** and **Etape de Lourantse** usually doing a roaring trade.

Practicalities

Crans Montana has managed to attract big spenders with designer shops, beautiful chalets and hotels, exclusive clubs and a fantastic, easy-going mountain. That said, there is some genuinely fantastic skiing to be had here.

Sleeping Crans Montana's tourist board (crans-montana.ch) has a bookable website where accommodation from self-catering through to five-star hotels can be reserved depending on dates and availability. We like the authentic **Hostellerie du Pas de l'Ours** (pasdelours.ch). The five-star **Hotel Royal** (hotel-royal.ch) should take care of those looking for some luxury.

Eating Sandwicherie Sucre Sal (T+41 (0)27-480 1214) is the cheapest place in town, **La Bergerie du Cervin** (T+41 (0)27-481 2180) is the fondue specialist, while **Au Gréni,** (T+41 (0)27-481 2443), is about as posh as posh gets.

Au pair/crèche Fleur des Champs (T+41 (0)27-481 2367) takes children up to seven, while **Halte-Gerderie P'tits Bouts** (T+41 (0)79-660 7620) caters for little ones up to eight.

Bars and clubs Après at **Punch Bar**, then head to the **New Pub**, then try the comically named **Number Two Bar** for late drinks. If you want to carry on, **Absolute** is the place to head.

Hire shop/rental Ski Set (crans-montana.skiset.com) do some brilliant deals if you book in advance, including free hire days and overall discounts.

Shopping In common with most of the other top-end Swiss resorts, Crans Montana is something of a shopper's heaven, with boutiques,

souvenirs and local delicacies all well catered for. If you're trying to keep the costs down, head for **Coop** and **Migros**.

Health and wellbeing CM overflows with wellness centres. Try the **Hotel Art de Vivre**'s Wellness centre (art-vivre.ch), **Alpage** at **Hotel Etrier** (hoteletrier.ch) or **Dabliu Beauty Farm** (dabliu.com).

Down days with kids Choose from swimming, bowling, the cinema (VO films are in English) or, if you feel like spoiling them, a helicopter flight over the Alps (eaglehelicopter.com).

Internet Plenty of options, with **Net Point**, **New Pub** or **Restaurant Farinet** and **Number Two Bar** all having terminals and Wi-Fi access.

Transfer options From Geneva grab a train to Sierre and take the funicular to Montana. Both can be booked through cmf.ch.

If you like this… try Klosters ▶▶ *p294*, St Moritz ▶▶ *p304*, Verbier ▶▶ *p308*.

try Klosters ▶▶ *p294*, St Moritz ▶▶ *p304*, Verbier ▶▶ *p308*.

Switzerland Crans Montana

LOCALS DO

✔ Shop and play golf.

✔ Sport good tans from all the sunbathing that goes on.

LOCALS DON'T

✘ Drive up the hill if they can help it.

✘ Worry about the lack of 'extreme' terrain.

OPENING TIMES

Early Dec to mid-Apr: 0830-1630

RESORT PRICES

Week pass: CHF301

Day pass: CHF56

Season pass: CHF869

DIRECTORY

Website: crans-montana.ch

Tourist office: T+41 (0)27 485-0404

Medical centre: T+41 (0)27 481-2040

Taxi: T+41 (0)27 481-5858

↘6 Davos

Town altitude 1560 m	Km of pistes 311 km		Funicular/cable ars 3/9		Terrain parks 3
Km to airport 150 km	Nursery areas 3				Glühwein factor ★☆☆
Airport Zürich	Blues 29		Gondolas/chairs 5/9		Ski in/ski out ★☆☆
Highest lift 3146 m	Reds 47		Drags 27		Environmental
Vertical drop 2030 m	Blacks 34		Night skiing yes		rating ★★★★★

PROS

- ✅ Accesses a large and varied ski area.
- ✅ Excellent for non-skiers as it offers all the facilities of a city.

CONS

- ❌ Fractured mountains mean a lot of time is spent commuting between them.
- ❌ Lacks 'authentic' ski village appeal.
- ❌ The only in-resort piste is a tricky black.

A working city with lots of varied skiing and alternative winter sports galore for non-skiers.

The Davos-Klosters ski area incorporates 300 km of pistes across five mountains on both sides of a valley. Parsenn is the largest and busiest mountain, accessed from Davos Dorf and Klosters. Its highest point is the Weissfluhgipfel (2844 m), where it drops into two expert runs, but the rest of the hill consists of open cruising terrain and long pistes. Madrisa is accessed from Klosters Dorf and has terrain mostly for beginners. On the other side of the valley, Pischa, reached by bus from Davos Dorf, is billed as the freeriding mountain; Jakobshorn, reached by gondola from Davos Platz, is popular with snowboarders; and Rinerhorn is good for families and rated by locals for off-piste. Pischa and Rinerhorn are the quietest – great for escaping the crowds.

Beginners South-facing Madrisa is the best mountain for beginners, but it is accessed from Klosters. Easier to reach is Bolgen, the Jackobshorn beginners' area, with plenty of terrain higher up once you've gained confidence. The Bünda

nursery area is a 10-minute hike from Davos Dorf and quite steep.

Intermediate Parsenn: wide, open pistes ideal for carving, idyllic tree-lined runs and some of Europe's longest reds down to Küblis and into Klosters. Madrisa: good, confidence-building blues and reds for tentative intermediates. Pischa: good for quiet cruising and for advanced intermediates looking for early off-piste experience. Jakobshorn is more challenging than Rinerhorn but both provide different and quieter slopes to Parsenn.

Expert Although low on black pistes, there are several off-piste itineraries (marked but unprepared and unpatrolled routes) and acres of off-piste. Parsenn: 'Wang' – the open, off-piste face of the Gotschnagrat; the black 13 and 16 into Wolfgang; the two blacks from the top of Weissfluhjoch. The itineraries on Madrisa and Jakobshorn are a joy in good conditions, particularly Jakobshorn into Mühle (or extended across to Sertig). Rinerhorn: the black 10 descends over 1000 m vertical – extend it by dropping in from the red 9b. Ski the trees either side of the gondola but look out for toboggans. Pischa: stick to the itineraries or book a guide.

Powder In addition to the itineraries, there's freeriding on all five mountains, meaning great variety. On the smaller mountains in particular, you'll find powder stashes two days after a storm. There are some great 'off the back' routes like Juonli on Rinerhorn to Sertig and Jakobshorn to Teufi, which are best tackled with a guide.

Trees Stick to the lower slopes of Parsenn and Rinerhorn.

Moguls Parsenn: the black 13 from Meierhoftäli to Wolfgang, under the Schwarzseealp chair and black 1 off Weissfluhgipfel, which is steep and bumpy.

Book a guide Guiding is with **Adventure Skiing** (T+41 (0)81-422 4825) or **Swiss Ski School** – ask for Michael, who knows the mountains like the back of his hand. Longer trips to Arosa and Gargellen in Austria are also possible.

Tuition There's **Swiss Ski School** and **New Trend**, which promises small classes.

Kids Swiss Ski School operates **Bobo Club** on Jakobshorn for skiers from four to seven years. There are good kids' areas too – **Madrisa Land** has a bouncy castle, magic carpet etc and Rinerhorn has a 'Dwarf Trail'.

Bad light Visit the **Institute for Snow and Avalanche Research** in Davos (not all material is translated into English, so a guide might be helpful).

Not to miss Parsenn's legendary red run to Küblis, 12 km long with a vertical drop of 2000 m – open to all levels, this is what skiing is all about.

Remember to avoid The black run into Davos Dorf at the end of the day – it gets crowded, icy, bumped out and you still have a walk into town at the end.

Relive a famous moment Watch the Spengler Cup (December) – the world's second oldest international ice hockey club tournament.

Pitstop and sunbathe Parsenn: the 'Schwendi huts' by Schifer are perfect for a break during the long Küblis run – **Freeriderlodge** and **Schwendihütte** are our favourites. **Parsennhütte** has a popular sun terrace. Jackobshorn: **Chalet Güggel** has fleece-covered day beds and cracking views. Rinerhorn: **Nülli's Schneebar** has live music.

Best mountain restaurant Parsenn: **Bruhin's Weissfluhgipfel** offers gourmet dining at altitude and our favourite Schwendi hut for eating is **Schwendi Ski und Berghaus**. Madrisa: **Berghaus Erika**. Jakobshorn: **Jatzhütte**. Rinerhorn: **Restaurant Spina** (T+41 (0)81-420 3101) does delicious *rösti*. **Walserhuus Sertig** (T+41 (0)81-410 6030) makes the ideal end to a long off-piste route (or scenic bus ride from Davos) to Sertig – reservations essential.

Practicalities

Before Davos became a ski resort, the clear mountain air helped convalescing tuberculosis sufferers, who stayed in large sanatoriums. Today the sanatoriums are plush hotels and Davos is a significant working city – Europe's highest – hosting prestigious events from the annual World Economic Forum to professional ice hockey's Spengler Cup. It's a long city, with the two main centres – Davos Dorf and Davos Platz – at either end of a 2-km strip of hotels, restaurants, shops, offices and homes. Platz is the centre of most activity.

Sleeping Most accommodation is booked through the tourist office (T+41 (0)81-417 6777; davosklosters. ch). Top of the range is the grand, five-star **Steigenberger Belvédère** (T+800-7846 8357, steinberger.com) with its large, newly renovated rooms and extensive spa facilities. The slick four-star **Waldhotel** (T+41 (0)81-415 1515; waldhotel-davos.ch) above town is peaceful, albeit slightly remote. Family-friendly **Hotel Cresta Sun** (T+41 (0)81-417 1616; cresta-hotels.ch) has separate three- and four-star buildings. **Davoserhof**, **Hotel Ochsen** and **Hotel Alte Post** in Platz are small, atmospheric and do good food. **Snowboarder's Palace** is a cheap hostel option.

Eating Vast choice – pick up a restaurant guide from the tourist office. Most gourmet restaurants are in hotels – notably **Mann und Co** (Waldhotel), **Flüela-Stübli** (Hotel Flüela) and **Restaurant Pöstli** (Morosani Posthotel) – apart from the Michelin-starred **Hubli's Landhaus** in the satellite village of Laret. At a more modest level, in Platz, **Pot au Feu** does French food in a rustic setting, **Al Ponte** has good pizza and

Bistro Gentiana is excellent. In Dorf, cosy **Bünderstübli** does local specialities and families like **Hotel Rössli**.

Au pair/crèche Madrisa, accessed from Klosters Dorf, is the main hub for childcare, with a **Baby Centre** (up to two years) and **Kids Club** (two to six years). Kinderland Pischa (T+41 (0)81-416 1313), at the top of the Pischa cable car, offers childcare (skiing optional) from three years.

Best après-ski **Bolgenschanz** by the Jakobshorn base station offers lively après-ski, while **Montana Bar** and **Paulaner's Bar** (Arabella Sheraton Hotel) by the Parsennbahn attract a marginally quieter crowd. Locals do coffee and pastries at **Café Schneider** in Platz or **Café Weber** in Dorf.

Bars and clubs Davos Platz is the hub of Davos's relatively subdued nightlife. **Cabanna Club**, **Cava Grischa** (Hotel Europe) and **Ex-Bar** are lively and go on till late. **Chämi Bar**, **Piano Bar** (Hotel Europe) and **Bar Bistro Angelo** are quieter, attracting an older audience.

Hire shop/rental Swiss Rent-a-Sport has an outlet by the Parsennbahn and **Top Secret** shop is a franchise, combining rental with tuition (New Trend ski school).

Shopping There's **Migros** supermarket, **Mölkerei** for local dairy products and various boutiques and souvenir shops.

Health and wellbeing The excellent **Eau-La-La** has pools, an outdoor jacuzzi and spa.

Down days with kids Davos has Europe's largest outdoor artificial ice-rink, with quality spectator sports played on it, a brilliant **Toy Museum** and a **Wintersports Museum**.

Internet Free access at the tourist office. **Café Carlo's** in Platz has Wi-Fi and **Oase** and **C-Bar** have computers.

Transfer options Fly to Zürich and take the (pre-booked) Davos-Klosters Express on Saturdays (davosklosters.ch) or fly to Friedrichshafen and book the daily Graubünden Express (graubuenden-express.com).

You can also ski here ... Parsenn, Madrisa, Jakobshorn, Rinerhorn, Pischa.

If you like this ... try Serre Chevalier ▶▶ *p180*, Cortina ▶▶ *p222*, Madonna di Campiglio ▶▶ *p234*.

⊚ **OPENING TIMES**

Mid-Nov to end Apr: 0815-1615

Ⓢ **RESORT PRICES (TopCard pass: Davos-Klosters, Flims-Laax, Lenzerheide and Valbella)**

Week pass: CHF285

Day pass: CHF65

Season pass: CHF680

ⓘ **DIRECTORY**

Website: davos.ch

Tourist office: T+41 (0)81-415 2121

Medical centre: T+41 900-003003

Pisteurs: T+41 (0)81-415 2133

Taxi: T+41 (0)81-401 1414

↘7 Engelberg

Town altitude	1050 m	Km of pistes	82 km	Funicular/cable	Terrain parks 1
Km to airport	90 km	Nursery areas	3	cars 1/2	Glühwein factor ★★★
Airport	Zürich	Blues	6	Gondolas/chairs 7/8	Ski in/ski out ★☆☆
Highest lift	3020 m	Reds	10	Drags 7	Environmental
Vertical drop	1970 m	Blacks	3	Night skiing yes	rating ★★★☆☆

PROS

- ✅ Incredible off-piste skiing and great party scene.
- ✅ Easy to reach from Zürich and Luzern.
- ✅ Good skiing facilities for children.

CONS

- ❌ Fills up with weekend visitors.
- ❌ The main lift is a schlep from town and it takes several lifts and 40 minutes to reach the top.
- ❌ Not ideal for beginners or intermediates.

An historic town with a great party scene and a mountain that's every freerider's dream.

Engelberg – 'the mountain of the angel' – was founded in 1120 by a Benedictine monk who heard an angel telling him to build a monastery where the town now lies. Today the monastery still stands and Engelberg echoes to the whoops of skiers here for incredible off-piste

skiing and one of the world's longest vertical descents.

Engelberg's skiing takes place on both sides of the valley – Brunni and Trübsee/Titlis – and on Fürenalp, which has one lift and is good for freeriders happy to hike. Brunni is small, south-facing and better suited for beginners and intermediates, while Titlis is the main ski area and divides into two – Titlis/Stand and Jochstock – halfway up the mountain at the Trübsee lake. Titlis itself is a magnificent 3238-m mountain. The ski area is magnificent too, with steeps, a vast glacier with crevasse-strewn runs, cliffs and long top-to-bottom runs.

Beginners Engelberg isn't ideal for you, with eight blue runs, virtually all accessed by T-bars. However, there's a nursery area in the village (Klostermatte) and the blues on Brunni and the Gerschnialp plateau below Trübsee are gentle and quiet.

Intermediate Although 60% of Engelberg's pistes are red, tentative intermediates will find the skiing limiting. Brunni has some good runs, particularly the long blue from Schonegg, and Jochstock has varied reds, but if you're not comfortable with off-piste or blacks, you'll quickly exhaust the terrain. Furthermore, travelling from the top of Klein Titlis to Stand involves tackling a tricky black or taking two lifts to get down.

Expert Where to start? Unmissable (with appropriate off-piste equipment) are: Laub – 1120 vertical metres of sheer, unadulterated off-piste joy; Galtiberg – nearly 2000 m of more varied off-piste; the Steinberg glacier route from Klein Titlis to Trübsee; and the east face of Jochstock. Brunni has some tree-skiing, particularly the Grünewald freeride route, which brings you out by a request train stop. Get a guide to show you round Fürenalp.

Powder The runs above are epic in powder – but start early to get tracks (resident Swedes hike up the hill at 0600). Shorter hits include the route marked as 2a 'planned downhill run' from Stand to Trübsee and routes into the Steinberg valley accessed off the Jochberg Express and Jochpass.

Trees Virtually non-existent on Titlis but there are enough on Brunni to entertain you for a flat-light morning.

Moguls The Rotegg yellow marked route from the base of Gletscherlift to the top of Stand.

Book a guide Essential to get the most out of Engelberg. **Outventure** (T+41 (0)41-611 1441) has guides who can negotiate their way across the Steinberg crevasses with their eyes closed.

Tuition Unless you're a child, Engelberg's not the best place to learn. Most tuition is for intermediates learning off-piste skills or experts requiring guides.

Kids Swiss Ski School has a ski-kindergarten for kids from three years and optional childcare after classes finish. **Prime Ski School** does private fast-track courses for beginners, 'New School' instruction and more. There are three kids' ski parks.

Bad light Exhaust the trees on Brunni before succumbing to the lure of Yucatan or take a day trip to Luzern.

Not to miss Engelberg is home to the world's only revolving cable car – the 'Rotair', which takes you up to 3020 m. Best avoided with a hangover ...

Remember to avoid The Rotegg black from the glacier to Stand is genuinely black. If in doubt, take the Ice Flyer back up and download in the Stand cable car.

Relive a famous moment Indians must think all mountains look like Titlis – Engelberg is where most of Bollywood's mountain scenes are filmed, including the Oscar-nominated *Lagaan*.

Pitstop and sunbathe Soak up the views at 3020 m from **Titlis Stübli**, watch skiers negotiate the Laub from **Ritz's** sun terrace and chill out at the trendy **Igludorf Bar** by Trübsee. The south-facing **Brunnihütte** is great for sunbathing and the food's good too.

Best mountain restaurant Titlis Stübli offers gourmet meals although there's a cheaper self-service restaurant and a sandwich bar as well. The **Ritz's** delicious cheese dishes are made courtesy of the cows that graze on the Laub, while **Skihütte Stand** has a cosy restaurant and basic self-service area.

☺ **LOCALS DO**

☑ Ski down Laub and have lunch at the Ritz.

☑ Do Happy Hour at Yucatan – it's legendary.

☑ Ski on weekdays when it's quiet.

☺ **LOCALS DON'T**

☒ Ski through the protected trees – you'll be fined.

☒ Forget Fürenalp for secret powder stashes.

☒ Sleep late on a powder day.

Switzerland Engelberg

Practicalities

The town is fairly compact, with the monastery at one end joined to the centre by the pedestrianized, cobbled Dorfstrasse. Many of the hotels are faded Victorian glories and the main lift station is a two-minute bus ride (15-minute walk) from the centre but this doesn't stop us rating Engelberg as one of our favourite resorts.

Sleeping Hotel Garni Alpenclub (T+41 (0)41-637 1243; alpenclub.ch) is a recently refurbished old building with only 11 rooms, most of which are inexpensive. However, there are a couple of beautiful, luxurious suites. **Hotel Waldegg** (T+41 (0)41-637 1822; waldegg-engleberg.ch), located high above the village, and central **Hotel Schweizerhof** (T+41 (0)41-637 1105; schweizerhof-engelberg.ch) are both fantastic. Our pick of the rest of the central properties is: **Hotel Belmont** (T+41 (0)41-637 2423; belmont-engelberg.ch); **Hotel Europe** (T+41 (0)41-639 7575; hoteleurope.ch) – a faded Victorian beauty; and **Hotel Engelberg** (T+41 (0)41-639 7979; hotel-engelberg.ch). **Hotel Bellevue** (T+41

OPENING TIMES

Mid-Nov to late May: 0830-1700

RESORT PRICES

Week pass: CHF260

Day pass: CHF59

Season pass: CHF840

DIRECTORY

Website: engelberg.ch

Tourist office: T+41 (0)41-639 7777

Medical centre: T+41 (0)41-637 0030

Pisteurs: T+41 (0)41-639 5050

Taxi: T+41 (0)78 666 5757

(0)41-639 6868; bellevue-engelberg.ch) is cheap and home to the Yucatan bar.

Eating **Beirialp** on Dorfstrasse does delicious pizzas, **Spannort** serves traditional Swiss dishes and **Hotel Garni Alpenclub** has a popular pizzeria and cosy 'cheese corner'. If you want to push the boat out, **Hess** (T+41 (0)41-637 0909), on Dorfstrasse just beyond the Schweizerhof, serves gourmet food in slick surroundings and offers private wine tastings in the wine cellar. **Schweizerhaus** dates back to the 17th century and does great fondue.

Au pair/crèche Ask the tourist office for daycare and babysitting services.

Best après-ski The Chalet at Titlis base station is packed on weekends. In town, the **Yucatan** opposite the train station is legendary – visit during Happy Hour (1700-1800) at least once. The adjacent **Eden Hotel Bar** is quieter – particularly the lounge at the front, which is also good for snacks.

Bars and clubs Yucatan keeps going till about midnight, when people move on to **Spindle Club**. **CCBaR** near the tourist office is quieter.

Hire shop/rental Titlis Sport has outlets at the base station and by Migros.

Lift tickets Avoid the queues at Titlis by buying your pass at the tourist office, train station and at most hotels.

Shopping If you like wine, visit the tiny **Seppi's Wystubli** wine store at the bottom of Terracestraße. **Co-op** and **Migros** are both by the tourist office.

Health and wellbeing The **Eienwäldli Wellness Centre** has pools, saunas etc. **Hotel Waldegg** has spa facilities.

Down days with kids Visit the **Sporting Park** with ice-rink, climbing wall etc and the **Cheese Factory** at the Monastery, where you can watch cheese being made.

Internet There's an internet café at **Okay Shop** by the Ramada and Wi-Fi in many of the hotels.

Transfer options Get a Swiss Rail Card and take the train from Zürich, Geneva or Basel airports via Luzern.

You can also ski here ... No local partners.

If you like this ... try St Anton ▶▶ p85, Chamonix ▶▶ p126, Andermatt ▶▶ p273, Verbier ▶▶ p308.

↘8 Flims-Laax

Town altitude	1100 m	Km of pistes	220 km	Funicular/cable		Terrain parks	1
Km to airport	153 km	Nursery areas	2	cars	0/4	Glühwein factor	★★★
Airport	Zürich	Blues	20	Gondolas/chairs	7/8	Ski in/ski out	★☆☆
Highest lift	3018 m	Reds	26	Drags	6	Environmental	
Vertical drop	1918 m	Blacks	5	Night skiing	yes	rating	★★★★★

PROS

- ✓ Large, well-planned area.
- ✓ Good for all levels.
- ✓ Great nightlife.

CONS

- ✗ Spread-out resort.
- ✗ Busy at start and end of day.
- ✗ Susceptible to bad weather in early season.

Relatively unknown to the UK, Flims-Laax has great terrain and a forward-thinking party scene.

Laax is a large, well-organized and rather picturesque resort, although it can be difficult to navigate until you're used to the layout. The wider Laax-Flims-Falera resort is known as the 'White Arena', although the area is dominated by the Crap Sogn Gion peak, and it is likely you'll spend most of your time navigating the runs around this peak and the eye-catching mountain restaurant that forms the resort's focal point.

Beginners There are two distinctive beginner-friendly areas, one in Flims and one in Falera, so early on it might be worth sticking to these wide, gentle slopes. If you're confident with turns, you'll enjoy some of the easier blues off the top of the Crap Sogn area, particularly the drag-accessed slopes around the Crap lift.

Intermediate Mid-level skiers will enjoy exploring Laax. There are two obvious, fun routes down from the Crap Sogn peak via the Plaun and Curnius chairs. These are long, with plenty of fun features. Equally worthy of investigation are the numerous reds off La Siala chair.

Expert Although out-and-out blacks are pretty thin on the ground, Laax is the kind of resort that tries to provide for top-level pass-buyers, as the numerous well-worked parks and pipes attest. So the blacks from La Siala and the top of the Vorlab are long and challenging enough to retain interest. You'll also enjoy the many options from the peak of Crap Sogn.

Powder In fresh snow Laax is a great resort as there is a lot of easily accessible off-piste terrain off the main lifts. Try the obvious bumps and pitches off the Curnius chair in the morning, before heading up to the Vorab side in the later afternoon. Itineraries off the Cassons peak and down from the Vorab Pign area are also serious freeski routes. A guide is probably advisable. Be aware that Laax is predominantly south facing, so the sun can dry things out quickly.

Trees Laax is high, so trees are only really found low down. In flat light, most

Switzerland Flims-Laax

😊 LOCALS DO

- ✓ Snowboard. Laax is awash with sideways standers.
- ✓ Explore the variety of the resort.
- ✓ Welcome visitors – it's a friendly place.

😠 LOCALS DON'T

- ✗ Get there first thing – the main lift up from Laax always has queues.

people stick to the Plaun chair although some awareness of the area is necessary to make the most of it. Stay low on the Crap Sogn side if in doubt. The mellow lower slopes in Flims also offer some definition.

Moguls Moguls form up on the glacier, but as it takes an age to get there look out for the steep pitch that usually bumps up beneath the Plaun chair. It gets busy though, so beware.

Book a guide Mountain Adventures AG (T+41 (0)81-927 7171) offer

individual or group lessons and are the local experts.

Tuition Again, **Mountain Adventures AG** take care of lessons for beginners.

Kids Laax is great for young skiers, and at the time of going to press children get two free trial lessons. There's also a dedicated children's ski area for really small kids.

Bad light Cabin fever will probably ensue if you stay in Laax itself, so hit the spa, explore Flims or head down the valley to Chur.

Not to miss An après session at the **Crap Bar**. It's friendly and a great way of getting into the rhythm of the place.

Remember to avoid If the presence of snowboarders gets your back up. Laax is one of the most snowboard-friendly resorts in Europe.

Relive a famous moment Laax hosts the UK Ski and Snowboarding Championships each winter, a great way of partying and skiing with some of the country's best. Check brits09.com for more information.

Pitstop and sunbathe The **No Name** café underneath the Crap Sogn peak is a cheap, popular spot for coffees, paninis and sunbathing. For something slightly more upmarket, the **Tegia Larnags** is also popular, as is **Tegia Curnius**, just next to the Curnius lift. Expect huge crowds outside enjoying the sunshine each lunchtime.

Best mountain restaurant Although there are prettier spots, such as **Tagia Curnius**, the huge restaurant at the summit of Crap Sogn Gion has great self-service food and is a convenient meeting place.

Practicalities

Flims-Laax-Falera is an example of three different places that have been linked by a lift system and then somewhat uncomfortably lumped together as one place. In reality, it is likely that you'll find yourself staying in either Laax or Flims. Of the two, Laax is little more than a base station with hotels and some apartments, although there has been expansion in recent years which has given it a more lively atmosphere. Flims is larger but we prefer Laax for the ease of getting up the mountain and its better resort feel. Falera is more suitable for couples and small families.

Sleeping The five-star **Grand Hotel Waldhaus** (T+41 (0)81-928 4848) was built in 1877 and is today an opulent, decadent number with the obligatory Wellness centre. There are three other accommodation options on-site as well, as part of the **Waldhaus Flims** resort (waldhaus-flims.ch). Opening for 2008-09, the **Rocks Resort** is the big news in town, a new purpose-built complex right next to the base which should provide Laax with a much-needed focal point. Other options include the **Hotel Signina** (T+41 (0)81-927 90 00), which enjoys a central position in Laax and has a fantastic restaurant; the similarly appointed **Laaxerhof** (laaxerhof.ch); and, if you fancy getting into the thick of the party action, the **Riders Palace** (riderspalace.ch). Be warned: a youthful crowd and raucous bar make it one for the night owls. The **Hotel Capricorn** (caprilounge.ch) is probably one of the cheaper options in town but has more of a hostel feel. In Falera, we like the **Hotel La Siala** (lasiala.ch).

Eating The restaurant at Park Hotel Waldhaus, **Epoca** (T+41 (0)81-928 48 48), serves local and international haute cuisine and is described as a 'gourmet temple'. The slightly upmarket **Pizzeria Pomodoro** (T+41 (0)81-911 1062) is probably the best of the many pizza joints in Flims. The **Living Room** (livingroomflims.ch) is a low-key, relaxed coffee/food shop serving Thai and local food. For an unusual experience, eat at the up-piste **Tegia Larnags** (T+41 (0)81-927 9910), next to the first gondola stop up from Laax, where you can enjoy fondues and other local specialties – then walk or ski down afterwards.

Au pair/crèche There are two crèches at each base station – one in Laax, one in Flims. Book through the **Mountain Adventures** ski school (T+41 (0)81-927 7171).

Best après-ski Without doubt it is the legendary **Crap Bar**. 'Crap' is the local word for peak and the prefix is everywhere in Laax. Located at the base station, it is where everyone congregates at the end of the day.

Bars and clubs Laax has a healthy, healthy nightlife scene, especially in Laax itself. **Crap Bar** is usually packed, while **Capri Lounge** at the Hotel Capricorn is also a favourite, and similar in feel to the **Living Room** in Flims. The **Lobby Bar** at the Riders Palace is a favourite with the younger crowd, while after-hours needs are fulfilled by the huge **Arena Nightclub** in the basement of the Riders Palace.

Hire shop/rental There are rental outlets at each base station, with **NTC Rent** at the Laax base station probably the easiest option. Book through the laax.com website.

Lift tickets You can pre-book tickets though Laax's sophisticated website, or at one of the main base stations.

Shopping Laax is expensive as a rule, and there is a only a pricey, derisory **Volg** in Laax itself. If you are self-catering, probably best to head to the nearby city of Chur for a cheaper resupply or hit the big **Co-op** in Flims.

Health and wellbeing With two swanky spas in town, pampering yourself is simple here. In Laax, the **Signina** has a full 'adventure pool' in the basement as well as further wellness facilities. In Flims, the **Waldhaus Park Hotel** has an extremely salubrious spa.

Down days with kids Not the greatest resort in the world to be stuck with bored kids, so we suggest taking a trip down the valley to Chur.

Internet As well as the many Wi-Fi networks in most hotels, you'll find dedicated facilities at the **Living Room** and **Riders Palace**.

Transfer options Trains from Zurich to Chur, and from there catch the regular PostAuto bus up to Flims and Laax (T+41 (0)81-256 3166).

If you like this ... try Morzine ▶▶ p172, Verbier ▶▶ p308.

⊚ OPENING TIMES

Nov to Apr: 0830-1630

⑤ RESORT PRICES

Week pass: CHF384

Day pass: CHF69

Season pass: CHF1411

ⓘ DIRECTORY

Website: laax.com

Tourist office: T+41 (0)81-920 8181

Medical centre: T+41 (0)81-921 4848

Pisteurs: T+41 (0)81-927 7001

Taxi: a-taxi.ch

↘9 Grimentz

Town altitude 1570 m	Funicular/cable
Km to airport 195 km	cars 0/1
Airport Geneva	Gondolas/chairs 0/3
Highest lift 2900 m	Drags 7
Vertical drop 1330 m	Night skiing no
Km of pistes 46 km	Terrain parks 1
Nursery areas 1	Glühwein factor ★☆☆
Blues 9	Ski in/ski out ★★☆
Reds 10	Environmental
Blacks 4	rating n/a

Beautiful, atmospheric village from which to explore the Val d'Anniviers ski area.

Practicalities

Grimentz is one of 12 villages in the stunning Val d'Anniviers. The small, family-friendly village, dotted with sun-blackened *raccards* (wheat storage barns) and ancient chalets, dates back to the 15th century. Grimentz is slightly larger than its neighbour Zinal but has direct access to a smaller ski area.

Sleeping Three-star B&B **Cristal** (T+41 (0)27-475 3291; cristalhotel.ch) offers a 'Dine Around' programme with local restaurants. Family-run **Becs de Bosson** (T+41 (0)27-475 1979; becsdebosson. ch) is basic but comfortable.

Eating Le Mélèze and **Becs de Bosson** offer local specialities. **Arlequin** has a *rösti* 'festival' on Wednesdays.

Bars and clubs Nightlife is quiet, particularly on weekdays. Locals go to **Chez Florioz** and **Le Country**.

Kids Snowli-club (T+41 (0)27-475 1493) on Bendolla cares for children from two years.

Transfer options Fly to Geneva, take a train to Sion (rhb.com), then a postal bus from there. A hire car is quite a good option here.

You can also ski here ... The Val d'Anniviers ski area: Grimentz, Zinal, St-Luc/Chandolin and Vercorin. Resorts are linked by (free) buses.

If you like this ... try Alpbach ▶▶ *p56*, Zürs ▶▶ *p95*.

⊚ **OPENING TIMES**
Early Nov to early Apr: 0830-1630

⊛ **RESORT PRICES (Val d'Anniviers ski pass – 220 km pistes)**
Week pass: CHF230
Day pass: CHF46
Season pass: CHF715

ⓘ **DIRECTORY**
Website: grimentz.ch
Tourist office: T+41 (0)27-475 1493
Medical centre: T+41 (0)27-475 2666
Pisteurs: T+41 (0)27-476 2000
Taxi: T+41 (0)79 628 6111

Grimentz's ski area has just 46 km of pistes – half blue, half red. It's a great spot for intermediates to progress on quiet and varied terrain.

Beginners Start with the long, winding blue from Bendolla to Grimentz (avoiding walkers and sledgers) before progressing slowly up the mountain.

Intermediate Build up confidence on the blues before tackling the steeper reds off the Lona T-bars. Spend a day each at St-Luc and Zinal.

Expert Like Zinal, the lure of Grimentz for expert skiers lies in its superb off-piste terrain, which is best explored with a guide. The long black Piste Lona is everything a black run should be and the Abondance itinerary will challenge most experts. Zinal has more expert terrain.

Tuition Swiss Ski School and International New School. Book in advance to secure an English-speaking instructor.

Bad light Go to Vercorin for trees.

Not to miss The spectacular views from the Roc d'Orzival. Christmas in Grimentz – it's possibly the most magical place to spend it.

↘10 Grindelwald

Town altitude 1034 m	**Km of pistes** 213 km	**Funicular/cable**		**Terrain parks** 2	
Km to airport 195 km	**Nursery areas** 3	**cars** 1/5		**Glühwein factor** ★★☆	
Airport Basel	**Blues** 24	**Gondolas/chairs** 2/18		**Ski in/ski out** ★☆☆	
Highest lift 2486 m	**Reds** 36	**Drags** 11		**Environmental**	
Vertical drop 1450 m	**Blacks** 12	**Night skiing** yes		**rating** ★★★★★☆	

PROS

- ✅ Breathtakingly beautiful scenery.
- ✅ Gentle cruising slopes for intermediates.

CONS

- ❌ Gondolas and trains are painfully slow and often overcrowded.
- ❌ Snow cover on lower slopes is unreliable.

Pretty village in a spectacular setting with mostly intermediate terrain.

This is my seventh season in Grindelwald – I love the community feel and awesome off-piste, which is only really touched by locals.

Stephen Scalzo, seasonnaire

Despite the fact that some of Europe's most spectacular peaks tower above Grindelwald, the resort itself is low and its slopes predominantly gentle. Most in-resort runs pass through trees, with the better snow higher up at the base of the Eiger, making for diverse territory and long valley runs. The ski area is divided in three: First (50 km of pistes accessed from the eastern end of Grindelwald); Kleine Scheidegg/Männlichen (100 km of pistes at the base of the Eiger); and neighbouring Wengen (linked by lift). Access to Kleine Scheidegg/Männlichen from Grindelwald requires a train or gondola ride from the western end of town, both of which take 30 minutes and suffer from queues at peak times.

Beginners Bodmi beginners' area on First often suffers from lack of snow, making Oberjoch a safer bet (although it requires downloading). Progress to the blues on Kleine Scheidegg and Männlichen.

Intermediate Excellent intermediate territory with long descents, varied terrain and steeper runs to progress to.

Start on First (try the long red 22), enjoy the quiet, tree-lined lower runs on Männlichen, carve down Kleine Scheidegg's blues and reds and challenge yourself on the Salzegg runs.

Expert With few black pistes, it's the off-piste that keeps expert skiers entertained. First is a good advanced playground and Männlichen is fun in good conditions.

Powder First and the upper slopes of Männlichen are good for tentative

powder skiers. Expert powder hounds should book a guide – routes include dropping from First down to Bort through the avalanche fences; the famous 'Whitehair' route off Salzegg under the Eiger to Alpiglen; and some challenging lines down Oberjoch.

Moguls Kleine Scheidegg's red 34 under Fallboden.

Tuition There are four schools and a private instructor agency. We like **Buri Sport**, which does rental and tuition. Contact the **Swiss Ski School** or **Mountaineering School** (T+41 (0)33-854 1280) for guiding.

Kids There are kids' areas on Bodmi and Männlichen.

Bad light There are trees on Männlichen's lower slopes

Not to miss The Jungfraujoch station, Europe's highest indoor train station. Expect incredible views of the Eiger and Jungfrau and lots of Japanese tourists.

Remember to avoid Trying to get on the lifts at Grund at 1000, especially at weekends.

Relive a famous moment The rotating Piz Gloria restaurant at the top of Schilthorn was the female-assassin training camp in *On Her Majesty's Secret Service* (1969).

Best mountain restaurant Try sausages and beer outside by Klein Scheidegg's **Schirmbar** or First's classy **Berghaus Bort**. The tiny **Stand Bar** and larger **Spycher** on Männlichen are great for sunny lunches and **Eigernordwand**'s terrace is popular.

LOCALS DO

- Drink 'Municafé' by the half litre (or litre) at Rancher Bar on First.
- Hike up Faulhorn on a powder day.

LOCALS DON'T

- Miss the trains to Kleine Scheidegg – they leave at 17 and 47 minutes past the hour.
- Ski slowly on the World Cup downhill Lauberhorn run.

 # Practicalities

Grindelwald is the epitome of 'Heidi country': a pretty village with a long mountaineering history that's dwarfed by the magnificent Eiger and Jungfrau. The main street buzzes year-round with international visitors here for the scenery, walking and tearooms as much as the skiing.

Sleeping Hotel Schweizerhof (T+41 (0)33-854 5858; hotel-schweizerhof.ch) is one of the more expensive hotels. Mid-range options include **Downtown Lodge** (T+41 (0)33-828 7730; downtown-lodge.ch) for youngsters and **Hotel Spinne** (T+41 (0)33-854 8888; spinne.ch) for nightlife. **Grindelwalder Hof** (T+41 (0)33-854 4010; grindelwalderhof.ch) is central with large rooms and apartments.

Eating Onkel Tom's Pizzeria near the First lift is good. **Spinne** is carnivore heaven while **Central Hotel Wolter** has great views and vegetarian food. **Café und Mehr (C&M)** does good snacks.

Au pair/crèche Murmeli (T+41 (0)77-414 9109) cares for children from six months. **Sunshine Nursery** (T+41 (0)33-853 0440) on Männlichen has no minimum age limit.

Bars and clubs Start on the mountain at Kleine Scheidegg's **TeePee Bar** before dropping into **C&M**, **Chalet Alter Post** (near First) or **Bistro Bar Memory**. Lively après continues at **Espresso Bar** (Hotel Spinne) and two nightclubs: **Mescalero** (Hotel Spinne) and **Plaza** (Hotel Sunstar). **Gepsi Bar** (Hotel Eiger) is quieter.

Shopping There's a surplus of shops selling Swiss Army knives and a large **Co-op**.

Hire shop/rental Buri Sport has stores by the train station and towards First. There are also 10 **Intersport** shops.

OPENING TIMES

Early Dec to mid-Apr: 0830-1600

RESORT PRICES

Week pass: CHF295

Day pass: CHF57

Season pass: CHF840

DIRECTORY

Website: myjungfrau.ch

Tourist office: T+41 (0)33-854 1240

Medical centre: T+41 (0)33-853 2515

Pisteurs: T162

Taxi: T+41 (0)79-215 1853

Health and wellbeing The sports centre by the tourist office has great facilities. **Hotel Belvedere** has an outdoor salt whirlpool.

Down days with kids The sports centre is popular as is the (free) **Alpine Bird Park** (T+41 (0)33-853 2655) at Wetterhorn.

Internet There's an internet corner at the sports centre and tourist office.

Transfer options Fly to Geneva or Zürich and take a train into Grindelwald via Interlaken. Alternatively, fly to Bern and take a shuttle bus (jungfrau-winter.ch).

You can also ski here ... Wengen, Mürren.

If you like this ... try Soldeu (Andorra), Alpbach ▶▶ *p56*.

↘11 Gstaad

Town altitude	1000 m	Funicular/cable cars	0/3
Km to airport	150 km		
Airport	Geneva	Gondolas/chairs	14/38
Highest lift	3000 m	Drags	28
Vertical drop	2050 m	Night skiing	yes
Km of pistes	250 km	Terrain parks	5
Nursery areas	23	Glühwein factor	★★★
Blues	24	Ski in/ski out	☆☆☆
Reds	15	Environmental	
Blacks	5	rating	★★☆☆☆

Large and luxurious, Gstaad is a Mecca for high society and the super-wealthy.

Rivalled by St Moritz, Gstaad is understated and sophisticated, with chalet-style buildings and a car-free centre. Runs are best suited to intermediates – although for many, skiing is secondary to socializing.

With 62 different lifts over six independent ski areas, Gstaad is part of the Glacier-Alpes Vaudoises ski area with stunning scenery, a wide range of skiing – and ample on-snow socializing.

Beginners Take the bus from town to Lauenen for sun-drenched blues.

Intermediate Reds cover the entire ski area – but Château d'Oex is perfect for escaping the Gstaad glitz.

Expert Blacks descend from the Les Diablerets glacier, plus off-piste exists in Saanenmöser and Schönried.

Tuition Snowsports Gstaad (gstaadsnowsports.ch).

Not to miss Heli-skiing with a guide or instructor, with **Air Glaciers** (airglaciers. ch) or **Heliswiss** (heliswiss.ch).

Remember to avoid Budgeting: Gstaad attracts Switzerland's super-wealthy – so expect to spend.

Practicalities 🛏🍴🚌

Sleeping A huge variety of accommodation, from B&Bs to quality self-catering apartments and hotel rooms, can be booked online at gstaad.ch. For prestige, **Gstaad Palace** (palace.ch) is king: doubles start at CHF1020.

Eating Chesery (chesery.ch) offers Asian-influenced cuisine, while **Rialto** (rialto-gstaad.ch) serves fine Italian. For traditional Swiss food go to **Rössli** (gasthausroessli.ch). **Café Pernet** (T+41 (0)33-744 5787) is relaxed and vegetarian friendly. The **Eagle Ski Club** (eagleskiclub.ch) serves 'the world's most expensive lunch' – a private members' restaurant on a private mountain, its annual membership costs CHF50,000!

Bars and clubs Go to the aptly named **FunFun Bar** (T+41 (0)33-744 6626) for après. The **Chlösterli** (chloesterli. com) has a lounge bar, club and bistro. **Richie's Pub** (T+41 (0)33-744 5787) is an English-style boozer. For pure glamour, the **Palace Hotel** has a bar, casino, cocktails and a club – the **GreenGo** (T+41 (0)33-748 5000).

Hire shop/rental Brand Sport und Mode (brandsport.ch), Edelweiss Sport (edelweisssport.ch) and **Hermanjat**

Sports (hermanja-gstaad.com) are in the town centre.

Transfer options Bern (60 km away) is the nearest airport, but Geneva (150 km) has more flights and is 85 minutes by car. Zürich (178 km), under two hours' drive away, is another option. From all airports, Gstaad is two hours by train (sbb.ch).

You can also ski here ... Balmberg, Langenbruck, Engadin/St Moritz and Kitzbühel all offer discounts with Gstaad season and multi-day tickets.

If you like this ... try Klosters ▶▶ *p294*, St Moritz ▶▶ *p304*.

◎ OPENING TIMES

Early Dec to mid-Apr: 0830-1630

Ⓢ RESORT PRICES (A TopCard pass covers the entire Gstaad area)

Week pass: CHF285

Day pass: CHF62

Season pass: CHF990

ⓘ DIRECTORY

Website: gstaad.ch

Tourist office: T+41 (0)33-748 8181

Medical centre: T+41 (0)33-744 1562

Taxi: T+41 (0)33-748 6666

Switzerland Gstaad

↘12 Klosters

Town altitude 1124 m	Km of pistes 305 km	Funicular/cable	Terrain parks 3
Km to airport 140 km	Nursery areas 2	cars 3/8	Glühwein factor ★☆☆
Airport Zürich	Blues 21	Gondolas/chairs 4/10	Ski in/ski out ★☆☆
Highest lift 2844 m	Reds 42	Drags 26	Environmental
Vertical drop 2034 m	Blacks 22	Night skiing yes	rating ★☆☆☆☆☆

PROS

- ✔ Pretty, atmospheric town.
- ✔ Gets more snow than Davos but accesses the same ski area.
- ✔ Excellent for families.

CONS

- ✘ Expensive.
- ✘ Fractured mountains mean a lot of time is spent commuting between them.

Quaint and sophisticated, Klosters accesses the vast Davos-Klosters ski area.

🙂 LOCALS DO

- ✔ Carry bus and train timetables with them to avoid lengthy waits.
- ✔ Reserve tables for lunch.

🙁 LOCALS DON'T

- ✘ Drive to the ski lifts.
- ✘ Care if you're rich or famous.

The Davos-Klosters ski area incorporates over 300 km of pistes across five mountains. The Gotschna gondola ascends from Klosters Platz to Parsenn, the largest and most varied mountain, while Madrisa is reached from Klosters Dorf and is ideal for beginners and families. The remaining three mountains – Jakobshorn, Pischa and Rinerhorn – are reached by train and/or bus. See Davos for further information about the skiing on all five mountains.

Beginners South-facing Madrisa is ideal for beginners, with plenty of blues and easy reds to progress to.

Intermediate Parsenn: wide, open pistes ideal for carving, idyllic tree-lined runs and some of Europe's longest reds down to Küblis and into Klosters. Madrisa: long, confidence-building blues and reds for tentative intermediates.

Expert The appeal of Davos-Klosters for expert skiers lies in the off-piste itineraries (marked but unprepared and unpatrolled routes) and off-piste. The benefit of staying in Klosters is that runs into the village are more challenging and you can

lap the off-piste off the red 24 down to Schwendi and on into the village.

Powder As you'll see from the Davos review, there are acres of excellent freeriding terrain.

Moguls Parsenn: the black 13 from Meierhoftäli to Wolfgang, steep black 1 off Weissfluhgipfel and under the Schwarzseealp chair.

Trees The red 21 into Klosters and Rinerhorn.

Book a guide Adventure Skiing (T+41 (0)81-422 4825) or **Swiss Ski School**.

Tuition Swiss Ski School and **Saas Ski School**, which has younger instructors and a less traditional approach.

Kids Swiss Ski School operates Bobo Club on Jakobshorn for skiers from four to seven years.

Bad light Stay low or visit Davos for the day.

Not to miss Parsenn's legendary 12-km-long, 2000-m vertical drop red

run to Küblis – open to all levels and what skiing is all about.

Remember to avoid Missing the après-ski at Gaudy's.

Relive a famous moment Or don't, in this case. Prince Charles had a close call in Klosters when a member of his party was killed in an avalanche in 1988.

Pitstop and sunbathe Freeriderlodge on Parsenn (Schifer) has great deckchairs, while Chalet Güggel on Jackobshorn goes even further with fleece-covered day beds. On Madrisa **Berghaus Erika**'s terrace gets busy.

Best mountain restaurant Parsenn: **Bruhin's Weissfluhgipfel** offers gourmet dining at altitude while **Schwendi Ski und Berghaus** does great *rösti*. Madrisa: **Berghaus Erika**. Jakobshorn: **Jatzhütte**. Rinerhorn: secluded **Restaurant Spina** (T+41 (0)81-420 3101) does delicious *röstis*.

Practicalities

It's easy to understand why the rich and royal like Klosters. The small village has luxurious accommodation, gourmet cuisine and that 'reassuringly expensive' feel. It accesses the same ski area as Davos but runs into the village are better and it gets more snow. Klosters Platz is the village centre while Klosters Dorf, a smattering of hotels by the Madrisa gondola, is a bus ride away. Trains between Klosters and Davos are included in your lift pass.

Sleeping Top of the range **Hotel Vereina** (T+41 (0)81-410 2727; vereinahotel.ch) provides friendly, unpretentious luxury and **Descent International** (descent.co.uk) has two chalets here. The beautifully frescoed, mid-range **Chesa Grischuna** (T+ 41(0)81-422 2222; romantikhotels. com/klosters) also has a separate, cheaper guesthouse. **Sweet Rustico Hotel** (T+41 (0)81-410 2288; rusticohotel. com) has just 10 rooms (ask for one at the back).

Eating Prince Charles's favourite hotel, the **Walserhof** (T+41 (0)81-410 2929), leads the gourmet way with two Michelin stars, closely followed by Hotel Vereina. **Chesa Grischuna** and **Hotel Wynegg** are more affordable. **Rustico** offers Euro-Asian cuisine and the **Prättiger Hüschi** fondue restaurant.

Au pair/crèche Madrisa has a **Baby Centre** (up to two years) and **Kids Club** (two to six years).

Bars and clubs There's great après-ski at the **Serneuser Schwendi Hütte** on red piste 21, **Gaudy's Graströchni** at the end of the same run and **Gotschnabar** by the gondola base station. Later on, (fairly subdued) action happens in the hotel bars: **Steinbock Bar**, **Chesa Grischuna**, **Cresta Bar**, **Rössli Bar** and **Piano Bar** before **Casa Antica** disco kicks in.

Hire shop/rental **Bardill Sport** has a rental and storage outlet by the Gotschna gondola and a clothing store in town.

Health and wellbeing Hotel Vereina's exquisite 1000-sq-m **Aquareina Spa** has herbal steam rooms, saunas, pool etc.

Down days with kids There's a long toboggan run but Davos has more facilities.

Internet There are computers at the tourist office and most hotels have Wi-Fi.

Transfer options Fly to Zürich and pick up a pre-booked Davos-Klosters Express on Saturdays (davosklosters.ch) or to Friedrichshafen and book the daily Graubünden Express (graubuenden-express.com).

You can also ski here ... Parsenn, Madrisa, Jakobshorn, Rinerhorn, Pischa.

If you like this ... try Lech ▶▶ *p73*, Zürs ▶▶ *p95*, Villars ▶▶ *p312*.

Switzerland Klosters

☺ OPENING TIMES
Mid-Nov to end Apr: 0815-1615

⑤ RESORT PRICES (TopCard pass: Davos-Klosters, Flims-Laax, Lenzerheide and Valbella)
Week pass: CHF285
Day pass: CHF65
Season pass: CHF680

① DIRECTORY
Website: klosters.ch
Tourist office: T+41 (0)81-410 2020
Medical centre: T+41 (0)81-330 4400
Pisteurs: T+41 (0)81-417 6150
Taxi: T+41 (0)81-416 7373

↘13 Les Diablerets

Town altitude 1151 m	Km of pistes 225 km	Blacks 3	Night skiing no
Km to airport 120 km	(Alpes Vaudoises)	Funicular/cable	Terrain parks 2
Airport Geneva	Nursery areas 1	cars 0/3	Glühwein factor ★☆☆
Highest lift 2970 m	Blues 20	Gondolas/chairs 0/6	Ski in/ski out ☆☆☆
Vertical drop 1819 m	Reds 23	Drags 14	Environmental
			rating ★★☆☆☆

PROS

- ✅ Snow all but guaranteed thanks to the glacier.
- ✅ Great for intermediates and families.
- ✅ Winter wonderland feel.

CONS

- ❌ Nightlife limited.
- ❌ A lot of drag lifts means it's not that suited for complete beginners.
- ❌ Main winter season ends early.

Inordinately pretty Swiss village safeguards surprisingly large and varied ski area.

Just an hour or so's drive from Geneva, French-speaking Les Diablerets is the type of cloyingly lovely resort for which descriptions such as 'chocolate box' were invented. With very few English-speakers in evidence, it is extremely popular with local Swiss who like the unchanged atmosphere of the town, while the enormous glacier that overlooks the town adds muscle to the entire Alpes Vaudoises region and attracts skiers the year round. For anybody looking for an untouched Swiss gem with a short transfer time, Les Diablerets must be a serious contender.

Les Diablerets is part of the Alpes Vaudoises region, although this appellation is somewhat formless, with a car needed if you want to take full advantage of it. With that in mind, it is likely that most visitors to Les Diablerets will spend most of their time exploring the in-bounds terrain, which is roughly split into three zones – Glacier 3000, Isenau and Meilleret.

Beginners Beginners will enjoy the gliding tree runs of Meilleret. Take the Vioz-Marots lift to the summit; from there you'll find numerous easy blues, including one that leads back down to the village when snow cover is strong. Over on Isenau, it's a similar story, although perhaps it is best to leave this till mid-week.

Intermediate Intermediates will enjoy this resort, and can spend the week building up to some of the more involved reds up on Glacier 3000. The routes to Villars are a great way of getting the legs back, but you'll probably find yourself drawn back to the more challenging terrain of Isenau most days, particularly that reached via the Floriettaz summit.

Expert With a lack of black runs on both 'regular' sides of the resort, the glacier will hold the most challenges. That said, you'll need a guide the first couple of times you try to negotiate some of the steeper routes; when you get it right there are some fantastic lengthy runs here. To really get the most out of your time here, you might do well to explore neighbouring Alpes Vaudoises resorts such as Gstaad.

☺ LOCALS DO

- ✅ Shred the glacier park in the autumn, to get the legs ready for the winter. It's a serious pre-season spot.
- ✅ Take part in the big end of season party at Oldenegg. It goes off.
- ✅ Ride Isenau in the spring sun.

☹ LOCALS DON'T

- ❌ Bother with the sledge run unless it's bulletproof ice.
- ❌ Forget to head to L'Ormonon for an after riding pint of Guinness.
- ❌ Miss the Flash and Fluo Jam Session on Isenau at the end of the winter. Dig out that neon …

Powder Glacier 3000 is a serious mountain environment, so much so that the tourist board publishes a guidebook detailing some of the popular itineraries. It means a guide is a must if you want to make the most of some fresh snowfall.

Moguls The Combe d'Auda on the glacier is a long, long run that takes in some killer moguls and deposits you on the road at Reusch. You'll have to get the bus home but it's worth it.

Tuition The local **Swiss Ski & Snowboard School** (T+41 (0)24-492 2002) takes care of lessons for adults and kids in a relaxed, friendly environment.

Kids The **Swiss Ski & Snowboard School** run the **Formule Club** kindergarten for youngsters.

Bad light Bad light scuppers much of the high ground and best terrain. Stay in Meilleret among the trees.

Not to miss One of the top-to-bottom descents on the glacier. In great snow, it'll remind you why you began skiing.

Remember to avoid The late season. Les Diablerets can suffer from a lack of snow once late March comes round, so stick to January and February for the best conditions.

Relive a famous moment Build something in town and you join a long list of architects to have helped Diablerets' architectural fame. Mario Botta, Switzerland's most influential designer recently added the new Botta 3000 restaurant on the glacier.

Best mountain restaurant The **Restaurant Botta 3000** (T+41 (0)24-492 0931) is a must. Designed by Mario Botta, the views are sublime and the food isn't bad either.

Practicalities

Sleeping Family-run **Hotel Les Sources** (T+41 (0)24-492 0100) is a firm Footprint favourite with clean rooms and great service, while nearby **Eurotel Victoria** (eurotel-victoria.ch) is huge and has spa facilities. For a lower-key option, the **Auberge de la Poste** (T+41 (0)24-492 3124) is as old as the French Revolution and has a convenient central location.

Eating Fare in Les Diablerets is strictly of the Swiss local variety – expect to eat fondue at least once. We like **Auberge de la Poste** (T+41 (0)24-492 3124) among the many hotel restaurants. For a change, try **L'Ormonan** (T+41 (0)24-492 3838) for that old favourite, the Alpine Chinese.

Au pair/crèche Les Diablerets tourism keep a comprehensive list of accredited babysitters that charge the uniform Swiss 'Red Cross' rate. Check diablerets.com for more information.

Bars and clubs Up on the glacier, **Roosters Bar** is popular for après-ski. In town, nightlife is hardly at a premium, but there are options: **MTB Bar** for pool and beers, **La Diabletine** or **L'Ormonan** for quiet drinks. **La Pote's** caters for the night owls.

Hire shop/rental Try **Snow Culture** (T+41 (0)24-492 1545) or the more traditional **Jacky Sport** (jackysports.ch).

Shopping This being Switzerland, there is a well-stocked **Co-op** and **Denner**, as well as the usual lovely local delis, bakeries and souvenir shops. Expect to leave with at least one item of Swiss Army memorabilia.

Health and wellbeing There is a solarium and a couple of beauty salons in Les Diablerets, but you're better off jumping in the car and heading to the

Ermitage Golf Hotel (ermitagegolf.ch) in nearby Gstaad.

Down days with kids The resort is proud of its family-friendly status, with kids under nine enjoying free access to the glacier and discounts in some local hotels (check alpes.ch for more details). The tourist board runs a range of down-day activities such as snowshoeing, ice-skating, curling and sledging – there is a 7-km sledge run!

Internet Wi-Fi comes as standard in most of the hotels in Les Diablerets, and bars such as **MTB** also have the facility.

Transfer options Our favourite – and the greenest way – of reaching the resort is to take the train. Check myswitzerland.com for more information.

You can also ski here ... Villars, Gryon, Gstaad, and the rest of the Alpes Vaudoises region.

If you like this ... try try Soldeu (Andorra), Alpbach ▶▶ *p56*.

Switzerland Les Diablerets

OPENING TIMES

Early Dec to mid-Apr: 0900-1630

RESORT PRICES

Week pass: CHF277

Day pass: CHF49

Season pass: CHF990

DIRECTORY

Website: diablerets.com

Tourist office: T+41 (0)24-492 3358

Medical centre: T144

Pisteurs: T+41 (0)24-492 3358

Taxi: T+41 (0)24-466 6767

⤵14 Leysin

Town altitude	1350 m	Km of pistes	60 km	Funicular/cable		Terrain parks	1
Km to airport	100 km	Nursery areas	3	cars	0/1	Glühwein factor	★★☆
Airport	Geneva	Blues	12	Gondolas/chairs	0/7	Ski in/ski out	★★☆
Highest lift	2205 m	Reds	5	Drags	6	Environmental	
Vertical drop	855 m	Blacks	2	Night skiing	no	rating	★★☆☆☆

With its sweeping views across Lake Geneva, little Leysin has some of the most impressive views in the Alps.

Let's be clear about this: Leysin is a pretty small resort, especially when compared to nearby Gstaad and even Les Diablerets. It means that the place remains slightly off the beaten track. And yet, there is an indefinable something about Leysin that enables it to seem more than the sum of its parts – perhaps because of its combination of closeness to Geneva, links to the Alpes Vaudoises area and some fun, surprisingly versatile skiing within its tight resort boundaries.

Leysin is small but should just about retain enough interest for a week's holiday. Most of the runs wind down pleasantly through the trees and fall smartly into the intermediate category. That said, there are some steep sections linking it all together and it is very easy to find more challenging terrain if you're looking for it.

Beginners You'll want to stay in the village really, specifically the dedicated nursery areas Valle Blanche and La Daille. Later, head up the Leysin-Tête d'Ai.

Intermediate Take the main Leysin Berneuse gondola up the hill to access the main area. There are some obvious top-to-bottom reds to tackle.

Expert You'll find the best terrain off the top of the Chaux de Mont, although dropping skier's left of the Ai-Berneuse chair also opens up some fairly challenging pitches. For the best terrain, though, you might want to spend the day exploring the glacier in Les Diablerets and some of the long itineraries.

Tuition Try leysinski.com for lessons in English.

Not to miss The views from the top of the Kuklos restaurants. On a clear day the views are outstanding.

Remember to avoid Beginners should definitely stay low until they're ready to try the higher slopes. Some of them funnel down into tricky cat tracks.

⚙ **OPENING TIMES**

Early Dec to mid-Apr: 0830-1630

💲 **RESORT PRICES**

Week pass: CHF266

Day pass: CHF49

Season pass: CHF770

🕐 **DIRECTORY**

Website: leysin.ch

Tourist office: T+41 (0)24-493 3300

Medical centre: T+41 (0)24-494 2010

Pisteurs: T+41 (0)24-557 1635

Taxi: T+41 (0)24-494 2555

Practicalities

Sleeping Swank it up in the four-star **Mercure Classic Hotel** (mercure.com), or book into the **Centrale Residence** (bonellihotels.ch) for the cheaper family option. Another option, the **Au Bel Air Hotel** (aubelair.ch), is right next to the lift.

Eating Le Leysin (T+41 (0)24-494 2315) is a firm Footprint favourite, while the restaurant at **Le Grand Chalet** (grand-chalet.ch) has fine dining and great views. We also like **La Farandole**, a great spot to check emails and relax with a coffee and a sandwich.

Bars and clubs It's a small place, so doesn't exactly compare with Chamonix or Méribel. Still, **Le Lynx** is the après-ski spot of choice and **Top Pub** ... is just that.

Hire shop/rental There are a few options, but try **Hefti Sports** (heftisports.ch) or **Endless Ride** (endless-ride.ch) which does ski and equipment hire.

Transfer options Along with the view, this is Leysin's trump card. It is a scant 100 km to Geneva, which makes a midweek or weekend flit a real possibility. The train remains the easiest and greenest option – check out myswitzerland.com.

You can also ski here ... Leysin is part of the loose Alpes Vaudoises area, meaning you could also ski Villars and Les Diablerets among others – see alpes.ch.

If you like this ... try Bansko ▶▶ *p104*, Risoul ▶▶ *p175*, Ruka ▶▶ *p254*.

↘15 Mürren

Town altitude 1650 m	Funicular/cable
Km to airport 150 km	cars 3/5
Airport Zürich	Gondolas/chairs 2/18
Highest lift 2970 m	Drags 16
Vertical drop 1329 m	Night skiing no
Km of pistes 213 km	Terrain parks 3
Nursery areas 6	Glühwein factor ★☆☆
Blues 23	Ski in/ski out ★☆☆
Reds 35	Environmental
Blacks 18	rating ★★★★☆

> *Mürren is a car-free village situated in possibly the world's most beautiful ski area with a wealth of off-piste skiing.*

Wengen's not-so-famous little sister Mürren is in the same Jungfrau ski region and has incredible Alpine village charm with the added appeal of being less crowded and less commercialized. During the winter months the village is buried in snow and inaccessible to vehicles so it's perfect for families, couples and those who really want to get away from urban life.

If you stay in Mürren, you will be on the doorstep of the Mürren/Schilthorn area of the Jungfrau ski region, which, in our opinion, is the best of the three areas. It has the highest accessible peak and the queues are far smaller than those in the other areas of the region. It's also great for experts.

Beginners Start off with a morning taking on the blues running down from the Schiltgrat peak then go for lunch at the **Sonnenburg** restaurant at the bottom of the Hindenburg run. You can then brave your first red run (if you haven't already done one) by skiing to the Maulerhubel lift where there are a couple more blue runs.

Intermediate You'll need to have your boots on by 0900 to beat the queue for the train that will take you from Lauterbrunnen to Kleine Scheidegg. The early start is worth it. There is a wealth of reds and easy blacks here to test your abilities and improve your technique.

Expert Start the day at the Schilthorn peak and from there ski down to the Muttleren, Riggli or Kandahar lifts. Between these three lifts and the Birg mid-station there are enough black runs and off-piste to keep you happy all morning. Finish off by skiing the famous Inferno Race route all the way down to Lauterbrunnen.

Tuition The Swiss Ski and Snowboard School (muerren.ch/skischule) in front of the Hotel Bellevue.

Bad light Most of the resort is very similar. Stick to the lower runs and it may be slightly clearer.

Not to miss Lunch in the legendary **Piz Gloria** restaurant on the Schilthorn – they filmed *On Her Majesty's Secret Service* here.

Remember to avoid The run down to Lauterbrunnen in the spring – it melts quickly and it's a long walk home!

Practicalities

Sleeping The four-star **Hotel Eiger** (T+41 (0)33-856 4545) is probably the best in the village. The **Eiger Guesthouse** (T+41 (0)33-856 5460; eigerguesthouse.com) costs as little as CHF45 for a bunk room.

Eating For intimate, genuine Swiss cooking go to **Stagerstuble** (T+41 (0)33-856 1316). Nearly every hotel has a decent restaurant but it is advisable to book.

Bars and clubs Youngsters go to **Blumenthal Disco/Bar** until 0300. For a more mature atmosphere go to **Hotel Eiger** bar or the **Regina Bar**.

Hire shop/rental Try Stager-Sport in the middle of town.

Transfer options Rail is best. Connect from Zürich, Geneva and Basel to Bern, then with two changes to Wengen. If you want to go in comfort you can get a very reasonably priced first-class 'round trip' ticket from any Swiss airport or border to any location (see myswitzerland.com).

You can also ski here ... No local partners.

If you like this ... try Samoëns ▶▶ *p179* and Wengen ▶▶ *p315*.

⊚ OPENING TIMES
Early Dec to mid-Apr: 0830-1720

⊛ RESORT PRICES
Week pass: CHF259

Day pass: CHF57

Season pass: CHF900

⊙ DIRECTORY
Website: jungfrauwinter.ch/wengen-muerren.ch

Tourist office: T+41 (0)33-856 8686

Medical centre: T+41 (0)33-826 2500

Doctor: T+41 (0)33-855 1710

Pisteurs: T+41 (0)33-855 4555

Taxi: T+41 (0)33-855 2480/1870

⬂16 Pontresina

Town altitude 1800 m	Km of pistes 350 km	Funicular/cable cars 4/7	Terrain parks 4	
Km to airport 200 km	Nursery areas 0	Gondolas/chairs 1/8	Glühwein factor ★★☆	
Airport Zürich	Blues 18	Drags 24	Ski in/ski out ★★☆	
Highest lift 3303 m	Reds 61	Night skiing yes	Environmental rating ★★☆☆☆	
Vertical drop 1750 m	Blacks 9			

A family-friendly Alpine village combining rustic charm with modern elegance. Pontresina has varied runs to suit all levels, and great off-piste terrain.

Pontresina is a sun-sure, self-contained resort located in the Upper Engadin valley of St Moritz. There is easy access to the nearby Diavolezza, Piz Lagalb, Languard, Corvatsch/Furtschellas and Corviglia-Marguns ski regions, plus the Bernina glacier.

Beginners There is only one area suitable for first timers and families, accessed by the Alp Languard ski lift and pony-powered San Spiert lift. There is also a Kinderland marked area of the **Snowsports School** for children's lessons.

Intermediate The Morteratsch glacier downhill run (Isla Persa) is the longest in the Engadine/St Moritz ski area at 10 km. Or try one of the Engadine's many night-skiing pistes, including the Glüna Plaina full-moon descent.

Expert Both the Diavolezza and Piz Lagalb cable cars head to some epic, monitored freeride areas – 2 km, big, dry, fog free and snow sure.

Tuition Snowsports Pontresina (snowsports-pontresina.ch).

Not to miss Free ice-skating on the Roseg glacier. December to February (T+41 (0)81 838 83 00, pontresina@estm.ch).

Remember to avoid Looking for a late-night club or boozer: Pontresina doesn't do après.

◷ OPENING TIMES

Early Dec to late Apr: 0830-1630

$ RESORT PRICES

Week pass: (6 days) local CHF203; area CHF437-561
Day pass: CHF75-92
Season pass: local CHF1944

◉ DIRECTORY

Website: pontresina.ch
Tourist office: T+41 (0)81-838 8300
Medical centre: T+41 (0)81-851 8111
Pisteurs: T117
Taxi: T+41 (0)79-786 1917

Practicalities

Sleeping The Grand Hotel Kronenhof (T+41 (0)81-830 3030; kronenhof.com) is a beautiful five-star hotel set in landscaped grounds, while **Hotel Walther** (T+41 (0)81-839 3636; hotelwalther.ch) is Pontresina's wellness hotel. Self-catering apartments for all budgets are available online from engadin-home.ch (T+41 (0)81-832 2525) and interhome.ch.

Eating Restaurant La Collina (T+41 (0)81-838 8585) serves refined Thai dishes. Gourmet **Restaurant Kronenstubli** (T+41 (0)81-830 3030) should placate the culinary vultures. **Pizzeria Piz Al** (T+41 (0)81-839 3900) is a cosy self-service while **Café & Restaurant Puntschell** (T+41 (0)81-838 8030) sells pastries, gateaux and sweets.

Bars and clubs Nightlife is subdued, with most bars situated in hotels. The best two are the 'Pöschtli' Keller (T+41 (0)81-838 9300) and the **Pitschna Scena** (T+41 (0)81-839 4580), which has a pub atmosphere, with food and live music on Thursdays.

Hire shop/rental Engadina Sport (engadinaasport.ch) is in the centre of town.

Transfer options The nearest airport is Milan, but Zürich, with a three-hour transfer time, is easier to fly to from the UK Budget airlines also fly to nearby Basel. Take the Swiss Rail train to Chur, then a Rhaetian Railway fast train to Pontresina (rhb.ch).

You can also ski here ... Corviglia-Marguns, Zuoz-Albanaz and Furtschellas.

If you like this ... try Alpbach ▶▶ *p56*, La Tania ▶▶ *p149*, Les Carroz ▶▶ *p155*.

↘17 Saas Fee

Town altitude 1800 m	**Km of pistes** 100 km	**Funicular/cable**		**Terrain parks** 2	
Km to airport 230 km	**Nursery areas** 2	**cars** 1/4		**Glühwein factor** ★★☆	
Airport Geneva	**Blues** 13	**Gondolas/chairs** 3/2		**Ski in/ski out** ★★☆	
Highest lift 3500 m	**Reds** 14	**Drags** 12		**Environmental**	
Vertical drop 1800 m	**Blacks** 5	**Night skiing** yes		**rating** ★★★★★★	

PROS

- ⊘ Insanely picturesque village with lively nightlife.
- ⊘ A cheaper, less crowded alternative to neighbouring Zermatt.
- ⊘ High altitude makes for excellent snow.
- ⊘ Family-friendly resort with plenty of beginner and intermediate terrain.

CONS

- ⊗ Much of the mountain is in shadow until at least February, making it cold and dark.
- ⊗ Limited expert terrain.
- ⊗ Lack of trees for flat-light days.

A beautiful town in a spectacular setting with snow-sure skiing, pumping nightlife and fantastic family facilities.

Saas Fee is arguably the most beautiful village in the Alps. Its winding, car-free streets are flanked by traditional Swiss chalets and cowsheds and dwarfed by 13 4000-m peaks, the 4545-m Dom and a glacier that seems to hang right above it. Saas Fee's quaint appearance belies a vibrant party scene, there are excellent restaurants and hotels, good non-skiing activities and it's an idyllic spot for families.

Saas Fee's glaciers provide excellent snow throughout the year but also limit the off-piste terrain and mean drag lifts are numerous (glaciers shift too much for chairlifts). However, you can't knock a 1700 m descent, long cruising reds, separate nursery slopes and one of Europe's best terrain parks.

Switzerland Saas Fee

Beginners Start at Staffelwald's dedicated nursery slopes, which are right by the village and free of speeding skiers, before progressing to the blues on Morenia.

Intermediate For intermediates, the appeal of Saas Fee lies in the high Alpine experience and long descents rather than clocking up miles. Favourites include 11a and 5 for carving and 9 for a steeper pitch.

Expert On-piste challenges are limited to completing the top-to-bottom runs without stopping, the handful of blacks and three excellent marked itineraries. Off-piste is essentially limited to guided ski touring.

Powder Powder in Saas Fee is a light, fluffy delight. The red 12 at Längfluh is quiet and you can dip into the sides of the piste. Hit the black 15a from Felskinn early for great lines.

Trees If you were a tree would you live 3500 m up on a glacier? We didn't think so. Expert skiers can shred a few trees on Plattjen off the 1a yellow itinerary.

Moguls The black 17 from Allalin, red 9 from Egginerjoch and red 11a from Spielboden get bumped out.

Book a guide A guide will show you the abundant off-piste that lurks between the crevasses. Contact the **Mountain Guide Office** (T+41 (0)27-957 4464).

Tuition **Swiss Ski School** is traditional while **Eskimos** school appeals to youngsters and promises smaller classes.

Kids Both ski schools offer various teaching options for kids from four years. The **Kids Fun Park** and **Beginner-Freestyle-Park** are popular with children. There are also excellent children's ski schools and nurseries in the nearby villages of Saas-Grund/Saas-Balen and Saas-Almagell.

Bad light Saas Fee isn't strong on trees, so soak in the **Bielen Leisure Centre**, bomb down the Feeblitz bobsleigh run, go sledging on Hannig, visit the **Allalin Ice Pavilion** and trace the village's growth (and glacier's shrinkage) through photos in the **Museum**.

Not to miss Small, local wine tastings held in the ancient 'fridge' chalets by the village entrance – ask the tourist office to book.

Remember to avoid Forgetting to ask your hotel for a reduction on your parking ticket when you check out.

Relive a famous moment Ken Russell's first feature film *Women in Love*, starring Oliver Reed and Glenda Jackson, was filmed here.

☺ LOCALS DO

✔ Avoid the queues for the AlpinExpress by taking the T-bar from the nursery slope up to the Felskinn cable car.

✔ Party long and hard in Popcorn and Nesties.

✔ Ski on Saturdays when it's changeover day and quiet.

☹ LOCALS DON'T

✘ Drive – cars are banned in the resort.

✘ Forget to wrap up warm – even if it's toasty in the village, the glacier is still bitterly cold.

✘ Forget to ski in January, when it's virtually empty.

Pitstop and sunbathe Watch the freestylers at the **Pitstop Bar** by the terrain park. **Popcorn Plaza**'s sun terrace comes complete with palm trees while indoors is super-cosy for bad-weather days.

Best mountain restaurant **Gletscher Grotte**, tucked in the woods on skier's left of the Felskinn cable car, is our favourite – it's rustic, quirky and does amazing cakes. **Britannia Hütte**, a short hike from Felskinn, is atmospheric while the large **Morenia** restaurant does good food.

Practicalities

Sleeping Saas Fee is a long town, with most lifts and the nursery slopes at the far end. Although some hotels run electric shuttles, families in particular should choose accommodation close to the lifts in order to avoid a 10-minute schlep. **Hotel Mistral** (T+41 (0)27-958 9211; hotel-mistral.ch) is opposite the slopes while **Hotel Alpin** (T+41 (0)27-957 1577; hotel-alpin.ch) is opposite AlpinExpress and popular with families. **Hotel Dom** (T+41 (0)27-958 7700; uniquedom.com) appeals to youngsters who frequent its bars (Popcorn and Living Room) and enjoy the PlayStations in each room. **Hotel du Glacier** (T+41 (0)27-958 1600; duglacier.ch) has large rooms and good spa facilities. If you want to do it in style, the five-star, family-owned **Alte Post** (T+41 (0)27-957 1515; my-saas-fee.ch) chalet sleeps six. It's Saas Fee's original 19th-century post office with slick new interiors. The excellent **Ferienart Resort & Spa** (T+41 (0)27-958 1900; ferienart.ch) is the only five-star hotel.

Eating Cheminée and Cäsar Ritz are the gourmet choices while true foodies will want to make the pilgrimage

---

---

to Markus Neff's Michelin-starred **Fletschhorn Waldhotel** (T+41 (0)27-957 2131), a 10-minute taxi ride from town. The **Ferienart** has six excellent restaurants, including an exceptionally good pizzeria, while **Spaghetteria** underneath Hotel Britannia is a cheaper Italian option. **Le Vieux Chalet** and **Hotel La Gorge**'s restaurant do Swiss dishes and **Kühstall Steakhouse** (by the village entrance) grills meat and seafood. Locals do lunch at **Tea Room Sporting** opposite Ferienart.

Au pair/crèche Contact the tourist office about the day-care centre (18 months to six years) and **Glückskäfer** (T+41 (0)27-225 8154) for babysitting.

Best après-ski The outdoor **Mühle** and **Blackbull** après-ski bars at the base of the slopes are packed with glühwein-sipping skiers. After sundown, head for **Popcorn** (a snowboarding shop by day and bar at night), **Nesties** and Hotel Metropol's **Crazy Night**.

Bars and clubs **Popcorn** is packed with locals, bands and DJs and **Crazy Night** attracts more youngsters. **Alpenbar**, **Happy Bar** and **The Living Room** are marginally quieter. **Popcorn** and **Poison** discos go on till late.

Hire shop/rental There are more rental shops than we could count – pick one that's near your hotel or the lifts so you can store kit there.

Lift tickets Buy your pass at the lift stations and tourist office. Check saas-fee.ch for packages that include pass and accommodation.

Shopping There's a large **Migros** for food and a surplus of ski shops.

Health and wellbeing Bielen Leisure Centre & Aqua Wellness has great

facilities. **Ferienart Spa** offers luxurious treatments and is open to non-residents.

Down days with kids Hotel Garni Imseng runs children's baking courses in the **Bakery Museum** on Tuesdays (T+41 (0)27-958 1258). The **Allalin Ice Pavilion** is worth a visit. There's also sledging, snow-tubing, ice-skating, the Feeblitz bobsleigh run and swimming (**Bielen Leisure Centre**).

Internet There's Wi-Fi at **Café Central** and **Hotel Dom** and computers at **Cyber Lion** just before Hotel Gorge.

Transfer options Fly to Zürich, Basel or Geneva and take a train to Visp, followed by bus (myswitzerland.com).

You can also ski here ... Saas-Grund, Saas-Almagell, Saas-Balen. A six-day ski pass gives you one day in Zermatt.

If you like this ... try Mayrhofen ▶▶ *p75*, Morzine ▶▶ *p172*, Arosa ▶▶ *p276*.

↘18 St Moritz

Town altitude 1822 m	**Km of pistes** 350 km	**Funicular/cable**	**Terrain parks** 2
Km to airport 211 km	**Nursery areas** 3	**cars** 3/7	**Glühwein factor** ★★☆
Airport Zürich	**Blues** 18	**Gondolas/chairs** 1/18	**Ski in/ski out** ★☆☆
Highest lift 3303 m	**Reds** 61	**Drags** 27	**Environmental**
Vertical drop 1503 m	**Blacks** 9	**Night skiing** yes	**rating** ★★★★☆☆

PROS

- ✅ The St Tropez of ski resorts, complete with '322 days of sunshine each year'.
- ✅ Good restaurants and nightlife.
- ✅ Empty pistes while glamorous visitors swig Veuve Clicquot from 1200-1500.
- ✅ Epic off-piste terrain, for those in the know.
- ✅ Spectacular mountain views from the pistes and resort.

CONS

- ❌ Expensive. Exceptionally.
- ❌ The sunshine can leave pistes bare and prone to moguls.
- ❌ The ostentatious wealth of many visitors will be a turn-off for some.

One of the world's glitziest, most expensive and supposedly sunniest resorts, combining cosmopolitan glamour with some excellent skiing.

St Moritz was the first town in the world to officially register its name together with a sun logo as a trademark back in 1986: 'St Moritz TOP OF THE WORLD' – a pretty punchy call. For over 150 winters St Moritz has been welcoming rich and famous visitors who come to ski, watch snow polo, speed down the legendary Cresta Run and spend large fortunes in luxury boutiques and spas.

St Moritz is part of the Engadin/St Moritz ski area – Switzerland's largest interconnected winter sports region, with 350 km of pistes spread over nine areas. St Moritz's three main ski areas are: Corviglia (large, accessed directly from town); Corvatsch (varied terrain, a 10-minute bus ride from town); and Diavolezza (challenging terrain, a 30-minute bus ride away). Ski buses are

efficient, making travel between the mountains pretty painless, although a hire car does facilitate exploration and parking is free. The further you stray from St Moritz, the quieter the mountains become, particularly so with Bernina, Lagalp, Muttas Muragl, Zuoz – small ski areas popular with families and locals.

Beginners South-facing Corviglia is your mountain of choice, despite the crowds. Salastrains is a good starting point, from where you can progress to the gentle blues around Corviglia.

Intermediate Over half of St Moritz's runs are red, with most blacks feasible for confident intermediates and the different mountains offering diverse terrain. Highlights include: Las Trais Fluors (Corviglia) for carving; the excellent snow and more challenging

reds off Piz Corvatsch; the winter wonderland Hahnensee black into St Moritz Bad (stopping at the Hahnensee restaurant for a drink); the high Alpine experience on Diavolezza; and quiet slopes on Lagalp. Confident intermediates will enjoy completing the 'Engadin Snow Safari' with the help of a free guide on Tuesdays (contact the tourist office for details) – ski under four 3000-m peaks and cover 99 km of pistes and 6666 m of altitude on Corvatsch and Diavolezza.

Expert On-piste challenges are limited although completing the 'Engadin Snow Safari' in a day is entertaining. There are however acres of barely touched, world-class off-piste. Our favourite routes include: the back bowls of Piz Nair; the face to the right of the Trais Fluors chair; the northwest face of Corvatsch; Diavolezza's Schwarzhang route and legendary freeride route across the

😊 LOCALS DO

- ✅ Ski on Furtschellas to escape the crowds on Corviglia and Corvatsch, particularly in spring when it gets more sun.
- ✅ Freeride at Diavolezza.
- ✅ Drink at the Stübli bar.

😠 LOCALS DON'T

- ❌ Ski on Corviglia on weekends or holidays – it's way too busy.
- ❌ Forget to bring their swimmers for the hot tub on Diavolezza.

Pers glacier and down the Morteratsch glacier; and the Lagalp route to La Rösa.

Powder Corvatsch and Lagalp are in the shade all morning, so start on Diavolezza. It's not uncommon to discover powder stashes days after a storm in St Moritz – book a guide to find them.

Trees Given the high altitude of all the mountains, these are limited to the lower slopes of Corvatsch.

Moguls Surprisingly few, given the number of fur-clad, knees-together skiers. There are some to the left of the Trais Flours chair and under the Lagalp cable car.

Book a guide Expert skiers should definitely book a guide to discover the off-piste routes named above as well as longer routes in the Roseg valley. Contact **St Moritz**

Experience AG (stmoritz-experience. ch) or **Bergsteigerschule Pontresina** (bergsteiger-pontresina.ch).

Tuition Swiss Ski School and **Suvretta Snowsports School** are the two options for ski school. Most guests take private lessons, so you could be lucky and get small classes.

Kids Swiss Ski School teaches kids at the Salastrains nursery area and prices include transport there by horse-drawn sleigh. It also runs the **Kinder Club** at Salastrains for non-skiing childcare.

Bad light Trees might be limited but alternative activities are not. Go walking on the lake, cross-country skiing or try the Cresta Run. You can book a passenger ride or take out limited membership with the **Cresta Run Tobogganing Club of St Moritz** (cresta-run.com) – giving you five runs during a winter season for CHF450.

Not to miss A midnight stroll on the frozen lake.

Remember to avoid Confusing St Moritz with a budget ski break destination.

Relive a famous moment Errol Flynn's Cresta Run performance was memorable for all the wrong reasons – he recorded the slowest time ever while letting out a 'high-pitched' scream all the way down. Beat his time and boast about it afterwards.

Pitstop and sunbathe Snuggle up on a double sun lounger at the aptly named El Paradiso on Corviglia, enjoy the afternoon sun and winter wonderland atmosphere at **Fuorcla Surlej** and **Hahnensee** on Corvatsch and bring swimmers for **Berghaus Diavolezza**, which has the highest jacuzzi in Europe.

Best mountain restaurant Mathis Food Affairs at the top of Piz Nair has undeniably excellent views and food although we still prefer the smaller El Paradiso or Alpina Hütte. On Corvatsch, **Alpetta** has delicious local dishes and **Fuorcla Surlej**'s fish soup is worth waiting for, while **Bergrestaurant Lagalb** has a cosy 'Stübli' at the back.

Practicalities

The compact centre of St Moritz (Dorf) is located above a frozen lake and essentially comprises two main streets and a small square. While it lacks the picturesque architecture of resorts like Kitzbühel, the views of the mountains are impressive. About five minutes from here lies St Moritz Bad, an ancient health spa that's now dominated by the Kempinski hotel but has some smaller, more affordable hotels.

Sleeping Most of St Moritz's hotels would bankrupt ordinary holidaymakers. Guarantee financial ruin by staying at **The Carlton** (T+41 (0)81-836 7000; carlton-stmoritz.ch), **Badrutt's Palace** (T+41 (0)81-837 1000; badruttspalace. com) or **Kempinski** (T+41 (0)81-838 3838; kempinski-stmoritz.com). Alternatively, mid-range **Hotel Hauser** (T+41 (0)81-837 5050; hotelhauser.ch) is central, family owned and fairly basic; **Garni Hotel Languard** (T+41 (0)81-836 0000; languard-stmoritz.ch) is a gorgeous B&B; **Hotel Eden** (T+41 (0)81-830 8100; edenstmoritz.ch) has great views. Hotel Laudinella (T+41 (0)81-836 0000; laudinella.ch) in St Moritz Bad is unpretentious and does great breakfasts. Chesa Guardalej (T+41 (0)81-836 6300; chesa-guardalej.ch) in Champfèr, a short bus ride from town, is a 'hotel village' – 92 rooms, three restaurants and a spa distributed over six houses. **Hotel Stille** (T+41 (0)81-833 6948; hotelstille.ch), located in woods near St Moritz Bad, claims to be 'the least expensive hotel in St Moritz'.

Eating There are plenty of expensive restaurants to choose from but reservations are essential. Favourites include the Michelin two-starred **Jöhri's Talvo** (T+41 (0)81-833 4455) in Champfèr, **NOBU** (T+41 (0)81-837

2800) and the rustic **Chesa Veglia** (T+41 (0)81-837 1000) in Badrutt's Palace. Less expensive, Hotel Hauser's **Roo Bar** restaurant does delicious meats cooked on hot stone and **Restaurant Engadin** (opposite Corviglia) offers affordable local dishes. **Hotel Laudinella** in St Moritz Bad houses six restaurants, including **Caruaso** which serves 60 types of pizza baked in a wood-fire oven. On the mountain, Corviglia's **Mathis Food Affairs** is a must for foodies, with brasserie, fine dining and a delicatessen.

Au pair/crèche There's no official nursery but most hotels offer child care. Check with the tourist office.

Best après-ski St Moritz is too civilized for après-ski in the traditional sense, with locals taking tea and pastries at **Hanselmann's** and saving themselves for later outings. Rare sightings of beer-drinking, ski-suited types are made at the Chantarella **Schirm Bar** and **Alpina Hütte** on Corviglia, **Finale** in Celerina and the outdoor bar at **Hotel Hauser**. **Bobby's Pub** in the Caspar Badrutt Shopping Gallery attracts a young crowd.

Bars and clubs Crystal Hotel's **Piano Bar** is good for civilized cocktails while locals whoop it up at **Stübli** (Hotel Schweizerhof), **Cava bar** (Hotel Steffani) and later at **King's Club** (Badrutt's) and **Vivai** (Hotel Steffani) discos. **Enoteca la Vigna** is good for quieter evenings and whisky lovers can choose between 1500 malts at the **Devil's Place** (Hotel Waldhaus am See).

Hire shop/rental We like **Corvatsch Sport** and **Corviglia Sport** at the respective base and mid-stations.

Shopping You can buy everything from a Purdey's rifle to Cartier diamonds. Co-

op's opening hours tend to be erratic, so check before you go.

Health and wellbeing People have been coming to St Moritz Bad since 1864 for spa treatments – the **Kempinski** continues the tradition in unbeatable (albeit slightly clinical) style. **Gut Training** (T+41 (0)81-834 4141) – fortunately 'gut' means 'good' in German – offers massage and physio.

Down days with kids Go for a walk on the lake, learn curling (on ice) or watch a film at **Cinema Scala**.

Internet There are several computers at **Bobby's Pub** and most hotels have Wi-Fi.

Transfer options Fly to Zürich and take the (scenic) train (sbb.ch) or shuttle (a-t-s. net). Book trains in advance with the Swiss Travel Centre (stc.co.uk).

You can also ski here ... St Moritz incorporates Corviglia-Piz Nair, Corvatsch-Furtscellas, Diavolezza-Bernina, Lagalb, Muttas Muragl, Zuoz.

If you like this ... try Kitzbühel ▶▶ p70, Chamonix ▶▶ p126, Cortina ▶▶ p222, Verbier ▶▶ p308.

⊚ OPENING TIMES

Mid-Nov to early May: 0830-1600

⊚ RESORT PRICES

Week pass: CHF311

Day pass: CHF67

Season pass (Engadin): CHF975

⊙ DIRECTORY

Website: stmoritz.ch

Tourist office: T+41 (0)81-837 3333

Medical centre: T+41 (0)81-836 3434

Pisteurs: T+41 (0)844 844 944

Taxi: T+41 (0)81-833 7272

Switzerland St Moritz

↘19 Verbier

Town altitude 1500 m	**Km of pistes** 192 km	**Funicular/cable**	**Terrain parks** 3
Km to airport 170 km	**Nursery areas** 2	**cars** 0/5	**Glühwein factor** ★★☆
Airport Geneva	**Blues** 12	**Gondolas/chairs** 9/24	**Ski in/ski out** ★★☆
Highest lift 3330 m	**Reds** 18	**Drags** 46	**Environmental**
Vertical drop 1830 m	**Blacks** 3	**Night skiing** no	**rating** ★★★★☆

PROS

- ✔ Recent investment in fast lifts.
- ✔ Loads of off-piste terrain.
- ✔ Fantastic après-ski, restaurants and nightlife.

CONS

- ✖ Mont Gelé lift is always shut.
- ✖ Not cheap.
- ✖ Can get quite busy.

Verbier combines Alpine high-society chic with a serious mountain and skiing for everybody.

One of Switzerland's heavy hitters, Verbier has managed to retain a lot of its indigenous character in the face of almost continual development – it is still a beautiful town. Recent soaring popularity might have blunted some of the place's vaunted exclusivity but it is still extremely popular with the great and the good, and the prices tend to reflect this. Thankfully, the mountain is a great leveller and the almost bewildering versatility of terrain continues to be Verbier's main draw, with ski bums toting transceivers and huge skis rubbing shoulders in the lift queue with Prada-wearing socialites. With four valleys to choose from, endless skiing options and a nightlife scene almost as famous as the powder, Verbier's fame is well deserved.

Verbier consists of three main areas: Verbier/Mont Fort, Savoleyres and Bruson. Verbier is the main sector, topping out at 3330 m, and is popular with the hardcore skiers and snowboarders for two main reasons: it's very high and there are lots of easily visible runs, faces, drops and couloirs to check out. Locals put first tracks in, and those unfamiliar with Verbier's off-piste often copy what they see. Savoleyres can be accessed by free buses, but the gondola up is slow. It's not as steep as the rest of Verbier, but is often clearer on cloudy days and has some fantastic pisted runs as well as some decent lines through the trees for those adventurous enough to explore. Bruson is worthwhile but requires taking a gondola, an infrequent bus, two chairlifts and a T-bar before you're high enough to get decent snow – the only time it gets really busy is when everything else is shut from avalanche risk. But the tree-skiing here is world class and a little hiking turns an area with few lifts into an expansive playground. It is also well worth the slog should you wish to ski around in relative solitude – something that Verbier is not exactly famed for.

☺ LOCALS DO

- ✔ Hike to out-of-the-way spots.
- ✔ Carry avalanche gear.
- ✔ Ask about conditions from the patrollers based in the Freeride Huts.

☹ LOCALS DON'T

- ✖ Eat a lot in the mountain restaurants.
- ✖ Get many early nights.
- ✖ Take a day off because it's snowing.

Beginners Les Esserts is the place for total beginners, but watch out for the drag lift. It's a separate slope on the No 2 bus route, surrounded by chalets at the top of the town. A cheaper, separate ski pass is available, which is advised. For those ready to advance, Le Rouge is the run to move up to – it's next door to the Les Esserts area. When you've mastered that, take a trip to Savoleyres to perfect turns on the long blue run down to the Le Taillay chair.

Intermediate For those wishing to improve their skiing – or simply to take a cruisy few runs – there's no better area than Savoleyres. Go anywhere apart from the tight trees on skier's right down the Etablons chair. Attelas all the way down to Medran is great for various different lines in fresh snow, steadily further away from the motorway piste. Alternatively, when everywhere else is tracked out, the Lac de Vaux and La Chaux are fun places to explore. If you're feeling a touch adventurous, there's always the intermediate lines in the funpark La Chaux to explore in the afternoon.

Expert The Col de Chassoure is home to the obligatory 'wall' run, which any self-respecting expert skier would always want to tick off the to-do list. Another must-do would be the Mont Gelé cable car, which has impressive runs in every direction. Technically, everything here is off-piste, but it's always tracked enough – and busy enough – to be generically described as a black run.

Powder Head up to Mont Fort as early as possible and bag a couple of runs down the front face, skier's right, before it gets really busy. With experience and someone with local knowledge, hike up past the cross at Mont Fort and drop off the backside down the Poubelle leading back to Siviez. Ride the lifts back up to Chassoure, then hike the ridge of Mont Gelé – it takes about 25 minutes once the boot pack has been stomped out.

Trees If you're looking for some of the best tree-skiing in the world, you'd best head to the Bruson area. It's a crawl to the top, with some of the oldest lifts in the 4 Valleys, but well worth the trek for the descent.

Moguls For those who like a full leg work-out, Verbier ticks a lot of boxes. If it hasn't snowed in a few days or more, then virtually every run off Mont Gelé, Mont Fort and the front face of the Chassoure Tortin could be classed as primo bump territory.

Book a guide Fantastically named **La Fantastique Guides** (T+41 (0)27-771 4141), the **Guides de Verbier** (T+41 (0)27-775 3363), or – if you want something more local – the **Adrenaline International Ski School (AISS)** (T+41 (0)27-771 7459), who use only Swiss guides.

Tuition La Fantastique Ski and Snowboard School and the **AISS** (see numbers above) both operate great schools. **New Generation** (T+41 (0)27-771-1181; skinewgen.com) is an award-winning school set up by Brits, while the **Ecole Suisse de Ski** (T+41 (0)27-775 3363) is the biggest operator in town.

Kids Under fives ski for free, and there's a discount for those up to 16. Verbier also runs a family pass, with savings of

up to 15%. Les Moulins, Les Esserts and Le Rouge areas are classified as family friendly.

Bad light If you're heading up the mountain, the trick here in flat light is to stay in the trees, so head for Bruson. If it is too hideous to do even that, Verbier's four museums and three art galleries should keep any culture vulture in rich pickings. For the sporty types, the **Fitness and Sports Centre**, with pool, squash and tennis courts, is probably the place to head.

Not to miss The Mont Fort Pub at least once for a proper Verbier night out.

Remember to avoid Going to the **Mont Fort Pub** every night – otherwise you won't get much time on the hill.

Relive a famous moment Where to start? Down a few shots at **Le Farinet** and join a list of celebs who have done likewise, from Princes William and Harry to the Beckhams, Phillip Schofield, James Blunt, Rick Astley, Ruby Wax and Les Dennis. Quite a mix, we're sure you'll agree.

Pitstop and sunbathe With the best views on the hill and a fantastic afternoon vibe, the **Bar 1936** is definitely the place to head.

Best mountain restaurant If you want great food in a rustic building with great views, the Savoleyres area is undoubtedly the place to be – **Buvette de la Marlenaz** and **Le Marmotte** are definite favourites, while **Le Carrefour** is the best for a good bit of grub and a couple of rays on the sun balcony while you're at it.

Practicalities

Sleeping Those with money to burn might like to know that **Chalet Cheyenne** (skiverbier.com) is available for CHF35,000 per week. At the other extreme, billing itself as the 'first atomic proof hostel in the world', **The Bunker** (thebunker.ch) is a functional, cheap option with 132 beds, all underground – not recommended for the claustrophobic. However, you do get use of the impressive Verbier Sports Centre built into the price. **Hotel les Touristes** (T+41 (0)27-771 2147; hoteltouristes-verbier.ch) is another cheap, friendly option (and the oldest hotel in town), while those looking for self-catered should try **Chalet Oliquin** (T+44 (0)7831 427778; chaletoliquin. com). Be aware you may have to book well in advance. The **Hotel Bristol** (bristol-verbier.ch) is centrally located and evenly priced (for Verbier!), as is the **Hotel Farinet** (hotelfarinet.com).

Eating En Bas at the **Pub Mont Fort** (T+41 (0)27-771 1834) is cheap and caters well for vegetarians. **Al Capone's** (T+41 (0)27-771 6774) is open for great pizza for lunch and dinner, while **Le**

Hameau (T+41 (0)27-771 4580) does an unbeatable CHF25 midday menu with a salad. For that truly authentic fondue vibe, there are two options: if you want to stay in town then it absolutely has to be **The Sonalon** (T+41 (0)27-771 6243). However, if you like your cheese to come with a bit of adventure, then book yourself into **La Marmotte** (T+41 (0)27-771 6834) – the restaurant is halfway up the mountain but they'll come and pick you up on a skidoo (the return journey is included, but many choose to sledge back to town).

Au pair/crèche Day-care centre **Les Schtroumpfs** (lesschtroumpfs.ch) employs qualified carers if your hotel doesn't offer childcare facilities.

Best après-ski Finish your day in classic Verbier style by stomping the ski boots on the tables of either the **Bar 1936** (directly below the Mayentzet chairlift), which is technically still on the slopes, or head into town to the **Fer à Cheval** (which regularly overflows into the street), **Le Farinet** (on a balcony overlooking the centre of town), or the ever-classic **Pub Mont Fort** (simply referred to as 'The Pub' by most). Expect live music, a fantastic atmosphere, and lots of shots wherever you go.

Bars and clubs The **Central T-Bar**, the **Crok No-Name Bar**, **King's**, **Le Farinet** and the **Pub Mont Fort** (whose slogan 'Still the original, Still the best' says everything) are all open until 0130. **The Icebox**, and **Casbah's** will take your money after that hour, while the **Coco Club** and **Farm Club** will probably bankrupt you by 0500.

Hire shop/rental Number One Sports and **Mountain Air** are the main ski shops although you'll find many more in the centre of town offering rentals and the latest hardware.

Shopping There are enough trinket shops to satisfy even the most ardent souvenir hoarder, as well as plenty of super-high-end boutiques from Prada to Gucci. For groceries head to the **Migros** just down from the main roundabout.

Health and wellbeing The **Centre Sportif** (T+41 (0)27-771 6601) has an indoor and outdoor pool plus all the latest sports centre accoutrements, while **The Verbier Touch** (T+41 (0)78-723 9674) offers specialist sports, relaxation or deep-tissue massage.

Down days with kids There's a **Glacier Museum**, the impressive **Verbier Castle** and the St Bernards' breeding kennels. Should the weather turn bad, there's always the indoor ice-rink or the cinema, which regularly plays English-language films – just look for a VO sticker (Version Originale).

Internet Check your emails in **Harold's**, **Pub Mont Fort**, **Verbier Beach** and the **Wonderbar** – all free Wi-Fi spots.

Transfer options Geneva is the nearest and easiest airport. From there take the train to Martigny and change for the Grand St Bernard Express, which will whisk you up to the resort. Trains are frequent, clean and very civilized. You can buy tickets at the station or purchase a **Swiss Transfer Service** from swisstravelsystem.com. Alternatively, **ATS** (a-t-s.net) provide shared minibus shuttles, and regular coach services run from Geneva during the winter months.

You can also ski here ... The 4 Valleys/Mont Fort pass includes Thyon, Veysonnaz, Siviez and Nendaz, on the same lift system.

If you like this ... try St Anton ▶▶ *p85*, Chamonix ▶▶ *p126*, Engelberg ▶▶ *p284*.

Switzerland Verbier

↘20 Villars

Town altitude	1300 m	Km of pistes	125 km	Funicular/cable cars	1/3
Km to airport	110 km	Nursery areas	2	Gondolas/chairs	3/11
Airport	Geneva	Blues	15	Drags	27
Highest lift	3000 m	Reds	19	Night skiing	yes
Vertical drop	900 m	Blacks	3		

Terrain parks	4	
Glühwein factor	★★☆	
Ski in/ski out	★★☆	
Environmental rating	★★☆☆☆	

PROS

- ✓ Easy to reach from Geneva.
- ✓ Excellent ski terrain and facilities for families.
- ✓ Expert terrain isn't skied, meaning fresh tracks for the few advanced skiers in resort.

CONS

- ✗ While Glacier3000 is snow-sure, Villars' slopes suffer from low altitude.
- ✗ Getting on the mountain requires a slow train ride or bus ride to the gondola.

A charming resort with old-school pedigree. Well-known as a family destination but underrated for its more challenging terrain.

So far my family has enjoyed three generations of winter and summer holidays in Villars. The beguiling views, all consuming feel-good factor and that special 'je ne sais quoi', which entices so many British families and romantic couples to return here every year, never seem to go away ... long may it continue!

Neil English, Winter Sports Correspondent for The Mail on Sunday

Villars could have been created for families and intermediates, with gentle, tree-lined, winter-wonderland pistes that lead right into the village. However, there's also enough here to keep experts happy, with accessible yet virtually deserted off-piste routes and steeper runs off the Diablerets glacier.

Beginners Start on the village nursery slopes before heading for the extensive Bretaye blues.

Intermediate Essentially, the entire ski area is open to intermediates and excellent for building technique and confidence. Enjoy the open Croix des Chaux slopes, the long red from Le Meilleret towards Vers l'Eglise and the Glacier3000, with its 5-km red down the Combe d'Audon.

Expert Villars offers some on-piste fun, mostly on Les Chaux and the glacier, but expert skiers come here for the off-piste. Descents are short but untracked, accessible and scenic. Locals' favourites

include cutting left off the Sodoleuvre-La Croix chair towards Taveyannaz (avoiding the out-of-bounds trees) and returning to the chair on the cross-country route and going skier's right of the short but steep Combe d'Orsay T-bar.

Powder Much of Villars' skiing is in the trees, while sections of the open bowls are unpisted, making it easy to drop into off-piste terrain under chairs like Petit

Chamossaire and Rasse-Chaux Ronde (the area is a golf course in summer).

Trees Trees are one of Villars' strengths, with tree-lined runs for all levels as well as tighter, more challenging tree-skiing for experts.

Moguls The black from the top of Les Chaux gets bumped out.

Book a guide Freeride routes best done with a guide include the Chamossaire, which drops off the back of Petit Chamossaire into Vers l'Eglise, and glacier routes like Pierre Meule and Le Dome – contact **Villars Expérience** (T+41 (0)24-495 4138).

Tuition Villars Ski School (villarsski. ch), Switzerland's first independent ski school, teaches the graduated-length method, using short skis to guarantee that beginners ski parallel on their first day.

Kids Children under nine can ski free and get free accommodation and ski lessons – visit villars.ch for details.

Bad light Stick to Les Mazots, Meilleret and the lower slopes on Les Chaux.

Not to miss The apres-ski in L'Arrivée, with delightful owners Roger Chappot (a former Swiss national hockey champion) and his wife Marlyse (a former figure-skating champion).

Remember to avoid Not asking a local to tell you the legend of the dragon in the Chavnonnes lake ...

Relive a famous moment David Coulthard and Jacques Villeneuve both own chalets in Villars – try keeping up with them on the slopes.

Pitstop and sunbathe Le Mazot, on Meillerets towards Les Diablerets, has a large terrace with dramatic views of the glacier, while **Le Roc**, at the top of the Roc d'Orsay lift, serves up excellent pizza and has a hot tub on the sun terrace (towels provided). The terrace at **Les Chaux** is a suntrap with views.

Best mountain restaurant Le Mazot, in addition to the views, does fantastic food including local *rösti* specialities

and steak tartare. The restaurant at Chavonnes overlooking the lake serves divine French food. **Auberge du Col de Soud** is the place to go for amazing omelettes, and beers on tap.

☺ LOCALS DO

- Enjoy post-skiing 'Turbos' (homemade glühwein with a shot of Wilhelmina pear liquor) in the Auberge du Col de Soud.
- Ski the La Gaine gully under Chaux Ronde on a powder day.

☹ LOCALS DON'T

- Take the slow, rattling rack-and-pinion train up the hill but take the gondola to Roc d'Orsay instead.
- Talk about their rich, famous and/or royal neighbours.
- Forget to reserve a table for dinner – particularly at Le Vieux Villars and Mon Repos.

Practicalities

Villars is a small, traditional town located on a south-facing balcony overlooking the Rhône valley. Surrounded by vast mountains, whose lower slopes are carpeted in conifers and dotted with chalets, Villars has attracted wealthy,

OPENING TIMES

Villars-Gryon late Dec to mid-Apr: 0900-1645; Glacier 3000 early Nov to end Apr: 0900-1645

RESORT PRICES

Week pass: CHF277

Day pass: CHF58

Season pass: CHF990

DIRECTORY

Website: villars.ch

Tourist office: T+41 (0)24-495 8113

Medical centre: T+41 (0)24-495 1400

Pisteurs: T+41 (0)24-495 8113

Taxi: T+41 (0)24-495 8484

international visitors for many years. Confident skiers should find accommodation close to the Roc d'Orsay gondola, while families and beginners are better off being near the funicular.

Sleeping Grand Hôtel du Parc (T+41 (0)24-496 2828; parcvillars.ch) is currently the only five-star hotel in town. While it is on the pistes and has spectacular views, its decor is very dated. We're holding out for a new five-star property that's being built as we write this. Meanwhile, we like the secluded La Renardière (T+41 (0)24-495 2592; larenardiere.ch), central **Hotel Alpe Fleurie** (T+41 (0)24-496 3070; alpe-fleurie.com) and family-friendly **Hotel Ecureuil** (T+41 (0)24-496 3737; hotel-ecureuil.ch). Contact the tourist office for details of various chalets and apartments, many of which are ski in/ ski out.

Eating Mon Repos, towards the neighbouring village of Gryon, has a lovely old chalet-style ambience and some of the best fine food in Villars at affordable prices. Visit at lunchtime for amazing views. Also excellent are **Le Vieux Villars** and **La Renardière**. **Restaurant du Soleil** in Chesières, just below Villars, has an imaginative menu with Asian dishes, fresh seafood and Swiss and French classics plus a great wine list. The chef at **Peppino**, in the Eurotel hotel, concocts delicious dishes using fresh alpine flowers that he and his staff pick from local pastures every other day. **Le Sporting**, **La Pizzeria** and **La Toscana** do good Italian food.

Au pair/crèche La Trottinette (T+41 (0)24-495 8888) nursery cares for kids up to six years. The tourist office has a list of babysitters.

Best après-ski Start off with piste-side glühweins at Le Bar below Chaux Ronde (look for the palm trees). If there's enough snow, ski down to L'Arrivée in town or have a drink on the terrace of **Auberge du Col de Soud** if you're taking the train down. L'Arrivée is a pint-sized après-ski chalet that's (officially) open from 1500 to 1930 pm (but often later) and serves local wines and snacks.

Bars and clubs Later on, the action kicks off at **Charlie's Bar**, **Central** and **Le Sporting** before dancing at **El Gringo** disco.

Hire shop/rental Holiday Mark offers specialist ski-boot fitting services. Staff at **Villars Ski Rental** are friendly and multilingual.

Health and wellbeing There's the public sports centre or **Serenity Beauty & Relaxation** (T+41 (0)24-495 1503) and Spa Les Fontaines de Pierre (T+41 (0)24-495 3888) for more luxurious treatments.

Down days with kids The sports centre has a swimming pool, bowling alley and ice-rink. There's also a sledge run in Villars and a Tele-Bob in nearby Frience.

Internet The BB Lounge internet café on Route des Hôtels.

Transfer options Fly to Geneva and take a private shuttle (resorthoppa.com) or train via Aigle (tpc.ch).

You can also ski here ... The Villars-Gryon-Diablerets-Glacier3000 ski pass comes automatically with passes of three days or more. Buy an Alpes Vaudoises ski area pass to access Leysin and Les Mosses.

If you like this ... try Arosa ▶▶ *p276*, Saas Fee ▶▶ *p301*.

↘21 Wengen

Town altitude	1274 m	Funicular/cable	
Km to airport	150 km	cars	3/5
Airport	Zürich	Gondolas/chairs	2/18
Highest lift	2970 m	Drags	16
Vertical drop	1329 m	Night skiing	no
Km of pistes	213 km	Terrain parks	3
Nursery areas	6	Glühwein factor	★★☆
Blues	23	Ski in/ski out	★☆☆
Reds	35	Environmental	
Blacks	18	rating	★★★★☆

With the imposing north face of the Eiger, Wengen is arguably one of the most stunning places to ski in the Alps.

☺ OPENING TIMES

Early Dec to mid-Apr: 0830-1720

ⓢ RESORT PRICES

Week pass: CHF259

Day pass: CHF57

Season pass: CHF900

ⓘ DIRECTORY

Website: jungfrauwinter.ch/wengen-muerren.ch

Tourist office: T+41 (0)33-855 1414

Medical centre: T+41 (0)33-826 2626

Pisteurs: T+41 (0)33-855 4555

Taxi: T+41 (0)33-855 1819

On the doorstep of Wengen is the Kleine Scheidegg/Mannlichen area of the Jungfrau ski region. Take the cable car from the centre of the village or the slightly longer but picturesque route on the train and you'll be skiing in under half an hour.

Beginners There are some lovely easy runs through the trees into Grindelwald. Up at Kleine Scheidegg you have an array of blues and easy reds. The blue all the way down back to Wengen is a must.

Intermediate Try the high-speed red down 1286 m in altitude to Grindelwald. You've got to ski the Lauberhorn downhill run all the way to the village.

Expert The Schilthorn side of the Jungfrau region is best for you. Get on all the blacks centred around the Birg mid-station.

Tuition There are a number of ski schools offering tuition in different languages.

Bad light The Mannlichen side is generally better as storms seem to blow down from the Eiger to Kleine Scheidegg more frequently. Try to stick to the runs in between the trees.

Not to miss Whether you can ski the black run down or not, you must eat at the revolving restaurant on the peak of the Schilthorn. Get the cable car down afterwards if you can't handle the run.

Remember to avoid The cable car when the crowds go up at 1000 – a nightmare.

Practicalities 🅿🏠🍴🚌

Accessible only by rail in the winter, Wengen's roads are mainly pedestrian pathways. The village is hugely popular with families, couples and tourists, drawn by the combination of classic architecture and a backdrop of views across and down the valley that makes Wengen one of the most beautiful Alpine villages in Switzerland.

Sleeping Splash out at **The Caprice** (T+41 (0)33-856 0606), go for the budget option at **Hotel Bernerhof** (T+41 (0)33-855 2721), or opt for **Hotel Brunner** (T+41 (0)33-855 2494), the best for ski-in.

Eating Try the *rösti* at **Baren** (T+41 (0)33-855 1419) and the steak at **Da Sina** (T+41 (0)33-855 3172).

Bars and clubs Go to **Tanne Bar** on the main street for a busy and lively atmosphere, or to **Crystal Bar**. Everyone ends up at **Tiffany's** for a late drink and dance.

Hire shop/rental Hotels offer discounts at certain hire shops so ask at reception when you arrive.

Transfer options Rail is best. Connect from Zurich to Bern then it's two changes to Wengen.

You can also ski here ...
Grindelwald, Mürren.

If you like this ... try Méribel ▶▶*p166*, Montgenèvre ▶▶*p170*.

↘22 Zermatt

Town altitude 1620 m	**Km of pistes** 313 km	**Funicular/cable cars** 2/7	**Terrain parks** 1
Km to airport 244 km	**Nursery areas** 5	**Gondolas/chairs** 6/9	**Glühwein factor** ★★☆
Airport Geneva	**Blues** 29	**Drags** 10	**Ski in/ski out** ★★☆
Highest lift 3899 m	**Reds** 72	**Night skiing** no	**Environmental**
Vertical drop 2279 m	**Blacks** 27		**rating** ★★☆☆☆

PROS

- ✅ High-altitude resort with generally reliable snow cover.
- ✅ Breathtaking views from the town and slopes.
- ✅ Exceptionally good food.
- ✅ Vast ski area with varied terrain for most levels including world-class off-piste.

CONS

- ❌ Lifts are invariably a bus, taxi ride or walk away from hotels.
- ❌ Expensive lift pass and hotels.
- ❌ Limited trees for bad-light days.
- ❌ Not ideal for beginners.

Zermatt has it all – an iconic mountain, a vast, high-altitude ski area, excellent dining, a pretty, car-free village and a good party scene.

Switzerland Zermatt

Like many other big-name resorts, Zermatt's ski area – the Matterhorn Ski Paradise – is vast, with just over 300 km of pistes, including Europe's highest run. It incorporates a glacier and accesses Cervinia in Italy, offering skiers of every level acres of terrain. The 'Paradise' comprises four areas: Rothorn (3103 m), Gornergrat (3089 m), Klein Matterhorn (3883 m) and Schwarzsee (2583 m). Significant investment in new lifts has reduced queues and there are free ski shuttles but lifts

😊 LOCALS DO

- ✅ Drink vast quantities of Café Fertig – coffee laced with schnapps.
- ✅ Appreciate the dangers of off-piste skiing and ski with caution.
- ✅ Avoid the painfully slow and crowded Gornergrat funicular by taking the Furi.

😟 LOCALS DON'T

- ❌ Find themselves wearing the chicken suit at the Hennu Stall after too many glühweins.
- ❌ Drive – Zermatt is a car-free resort. (Park at Täsch and take the train from there.)

are spread across town, so you'll find yourself schlepping through town fairly frequently.

Beginners Although there are nursery slopes on Blauherd and gentle blues on the Klein Matterhorn glacier, they're limiting and reaching them involves several time-consuming lifts. Furthermore, you miss out on skiing into the village.

Intermediate Intermediate terrain is spread thoughout the area, with slow and tiring travel between mountains, so we advise skiing one each day. Get up on Rothorn early for deserted red

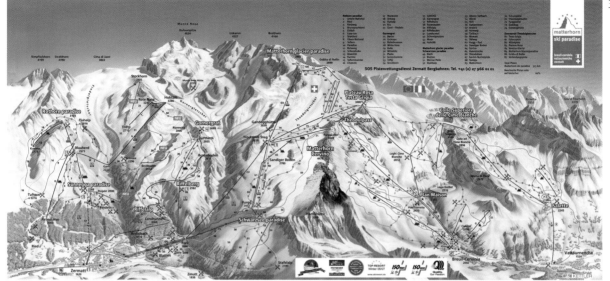

cruisers and magnificent views. The lower slopes on Gornergrat are varied and tree-lined while the upper slopes are suitable for confident intermediates. Schwarzsee and Klein Matterhorn glacier offer predominantly gentle, open reds with staggering views. Finally, the skiing on Cervinia is ideal for intermediates, so ensure you spend at least a day cruising there.

Expert Advanced skiers, particularly freeriding ones, love Zermatt (and Stockhorn in particular) with good reason. There are great long reds (Rothorn-Furi, Hohtali-Furi, Trockener Steg-Zum See), blacks are challenging and varied, there are some excellent marked 'ski runs' (routes marked on the hill but not prepared or patrolled) and there's more off-piste terrain than you can shake a ski pole at – conditions permitting. However, even if there's enough snow to cover Zermatt's rock gardens, off-piste skiing here involves rocky outcrops and small cliffs. Favourite routes to approach with caution and/or a guide: the Rothorn itineraries; the 1100-m vertical drop on Stockhorn and its various lines, particularly when you hike from Rote Nase; hiking the ridge from Gornergrat to ski into Gant; and the itineraries above Furgg and below Schwarzsee.

Powder Beware of rocks – a friend of ours destroyed two pairs of skis in one March week. If you hit Zermatt in good conditions, ski the marked itineraries first thing (they get tracked out quickly) before exploring further afield with a guide.

Trees There are a handful of tree-lined runs on Riffelalp and Sunegga's lower slopes. Experts should try the top of the 'National' black from Blauherd to Patrullarve and underneath the Blauherd chair (in good snow cover).

Moguls The marked itineraries off Stockhorn down to Gant become long,

steep bump runs a few days after a storm. The reds under Trockener Steg are less steep.

Book a guide With such a vast ski area, a guide is worthwhile for all levels in order to orientate yourself on the mountain. Expert skiers will certainly benefit, exploring routes off Rothorn and Stockhorn, tackling Schwarztor and ski touring up various 3000 m-plus peaks in the region. There's also heli-skiing, for vertical drops of over

2500 m. Contact the **Alpine Center** (alpincenter-zermatt.ch).

Tuition In addition to the **Swiss Ski School**, there's **Stoked**, a snowboard/ski school to provide small, fun classes with mostly English-speaking instructors.

Kids Stoked runs the **Snowflakes Kids Club** (4-12 years) on Schwarzsee and Swiss Ski School operates **Snowli-club Riffelberg** (4-6 years).

Bad light Given the lack of trees, we recommend a visit to the **Alpine Museum** followed by a large lunch.

Not to miss Stopping regularly to admire the spectacular views (you can see 38 4000 m peaks from Klein Matterhorn) and indulging in long lunches.

Remember to avoid Skiing down the black Furgg to Furi run at the end of the day if you're tired – it gets icy and crowded.

Relive a famous moment Zermatt is home to Switzerland's highest peak, the Dufourspitze (4634 m), as well as the Matterhorn. Lincolnshire man Charles Hudson was one of the first to summit Dufourspitze in 1855 but he died 10 years later during Edward Whymper's controversial first ascent of the Matterhorn. He's buried in Zermatt's churchyard.

Pitstop and sunbathe Restaurant **Tufternalp** (below Blauherd) has excellent views of the Matterhorn and a feeding trough that attracts deer. Enjoy a glühwein at the **Gandegghütte** above Trockener Steg – it's remote but the location, sandwiched below the Klein Matterhorn and beside the glacier, is worth sidestepping to reach it.

Best mountain restaurant Treat yourself to at least one meal in **Chez Vrony** (T+41 (0)27-967 2552), near Findeln, which mixes traditional with Heston Blumenthal-esque experimental, and **Zum See** (T+41 (0)27-967 2045), which is one of Zermatt's culinary institutions – booking is essential. Findeln is home to two other excellent restaurants: **Paradies** and **Findlerhof** (aka **Franz & Heidi's**). More affordable treats include the **Tufternalp**, **Riffelberg** and **Restaurant Furri**. Finally, pop over to Cervinia for genuine Italian pasta.

Practicalities

As you stand on the snowy, bustling square outside Zermatt's train station, staring open-mouthed at the Matterhorn towering above the village, you know you're in for a treat. Zermatt fully deserves its status as one of the world's best winter resorts, combining excellent, mixed-ability skiing on high, snow-sure slopes with breathtakingly beautiful scenery, a traditional village, some of the world's best altitude dining and good nightlife. You won't save money or lose weight if you come here but you will have a fantastic winter experience.

Sleeping Most accommodation in Zermatt is in hotels but luxury chalet operator **Descent International** (UK T+44 (0)20-7384 3854; descent.co.uk) runs two stunning chalets here. The five-star **Zermatterhof** (T+41 (0)27-966 6600; matterhorn-group.ch) is a classic luxury hotel, while **Omnia** (T+41 (0)27-966 7171; the-omnia.com) is chic and trendy. **Aparthotel Zurbriggen** (T+41 (0)27-966 3838; zurbriggen.ch), owned by legendary Swiss skier Pirmin Zurbriggen, offers slick apartments with breakfast. Four-star **Hotel Alex** (T+41 (0)27-966 7070; hotelalexzermatt.com) is right by the lifts and has great food. The mid-range **Hotel Poste** (T+41 (0)27-967 1931) largely makes up for much-needed redecoration with excellent food, friendly owners and its party-central location. The **Youth Hostel** (T+41 (0)27-967 2320; youthhostel.ch/zermatt) is clean, central and affordable.

Eating There are some 100 restaurants in Zermatt, so you won't go hungry. There are more gourmet restaurants in Zermatt than in any other resort. In brief, therefore, three restaurants are particularly well known: **Rôtisserie La Broche** (Zermatterhof), the Michelin-

starred **Le Gourmet** (Hotel Alpenhof) and **Le Corbeau d'Or** (Hotel Mirabeau). Also excellent are **Le Mazot** – small, overlooks the river and serves melt-in-the-mouth lamb – and romantic **Spycher** opposite. We also like **Stockhorn, Café DuPont** and **Whymperstube** (Monte Rosa Hotel) for fondues and other Swiss specialities. **Old Zermatt** on the river serves locally caught fish, **Elsie's Bar** is a two-storey pub offering posh seafood, **Hotel Post** has two Italian restaurants – **Pizzeria Broken** and **Old Spaghetti Factory** – both of which are great fun. **Bahnhof Buffet Panorama** does good value set menus.

Au pair/crèche **Kinderparadeis** looks after non-skiing children from two years in an indoor playground. Ask the tourist office for babysitting services.

Best après-ski Action starts on the mountain at **Simi, Hennu Stall** and **Zum See** towards Furri and **Othmar's Hütte** and **Olympic Bar** on Rothorn/Sunnegga. In town, locals head for **North Wall Bar, Brown Cow** and **Papperla**, all of which continue until late. **Elsie's Bar** and **Joseph's Wine Bar** (Hotel Mirabeau) are popular with more mature visitors.

Bars and clubs North Wall Bar, **Grampi's Pub** and **Papperla** (and affiliated nightclub **Schneewitchen**) are all loud and late and come with hangover guarantees, as does **Hotel Poste**, which incorporates restaurants, bars and disco under one roof. **Pollox T-Bar** is also a good disco. The über-trendy **Vernissage** above the cinema is ideal for cocktails and light snacks.

Hire shop/rental All the shops offer the same prices for equipment. **Julen Sport** on Hofmattstrasse is large with helpful staff. **Flexrent** is at the Rothorn base station.

Shopping There's a **Co-op** by the train station, a smaller supermarket in the main square and plenty of souvenir shops and boutiques.

Health and wellbeing You'll find virtually any treatment you can imagine here – visit gesundheit-zermatt.ch for more information.

Down days with kids Visit the **Ice Grotto** on Klein Matterhorn and **Alpine Museum** in town, watch a film at the cinema or take a (free) guided walk around town (ask at the tourist office).

Internet Stoked Snowboard School has terminals in the basement and many hotels have Wi-Fi.

Transfer options Fly to Geneva and take a train to Zermatt (sbb.ch). Book tickets in advance at **Swiss Travel Centre** (stc.co.uk).

You can also ski here ... Cervinia, Valtourneche (Italy).

If you like this ... try Chamonix ▶▶ *p126*, St Moritz ▶▶ *p304*, Verbier ▶▶ *p308*.

Switzerland Zermatt

◉ OPENING TIMES

Open year round: Nov to May: 0830-1650 Jun to Oct: 0730-1500

⑤ RESORT PRICES (Zermatt/International pass with Cervinia)

Week pass: CHF350/CHF394

Day pass: CHF71/CHF80

Season pass: CHF1400/CHF1530

ⓘ DIRECTORY

Website: zermatt.ch

Tourist office: T+41 (0)27-966 0101

Medical centre: T+41 (0)27-967 1188

Pisteurs: T+41 (0)27-966 0101

Taxi: T+41 (0)84-811 1212

↘23 Zinal

Town altitude 1670 m	Funicular/cable
Km to airport 200 km	cars 0/1
Airport Geneva	Gondolas/chairs 0/2
Highest lift 2895 m	Drags 6
Vertical drop 1225 m	Night skiing no
Km of pistes 70 km	Terrain parks 1
Nursery areas 2	Glühwein factor ★★☆
Blues 6	Ski in/ski out ★★☆
Reds 11	Environmental
Blacks 4	rating n/a

Tiny, quiet village dwarfed by spectacular mountains – ideal for short breaks.

Zinal has 70 km of mostly intermediate pistes and a large freeride area. Confident skiers will find enough to enjoy when they explore other Val d'Anniviers resorts, but it does feel small.

Beginners Beginners might find Zinal's blues daunting, preferring to start off on the lower slopes of St-Luc and gentle blues on Grimentz before enjoying the high Alpine environment.

OPENING TIMES

Early Nov to early Apr: 0830-1630

RESORT PRICES (Val d'Anniviers ski pass – 220 km pistes)

Week pass: CHF230

Day pass: CHF46

Season pass: CHF715

DIRECTORY

Website: zinal.ch

Tourist office: T+41 (0)27-475 1370

Medical centre: T+41 (0)27-475 2666

Pisteurs: T+41 (0)27-475 1870

Taxi: T+41 (0)79-628 6111

Switzerland Zinal

Intermediate Varied terrain to build on technique and learn off-piste skills. The 1211-m-long descent from Combe Durand via Piste de l'Aigle is a joy.

Expert A well-kept off-piste secret, Zinal has some truly great routes. The (genuinely) black Piste du Chamois to Grimentz is a dream in powder, as is the Freeride zone. Book a guide to discover more (anniviers-montagne.ch).

Tuition Swiss Ski School teaches all levels and kids from four years at Snowli Park on Sorebois.

Bad light Go to Vercorin for trees.

Not to miss A guided snowshoe tour into the Zinal glacier (T+41 (0)27-475 1370).

Remember to avoid Missing the last bus back to Zinal – keep a timetable on you.

Practicalities

At 1670 m, Zinal is the highest of 12 villages in the Val d'Anniviers, nestled at the foot of the 3668-m Besso and surrounded by the 'Imperial Crown' – five mountains over 4000 m, including the Matterhorn.

Sleeping Hotel Le Besso (T+41 (0)27-475 3165; lebesso.ch), built in 1895, has 10 rooms and a comfy wine bar-cum-sitting room. L'Europe (T+41 (0)27-475 4404; europezinal.ch) is popular with families.

Eating Le Besso serves gourmet food for very reasonable prices. Crêperie La Versache is popular for lunch.

Bars and clubs You don't come here to party. Enjoy quiet drinks at Le Pub, Le Besso and Le Trift. Discothèque l'Alambic can get busy at weekends.

Kids Les Pitchouns (T+41 (0)78-679 6891) offers day care for children from 18 months (closed on Saturdays).

Transfer options Fly to Geneva, take a train to Sion (rhb.com) and postal bus from there.

You can also ski here ... The Val d'Anniviers ski area: Grimentz, Zinal, St-Luc/Chandolin and Vercorin. Resorts are linked by (free) buses.

If you like this ... try Zürs ▶▶ *p95*, Saas Fee ▶▶ *p301*.

Index

Countries are indicated in brackets: **And** = Andorra; **Bul** = Bulgaria; **Aus** = Austria; **Fin** = Finland; **Fr** = France; **It** = Italy; **Nor** = Norway; **Slo** = Slovenia; **Sp** = Spain; **Swe** = Sweden; **Swi** = Switzerland

Index

Photography credits

P 2: Pally Learmond

P 6: (top) Matt Barr; (bottom) Gabriella Le Breton

P 8-9: Pally Learmond

P 10: (bottom right) M Reyboz; (top left) Monica Dalmasso; (top right) Christian Perret; (bottom left) James Crompton

P 12: J Schneider

P 13: Ferienregion St. Johann in Tirol

P 16: ABS-Airbag.com

P 18: Andrew Hingston

P 19: Tam Tam Photo

P 20: James McPhail

P 24: (top) Monterosa Ski Archive; (bottom) Nuts.fr

P 25: Zürs Tourism

P 27: Monterosa Ski Archive

P 28: Nuts.fr

P 29: (top) La Rosiere Tourism; (bottom left and bottom right) nuts.fr

P 30: (bottom) Meribel Tourism; (top) Credit Les Arcs Tourism

P 31: Credit G Lansard

P 32-33: Marc Gasch

P 35, 36: Vallnord

P 37: skiandorra.ad

P 38, 39: Vallnord

P 41: skiandorra.ad

P 44, 45: Baqueira-Beret

P 46, 47: Giles Birch

P 48-49: Ötztal Tourismus (Bernd Ritschel)

P 51: Lech Zürs Tourism

P 52: TVB St. Anton am Arlberg

P 53: Alex Kaiser

P 55: Zürs Tourism

P 56, 57: Alpbachtal Seenland Tourism

P 58: Gasteinertal Tourismus

P 60; Bad Klein Kircheim

P 61: TVB Wilder Kaiser

P 63, 64: Innsbruck Tourism

P 65: TVB Innsbruck

P 66: Ischgl Tourism

P 68, 69: Ischgl Tourism

P 70: Kitzbühel Tourismus

P 72: Albin Niederstrasser

P 73: (top) Gabriella Le Breton; (bottom) Xandi Kreuzeder

P 75: Credit Mayrhofen

P 76, 77: Mayrhofen

P 78: (top) Ötztal Tourismus (Bernd Ritschel); (bottom) Ötztal Tourismus

P 80: VB Saalbach Hinterglemm

P 82: VB Saalbach Hinterglemm

P 83: Ötztal Tourismus (Isidor Nösig)

P 84: Ötztal Tourismus (Bernd Ritschel)

P 85: TVB St. Anton am Arlberg

P 86: Gabriella Le Breton

P 89: Archive: Cable Car Company

P 90: (left) stubaier gletscher.com; (right) Martin-Hesse

P 91: Martin-Hesse

P 92: Kitzbüheler Alpen Brixental

P 93, 94: Zell am See Kaprun

P 95: Zürs Tourism

P 96-97: SC Vogel

P 99, 100: Slovenia.info

P 101, 103, 104, 106: James McPhail

P 107: Balkan Holidays

P 108, 109: Slovenia.info

P 111: SC Vogel

P 112-113: François Maire

P 115: Jeremie Pontin

P 116: P. Royer

P 117: (top) Marc Buscail; (bottom) David Machet

P 120: François Maire

P 122: François Maire

P 123: Avoriaz Tourism

P 125: M Reyboz

P 126: Chris Moran

P 127: OT Chamonix

P 128: Chris Moran

P 130: C Tatin

P 131: Thiebaut

P 132: Vuarand

P 133, 135: Patrick Pachod

P 136-137: C Arnal

P 137: P Labeau

P 138, 139: Greg Dieu

Ps 140, 141, 142: OT La Grave-La Meije

P 146: B Chaveau

P 148: duodecim.com

P 149: OT Tania

P 150: Mike Steegmans

P 153: Scalp

P 156: Bruno Longo

P 159, 160: Les Gets

P 161: Les Houches/Mario Colonel

P 162, 163: G Lansard

P 164: nuts.fr (JP Noisillier)

P 165: V. Pawlowski

P 166: JM Gouedard

P 167, 168: Greg Funnell

P 170: Molle

P 171: Méribel.net

P 172: (left) OT Morzine; (right) OT Morzine (F. Reinhart)

P 175: M Durand

P 176: Duodecim

P 177: G Lansard

P 178: A Royer

P 179: OT Samoens

P 180, 181: Zoom Agency

P 182: Zoom Agency

P 185, 186: Monica Dalmasso

P 189, 190, 191: nuts.fr

P 193: OT Val Thorens (J. Schneider)

P 194: OT Val Thorens (D. Daher)

P 196: (top) MRV; (bottom) Anna Frejus

P 198-199: Laurin Moser South Tyrol Marketing

P 201, 202: Monterosa Ski Archive

P 203: Natalie Mayer

P 204: (top) Cortina Tourism; (bottom) James Crompton

P 205, 206, 207: Monterosa Ski Archive

P 208: Alta Badia Tourism

P 209: Gabriella Le Breton

P 210, 211: Bardonecchia Ski

P 213: Campitello ski area

P 214: Flavio Faganello

P 215: Gianni Zotta

P 216: (left) Cervinia Tourism; (right) Danny Milano

P 218, 218-219: Monterosa Ski Archive

P 220, 221: Turismo Torina

P 222-223, 224: Cortina Tourism

P 226, 227: James Crompton

P 228, 229: Monterosa Ski Archive

P 230, 231: La Thuile

P 232: Gene Darkwin

P 233: A. Incontri

P 234: Azienda per il Turismo Spa Madonna di Campiglio Pinzolo Val Rendena

P 235: Natalie Mayer

P 236, 237: Monterosa Ski Archive

P 238: James Crompton

P 239: Plan de Corones

P 241: Sauze Tourism

P 242: Sestriere

P 243: Val Gardena Tourism

P 244-245: Jonas Kullman

P 247: Levi Tourism

P 248: Mattias Johansson

P 249: Riksgransen Tourism

P 252, 253: Levi Tourism

P 254: Kimmo Salminen

P 255: Nils Erik Kjellmann

P 256: Hemsedal Turistkontor/Simen Berg

P 257: Hemsedal Turistkontor

P 259: Esben Haakenstad

P 260: Henrik Trygg

P 261: Per Eriksson

P 262: Mattias Johansson

P 263: (top) Mattias Johansson; (bottom) Matt Barr

P 264-265: Robert Bosch

P 267: JUNGFRAU REGION MARKETING AG

P 268: Engelberg Tourism Engelberg, Switzerland

P 269: (top left, bottom right) Oliver Ritz; (bottom left) Chris Moran

P 271: Zermatt Tourismus

P 273, 274, 275: Andermatt Gotthard Tourism

P 276: Arosa Tourism

P 277: Champery Tourism

P 278: Crans Montana Tourism

P 280, 281, 282, 283: swiss-image.ch

P 284: Engelberg Tourism

P 285: (right) James McPhail; (left) Engelberg Tourism

P 286: Engelberg Tourism

P 287: Weisse Arena Gruppe, Laax

P 288: Christian Stadler

P 290: Grimentz Tourism

P 291, 292: Grindelwald Tourism

P 293: Gstaad Saanenland Tourismus

P 294, 295: swiss-image.ch

P 296: Les Diablerets Tourism

P 300: Torsten Kruger

P 301, 302, 303: Saas Fee Tourism

P 305, 306: Christian Perret/St Moritz Tourism

P 306: Christian Perret

P 308, 310: Verbier Tourism

P 312, 313, 314: Villars Media

P 315: Wengen

P 316-317: James McPhail

P 317: Mattias Fredriksson

P 318: Zermatt Tourismus

P 320, 321: Coeur du VALAIS

Tread your own path

Saddle up, check the view, ride the world

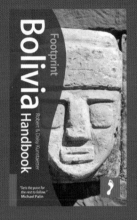

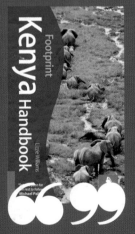

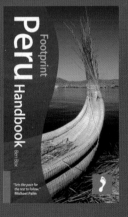

Credits

Footprint credits

Text editor: Tim Jollands
Editorial Assistant: Alice Jell
Production: Angus Dawson
Page layout: Lapiz Digital Services, Chennai, India

Managing Director: Andy Riddle
Publisher: Patrick Dawson
Commissioning Editor: Alan Murphy
Editorial: Sara Chare, Ria Gane, Jenny Haddington, Felicity Laughton, Nicola Gibbs
Cartography: Robert Lunn, Kevin Feeney, Kassia Gawronski, Emma Bryers
Design: Mytton Williams
Sales and marketing: Liz Harper, Hannah Bonnell
Advertising: Renu Sibal
Business Development: Zoë Jackson
Finance and Administration: Elizabeth Taylor

Maps ☻ Netmaps, SA. 2008
http://www.digitalmaps.co.uk

Photography credits

Title page: Pally Learmond
Front cover: Snow Images, Mark Junak (Tignes)
Back cover: Friedrich Schmidt (St Anton)

Print

Manufactured in Italy by EuroGrafica
Pulp from sustainable forests

Footprint Feedback

We try as hard as we can to make each Footprint guide as up to date as possible but, of course, things always change. If you want to let us know about your experiences – good, bad or ugly – then don't delay, go to www.footprintbooks.com and send in your comments.

Every effort has been made to ensure that the facts in this guidebook are accurate. However, travellers should still obtain advice from consulates, airlines etc about travel and visa requirements before travelling. The authors and publishers cannot accept responsibility for any loss, injury or inconvenience however caused.

Publishing information

Footprint Skiing Europe
1st edition
© Footprint Handbooks Ltd
November 2008

ISBN 978-1-906098-44-5
CIP DATA: A catalogue record for this book is available from the British Library

® Footprint Handbooks and the Footprint mark are a registered trademark of Footprint Handbooks Ltd

Published by Footprint

6 Riverside Court
Lower Bristol Road
Bath BA2 3DZ, UK
T +44 (0)1225 469141
F +44 (0)1225 469461
discover@footprintbooks.com
www.footprintbooks.com

Distributed in North America by

Globe Pequot Press

The colour maps are not intended to have any political significance.